Mariology at the Beginning of the Third Millennium

Theology at the Beginning of the Third Millennium
Series Preface

Theology at the Beginning of the Third Millennium is a new series of theological monographs which seek to examine the *status quaestionis* of various sub-disciplines within the field of theology in this second decade of the third millennium and some half a century after the conclusion of the Second Vatican Council. While the impetus for the series has come from scholars at the University of Notre Dame (Australia), the Catholic Institute of Sydney, and Campion College (Sydney), contributors to the volumes come from a diverse array of theological academies. A feature of the series is the fact that although the majority of the contributors are situated within the Catholic intellectual tradition, scholars from other traditions are also welcome.

The various sub-disciplines which form the subject of each volume are examined from the perspective of scripture scholarship, fundamental, systematic and dogmatic theology, spirituality, historical theology, ecumenical and pastoral theology and the theology of culture. This is consistent with the Balthasarian metaphor that "Truth is Symphonic" and thus created by an harmonious integration of different disciplines or "sections" of the theological orchestra. Consistent with the charism of St. James the contributors share a high degree of respect for the deposit of the faith, a Johannine interest in integrating spirituality and mystical theology with dogmatic and fundamental theology, a Pauline sensitivity to the influence of the Holy Spirit, a Petrine interest in official magisterial teaching and, above all, a Marian disposition of receptivity to the Divine *Logos*.

Mariology at the Beginning of the Third Millennium

EDITED BY
Kevin Wagner
M. Isabell Naumann
Peter John McGregor
AND
Paul Morrissey

☙PICKWICK *Publications* · Eugene, Oregon

MARIOLOGY AT THE BEGINNING OF THE THIRD MILLENNIUM

Theology at the Beginning of the Third Millennium

Copyright © 2017 Wipf and Stock Publishers. All rights reserved. Except for brief quotations in critical publications or reviews, no part of this book may be reproduced in any manner without prior written permission from the publisher. Write: Permissions, Wipf and Stock Publishers, 199 W. 8th Ave., Suite 3, Eugene, OR 97401.

Pickwick Publications
An Imprint of Wipf and Stock Publishers
199 W. 8th Ave., Suite 3
Eugene, OR 97401

www.wipfandstock.com

PAPERBACK ISBN: 978-1-5326-0143-9
HARDCOVER ISBN: 978-1-5326-0145-3
EBOOK ISBN: 978-1-5326-0144-6

Cataloguing-in-Publication data:

> Names: Wagner, Kevin. | Naumann, M. Isabell Naumann | McGregor, Peter John | Morrissey, Paul.
>
> Title: Mariology at the beginning of the third millennium / edited by Kevin Wagner, M. Isabell Naumann, Peter John McGregor, and Paul Morrissey.
>
> Description: Eugene, OR: Pickwick Publications, 2017 | Series: Theology at the Beginning of the Third Millennium | Includes bibliographical references.
>
> Identifiers: ISBN 978-1-5326-0143-9 (paperback) | ISBN 978-1-5326-0145-3 (hardcover) | ISBN 978-1-5326-0144-6 (ebook)
>
> Subjects: LCSH: Mary, Blessed Virgin, Saint—Theology | Mary, Blessed Virgin, Saint | Mary, Blessed Virgin, Saint—Devotion to

Classification: BT613 W146 2017 (print) | BT613 (ebook)

Manufactured in the U.S.A.   04/20/17

Contents

Contributors | vii

Preface—*Paul Morrissey* | xi

1. Mariology at the Beginning of the Third Millennium | 1
   —*M. Isabell Naumann ISSM*

2. The Virgin Mary in Ancient Christian Tradition | 32
   —*Fr. Joseph Azize*

3. Theotokoupoleis: The Mother of God as Protectress of the Two Romes | 51
   —*Mario Baghos*

4. Mariology of John Paul II: An Overview | 78
   —*Mariusz Biliniewicz*

5. Marian Arks Cut Adrift: The Post-Roman Catholic Development of Two Australian Marian Apparitional Movements | 98
   —*Bernard Doherty*

6. How is Mary a Seat of Wisdom? A Spatial Exploration | 122
   —*Renée Köhler-Ryan*

7. Revisiting the Marian Dimension of Ignatian Spirituality | 140
   —*Robin Koning SJ*

8. Mary as Priest, Prophet, and King | 163
   —*Peter John McGregor*

9. Luke 1:26–38 as a Model of Dialogue | 183
—*M. Isabell Naumann ISSM*

10. Marian Epistemology | 194
—*Matthew John Paul Tan*

11. Mary the Temple of Scripture: The Biblical Art of Sacred Circumlocution | 209
—*Robert Tilley*

12. Towards a Patristic Theology of Barrenness | 226
—*Kevin Wagner*

13. Lex Orandi, Lex Credenda. Dulia, Hyperdulia, et Latria | 243
—*Christopher John Wolter*

Contributors

Fr. Joseph Azize is a priest in the Maronite Catholic Church. He obtained a law degree and PhD in ancient history from the University of Sydney. In addition to some popular books and articles, he has published academically in ancient history, law, and most recently, has focused on pre-Nicene Church history. He has a special interest in Christian Antioch and the Greek and Syriac language traditions which were centered upon it. His most recent articles have contended that the ancient evidence for Jesus' institution of the Eucharist at the Last Supper, and the early development of a threefold ecclesiastical hierarchy are reliable.

Dr. Mario Baghos was Lecturer in Church History at St. Andrew's Greek Orthodox Theological College, and is a member of the Australian Association for Byzantine Studies. He received his PhD in Studies in Religion from the University of Sydney, and his research interests include religious and Christian symbolism in ancient and medieval cities, and ancient and modern representations of Christian saints.

Dr. Mariusz Biliniewicz holds an MA in biblical theology from the Pontifical Theological Faculty in Wrocław, Poland and a PhD in systematic theology from the Milltown Institute of Theology and Philosophy in Dublin, Ireland. He is currently a Lecturer in Theology at the University of Notre Dame, Australia—Sydney.

Dr. Bernard Doherty is currently Adjunct Lecturer in History and New Religions at St. Mark's National Theological Centre, School of Theology, Charles Sturt University, Canberra, Australia. He is a graduate of Macquarie

University. Following his PhD, Bernard was a postdoctoral fellow at the Institute for Studies of Religion at Baylor University in the United States where he worked on a series of projects on new religious movements in Australia and abroad and on applying social science methodologies to the study of early Christianity. Bernard has published in a number of academic journals including the *Journal of Religious History*, *Nova Religio*, the *International Journal for the Study of New Religions*, the *Alternative Spirituality and Religions Review*, *Phronema*, and the *Journal of the Australian Catholic Historical Society*. Bernard's research interests are wide-ranging and include new religious movements, patristics, Australian religious history, Church and State issues, religion and the media.

Dr. Renée Köhler-Ryan is a Senior Lecturer in Philosophy at University of Notre Dame Australia. Her publications reflect her academic interests in the ideas, art, and architecture of the Middle Ages, issues surrounding philosophy of the human person, political philosophy, philosophy of culture, and the dynamic relationship between faith and reason in the Catholic intellectual tradition.

Rev. Dr. Robin Koning SJ is an Australian Jesuit priest and Adjunct Scholar at Jesuit Theological College, Parkville, Victoria. His academic interests include Bernard Lonergan, Ignatian spirituality, Christology, and theological method.

Dr. Peter John McGregor is a lecturer at the Catholic Institute of Sydney. He has some thirty years experience in evangelization, catechesis, and religious education. Peter has academic qualifications in arts, education, and theology, and his research has been published in theological journals such as *New Blackfriars*, the *Irish Theological Quarterly*, *Pro Ecclesia* and *Radical Orthodoxy*. He completed his PhD (summa cum laude) in 2013 with a thesis entitled "Heart to Heart: The Spiritual Christology of Joseph Ratzinger," for which he received the Australian Catholic University's 2013 Vice Chancellor's Award for Excellence in the PhD thesis. In 2016 a revised version of this thesis was published under the same title. He is a member of the Emmanuel Community (Communauté de l'Emmanuel), a community of lay people, priests and consecrated people within the Catholic Church. Peter is married, and has two children.

Dr. Paul Morrissey STD is President of Campion College, Australia's first Higher Education institution devoted to the study of the liberal arts. He holds a Pontifical Doctorate in Theology from the Sydney College of

Divinity and a Licentiate in Sacred Theology from the Lateran in Rome. He is Adjunct Associate Professor of Theology in the School of Philosophy and Theology, University of Notre Dame, where he taught theology for eight years. Paul is married with seven children.

Dr. M. Isabell Naumann ISSM STD is a member of the Secular Institute of the Schoenstatt Sisters of Mary (ISSM) and holds a doctorate in sacred theology. She is the Academic Dean of Studies at the Seminary of the Good Shepherd, Sydney; teaches systematic theology at the Catholic Institute of Sydney and is an Adjunct Professor in Systematic Theology at the John Paul II Institute for Marriage and Family in Melbourne, and at the University of Notre Dame, Sydney. She serves on various national and international academic boards and councils including the Pontifical Council for Culture, Rome.

Dr. Matthew John Paul Tan is the Felice and Margredel Zaccari Lecturer in Theology and Philosophy at Campion College, Australia, and a sessional lecturer in theology at the John Paul II Institute for Marriage and Family in Melbourne. He completed his doctorate in theology at the Australian Catholic University, and his licentiate in sacred theology at the Pontifical University of St. Thomas Aquinas, Rome. He is the author of *Justice, Unity and the Hidden Christ* (Pickwick, 2014) and *Redeeming Flesh: The Way of the Cross with Zombie Jesus* (Cascade, 2016). He is the editor of the theological blog, *The Divine Wedgie*.

Dr. Robert Tilley is a lecturer in biblical studies at both the Catholic Institute of Sydney and The University of Notre Dame, Australia and also lectures in Catholic adult education in the areas of theology and the arts. He holds a BA, MA, and a BD from the University of Sydney. Dr. Tilley received his doctorate from the University of Sydney with a thesis entitled "Reading the Sacred Text." In 2007, Dr. Tilley published *Benedict XVI and the Search for Truth* and is currently working on a book on Job, a critique of negative theology in the light of justice, and another on St. Paul's understanding of grace as a theology of inclusion.

Dr. Kevin Wagner is a lecturer in theology at the University of Notre Dame, Australia—Sydney. His PhD was completed at the John Paul II Institute for Marriage and Family (Melbourne) under the supervision of Dr. Adam G. Cooper. Kevin's thesis focused on the conversion of the fourth/fifth-century Neo-Platonist bishop Synesius of Cyrene and those qualities of traditional Greek *paideia* that best facilitate truth-seeking. Kevin was previously the

Director of the Emmanuel School of Mission in Rome, a role he shared with his wife. He has a background in secondary school teaching and has taught mathematics, religious education, and information technology at both government and Catholic schools in Sydney, Melbourne, and London.

Christopher John Wolter is an Associate Lecturer in the School of Philosophy and Theology at the University of Notre Dame, Australia—Sydney, and a doctoral candidate. From 1999 to 2004 Chris completed a Bachelor of Theology, in Victoria. In 2006–8, he completed a Bachelor of Fine Arts degree at Sydney's National Art School. In 2009 Chris took up work at UNDA—Sydney in a service role and in 2010 he began tutoring in theology. From there he has gone on to become a fulltime member of the core curriculum teaching team. His PhD thesis combines liturgical theology with the philosophy and theology of aesthetics.

Preface

—Paul Morrissey

When studying for my undergraduate degree in theology, the Virgin Mary was not given a high priority. The study of Mary was reduced to the last few weeks of a year-long course in Christology, the focus of which was an overview of Marian dogmas as well as the portion of the chapter in *Lumen Gentium* on Mary. Since the Second Vatican Council the place of Mary in theology and generally in the life of the Church has been at times muted. This is perhaps understandable given the debates concerning Mary's "place" in the documents of Vatican II (see, in this collection, Isabell Naumann's chapter, "Mariology at the Beginning of the Third Millennium.") In an ecumenical age, it was argued, the Church needed a less triumphalist Mariology and piety with a greater focus on Mary as model disciple. In certain respects this has led to a dichotomy between the continued Marian piety of many faithful (and, truth be told, the piety of the post-conciliar popes) and a theological timidity concerning Mary.

This collection of chapters, in the Australian context at least, seeks to address the current situation of Marian studies. Taken as a whole these chapters represent a welcomed call for renewal and reawakening in Mariology. The collection is also delightfully eclectic, both in terms of topics covered but also in terms of the denominational and academic backgrounds of the authors. Notwithstanding this variety there are some themes through which we can group the chapters: the context of contemporary Mariology; Mariology and Scripture; Mary and dogmatic theology; spirituality and Mariology; and, finally, art, liturgy, and Mary.

There are three chapters that fall within the parameters of the context of Marian studies today. Isabell Naumann's chapter, "Mariology at the Beginning of the Third Millennium," offers a valuable overview of the current state of Marian studies and devotion. While decrying the current state of Mariology in the academy, Naumann sees signs of hope and she calls for a renewed Mariology that is integrated more fully with Christology, ecclesiology, pneumatology, and theological anthropology. In his chapter, Mariusz Biliniewicz also looks at the context of recent Mariology, but with a specific focus on John Paul II. In a very different and interesting way, Bernard Doherty, offers some context regarding recent Mariology and piety in his essay, "Marian Arks Cut Adrift: The Post-Roman Catholic Development of Two Australian Marian Apparitional Movements." Doherty's chapter is historical/sociological rather than theological, but he places the rise of many Marian "sects" in the post-conciliar era within the context of the perceived Marian silence in the church. Doherty demonstrates that these apparitional movements are characterized by a return to a more traditionalist and triumphalist Mariology and piety, and remain a very difficult phenomenon for the institutional Church.

The chapters from Fr. Azize, Robert Tilley, and Isabell Naumann explore Marian scriptural themes. Fr. Azize argues against a reductive interpretation of Mary that is often the result of the Marian silence in Mark's Gospel, especially when it is considered the first Gospel written. Robert Tilley calls for a deeper and more thematic interpretation of Scripture; that is, to see the architectural whole rather than small fragments. The most important work of architecture in the Bible is the temple, the mediator of God's glory, and, Tilley argues, the person of Mary can be seen as the temple of Scripture, the preeminent mediator of the Logos. In her chapter entitled, "Luke 1:26–38 as a Model of Dialogue," Isabell Naumann shows that the Annunciation to Mary is an archetype of the dialogue between God and humanity.

Under the theme of dogmatic theology is Peter McGregor's chapter, "Mary as Priest, Prophet, and King." McGregor provides a very helpful and quite innovative demonstration of how Mary fulfills the threefold mission of Christ as outlined in *Lumen Gentium*; a mission to which all Christians are called. Matthew Tan is similarly innovative in his chapter arguing that Mary's discipleship represents a way of knowing that can offer a corrective to the Church accepting modern epistemological assumptions which inhibit its evangelical mission.

An important dimension of Mariology is spirituality. Robin Koning, SJ, gives a wonderful overview of the Marian influence on St. Ignatius of Loyola, particularly looking at the importance of Mary in his spiritual exercises. He argues that the well intentioned and ecumenically motivated muting of Mary in some contemporary presentations of the exercises represents an impoverishment and not something true to the vision of Ignatius. Mario Baghos in his chapter, "Theotokoupoleis: The Mother of God as Protectress of the Two Romes," asks us to consider the role of saints, and particularly Mary, as patrons, not just of churches, but of cities. Kevin Wagner's chapter focusses on patristic writings and seeks to establish a spirituality of barrenness highlighting the link between writings on childlessness and consecrated virginity (as symbolized most particularly in Mary). Wagner's discussion is most apt in our times when ethical questions surrounding fertility are very much to the fore.

Finally we have in this collection a focus on art and liturgy. Renée Köhler-Ryan, in her chapter, "How is Mary a Seat of Wisdom? A Spatial Exploration," explores the medieval iconography of Mary as seat of wisdom, an iconography that thrived in the twelfth century. This iconography, argues Köhler-Ryan, points to the ways that Mary is wise and that her wisdom is ultimately grounded in a *participated theonomy*. A particularly important ecumenical question in Mariology is Mary's place in liturgy and prayer. Chris Wolter, in "Lex Orandi, Lex Credenda: Dulia, Hyperdulia, et Latria," gives a helpful clarification between worship and honor, while also demonstrating how the Western church has liturgically venerated Mary in light of its belief.

What is clear in this collection of chapters is that Mary has an intrinsic role in the ongoing life of the Church. Mariology needs to be renewed in order that the Church can remain faithful to her mission of bearing the Word and giving him to the world. This renewal touches on all aspects of Christian thought and life, as these chapters demonstrate. It is the hope of the editors that what is contained herein will contribute to a renewal of Mariology for the twenty-first century.

1

Mariology at the Beginning of the Third Millennium

—M. Isabell Naumann ISSM

According to the document The Virgin Mary in Intellectual and Spiritual Formation, *"the dignity and importance of Mariology . . . derive from the dignity and importance of Christology, from the value of ecclesiology and pneumatology, from the meaning of supernatural anthropology and from eschatology: Mariology is closely connected with these tracts" (22). The Second Vatican Council marked a turning point in the Church's approach to her own identity and mission, which consequently affected Marian theology and spirituality. What emerged from the conciliar discussion and from post-conciliar magisterial documents, in particular from the writings of the recent popes, suggests a balanced approach toward a more integrated Mariology. Mary represents in a tangible and personal form the Church's own identity, activity, and goal. This more integrated picture of Mary and the Church has raised and opened up many issues, which necessarily involve further investigation and development. Contemporary Marian studies—enriched by a biblical rediscovery of Mary's unique role—reflect upon hermeneutical-cultural, anthropological-historical, Mariological-ecclesiological, ecumenical and related aspects.*

Mariology at the Beginning of the Third Millennium

Where do Mariology, Marian studies, and Marian devotion stand in contemporary culture and climate? Why are Mary, the Mother of God, and the Church's teaching about her largely considered irrelevant and often reduced to what, for example, Barth referred to as an "excrescence, a diseased construct of theological thought"[1] (within the Catholic Church). In fact, why is there no mention or merely an inconsequential reference to Mary or Marian studies in tertiary religious studies curricula, contemporary theological publications, and related studies?

In part it might be due to the prevailing concept of scientific theology which is unable to tolerate any Marian reference in what is classed as theology's legitimate parameter. And regrettably, so an eminent contemporary scholar says, "evolving in scholastic categories for too long and sometimes with the self-deceptive ambition of acting scientifically, Mariology may have unwittingly contributed to its own demise in the eyes of representatives of other theological disciplines."[2]

Furthermore, within the ecumenical context,[3] for fear of theological misunderstanding, Mary and Marian studies are frequently considered as a point of contention and hindrance, or Mary is relegated to a *persona insignificante* in theological discourse as such.[4]

Another reason why Marian theology is often shunned in academic circles is the perception of it as being nothing more than popular religious fervor and devotions, growing out of an emotional and irrational desire for ritual observances and sentimental practices. More devotional than spiritual, its theological grounding seems rather weak and inadequate, and

---

1. Barth, *Kirchliche Dogmatik*, 153.
2. Roten, "How can Spirituality be Marian," 7–9.
3. Here in reference to the ecumenical context of the Christian denominations of the West.
4. Bliss, "The Role of Mary in Ecumenical Relations between the Catholic Church and Her Major Ecumenical Partners," 84–100; Blancy et al., *Mary in the Plan of God and in the Communion of Saints*, 122–28; Roten, "How can Spirituality be Marian," 8; Dittrich, *Protestantische Mariologie-Kritik*; Seybold, *Maria im Glauben der Kirche*, 11–12; Wickert, "Freiheit von Sünde-Erhöhung zu God," 59–85; see also Seybold, "Nach-Frage," 132–43; Gentle, "The Blessed Virgin Mary's Cooperation in the Redemption," 40–58; Largo Domínguez, "María y la esperanza en la Declaración ecuménica de Seattle," 309–28; Garrapucho, "La madre de Jesús en el actual diálogo ecuménico," 51–68; De Bhaldraithe, "The Challenge of the ARCIC Agreement on Mary," 21–36; Wicks, "The Virgin Mary in Recent Ecumenical Dialogues," 25–57; Unterseher, "Mary in Contemporary Protestant Theological Discourse," 194–212; Brown at. al., *Mary in the New Testament*, 7–31.

hence all that sounds somehow "Marian" is consigned to a level of superficial popular piety, good enough to placate the religious conscience of the masses.[5]

And finally there are those who, out of existential and gender related reasons, see Mary either as a patriarchal construct or as an impossible ideal to reach out to. Her portrayal is over-laden with reminiscences of an era when Mary was presented as the exalted and remote heavenly queen who, at the same time, served as a demanding and overbearing model of moral perfection.[6] Being faced with such a highly elevated model, human beings, struggling with the consequences of original sin within one's own and other's frailty, and the social fragmentation of human life, resent Mary as an oppressive figurehead of an unattainable ideal, rather than embrace her as a loving mother, sister, and companion.[7]

Having indicated several negative facets of contemporary Mariology, there are at the same time positive signs, a strong re-discovery of Mary,[8] for example, within the younger generation, in newly established Associations of Apostolic life, and in the so called ecclesial movements which—founded in the conciliar teaching of Vatican II, within their own unique charismas—influence new approaches and appreciation of the Mother of God.[9]

---

5. Roten, "Popular Religion and Marian Images," 62–120; Roten, "How Can Spirituality Be Marian," 8; Sapitula, "Marian Piety and Modernity," 399–424; McDannell, *Material Christianity*; Mondéjar, Mallía, Izquierdo Gil, "Presencia Mariana y experiencia de María en varios continents," 297–306; Jones, *Empowered with Mary*; Greenacre et al., *Maiden, Mother and Queen*; Holler, "The Origins of Marian Devotion in Latin American Cultures in the United States," 108–27.

6. Johnson, *Truly Our Sister*, 18–43, 261–74; Johnson, "The Marian Tradition and the Reality of Women," 85–107; Clark, "Women, Gender, and the Study of Christian History," 395–426; Gebara and Bingemer, *Mary—Mother of God, Mother of the Poor*; McDannell, "Feminist Mariologies," 527–67.

7. Roten, "How Can Spirituality be Marian," 9; Rubin et al., *Mother of God*, 303–10; Beattie, *God's Mother, Eve's Advocate*, 71–86; Beinert, *Unsere Liebe Frau und die Frauen*, 11–26, 65–110; Gössmann, "Mariologische Entwicklungen im Mittelalter," 63–85; Kimberly, "Pentecostal Women," 404–12.

8. See in particular the studies by Kereszty, "Toward the Renewal of Mariology," 779–99; Serra, "María, figlia del Padre," 293–308; Flores, "Mary, the Virgin," 47–113; Flores, "Jesus Christ, the Only-Begotten Son of the Father and of the Virgin Mother," 143–234; Reynolds, *Gateway to Heaven*; Boss, *The Spirit of Mary*; Gubler, *Maria: Mutter, Prophetin, Himmelskönigin*; Ziegenaus, *Geboren aus der Jungfrau Maria*, 19; García Llata, "Esperanzas y cumplimientos en la historia de María," 233–50; García Paredes, "María en la espiritualidad del siglo XXI," 35–50; Colzani, "Il ruolo di Maria nell'antropologia teologica postconciliare," 67–89; Roten, "From Gatherer to Sender," 193–214.

9. For example, Christian Life Movement, Communauté "Rejouis-Toi," Communion and Liberation, Community of Sant'Egidio, Focolare, Community of the

Following these observations we may assert that Mary too—drawn into the fate of her Son, both now and then—becomes a *sign of contradiction*. She is either honored and loved or hated and despised . . . but she is a person to be reckoned with because of her significant ongoing role in the history of salvation and in the life of the *people of God*.

The Significance of Marian Theology

Speaking of the importance of Mary in his comprehensive five-volume work *Dogma (Katholische Dogmatik)*, M. Schmaus rightly states, that

> in Mariology all theological strands are linked together—the christological, ecclesiological, anthropological and eschatological—and almost all theological discussions of the present time are fused in it. Mariology then becomes the point of convergence for all important theological statements.[10]

The magisterial document *The Virgin Mary in Intellectual and Spiritual Formation* concurs similarly, concluding that

> the dignity and importance of Mariology . . . derive from the dignity and importance of Christology, from the value of ecclesiology and pneumatology, from the meaning of supernatural anthropology and from eschatology: Mariology is closely connected with these tracts.[11]

Numbers 23–26, 32–33 expound further this point. In reference, then, to the above, the significance of Mariology lays in its *locus* and *telos*, so well presented in the conciliar document *Lumen gentium*.

The Contribution of Vatican II to Mariology

Considering Vatican II within the context of the development of Mariology particularly in its relatedness to ecclesiology, it was the task of the Council (expressed in both *Lumen gentium* and the proclamation *Mary, Mother of the Church*) to balance the somewhat prevailing perspective of contemplating

---

Béatitudes, Couples for Christ, Communauté de l'Emmanuel, Neo-Catechumenate, Secular institutes (Caritas Christi, Secular Franciscan Order, Secular Institutes of Schoenstatt).

10. Schmaus, *Katholische Dogmatic* V, 7.

11. Congregation for Catholic Education, *The Virgin Mary in Intellectual and Spiritual Formation*, 22.

Mary's relationship with the Church and her place in the Church in vertical/horizontal categories (in terms of being placed "against"). Mary, in her uniqueness as mother, helpmate, and associate of Christ in the entire work of redemption,[12] transcends such categories: as the *pre*-redeemed person, the immaculate original personification of the Church. The conciliar document *Lumen gentium* describes her as the most excellent member and model of the Church, and at the same time the Mother of the Church, who is active as the educator of *all* the members.[13]

Furthermore, the Council did not intend to present a complete doctrine on Mary but to give a carefully compiled treatise on the role of Mary in the mystery of the Incarnate Word and the Mystical Body.[14] As such, there is in chapter 8 the first unified and most extensive presentation of a Mariology given by a Council. The text shows a powerful coherence of the mystery of Christ with the mystery of the Church; Mary is drawn into this mystery through the grace of Christ,[15] because an authentic theology of Mary must lead to a deeper understanding of the essence of the Church.[16]

Chapter 8 of Lumen gentium

It is significant that the Marian chapter became the final chapter of the Dogmatic Constitution on the Church.[17] The first chapter gives an exposition of the mystery of the Church, how this mystery is then unfolded in the *People of God*, in the hierarchical framework, and in the laity. The pondering of the

12. Kentenich, *Oktoberwoche*, 278.

13. See in this context Beinert, "Maria im Geheimnis Christi und der Kirche," 284–309; Egbuonu, *Vatican II on Mary*; Hogan, "Mary and the Catholic Charistmatic Renewal 1971–1978," 237–372.

14. *Lumen gentium*, no. 54.

15. *Lumen gentium*, nos. 53, 60.

16. Maccquarie, *Mary for all Christians*, 113. See also the following studies: Greshake, *Maria-Ecclesia*; Hälbig, *Die Krönung der Braut*. For the following see Naumann, *Cum Maria ad altare*, 118–46.

17. Concerning the conciliar context see Jelly et al., "The Theological Context of and Introduction to Chapter 8 of *Lumen gentium*," 43–265; Beinert, "'Maria im Geheimnis Christi und der Kirche," 284–424; Sales, "La bienheureuse Vierge Marie au Concile œcuménique de Vatican II," 498–519. For a critical Protestant assessment: Blanshard, *Paul Blanshard on Vatican II*, 172–81; Fairweather, "The Church," 80–82. Pertaining to some of the leading pariti, see the following studies: Roten, "Mary—Personal Concretization of the Church," 242–321; Kyte, *The Joy of a Covenant Fulfilled*; De Luis Carballada, "La maternidad sacramental de María," 85–102; Mariño, "Rahner: María, oyente de la palabra, Madre del Señor y hermana nuestra," 11–30; Fritz, "Konkrete Dogmatik," 733–35; Martínez, "La Virgen María en los escritos de Yves Congar," 31–60.

mystery of the Church in the first chapter is presented in the final chapter in a personalized manner in the figure of Mary and her place in the mystery of Christ and of the Church.

The developmental stages of the Marian schema, from an independent schema until its insertion into the Constitution on the Church, reflect the Council's emphasis on integration, unity, and reorientation of the sources of Christianity.

The Council integrated the mysteries of our faith into the one unifying mystery of salvation, Jesus Christ, who extends the saving efficacy of his resurrection to all people through the Church, his sacrament on earth.[18]

By integrating Mariology into ecclesiology, Mary as an icon represents, in her person and the pertinent teaching about her, the mystery of Christ in the Church and its immeasurable effect on humankind in salvation history. Thus, Mariology has been approached not deductively,[19] but from the center of the mystery of salvation[20] and in this the traditional Mariological statements have been christologically and ecclesiologically integrated and rearranged.[21]

This salvation-historical perspective is seen as a truly *new theological perspective*.[22]

---

18. *Lumen gentium*, nos. 1–8.

19. De Fiores, "Mary in Postconciliar Theology," 471; Napiorkowski, "The Present Position in Mariology," 52–62, 59. See also Courth, "Maria—heute neu gefragt?," 40–50; Muehlen, "Neuorientierung und Krise der Mariologie in den Ausssagen des Vaticanums II," 19–53; Masciarelli, "Antropolgia e Mariologia dopo il Vaticano II," 129–67; Del Gaudio, "La dimensione antropologica della Mariologia del Concilio Vaticano II," 11–48.

20. Meo, "Councilio Vaticano II," 387. Courth writes: "Von einem bloß symbolisch gefaßten Marienbild her läßt sich letztlich nur die generelle Aussage über die männlich-weibliche Struktur des Menschen machen, nie aber eine subjekthafte . . . . Genau das aber ist Inhalt der besonders durch Mariens Mutterschaft konkretisierten biblischen Glaubensgewißheit: jeder einzelne Mensch besitzt von Gott her eine unbedingte Unvertauschbarkeit in seiner Aufgabe für die Geschichte des Heils. Personalität als unverwechselbarer Selbstand läßt sich in dieser strikten Form dann halten, wenn ich an das geschichtlich ereignishafte Handeln Gottes glaube, wodurch jeder Mensch in direkte Unmittelbarkeit zu ihm tritt und darin ueber den Tod hinaus auch gehalten wird. Und damit sind menschliche Unantastbarkeit und Freiheit grundgelegt . . . . Die Heilsgeschichte mit der Menschwerdung Christi aus Maria als Scheitelpunkt veranschaulicht und bestärkt diese personale und zugleich gemeinschaftliche Sicht des Menschen." Courth, "Maria-heute neu gefragt?," 50 and "Marienglaube-Marienverehrung," 137–47.

21. Napiorkowski, "The Present Position in Mariology," 52–62; Del Corazón, "Los Principíos Mariologicos en el Capitulo Mariano del Concilio Vaticano II," 291–308.

22. Meo, "Councilio Vaticano II," 387. Comparing the first with the last text of the schema, the "main draftsmen" Philips and Balîc acknowledged that the first was more orientated on the magisterial teaching while the last one [actual Chapter VIII of *Lumen*

> The person, the mission, the privileges of Mary, and also the devotion offered to her, are not considered in themselves or in relation to her dignity as Mother of God. Rather, the whole treatment is developed and expanded in the broader framework of the history of salvation.[23]

This new perspective, presenting the Mother of God at her rightful place in salvation history, shows her as the example of the human person cooperating with grace in the work of salvation and also as the example of the Church, the sign and effective instrument of salvation.[24] She portrays the *acting person and the acting ecclesial community* and hence, evidences dimensions of anthropological and ecclesiological dynamics, which are important elements for contemporary research and discussion on Mary, particularly within the *ecumenical dialogue*.[25]

At the closing of the Third Session of the Council, Pope Paul VI not only confirmed Mary's place as type and model[26] of the Church, as expressed in chapter 8 of *Lumen Gentium*, but also promulgated her place as "*our mother in the order of grace*"[27] through the solemn proclamation of Mary as Mother of the Church.[28]

The Marian teaching of Vatican II is well summarized in the magisterial document *The Virgin Mary in intellectual and spiritual formation*:

> The importance of Chapter VIII of *Lumen gentium* lies in the value of its doctrinal synthesis and in its formulation of doctrine about the Blessed Virgin in the context of the mystery of Christ and of the Church. In this way the Council allied itself to the patristic tradition which gives a privileged place to the history of salvation in every theological tract; stressed that the Mother of the Lord is not a peripheral figure in our faith and in the panorama of theology; rather, she, through her intimate participation in the history of salvation, "in a certain way unites and mirrors

---

gentium] was placed in the framework of salvation history. Philips, "Pourtant, nous pouvons affirmer avec le Père Balic," Philips, *L'Eglise et son Mystère au le Concile du Vatican*, 210.

23. Meo, "Councilio Vaticano II," 386–87.

24. See in particular *Lumen gentium*, no. 65.

25. Next to Chapter VIII, Mary is mentioned once more in *Lumen gentium*, no. 50, and in the following documents: *Sacrosanctum concilium*, no. 103; *Unitatis redintegratio*, nos. 15, 20; *Nostra aetate*, no. 3; *Ad Gentes*, no. 4; *Apostolicam actuositatem*, no. 4; *Optatam totius*, no. 8; *Perfectae caritatis*, no. 25; and *Presbyterorum ordinis*, no. 18.

26. *Lumen gentium*, nos. 63, 65.

27. Ibid., no. 61.

28. Acta Synodalia III, VIII (Sessio Publica V), 915.

within herself the central truths of the faith";[29] [and] formulated a common vision for the different positions about the way in which Marian matters are to be treated.[30]

Aspects of Mary and the Church in Post-conciliar Magisterial Documents

The dimensions of Mary's relatedness to the Church, flowing from her union with Christ, as presented in chapter 8 of *Lumen gentium*, and Pope Paul VI's proclamation of Mary's title Mother of the Church, are reiterated in the *Catechism of the Catholic Church*.[31]

Closely related and further expounding on the conciliar document in particular are the magisterial documents *Marialis Cultus*, *Signum Magnum*, and *Redemptoris Mater* which shall be considered here briefly.[32]

29. *Lumen gentium*, no. 65.
30. *The Virgin Mary in intellectual and spiritual formation*, 5.
31. *Catechism of the Catholic Church*, nos. 963–75. In the Catechism the mystery of Mary is related primarily to the Trinitarian mystery. [See the following references of Mary's relationship with the Father, nos. 144, 273 and 411; with the Son, nos. 484–507 and 618; with the Holy Spirit, nos. 721–28, 733, 829, 963–75.] Her relationship with the Church is within the section devoted to the Holy Spirit, which immediately links the establishment of the Church at Pentecost with the Incarnation of the Word through Mary's cooperation. ["I believe in the Holy Spirit," nos. 683–1065.] As the spotless Bride, Mary is the example of the Church's holiness, and in this the Marian dimension of the Church precedes the Petrine [no. 773]. The Catechism further presents Mary as the exemplary realization of the Church, and her eschatological icon and preeminent sign of hope (τυπος) [nos. 967, 972]. The Catechism brings out the unity between the Immaculate Conception and the Assumption of Mary, nos. 965 and 966.] Mary's undivided unity with Christ marks her pilgrimage of faith and perseverance in faith [no. 964] and her motherhood of the Church [nos. 963 and 967–69]. See also Buby, *Mary of Galilee*, 216–22. For a critical assessment of the Mariological content of the Catechism, see Farrell, "The Catechism's Approach to the Blessed Virgin Mary," 39–46. For a less favorable response to the Catechism's use of the title Mary, Mother of the Church, see Wagner, "Maria-Mutter und Mittlerin," 180–85 [The author's arguments demonstrate somewhat incorrect research data when comparing her sources!], and "Ein Kirchenbild für unsere Zeit?," 533–46.
32. For the purpose of this overview it shall suffice to consider these major magisterial Marian documents. From the wealth of other studies concerning the Mary-Church relationship, see for example, Kirwin, "Mary's salvific role compared with that of the church," 29–43; Lubac, *The Church: Paradox and Mystery*, 54–67; Thornhill, *Sign and Promise*, 220–34; Carr, "Mary in the Mystery of the Church," 5–32; Forte, *Maria, Mutter und Schwester des Glaubens*, 201–9; Strada, *María y nosotros*, 125–72; Esquerda Bifet, "María, Tipo de la Iglesia," 187–239; and "Sentido escatologico de la Tipologia Mariana," 103–15; Courth, "Marienglaube-Marienverehrung," 136–47; Neuner, "Maria, Urbild der Kirche," 442–50. See also Koehler, "Mary's spiritual Maternity after the

Pope Paul VI re-emphasizes Mary's role as model and mother of the Church in *Signum Magnum* and in *Marialis Cultus*.[33]

In *Signum Magnum* the Pope writes: "Mary is the Mother of the Church—not only because she is the mother of Jesus Christ and his closest associate in 'the new economy . . .' but also because she 'shines as the model of virtues for the whole community of the elect.'"[34] She participated in the Son's sacrifice for our redemption in such intimate fashion that he designated her the mother not only of John the apostle but also—it seems legitimate to say this—of the human race, which he somehow represented.[35] Now in heaven she carries on her motherly role, "helping to nourish and foster the divine life in the souls of redeemed men. This truth is a most consoling one, and God in his wisdom has made it an integral part of the mystery of human salvation."[36]

Again, in *Marialis Cultus*, which places emphasis on the *integration of Marian devotion into Christian worship*, the central understanding of Mary is given in her being the pre-eminent member of the Church, a shining example and the loving mother.

The introduction points already to the centrality of Mary in the mystery of the Church:

> The Church's reflection today on the mystery of Christ and on her own nature has led her to find at the root of the former and as a culmination of the latter the same figure of a woman: the Virgin Mary, the Mother of Christ and the Mother of the Church. And the increased knowledge of Mary's mission has become joyful veneration of her and adoring respect for the wise plan of God, who has placed within his family [the Church], as in every home, the figure of a woman, who in a hidden manner and in a spirit of service watches over that family.[37]

The *interrelatedness between the Church and Mary* is expressed in the following text:

> The faithful will be able to appreciate more easily Mary's mission in the mystery of the Church and her preeminent place in the

---

Second Vatican Council," 39–68; Langella, "Maria Paradigm antropologico nella teologia postconciliare," 3–10.

33. Pope Paul VI, *Signum Magnum*, 465–75; and *Marialis Cultus*.
34. *Signum Magnum*, part I.
35. *Lumen gentium*, no. 58.
36. *Signum Magnum*, part I.
37. *Marialis Cultus*, Introduction. For the concept of "living memory" in *Marialis Cultus*, see Roten, "Memory and Mission," 86–88.

> communion of saints if attention is drawn to the Second Vatican Council's reference to the fundamental concepts of the *nature of the Church as the Family of God, the People of God, the Kingdom of God and the Mystical Body of Christ*. This will also bring the faithful to a deeper realization of the brotherhood which unites all of them as sons and daughters of the Virgin Mary, "who with a mother's love has cooperated in their rebirth and spiritual formation," and as sons and daughters of the Church. . . . They will also realize that both the *Church and Mary collaborate to give birth to the Mystical Body* of Christ since "both of them are the Mother of Christ, but neither brings forth the whole [body] independently of the other."[38] Similarly the faithful will appreciate more clearly that the action of the Church in the world can be likened to an extension of Mary's concern.[39]

In *Redemptoris Mater*, Pope John Paul II gives an *original synthesis* of essential elements of chapter VIII of *Lumen gentium, Marialis Cultus, Signum Magnum, Christi Matri*[40] and his personal reflections regarding Mary and the Church.[41] Primarily in the consideration is Mary's exceptional *pilgrimage of faith* in which she "advanced, faithfully preserving her union with Christ.[42] In this way the *twofold bond* which unites the Mother of God *with Christ and with the Church* takes on historical significance."[43]

Ecclesiologically the Pope speaks within "the redemptive economy of grace"[44] of

> a unique correspondence between the moment of the Incarnation of the Word and the moment of the birth of the Church. The person who links these two moments is Mary: Mary at Nazareth and Mary in the Upper Room at Jerusalem. In both cases her discreet yet essential presence indicates the path of "birth from the Holy Spirit." Thus she who is present in the mystery of Christ as Mother becomes—by the will of the Son and the power of

---

38. Isaac of Stella, *Sermo* LI, "In Assumptione B. Mariae," in PL, 1863A.

39. *Marialis Cultus*, no. 28.

40. Pope Paul VI, *Christi Matri*, 745–49.

41. Roten considers *Redemptoris Mater* under the aspect of "the dynamic memory" of Mary, in Roten, "Memory and Mission: A theological reflection on Mary in the paschal mysteries," 88–91.

42. *Lumen gentium*, no. 58. See in this context also Petri's comments to aspects of *Redemptoris Mater*. Petri, "Die Stellung Marias in der Kirche," 39–49.

43. *Redemptoris Mater*, no. 5. The frequency of the phrase "pilgrimage of faith" provides a certain dynamic dimension to the encyclical letter, for example, nos. 2, 6, 17, 18, 28, 39, 40, 49.

44. *Redemptoris Mater*, no. 24.

the Holy Spirit—present in the mystery of the Church. In the Church too she continues to be *a maternal presence*."[45]

Mary as the believer par excellence is present in the "ecclesial journey or pilgrimage through space and time, and even more through the history of souls";[46] she is present when that journey—"the *Church's pilgrimage through the history of individuals and peoples*"—begins at Pentecost, yet Mary's journey of faith began already at the Annunciation.[47]

The triad of Annunciation-Golgotha-Pentecost comes into perspective, as Mary, who is united in prayer with the disciples in the Upper Room "'goes before them,' 'leads the way' for them. The *moment of Pentecost* in Jerusalem had been prepared for by the *moment of the Annunciation* in Nazareth, as well as by the Cross. In the Upper Room, Mary's journey meets the Church's journey of faith."[48]

The *indissoluble unity of Mary with the mystery of Christ is constitutive of her indissoluble unity with the Church*, therefore at "the basis of what the Church has been from the beginning, and of what she must continually become from generation to generation, in the midst of all the nations on earth" is *Mary, the believer* (Luke 1:45).[49] It is precisely her "faith which marks the beginning of the new and eternal Covenant of God with man in Jesus Christ"[50]; and

> this *heroic faith* of hers *precedes* the apostolic *witness* of the Church, and ever remains in the Church's heart, hidden like a special heritage of God's revelation. All those who from generation to generation accept the apostolic witness of the Church share in that mysterious inheritance and in *a sense share in Mary's faith*.[51]

Thus "she offers hope to those . . . who are still on the journey." She is at the same time "an *icon of fidelity for the Church as a whole*, a concrete symbol of

---

45. Ibid.
46. Ibid., no. 25.
47. Ibid., no. 26.
48. Ibid.
49. Ibid., no. 27.
50. Ibid. See also the second last paragraph of no. 28.
51. Ibid., no. 27. It is perhaps in this perspective where Mary's significance is shown in ecumenical-ecclesiological dialogue; but here too holds true what Jelly writes: "Not only do we Catholics have to present our Madonna in the clearest light possible, reflecting the best in our Tradition, but we too must learn from our fellow Christians not only their problems with our Marian doctrines and devotions, but also their own traditions about her place in the church." Jelly, *Madonna: Mary in the Catholic Tradition*, 114.

hope that the Church as a whole may not stray from the path of truth and faithful action in response to the Gospel."[52]

Mary's presence in the mystery of the Church is *more than that of a model and figure*, because "the Church's mystery also consists in generating people to a new and immortal life: this is her motherhood in the Holy Spirit. And here Mary is . . . much more." For, "*with maternal love she cooperates in the birth and development*" of the sons and daughters of Mother Church."[53] Christ's word from the cross (cf. John 19:26–27), which determines Mary's place in the life of the faithful, expresses "the *new motherhood* of the Mother of the Redeemer: a spiritual motherhood."[54]

In this context the Pope speaks of a "Marian dimension of the life of Christ's disciple," that is, Mary's motherhood is "a gift which Christ himself makes personally to every individual. . . . At the foot of the Cross there begins that special entrusting of humanity to the Mother of Christ."[55] Like the apostle John, the Christian who responds to this *gift*

> "welcomes" the Mother of Christ "into his own home" and brings her into everything that makes up his inner life, that is to say into his human and Christian "I." . . . This filial relationship, this self-entrusting of a child to its mother, not only has its *beginning in Christ* but can also be said to be *definitively directed toward him*.[56]

The Church always maintains a close link with Mary "which embraces, in the saving mystery, the past, the present and the future, and venerates her as the *spiritual mother of humanity and the advocate of grace*."[57]

Concluding these considerations, the following can be said: The Second Vatican Council indeed marked a turning point in the Church's approach to her own identity and mission which consequently affected Marian theology and spirituality. What emerged from the conciliar discussion and from post-conciliar magisterial documents, in particular from the writings

---

52. Hines, "Mary and the Prophetic Mission of the Church," 287–88.

53. *Redemptoris Mater*, no. 44.

54. A motherhood, "born from the heart of the Paschal Mystery of the Redeemer of the world. It is a motherhood in the order of grace, for it implores the gift of the Spirit who raises up the new children of God, redeemed through the sacrifice of Christ: that Spirit who together with the church Mary too received on the day of Pentecost. Her motherhood is particularly noted and experienced by the Christian people . . . at the liturgical celebration of the mystery of the redemption. Mary guides the faithful to the Eucharist." *Redemptoris Mater*, no. 44.

55. *Redemptoris Mater*, no. 45.

56. Ibid., nos. 45–46.

57. Ibid., no. 47. Also Roten, "Memory and Mission," 126.

of the recent popes, suggests a balanced approach toward a more integrated Mariology.[58]

Mary *represents* in a *tangible and personal form* the Church's own identity, activity and goal. This more integrated picture of Mary and the Church has raised and opened up many issues, which necessarily involve further investigation and development.

Aspects of Post-conciliar Developments in Non-magisterial Documents

Based on the conciliar teaching, Catholic Marian theology has, contrary to numerous negative reactions, further developed during the post-Vatican II era, thanks not only to outstanding magisterial works, but also to eminent Mariologists, Marian academic institutions, ecumenical commissions, academic professional societies, and periodicals.[59]

Contemporary Marian studies—enriched by a biblical rediscovery of Mary's unique role—reflect upon hermeneutical-cultural, anthropological-historical, Mariological-ecclesiological, ecumenical, liturgical, and related aspects. De Fiores gives a substantial presentation of these aspects. He points out three distinct pathways of developments of post-conciliar Mariology that were inaugurated by Vatican II. He points out *renewal, recovery,* and *cultural encounter.*[60]

---

58. Just as in pre-conciliar writings the relationship was restricted to Mary's model character and this predominantly for the lay faithful, for example, Semmelroth, so in post-conciliar Mariological-ecclesiological writing there is a danger of limiting Mary's relationship with the Church in metaphorical, symbolical terms. Here, the writings of Pope Paul VI and Pope John Paul II propose significant perspectives for a more balanced view. For the different "perspective" see Coyle, "Marian Theology Today," 134–49; Hauke, "Freiheit und Gehorsam im Marienbild feministischer Theologien," 85–104. Although "the language about Mary is always immediately transferable to language about the church within that threefold dialectic of archaeology, teleology, and eschatology," so Chapman says that, "the person of Mary is never lost; the two are simply transcended by the power of a uniting metaphor that discovers that the two are in fact one in Being." Chapman, "Mary as Metaphor," 39.

59. De Fiores "Mary in Postconciliar Theology," 469–539; Phan, *Mary in Recent Theology and Piety*. Academic Journals: *Ephemerides Mariologicae, Marian Studies, Theotokos, Études Mariales, Marianum, Theotokos: Ricerche interdisciplinary di Mariologia.*

60. De Fiores, "Mary in Postconciliar Theology," 477–522; Gómez, *Mary, Virgin and Mother in Theology and Devotion*; Gambero, *Mary and the Fathers of the Church*; Gambero, *Mary in the Middle Ages*; Miravalle, *Mariology*; Perry et al., *The Blessed Virgin Mary*; Boss, *Mary: The Complete Resource*; The Pontifical International Marian Academy, *The Mother of the Lord*.

While the focus of *renewal* is primarily on Mary's place in Christology and ecclesiology (for example, Marian references in Sacred Scripture and the Marian dogmas), based on advanced doctrinal and exegetical findings[61] as well as historical, linguistic, liturgical, ecumenical, and studies of human sciences[62]; *recovery* focuses above all on the relationship between Mary and the Holy Spirit, the pneumatological dimension, and Mary's role within the people of God, Christian living, and Marian devotion.[63]

In *cultural encounter* the areas of Mary and culture/s,[64] feminism,[65] theological anthropology,[66] liberation-theological questions,[67] interreligious

---

61. De Fiores, "Mary in Postconciliar Theology," 477–522; Phan, *Mary in Recent Theology and Piety*; Brown et al., *Mary in the New Testament*; Buby, *Mary of Galilee*; Blanco Pacheco, "'Derriba del trono a los poderosos y enaltece a los humildes' (Lc 1,52)," 347–60; Santiago, *Evangelio de Lucas*; Aparicio Rodríguez, "Los dones del Espíritu Santo a María, templo del Espíritu," 203–18; Carreón and Luna, "Estructura del Magnificat," 122–38; Rossier, "Kecharitomene (Lk. 1:28) in the Light of Genesis 18:16–33," 159–83; Pavía, *Y el angel anunció a María*.

62. McLoughlin et al. *Mary for Earth and Heaven*; Unterseher, "Mary in Contemporary Protestant Theological Discourse," 194–212; Denaux et al., *Studying Mary*; Anglican and Roman Catholic International Commission, "The Seattle Statement Mary: Grace and Hope in Christ"; Blancy et al., *Mary in the Plan of God and in the Communion of Saints*; Gentle, "The Blessed Virgin Mary's Cooperation in the Redemption," 40–58; Largo Domínguez, "María y la esperanza en la Declaración ecuménica de Seattle," 309–28; Garrapucho, "La madre de Jesús en el actual diálogo ecuménico," 51–68; Genig, "A Forgotten Word and a Forgotten Woman," 52–72; Kimball, "The Influence of Scripture in the Marian Ecumenical Exchange in the 20th and 21st Centuries," 95–126; Greenacre at al, *Maiden, Mother and Queen*; Harán et al., *La cooperación del cristiano con la gracia (cooperación de María y de la iglesia) en una perspectiva ecuménica*; Sherlock, "The Anglican and Roman Catholic Ecclesial Traditions," 362–79.

63. De Fiores, "Mary in Postconciliar Theology," 477–522; Phan, *Mary in Recent Theology and Piety*; Baril, *The Feminine Face of the People of God*; Ratzinger, *Daughter Zion*; Manelli, "La 'Presenza' dell'Immacolata nella vita spirituale," 159–223; Dunn, *Finding Grace with God*; Cabello, "María, madre del Buen Consejo," 259–76.

64. Chua, *Theological-Spiritual Reflection on the Role of Mary*; De Fiores, *Dios nos habla a través de María*; Adingra, *La place et le rôle de Marie dans l'église-famille de Dieu en Afrique*; Shahada Sharelle, *Noble Women of Faith*; Clarke, *The Virgin Mary and Catholic Identities in Chinese History*; Mondíjar et al. "Presencia Mariana y experiencia de María en varios continentes," 297–306; Largo Domínguez, "El dios de María," 57–88. See here in particular the excellent study by Boff, *Mariologia Sociale*, 122–255 and 284–91.

65. Levine, *A Feminist Companion to Mariology*; Beattie, *God's Mother, Eve's Advocate*; Calloway, *The Virgin Mary and Theology of the Body*; Johnson, *Truly our Sister*; Maeckelberghe, *Desperately Seeking Mary*; Hultin, "A New Web for Archne and a New Veil for the Temple," 209–23; Hamington, *Hail Mary?*; Malick, "An Examination of Jesus's View of Women through Three Intercalations in the Gospel of Mark," 4–15.

66. Donald, *The Virgin Mary and Theology of the Body*; Hearden, *Mary: God-Bearer to a World in Need*; Boff, *The Maternal Face of God*; Cunneen, *In Search of Mary*.

67. *Documento de Puebla III Conferencia General del Episcopado Latinoamericano*; Gebara, *Mary, Mother of God, Mother of the Poor*.

dialogue,⁶⁸ aesthetics, art, film, and contemporary discussions of dogmatic statements like Mary and the role of women—to mention a few—are investigated.⁶⁹

Similarly, the document *The Virgin Mary in Intellectual and Spiritual Formation*, mentions these areas. These include new frontiers for Mariology that are opened up by *biblical exegesis of intertestamental literature*; in the *field of dogmatic theology*, with "the insights of biblical exegesis . . . and tradition . . . the critical study of the historical circumstances in which these dogmas were defined, and of the language in which they were formulated"; in evaluation of *Marian liturgical expressions and devotion*; in the field of *ecumenism and inter-religious discourse*; anthropology with the subject of "Mary and women"; the *pneumatological* dimension, "the problem of *inculturation* of Marian doctrine, forms and Marian piety and the area of *pastoral service*."⁷⁰

The Cultural-symbolic Significance of Mary

The above mentioned dimensions need to be translated into categories of contemporary mentality and existential concern, therefore from an ecclesial perspective it is particular important to mention the *cultural-symbol significance of Mary*.

As *Christ* was born into a particular culture, concretized in Mary, so every acceptance of Christ in a culture must bear *Marian features*. And the original image every culture can relate to is that of *Mother and child*. (We will return to this image in the next part.)⁷¹

The *history of Christianity* effectively illustrates the intricate correlation between culture and Sacred Scripture, "Christianity must embody itself in appropriate cultural forms; for a faith that does not become culture is a faith not fully received."⁷²

---

68. Hearden, "Ambassador for the World," 18–38; Sullivan, "Mary's Virginity as the Sign of Her Faith," 1–25; Carroll, "Mary/Maryam, Woman of Faith for Christians and Muslims," 30–35; Abbud, *Mary in the Quran*; Reck, "The Annunciation to Mary," 355–83; Mahmutćehajić, *Praised and the Virgin*; Hearden, "Lessons from Zeitoun," 409–26.

69. De Fiores, "Mary in Postconciliar Theology," 477–522; Phan, *Mary in Recent Theology and Piety*; Thompson, "Virgin-Mother Mary and Virgin-Mother Church," 325–48; Altmann, "Right and Left in Art," 223–38.

70. Congregation for Catholic Education, *The Virgin Mary in Intellectual and Spiritual Formation*, 10–16, 32–33.

71. For the following I am particularly indebted to Roten, *Contemporary Culture, the Trinity and Mary*; Roten, "Mary: Woman of Faith," 4–24.

72. Roten, *Contemporary Culture, the Trinity and Mary*, and "Mary: Woman of Faith," 14–18. Pope John Paul II, *Redemptoris Missio*, nos. 52–54.

History also shows that *"cultural Christianity,* the glue that sealed for centuries the unity between Church and world, has lost its cohesive power in some parts of the Church (Europe, North American, Latin America) or was never really present and active in others (India, Africa, China)."[73]

To counteract the progressive dissolution of its identity as world Church, the Church is in need of a higher cultural profile, a *transformational model,* by "taking the person as one's starting-point and always coming back to the relationships of people among themselves and with God"[74] in order to render the truth of the gospel culturally (spiritually, sociologically, and psychologically) meaningful.[75]

Although the *gospel and evangelization* are not identical with culture and *above any culture* (supra-cultural), they are capable of permeating them without becoming subject to them. To ensure a full evangelization of culture/s they have to be regenerated by an encounter with the gospel.[76] Acknowledging the originality of each culture, while at the same time accentuating their inadequacies (partly in respect to the divine order) the Church rejects any cultural relativism but promotes inculturation, based on one of the most important criteria in assessing culture, that of its compatibility with the gospel and communion with the universal Church.[77]

It is within these parameters (Christianity and culture) that the central event of the *Incarnation of the God-Man* where "Mary and contemporary culture come together and explain themselves in mutuality and interdependence."[78]

Incarnation understood in anthropological perspective operates according to a model of receiving and giving, meaning the laws of life both biological and spiritual. Where *truth and love* come together in a person, faith extends, accommodates and becomes adaptable and *truly Marian and ecclesial* because it will concentrate and be centered on *being for,* being for God being for the other, "called to exist for others, to become a gift."[79]

---

73. "The split between the Gospel and culture is without a doubt the drama of our time, just as it was of other times." *Evangelii Nuntiandi,* no. 20; Roten, *Contemporary Culture, the Trinity and Mary*; Roten, "Mary: Woman of Faith," 14–18.

74. *Evangelii Nuntiandi,* no. 20. ["What matters is to evangelize man's culture and cultures, in the wide and rich sense which these terms have in *Gaudium et spes* (53), always taking the person as one's starting-point and always coming back to the relationships of people among themselves and with God."]

75. Roten, *Contemporary Culture, the Trinity and Mary.*

76. *Evangelii Nuntiandi,* no. 20.

77. Roten, *Contemporary Culture, the Trinity and Mary,* 2–3.

78. Ibid., 4.

79. *Mulieris Dignitatem,* no. 7; see also Rossi Espagnet, "Densitá antropologica della

Here lies one of the foundational reasons for Mary's cultural charism and incarnational impact on culture. Her whole life is based on the sincere gift of self, and her call to exist for others and to become gift.[80]

Mary's portrayal at the Incarnation is that of *culture made individual person and mother* into which the second person of the Holy Trinity incarnates as Jesus Christ. And, the understanding of the *Christ event* as ongoing incarnation (wherever the mystery of Christ is object of cultural transfer, reassessment, and inculturation) invariably makes of *Mary a witness to and a guardian* of this reality and its intrinsic correlation to all aspects of human life.[81]

The close connection between Mary, as the mother of God incarnate and redeemer of humankind, and Mary as the universal archetype of mother and of motherliness is of trans-cultural (common to all human beings) importance. It places her, the mother of life eternal, in a uniquely privileged position to promote and sustain Christian evangelization and inculturation.[82]

Contemporary theological reflections on Mary's cultural charism and its incarnational impact offer some *fascinating images of Mary*. Based on these essential Catholic yet cultural-diverse studies, Roten mentions in particular four prominent contemporary cultural images of Mary[83]: The *vitalist* image of Mary in Africa, the *spiritual* image of Mary in Asia (in particular India), the strongly *socially* oriented image of Mary in Latin America, and the *personalist* image of Mary in Western culture, mainly the North Atlantic culture (Western Europe and North America).

---

figura di Maria nella '*Mulieris dignitatem*,'" 49–65.

80. Roten, "Mary: Woman of Faith," 16–18.

81. Ibid.

82. Ibid. (The archetype of the mother is a universal archetype of the human psyche.)

83. Ibid. Within this context see also Muzumanga, "Naissance du Fils de Dieu et Immaculée Conception en Afrique," 69–104; Adingra, *La place et le rôle de Marie dans l'église-famille de Dieu en Afrique*; Chigumira, "Mary as a Symbol of Inspiration for the Empowerment of Southern African Christian Women Disproportionately Infected/Affected by HIV and AIDS," 117–38; Uzumanga, "Marie entre l'Ancienne et la Nouvelle Évangélisation de l'Afrique," 295–320; Sapitula, "Marian Piety and Modernity," 399–424; Bitoy, "Tender Mother, Gentle Revolutionary," 435–44; Shahada. *Noble Women of Faith*; Clarke, *The Virgin Mary and Catholic Identities in Chinese History*; Armanski, *Die großen Göttinnen*; Fernández García, "Presencia de Mar a en la mission evangelizadora," 447–54; Mondíjar, "Presencia Mariana y experiencia de María en varios continentes," 297–306; Largo Domínguez, "El dios de María," 57–88; Pissarek-Hudelist, "Maria—Schwester oder Mutter im Glauben?" 146–67; The Pontifical International Marian Academy, *The Mother of the Lord*, 109–12; Beinert, *Unsere Liebe Frau und die Frauen*, 139–68; Boff, *Mariologia Sociale*, 122–55; 284–91.

The *African image of Mary* is a manifesto for life reflecting the goodness and beauty of life, of life received, celebrated and passed on, of life treasured and shared in community; life in this world as promise and anticipation of the eternal life to come. Mary embodies this holy vitalism as mother and guardian of life, manifesting faith as life and communion of life. The Marian figure of some of the *Asian cultures* conveys a strong ecumenical note. She is a highly spiritual figure inviting the communion of spirits, pointing to unity beyond diversity, inviting reconciliation and communion in the transcendent. In the Asian representation of Mary we find the relational and unifying character of spirit and love. *Mary of Latin America* is both the Mother of Sorrows and Our Lady of the Magnificat. She is a symbol of sacrificial love with a strongly incarnational purpose, embodying hope, change, transformation and social justice; she stands for righting the wrongs of the past and embodies the dawn of a better future. Thus, in the Latin-American understanding of Mary there is a strong incarnational thrust of faith. Contemporary *North Atlantic culture* has discovered Mary as one of us: a sister figure, a companion on our pilgrimage to God, our *alter ego* and the figurehead for many causes and a variety of situations. The eschatological thrust of faith as remembered in Mary's companionship on our pilgrimage to God is prominent.[84]

Roten further asserts that although, being aware of the limitations and the stereotypical character of these images, culture is at all levels typical by nature, and has a typifying tendency and character. The symbolic expression and value of these images lead to further investigation into their engendering importance for the evangelizing mission of the Church in the third millennium.[85]

The Image of Mother and Child as Theo-cultural Synthesis

A most pertinent presentation of Mary's persona and faith, and her theological and cultural identity can be seen in the image of *mother and child*. It highlights Mary's historical role as Theotokos, and the human archetype perceived in the affective relationship with Mary.[86]

> The icon of mother and child is probably the most powerful symbol and one of the best syntheses of Christianity. It brings together . . . the many facets of God's self-revelation to the world.

---

84. Roten, "Mary: Woman of Faith," 4–24.
85. Ibid., 16–17.
86. Ibid., 17.

> It stresses in particular the unbreakable unity . . . between God and humankind. Symbol of the Incarnation, the icon of Mother and Child suggests and anticipates in subtle ways the semantics of redemption: God gives himself away (manifests himself as a child); he identifies with the little ones to give them new stature and heightened self-understanding (represented in the adult figure of a mother).[87]

The image of *Mother and child* not only portrays how Christ is growing in us so that we might be able to grow in him, it is in particular a living testament of love, speaking without ceasing of God's loving self-giving, and the loving reception this gift was given in Mary's heart and womb. This image is an unvarying reminder of God's everlasting love directed to the whole world at all times and a constant and living witness to the divine-human unity. It testifies to the ever-active presence of the Spirit in Mary's life. With its universal cultural appeal the Mother-Child representation is the symbol of love and life, able to cross all borders of human understanding, and uniting humanity in some of its most fundamental values and concerns.[88]

To sum up these reflections we may turn to von Balthasar's words:

> The image of Mary [Mother and Child] is incontestable, and even to nonbelievers it represents a treasure of inviolable beauty, even when it is understood not as an image of faith but only as a sublime symbol interpreted according to universal human categories.[89]

Multicultural as we are in our Western society, it becomes obvious that, from an ecclesiological and theological-anthropological perspective, enriched, as mentioned, by its cultural impetus, Mariology can provide a significant point of unity in diversity.

Conclusion—The Ecclesial Context of Mariology (for the Third Millennium)

Having considered aspects of post-Vatican II Mariology with a particular focus on Mary's cultural significance, we may return to our starting point

---

87. Ibid.

88. Ibid., 18.

89. Balthasar, *The Glory of the Lord*, 562. Our ecclesial tradition makes evident that a "faith which does not encompass the whole of human reality will be neither dynamic nor incarnational. It will be sectarian but not cultural; it will abandon its truly Catholic character, and no longer deserve the name of Marian faith." Roten, "Mary: Woman of Faith," 18.

of what may be poised as a question "Is there a place for Mary/Mariology in the Third Millennium?"

The answer may come from the Church's own self-understanding. Called by God "to become the principle of all that belongs to the Church"[90] (God's *Wort* und the human *Antwort*), von Balthasar rightly sees in Mary the archetypical realization of the Church[91] and thus "the true and universal, fundamental spirit of all the individual charisms"[92] in the Church. The essential attitude which constitutes Mary's archetypal character is convincingly given by Ratzinger, when he writes:

> God's word to Mary "is pure *Yes*, just as she herself stands before him as a pure *Yes*" (freedom from original sin). "This correspondence of God's *Yes* with Mary's *Yes* . . . denotes that Mary reserves no area of being, life, and will for herself as a private possession: instead, precisely in the total dispossession of self (what von Balthasar terms *de-privatized*),[93] in giving herself to God, she comes to the true possession of self."[94]

She stands at the cross [John 19:25–27] already redeemed through the cross. In this she becomes (under the cross), "bride, the quintessence of the Church."[95]

> As the helpmate of the New Adam she gives her spiritual consent and receives the gift of his redemptive grace in lieu of the Church and for her. She, who perfectly received her Son in her heart and body, now receives him as the Immaculate Church, in faith and love always.[96]

This, her *all comprehensive fiat*—in its perfection unequalled—becomes the all-embracing, protective and directive form for the whole ecclesial life, the interior form of *communio*, in so far as this is an unlimited mutual

---

90. Balthasar, *Explorations in theology: Creator Spirit*, 295.
91. Ibid.
92. Ibid.
93. Balthasar, *The Glory of the Lord*, 341; Roten, "How Can Spirituality be Marian?," 50.
94. Ratzinger, *Daughter Zion*, 70. See also Lohfink, *Maria—nicht ohne Israel*.
95. Roten, "Memory and Mission: A Theological Reflection on Mary in the Paschal Mysteries," 100 (Balthasar and Speyr, *Au coeur du mystère rédempteur*, 62.).
96. Roten, "Memory and Mission," 100; Balthasar, *Church and World*, 137 and *Razing the Bastions*. See here also the excellent study by Oster, *Person und Transsubstantiation*, 39–41; 431–73.

acceptance. And in this, her *Christoform* attitude becomes *foundational for the communio fidelium*.⁹⁷

The receptivity of Mary's faith, her Yes, is not passive or submissive in its

> openness, but rather, is characterized by an active fecundity. Her perfect (unconditional) act of faith is what opens the door to the Incarnation of the Word in her fruitful womb—a paradigm that holds true for all believers who must "give birth" to Christ in the womb of their own hearts through faith.⁹⁸

It is "*Mary's subjective act of faith*, therefore, that becomes the ground for the subjective act of the Church as such, as well as the *ground for each individual act of faith*."⁹⁹ In effect, we can say, that Mary's initial yes grew into a *permanent Fiat-structure* for the *ecclesial community*. As such, this *Fiat*-structure comes alive, grows and matures through the theological virtues of faith, hope and charity, consequently emphasizing the strongly incarnational character of our *ecclesial* beliefs and behavior.¹⁰⁰ The holiness of the Church finds its ground and personal center, in the *point vierge*, in *Mary's Immaculate Conception*.¹⁰¹

Considering the theological-anthropological perspective of the *human person as imago Dei*, which points to the fact that "personhood is distinct from mere self-aware 'subjectivity'" and that "every human person, exists in the order of grace as '*one who is sent*' by God with a specific 'task,'"¹⁰²—called

---

97. Balthasar, *Der antirömische Affekt?*, 173. See also McPartlan, "Mary and Catholic-Orthodox Dialogue," 12; Roten, "Memory and Mission," 81.

98. Chapp, *The God who speaks*, 208.

99. Ibid.; Huguet, "Anthropologie de l'espérance, Appelés à une vivante espérance (1P 1,3)," 45–53.

100. Roten, "How can Spirituality be Marian," 11.

101. Wright, *Mary and the Catholic Imagination*, 61–71. Chapp, *The God who speaks*, 208. Roten succinctly illustrates this when he distinguishes that Mary is not only an "actor in the event and process of salvation history" but also as the "recipient of salvation, and thus a redeemed creature. This fully graced person—the Immaculata—is indeed both a 'fully and perfectly redeemed person' and the 'ideal of faith.' . . . Redeeming grace was given to her in abundance, but it needed to be received in faith and lived out in obedience." Roten, "Marian Devotion for the New Millennium," 61–62. See also Rahner, "The Immaculate Conception," 206–7 and *Mary, Mother of the Lord*, 44–47; Ratzinger, *Daughter Zion*, 69; Novotny, "Making Mary's Yes Our Own," 101–22. According to Balthasar, Mary's interaction with God is the exemplary event of the God-human relation—encouraging every person to creatively participate fully in the glorious liberty of the children of God. Von Balthasar, *Church and World*, 132–37.

102. Balthasar, "On the Concept of Person," 18. See also Walker, "Personal Singularity and the Communio Personarum," 457–79; Ratzinger, "Concerning the Notion of

as *acting person to active participation*. This *being sent* becomes concrete in the context of human history and where the individual person—in her/his distinctness and dignity—is called to respond to God's gift of freedom by either affirming or denying God's offer, creation and self.[103] At the same time, human personhood is fundamentally oriented to the "other" in such a way as to find its truest inner fulfillment in the *kenotic gift of self to the other* something analogous to the perichoresis of the Trinitarian relation. The God-given "mission" of the individual person is essentially and socially oriented to all other God-given "missions"[104] and therefore is dialogical and communal. Thus, in an archetypal and culturally significant fashion, Mary, in her response to God in the continuous dialogic event—Trinitarian freedom and Mary's human freedom—is the *theological person, the person with God*[105] for the third millennium.

It is for this reason that von Balthasar's words are also valid for today:

> Without Mariology Christianity threatens imperceptibly to become inhuman. The Church becomes functionalistic, soulless, a hectic enterprise without any point of rest, estranged from its true nature by the planners. And because, in this manly-masculine world, all that we have is one ideology replacing another, everything becomes polemical, critical, bitter, humorless, and ultimately boring, and people in their masses run away from such a Church.[106]

Person in Theology," 452–53.

103. Naumann, "Mary as the Anthropological Model in the Thought of J. Kentenich," 31–47. See also Di Noia, "Imago Dei—Imago Christi," 276; Ackermann, "The Church as Person in the Theology of Hans Urs von Balthasar," 241–42.

104. Schindler, "Luigi Giussani on the 'Religious Sense' and the Cultural Situation of Our Time," 103.

105. Novotny, "Making Mary's Yes Our Own," 101–3. Roten succinctly illustrates this when he distinguishes Mary not only as an "actor in the event and process of salvation history" but also as the "recipient of salvation, and thus a redeemed creature. This fully graced person is indeed both a 'fully and perfectly redeemed person' and the 'ideal of faith,' and thus is justly acclaimed as the 'personal summit of the faithful' . . . Redeeming grace was given to her in abundance, but it needed to be received in faith and lived out in obedience patterned on the Fiat of the Annunciation." Roten, "Marian Devotion for the New Millennium," 61–62. See also: Naumann, "Pentecost: between Hope and Expectation," 164–65; Rahner, "The Immaculate Conception," 201–13.

106. Balthasar, *Elucidations*, 72.

Bibliography

Ackermann, Stefan. "The Church as Person in the Theology of Hans Urs von Balthasar." *Communio* 29 (2002) 238–49.
Acta Synodalia Sacrosancti Concilii oecumenici Vaticani II. Rome: Polyglottis Vatican 1970–86.
Abbud, Hosn. *Mary in the Quran: A Literary Reading*. Routledge Studies in the Qur'an. Abingdon, UK: Routledge, 2013.
Adingra, Eugène. "La place et le rôle de Marie dans l'église-famille de Dieu en Afrique: sur la base du rôle de la mère dans la famille africaine en général." PhD diss., Dayton, OH: International Marian Research Institute, 2014.
Altmann, Simon L. "Right and Left in Art: The Annunciation." *Empirical Studies of the Arts* 31 (2013) 223–38.
Anglican and Roman Catholic International Commission. *Mary: Grace and Hope in Christ. The Seattle Statement of the Anglican-Roman Catholic International Commission*. Edited by Bolen, Donald and Gregory Cameron. London: Continuum, 2006.
Armanski, Gerhard. *Die großen Göttinnen: Isis (und Maria), Aphrodite, Venu*. Würzburg: Königshausen und Neumann, 2013.
Balthasar, Hans Urs von, and Adrienne von Speyr. *Au coeur du mystère rédempteur*. Chambray: Éditions CID, 1980.
Balthasar, Hans Urs von. *Der antirömische Affekt: Wie lässt sich das Papstum in der Gesamtkirche integrieren?* Einsiedeln/Trier: Johannes, 1989.
———. *Church and World*. New York: Herder and Herder, 1967.
———. *Elucidations*. London: SPCK, 1975.
———. *Explorations in Theology: Creator Spirit. Vol. 3*. San Francisco: Ignatius, 1993.
———. *The Glory of the Lord. Vol I. Seeing the Form*. Translated by Erasmo Leivà-Merikakis. San Francisco: Ignatius, 1982.
———. *Razing the Bastions*. San Francisco: Ignatius, 1993.
Barth, Karl. *Kirchliche Dogmatik*. Vol I. Zurich: Theologischer Verlag, 1993.
Beattie, Tina. *God's Mother, Eve's Advocate*. London: Continuum, 2004.
Beinert, Wolfgang. "Maria im Geheimnis Christi und der Kirche." In *Communio Sanctorum. Einheit der Christen-Einheit der Kirche. Festschrift für Bischof Paul-Werner Scheele*, edited by Josef Schreiner, und Klaus Wittstadt, 284–309. Würzburg: Echter, 1988.
———. *Unsere Liebe Frau und die Frauen*. Freiburg: Herder, 1989.
Bitoy, Jonathan A. "Tender Mother, Gentle Revolutionary: Mary in the Life of the Filipinos." *Ephemerides Mariologicae* 63 (2013) 435–44.
Blanco Pacheco, Severiano. "'Derriba del trono a los poderosos y enaltece a los humildes' (Lc 1,52)." *Ephemerides Mariologicae* 63 (2013) 347–60.
Blancy, Alain, Maurice Jourjon, and the Domes Group. *Mary in the Plan of God and in the Communion of Saints*. Mahwah, NJ: Paulist, 2002.
Bliss, Frederick. "The Role of Mary in Ecumenical Relations between the Catholic Church and Her Major Ecumenical Partners." In *Mary, Woman of Faith. Proceedings from the 3rd Asia Oceania Mariological Conference, Manaoag, Pangasina*, edited by Roland D. Mactal, 84–100. Dagupan City, Philippines: Archdiocese of Lingayen-Dagupan, 2013.

Boff, Clodovis M. *Mariologia Sociale: Il significato della Vergine per la società*. Biblioteca di teologia contempranea 136. Brescia: Editrice Queriniana, 2007.

Boff, Leonardo. *The Maternal Face of God*. San Francisco: Harper & Row, 1987.

Boss, Sarah J., ed. *Mary: The Complete Resource*. London: Continuum, 2007.

———. *The Spirit of Mary*. New Haven, CT: Yale University Press, 2012.

Brown, Raymond, et al., eds. *Mary in the New Testament: A Collaborative Assessment by Protestant & Roman Catholic Scholars*. Mahwah, NJ: Paulist, 2000.

Buby, Bertrand. *Mary of Galilee* I–III. New York: Alba House, 1994, 1995, 1997.

Calloway, Donald H., ed. *The Virgin Mary and Theology of the Body*. West Chester, PA: Ascension, 2007.

Carreón Luna, Manuel. "Estructura del Magnificat," *Efemerides Mexicana* 82 (2010) 122–38.

Carroll, Sandra. "Mary/Maryam, Woman of Faith for Christians and Muslims: Pertinent Perspectives for Religious Educators." *Religious Education Journal of Australia*, 28 (2012) 30–35.

Catechism of the Catholic Church. Homebush, NSW: St. Pauls, 1994

Chapman, Mark E. "Mary as Metaphor: A Linguistic Proposal for the Recovery of Ecclesiology." *Currents in Theology and Mission* 20 (1993) 29–39.

Chapp, Larry S. *The God Who Speaks: Hans Urs von Bathasar's Theology of Revelation*. San Francisco: International Scholars, 1996.

Carr, Anne. "Mary in the Mystery of the Church: Vatican Council II." In *Mary According to Women*, edited by Carol-Francis Jegen, 5–32. Kansas City, MO: Leaven, 1985.

Chigumira, Godfrey. "Mary as a Symbol of Inspiration for the Empowerment of Southern African Christian Women Disproportionately Infected/Affected by HIV and AIDS." *Black Theology: An International Journal* 12 (2014) 117–38.

Chua, Celia. *Theological-Spiritual Reflection on the Role of Mary in the Concept of Trinitarian and Ecclesiological Communion Applied to a Family-ecclesio Model in Taiwan*. Rome: International Mariological Congress, 2000.

Clarke, James. *The Virgin Mary and Catholic Identities in Chinese History*. Hong Kong: Hong Kong University, 2013.

Clark, Elizabeth A. "Women, Gender, and the Study of Christian History." *Church History* 70 (2001) 395–426.

Colzani, Gianni. "Il ruolo di Maria nell'antropologia teologica postconciliare." *Theotokos: Ricerche interdisciplinary di Mariologia* 21 (2013) 67–89.

Congregation for Catholic Education. *The Virgin Mary in Intellectual and Spiritual Formation*. Rome, March 25, 1988.

Courth, Franz. "Marienglaube-Mari-enverehrung: Dogmatische Überlegungen zu aktuellen Fragen." *Münchener Theologische Zeitschrift* 31 (1980) 137–47.

———. "Maria–heute neu gefragt?" *Trierer Theologische Zeitschrift* 96 (1984) 40–50.

Cunneen, Sally. *In Search of Mary: The Woman and the Symbol*. New York: Ballantine, 1996.

Coyle, Kathryn. "Marian Theology Today: Reinterpreting the Symbols." *East Asian Pastoral Review* 26 (1989) 134–49.

De Bhaldraithe, Eoin. "The Challenge of the ARCIC Agreement on Mary." *Doctrine and Life* 60 (2010) 21–36.

De Fiores, Stefano. *Dios nos habla a través de María. Las apariciones Marianas en nuestro tiempo*. Madrid: San Pablo, 2013.

———. "Mary in Postconciliar Theology." In *Vatican II. Assessment and Perspectives. Twenty-five years After: 1962–1987*, 3 vols, edited by René Latourelle, vol. I, 1–471. Mahwah, NJ: Paulist, 1988.

De Luis Carballada, Ricardo. "La maternidad sacramental de María: La Mariología de Edward Schillebeeckx. " *Ephemerides Mariologicae* 62 (2012) 85–102.

Del Gaudio, Daniela. "La dimensione antropologica della Mariologia del Concilio Vaticano II." *Theotokos: Ricerche interdisciplinary di Mariologia* 21 (2013) 11–48.

Denaux, Adelbert and Nicolas Sagovsky. *Studying Mary: Reflections on the Virgin Mary in Anglican and Roman Catholic Theology and Devotion*. The ARCIC Working Papers. London: T. & T. Clark, 2007.

Di Noia, Anthony. "Imago Dei—Imago Christi: The Theological Foundations of Christian Humanism." *Nova et Vetera* 2 (2004) 267–78.

Dittrich, Achim *Protestantische Mariologie-Kritik: Historische Entwicklung bis 1997 und dogmatische Analyse*. Mariologische Studien 11. Regensburg: Franz Pustet, 1998.

Documento de Puebla III. Conferencia General del Episcopado Latinoamericano. Online: http://www.celam.org/doc_conferencias/Documento _Conclusivo_ Puebla.pdf.

Dunn, Rose E. *Finding Grace with God: A Phenomenological Reading of the Annunciation*. Eugene, OR: Pickwick, 2014.

Egbuonu, Douglas Nnamdi. *Vatican II on Mary: The Case for the Definition of the Spiritual Motherhood of Mary*. Bloomington, IN: Author House, 2014.

Escudero Cabello, A. "María, madre del Buen Consejo. Eco de una Mariología de la acción escatológica." *Ephemerides Mariologicae* 63 (2013) 259–76.

Esquerda Bifet, Juan. "María, Tipo de la Iglesia." *Estudios Marianos* XXXI (1968) 187–239.

———. "Sentido escatologico de la Tipologia Mariana," Estudios Marianos XXXIX (1974) 103–15.

Fairweather, Eugene. "The Church." In *The Second Vatican Council: Studies by Eight Anglican Observers*, edited by Bernard C. Pawley, 54–83. London: Oxford, 1967.

Farrell, Marie. "The Catechism's Approach to the Blessed Virgin Mary." In *The New Catechism: Analysis and Commentary*, edited by Andrew Murray, 39–46. Catholic Institute of Sydney. Brookvale, NSW: Prior, 1994.

Fernández García, B. "Presencia de Mar a en la mission evangelizadora." *Ephemerides Mariologicae* 60 (2010) 447–54.

Flores, Deyanira. "Jesus Christ, the Only-Begotten Son of the Father and of the Virgin Mother: Mary's Virginity from a Trinitarian Perspective." *Marian Studies* 58 (2007) 143–234.

———. "Mary, the Virgin: Completely and Permanently Transformed by God's Grace: The Meaning and Implications of Luke 1:28 and of the Dogma of the Immaculate Conception for Mary's Spiritual Life." *Marian Studies* 55 (2004) 47–113.

Forte, Bruno. *Maria, Mutter und Schwester des Glaubens*. Zürich: Benziger, 1990.

Fritz, Peter J. "Konkrete Dogmatik: Die Mariologie Karl Rahners." *Theological Studies* 74 (2013) 733–35.

Gambero, Luigi. *Mary and the Fathers of the Church: The Blessed Virgin Mary in Patristic Thought*. San Francisco: Ignatius, 1999.

———. *Mary in the Middle Ages: The Blessed Virgin Mary in the Thought of the Medieval Latin Theologians*. San Francisco: Ignatius, 2005.

García Llata, Carlos. "Esperanzas y cumplimientos en la historia de María." *Ephemerides Mariologicae* 62 (2012) 233–50.

García Paredes, José Cristo Rey"María en la espiritualidad del siglo XXI." *Ephemerides Mariologicae* 60 (2010) 35–50.

Garrapucho, Fernando R. "La madre de Jesús en el actual diálogo ecuménico." *Ephemerides Mariologicae* 60 (2010) 51–68.

Gebara, Ivone, and Maria Clara Bingemer. *Mary—Mother of God, Mother of the Poor*. Maryknoll, NY: Orbis, 1989.

Genig, Joshua D. "A Forgotten Word and a Forgotten Woman: A Lutheran Attempt at Regaining the Sacramentality of Scripture by Way of the Annunciation to Mary." *Marian Studies* 61 (2010) 52–72.

Gentle, Judith Marie. "The Blessed Virgin Mary's Cooperation in the Redemption: An Ecumenical Perspective." *Marian Studies* 59 (2008) 40–58.

Gössmann, Elisabeth. "Mariologische Entwicklungen im Mittelalter." In *Maria für alle Frauen oder über allen Frauen?* edited by Elisabeth Gössmann et al., 63–85. Freiburg: Herder, 1989.

Gómez, Felipe, S.J. *Mary, Virgin and Mother in Theology and Devotion*. Makati City: St. Pauls, 2011.

Greenacre, Roger and Colin Podmore, *Maiden, Mother and Queen: Mary in the Anglican Tradition*. Norwich: Canterbury, 2013.

Greshake, Gisbert. *Maria-Ecclesia: Perspektiven einer Marianisch grundierten Theologie und Kirchenpraxis*. Regensburg: Friedrich Pustet, 2014.

Gubler, Marie-Louise. *Maria: Mutter, Prophetin, Himmelskönigin*. Stuttgart: Katholisches Bibelwerk, 2008.

Hälbig, Klaus W. *Die Krönung der Braut: Gottes Vermählung mit der Welt in Maria*. Sankt Ottilien: Eos, 2014.

Hamington, Maurice. *Hail Mary? The Struggle for Ultimate Womanhood in Catholicism*. Hoboken, NJ: Taylor and Francis, 2014.

Harán, Alson and Javier Pedrito. *La cooperación del cristiano con la gracia (cooperación de María y de la iglesia) en una perspectiva ecumenical*. Dayton, OH: Semacon Foundation, 2013.

Hauke, Manfred. "Freiheit und Gehorsam im Marienbild feministischer Theologien." In *Maria: Gehorsam und Freiheit im Urbild der Kirche. Eine Veröffentlichung des Internationlen Mariologischen Arbeitskreises Kevelaer*, edited by German Rovira. 85–104. Aschaffenburg: Verlag Ursula Zöller, 1994.

Hearden, M., Kimball, V. M., eds. *Mary: God-Bearer to a World in Need*. Eugene, OR: Pickwick, 2013.

Hearden, Maura. "Ambassador for the World: Mary as a Bridge for Dialogue between Catholicism and Islam." *Journal of Ecumenical Studies* 41 (2004) 18–38.

———. "Lessons from Zeitoun: A Marian Proposal for Christian-Muslim Dialogue." *Journal of Ecumenical Studies* 47 (2012) 409–26.

Hines, Mary E. "Mary and the Prophetic Mission of the Church." *Journal of Ecumenical Studies* 28 (1991) 281–99.

Hogan, Robert. "Mary and the Catholic Charistmatic Renewal 1971–1978." *Marian Library Studies* 29 (2011–2012) 237–372.

Holler, Stephan. "The Origins of Marian Devotion in Latin American Cultures in the United States," *Marian Studies* 46 (1995) 108–27.

Huguet, Marie-Thérès. "Anthropologie de l'espérance, Appelés à une vivante espérance (1P 1, 3)," In *Llamados 'a una esperanza viva' (1P 1,3), Actos del Congreso Mariológico Mariano Internacional de Sevilla, 27–30 de mayo 2014*, edited by Stefano M Cecchin, 33–55. Ciudad del Vaticano: Pontificia Academia Mariana Internationalis, 2015.

Hultin, Jeremy F. "A New Web for Archne and a New Veil for the Temple: Women and Weaving from Athena to the Virgin Mary." In *Women and Gender in Ancient Religions: Interdisciplinary Approaches*, edited by S. P. Ahearne-Kroll et al., 209–23. Tübinger: Mohr Siebeck, 2010.

Isaac of Stella. Sermo LI, "In Assumptione B. Mariae" *Patrologia Latina* 194 edited by J. -P. Migne, 1862–66. Paris: Migne, 1855.

Jelly, Frederick et al. *Madonna: Mary in the Catholic Tradition*. Huntington, IN: Our Sunday Visitor, 1986.

———. "The Theological Context of and Introduction to Chapter 8 of Lumen gentium." *Marian Studies*, 37 (1986) 43–265.

Johnson, Elizabeth. "The Marian Tradition and the Reality of Women," In *Horizons on Catholic Feminist Theology*, edited by Joann Wolski Conn and Walter E. Conn, 85–107. Washington, DC: Georgetown University Press, 1992.

———. *Truly Our Sister: A Theology of Mary in the Communion of Saints*. New York: Continuum, 2003.

Jones, Barbara. *Empowered with Mary*. New Orleans: Pelican, 2000.

Kentenich, Josef, *Oktoberwoche*. Vallendar-Schönstatt: Schönstatt-Verlag, 1950.

Kereszty, Roch A. "Toward the Renewal of Mariology." *Nova et Vetera* 11 (2013) 779–99.

Kimball, Virginia M. "The Influence of Scripture in the Marian Ecumenical Exchange in the 20th and 21st Centuries: A Meeting Point of Dialogue." *Marian Studies* 61 (2010) 95–126.

Kimberly, Erwin A. "Pentecostal Women: Chosen for an Exalted Destiny." *Theology Today* 68 (2012) 404–12.

Kirwin, George F. "Mary's Salvific Role Compared With That of the Church." *Marian Studies* 25 (1974) 29–43.

Koehler, Theodore A. "Mary's Spiritual Maternity after the Second Vatican Council." *Marian Studies* 23 (1972) 39–68.

Kyte, Gabriel J. "The Joy of a Covenant Fulfilled: The Mariology of Pope Benedict XVI." MA thesis, St. Joseph's Seminary, Yonkers, NY, 2014.

Langella, Alfonso. "Maria Paradigm antropologico nella teologia postconciliare." *Theotokos: Ricerche interdisciplinary di Mariologia* 21 (2013) 3–10.

Largo Domínguez, Pablo. "El dios de María: un Dios para nuestra generación." *Ephemerides Mariologicae* 63 (2013) 57–88.

Levine, Amy-Jill, and Maria Mayo Robbins, eds. *A Feminist Companion to Mariology*. Cleveland, OH: Pilgrim, 2005.

———. "María y la esperanza en la Declaración ecuménica de Seattle." *Ephemerides Mariologicae* 62 (2012) 309–28.

Lohfink, Gerhard, and Ludwig Weimer. *Maria-nicht ohne Israel: Eine neue Sicht der Lehre von der Unbefleckten Empfängnis*. Freiburg: Herder, 2008.

Lubac, Henri de. *The Church: Paradox and Mystery*. New York: Alba House, 1969.

Macquarie, John. *Mary for All Christians*. Glasgow: Harper Collins, 1990.

Maeckelberghe, Els. *Desperately Seeking Mary: Feminist Appropriation of a Traditional Religious Symbol*. Kampen, The Netherlands: Pharos, 1991.

Mahmutćehajić, Rusmir. *Praised and the Virgin*. Philosophy of Religion. World religions, Vol. 3. Boston: Brill, 2014.

Malick, David E. "An Examination of Jesus's View of Women through Three Intercalations in the Gospel of Mark." *Priscilla Papers* 27.3 (2013) 4–15.

Manelli, Stefano M. "La 'Presenza' dell'Immacolata nella vita spiritual." *Immaculata Mediatrix: Rivista Internazionale di Teologia Mariana* 13 (2013) 159–223.

Martínez, Manuel A. "La Virgen María en los escritos de Yves Congar." *Ephemerides Mariologicae* 62 (2012) 31–60.

Mariño, Maria Jose. "K. Rahner: María, oyente de la palabra, Madre del Señor y hermana nuestra." *Ephemerides Mariologicae* 62 (2012) 11–30.

Masciarelli, Michaele G. "Antropolgia e Mariologia dopo il Vaticano II." *Theotokos: Ricerche interdisciplinary di Mariologia* 21 (2013) 129–67.

McDannell, Colleen. *Material Christianity: Religion and Popular Culture in America*. New Haven, CT: Yale University, 1995.

McDonnell, Kilian. "Feminist Mariologies: Heteronomy/Subordination and the Scandal of Christology," *Theological Studies* 66 (2005) 527–67.

McLoughlin, William, et al., eds. *Mary for Earth and Heaven: Papers on Mary and Ecumenism Given at International Congresses of the Ecumenical Society of the Bl. Virgin Mary at Leeds (1998), Oxford (2000) and Conferences at Walsingham (1997), Maynooth (2001)*. Leominster, UK: Gracewing, 2002.

McPartlan, Patrick. "Mary and Catholic-Orthodox Dialogue." *One in Christ* 34 (1998) 3–17.

Meo, Salvatore. "Concilio Vaticano II." In *Nuovo Dizionario di Mariologia*, edited by Stefano De Fiores et al., 379–94. Milano: Edizioni Paoline, 1985.

Migne, Jacques Paul, ed. *Patrologia Latina*. Paris: Migne, 1844–55.

Miravalle, Mark, ed. *Mariology: A Guide for Priests, Deacons, Seminarians and Consecrated Persons*. Goleta, CA: Queenship, 2007.

Mondéjar, Carmen, et al. "Presencia Mariana y experiencia de María en varios continentes." *Ephemerides Mariologicae* 60 (2010) 297–306.

Muehlen, Heribert. "Neuorientiering und Krise der Mariologie in den Ausssagen des Vaticanums II." *Catholica* 20 (1966) 19–53.

Muzumanga, F. "Marie entre l'Ancienne et la Nouvelle Évangélisation de l'Afrique." *Ephemerides Mariologicae* 64 (2014) 295–320.

———. "Naissance du Fils de Dieu et Immaculée Conception en Afrique." *Ephemerides Mariologicae* 60 (2010) 69–104.

Napiorkowski, Stanislaw. "The Present Position in Mariology." *Concilium* 9 (1967) 52–62.

Naumann, Isabell. *Cum Maria ad altare: Toward an Integration of Mariology and Ecclesiology*. Waukesha, WI: Lithoprint, 1999.

———. "Mary as the Anthropological Model in the Thought of J. Kentenich." *Ephemerides Mariologicae* 59 (2009) 31–47.

———. "Pentecost: Between Hope and Expectation." In *Llamados 'a una esperanza viva' (1P 1,3). Actos del Congreso Mariológico Mariano Internacional de Sevilla, 27–30 de mayo 2014*, edited by Stefano M., 127–67. Ciudad del Vaticano: Pontificia Academia Mariana Internationalis, 2015.

Neuner, Josef. "Maria, Urbild der Kirche." *Geist und Leben* 69 (1996) 442–50.

Novotny, Ronald. "Making Mary's Yes Our Own: A Study of Theological Personhood." *Marian Studies* 56 (2005) 101–22.

Oster, Stefan. *Person und Transsubstantiation: Mensch-Sein, Kirche-Sein und Eucharistie—eine ontologische Zusammenschau.* Freiburg: Herder, 2011.

Pavía, Antonio. *Y el angel anunció a María.* Madrid: San Pablo, 2013.

Perry, Tim, and Daniel Kendall, SJ. *The Blessed Virgin Mary.* Guides to Theology. Grand Rapids: Eerdmans, 2013.

Petri, Heinrich. "Die Stellung Marias in der Kirche." In *Maria und der Heilige Geist: Beiträge zur pneumatologischen Prägung der Mariologie,* edited by Anton Ziegenaus, 39–49. Regensburg: Verlag Friedrich Pustet, 1991.

Phan, Peter C. *Mary in Recent Theology and Piety: The View from the Unites States of America.* International Mariological Congress. Rome, 2000.

Philips, Gerard. *L'Eglise et son Mystère au le Concile du Vatican: Histoire texte et commentaire de la constitution "Lumen gentium."* 2 vols. Paris: Cerf, 1967–68.

Pissarek-Hudelist, Herlinde. "Maria—Schwester oder Mutter im Glauben?" In *Maria für alle Frauen oder über allen Frauen?,* edited by Elisabeth Gössmann et al., 146–67. Freiburg: Herder, 1989.

Pontifical International Marian Academy. *The Mother of the Lord: Memory, Presence, Hope. Presenting a Review of the Actual Questions Facing Mariology Today.* Translated by Thomas Thompson. Staten Island, NY: St. Paul's, 2007.

Pope John Paul II. Apostolic Letter *Mulieris Dignitatem.* Online: http://w2.vatican.va/content/john-paul-ii/en/apost_letters/1988/documents/hf_jp-ii_apl_19880815_mulieris-dignitatem.html

Pope John Paul II. Encyclical *Redemptoris Missio.* Online: http://w2.vatican.va/content/john-paul-ii/en/encyclicals/documents/hf_jp-ii_enc_07121990_redemptoris-missio.html.

Pope Paul VI. Apostolic Exhortation *Evangelii Nuntiandi.* Online: http://w2.vatican.va/content/paul-vi/en/apost_exhortations/documents/hf_p-vi_exh_19751208_evangelii-nuntiandi.html

———. Apostolic Exhortation *Marialis Cultus.* Online: https://w2.vatican.va/content/paul-vi/en/apost_exhortations/documents/hf_p-vi_exh_19740202_marialis-cultus.html

———. Apostolic Exhortation *Signum Magnum.* Online: http://w2.vatican.va/content/paul-vi/en/apost_exhortations/documents/hf_p-vi_exh_19670513_signum-magnum.html

———. Encyclical *Christi Matri.* Online: http://w2.vatican.va/content/paul-vi/en/encyclicals/documents/hf_p-vi_enc_15091966_christi-matri.html

Rahner, Karl. "The Immaculate Conception," *Theological Investigations* I. 201–13. London: Darton, Longman & Todd, 1974.

———. *Mary, Mother of the Lord.* New York: Herder & Herder, 1964.

Ratzinger, Joseph. "Concerning the Notion of Person in Theology." *Communio* 17 (1990) 439–54.

———. *Daughter Zion: Meditations on the Church's Marian Belief.* San Francisco: Ignatius, 1983.

Reck, Jonathan M. "The Annunciation to Mary: A Christian Echo in the Qur'ān." *Vigiliae Christianae* 68 (2014) 355–83.

Reynolds, Brian. *Gateway to Heaven: Marian Doctrine and Devotion, Image and Typology in the Patristic and Medieval Periods.* Hyde Park, NY: New City, 2012.

Rodríguez Aparicio, Jorge H. "Los dones del Espíritu Santo a María, templo del Espíritu." *Ephemerides Mariologicae* 63 (2013) 203–18.

Rossier, François. "Kecharitomene (Lk. 1:28) in the Light of Genesis 18:16–33: A Matter of Quantity." *Marian Studies* 55 (2004) 159–83.
Rossi Espagnet, Carlo. "Densitá antropologica della figura di Maria nella' *Mulieris dignitatem.*" *Theotokos: Ricerche interdisciplinary di Mariologia* 21 (2013) 49–65.
Roten, Johann. *Contemporary Culture, the Trinity and Mary*. International Mariological Congress. Rome, 2000.
———. "From Gatherer to Sender: Plaidoyer for a New Marian Dynamism." *Ephemerides Mariologicae* 64 (2014) 193–214.
———. "How Can Spirituality be Marian." *Marian Studies* 52 (2001) 7–52.
———. "Mary—Personal Concretization of the Church—Elements of Benedict XVI's Marian Thinking." *Marian Studies* 57 (2006) 242–321.
———. "Mary: Woman of Faith: Its Biblico-Theological Foundations." In *Mary, Woman of Faith. Proceedings from the 3rd Asia Oceania Mariological Conference, Manaoag, Pangasina*, edited by Roland D Mactal, 4–24. Dagupan City, Philippines: Archdiocese of Lingayen-Dagupan, 2013.
———. "Marian Devotion for the New Millennium." *Marian Studies* 51 (2000) 52–95.
Roten, Johann, "Popular Religion and Marian Images." *Marian Studies* 45 (1994) 62–120.
Rubin, Miri. *Mother of God: A History of the Virgin Mary*. London: Penguin, 2010.
Sacrado Corazón, Enrique del. "Los Principíos Mariologicos en el Capitulo Mariano del Concilio Vaticano II." *Estudios Marianos* 27 (1966) 279–333.
Sales, Michel. "La bienheureuse Vierge Marie au Concile œcuménique de Vatican II." *Nouvelle Revue Theologique* 107 (1985) 498–519.
Santiago, Garcia. *Evangelio de Lucas*. Colección Commentarios de la NBJ 2. Bilbao: Desclée de Brouwer, 2012.
Sapitula, Manuel Victor. "Marian Piety and Modernity: The Perpetual Help Devotion as Popular Religion in the Philippines." *Philippine Studies: Historical and Ethnographic Viewpoints* 62 (2014) 399–424.
Schindler, David. "Luigi Giussani on the 'Religious Sense' and the Cultural Situation of Our Time." *Communio* 25 (1998) 141–50.
Schmaus, Michael, *Katholische Dogmatik*. Vol V. Mariologie. München: Herder, 1973.
Serra, Aristide. "María, figlia del Padre: Appunti preliminary biblico-giudaici." *Ephemerides Mariologicae* 63 (2013) 293–308.
Shahada Sharelle, Haqq. *Noble Women of Faith: Asiya, Mary, Khadija, Fatima*. Clifton, NJ: Tughra, 2013.
Sherlock, Charles. "The Anglican and Roman Catholic Ecclesial Traditions: The Heritage of *Unitatis Redintegratio*." *International Journal for the Study of the Christian Church* 14 (2014) 362–79.
Seybold, Michael, ed. *Maria im Glauben der Kirche*. Extempralia: Fragen der Theologie und Seelsorge, edited by Theodor Mass-Ewerd and Michael Seybold, Band 3. Eichstätt-Wien: Franz-Sales, 1985.
Strada,Angelo L. *María y nosotros, Manual de teólogia y espiritualidad Marianas*. Buenos Aires: Editorial Claretiana, 1985.
Sullivan, Patricia A. "Mary's Virginity as the Sign of her Faith: A Study of the Nature-Grace Dynamic." *Marian Studies* 58 (2007) 1–25.
Tanner, Norman P., ed. *Decrees of the Ecumenical Councils*. 2 vols. London: Sheed & Ward, 1990.

Thompson, Thomas. "Virgin-Mother Mary and Virgin-Mother Church: Liturgical Perspectives." *Marian Studies* 58 (2007) 325–48.

Thornhill, John. *Sign and Promise: A Theology of the Church for a Changing World*. London: Collins Liturgical, 1988.

Unterseher, Cody R. "Mary in Contemporary Protestant Theological Discourse." *Worship* 81 (2007) 194–212.

Wagner, Marion. "Ein Kirchenbild für unsere Zeit? Ekklesiologische Aussagen des neuen Weltkatechismus." *Stimmen der Zeit* 118 (1993) 533–46.

———. "Maria-Mutter und Mittlerin: Die Marienenzyklika Papst Johannes Paul II. und der ökumenische Dialog über Maria." *Trierer Theologische Zeitschrift* 101 (1992) 172–89.

Walker, Adrian. "Personal Singularity and the Communio Personarum: A Creative Development of Thomas Aquinas' Doctrine of Esse Commune." *Communio* 31 (2004) 457–79.

Wickert, Ulrich, "Freiheit von Sünde-Erhöhung zu God." In *Maria im Glauben der Kirche*. Extempralia: Fragen der Theologie und Seelsorge, edited by Theodor Mass-Ewerd and Michael Seybold, Band 3, 59–85. Eichstätt-Wien: Franz-Sales, 1985.

Wicks, Jared. "The Virgin Mary in Recent Ecumenical Dialogues." *Gregorianum* 81 (2000) 25–57.

Wright, Wendy M. *Mary and the Catholic Imagination*. 2010 Madeleva Lecture in Spirituality. Mahwah, NJ: Paulist, 2010.

Ziegenaus, Anton, ed. *Geboren aus der Jungfrau Maria: Klarstellungen*. Mariologische Studien 19. Regensburg: Pustet, 2007.

2

The Virgin Mary in Ancient Christian Tradition

—Fr Joseph Azize

What were the earliest Christian traditions concerning Mary the Mother of Jesus? Considering the New Testament, then the other evidence (e.g., Ignatius of Antioch, the Ascension of Isaiah, the Odes of Solomon, the Protoevangelium of James, and the Gospel of Philip), it emerges that there is significant evidence for continuity. In particular, Matthew 1:25 is consistent with the ancient tradition of the perpetual virginity of Mary. Since texts such as Philip are in polemic with this tradition, we may speak of a mainstream or even "orthodox" tradition of Christianity. The study also challenges the standard view that Mark 3 depicts Mary in a negative light. Methodologically, it is submitted, to study the figure of Mary in ancient history, we must consider how the New Testament materials were read in the ancient world.

1. The Gospel of Mark, and Mary

First of all, I must state my assumptions. I accept, as highly probable and more satisfactory than rival conjectures, the thesis that the earliest of the canonical Gospels is Mark, and that both Matthew and Luke used his text.[1] Mark's Gospel is focused on Jesus, whose passion and res-

---

1. This is a fundamental assumption for many scholars, e.g., Guelich, *Mark*, xli.

urrection form its lengthy climax. Mark unequivocally mentions Mary only in 3:31–35 and 6:1–4. I shall not consider the possibility that she is the Mary of 15:40 and 47, and 16:1.[2] In the NAB translation, the relevant sections read

> He came home. Again [the] crowd gathered, making it impossible for them to even eat. When his relatives heard of this they set out to seize him, for they said, "He is out of his mind." The scribes who had come from Jerusalem said, "He is possessed by Beelzebul." (Mark 3:20–22a)

After the "kingdom divided against itself" pericope, the Gospel continues:

> His mother and his brothers arrived. Standing outside they sent word to him and called him. A crowd seated around him told him, "Your mother and your brothers [and your sisters] are outside asking for you." But he said to them in reply, "Who are my mother and [my] brothers?" And looking around at those seated in the circle he said, "Here are my mother and my brothers. [For] whoever does the will of God is my brother and sister and mother." (Mark 3:31–35)

Mark has Jesus travel and then return to Nazareth:

> He . . . came to his native place, accompanied by his disciples. When the Sabbath came he began to teach in the synagogue, and many who heard him were astonished. They said, "Where did this man get all this? What kind of wisdom has been given him? What mighty deeds are wrought by his hands! Is he not the carpenter, the son of Mary, and that brother of James and Joses and Judas and Simon? And are not his sisters here with us? And they took offence at him. Jesus said to them, "A prophet is not without honor except in his native place and among his own kin and in his own house." (Mark 6:1–4)

Most scholars see a certain criticism of Mary and the brethren here, or at least a depiction of them as having a negative attitude to Jesus. Typical is Zervos:

> Mark's Gospel . . . presents the relationship between Jesus and his family, Mary included, in a negative light. In Mark 3:21, "when his family heard [of Jesus' activities], they went out to restrain him, for people were saying, 'He has gone out of his mind'"; in 3:31–35 Jesus denies his biological family in favor of

---

2. This is, however, argued by Fenton, "Mother of Jesus," *passim*.

those around him who do the will of God. . . . Finally, in Mark 6:4 Jesus includes his derogatory statement.³

Representative of a different view, rarely voiced, is Lamarche, who asks:

> En insistant si souvent sur les limites de Pierre, des apôtres, de la famille de Jésus, peut-être même de sa mère, Marc veut-il critiquer et dénigrer tous ces personnages ou a-t-il un autre but?⁴

Lamarche concludes that in chapter 3 Mark is not criticizing Mary and his brothers but rather showing that those who were closest to Jesus did not comprehend his mystery.⁵ We must now examine the relevant passages and place them in their context.

2. Mark 3

The translation "his relatives" in 3:21 for *hoi par'autou* is acceptable, and is favored by recent translations. However, "his relatives" is not a literal translation of *hoi par'autou*,⁶ despite the fact that many scholars take the identification of *hoi par'autou* as being Jesus' mother and brothers as so obvious that it needs no argument.⁷ Leaving but one word in the Greek, it is literally "those *para* him." Since that much is scarcely controversial, the main issue in translating must be the force of *para* with the genitive. Bortone states that this preposition "pointed to one side of the referent object, and thus indicated a region, while direction or want of it was indicated by the case."⁸ He states that with the genitive, it had ablative force, e.g., *para basileos*, "from the court of the king."⁹

On first principles, then, *hoi par'autou* might be thought to mean something such as: "those who were by him." However, phrases often have unexpected nuances. And so it is with this one. *BDAG* states: "The Koine also uses this expr. to denote others who are intimately connected w.

---

3. Zervos, "Christmas with Salome," 77–78.
4. Lamarche, *Evangile de Marc*, 20.
5. Ibid., 126–27.
6. For example, Donahue and Harrington, *Gospel of Mark*, 128–29.
7. Even Fenton, whose article is specifically on Mary in the Gospel of Mark, makes this assumption: Fenton, "Mother of Jesus," 434.
8. Bortone, *Greek Prepositions*, 144.
9. Ibid., 144. Robertson, *Grammar of the New Testament*, 614 comes to a similar conclusion.

someone, e.g. *family, relatives . . . ,*" and then cites Mark 3:2.[10] Lane translates the term as "friends," and comments:

> Because the expression is clearly colloquial it is difficult to be certain of its exact nuance. The translation "his friends" or "associates" is (often) adopted. . . . Moule argues that a less direct association than family may be inferred from a comparison of the prepositions *para* and *hupo*. The latter preposition expresses a more intimate relation, so that *para* would possibly mean a group of disciples or friends. Papyri support for the rendering "friends," "neighbors," "associates" is not lacking . . . (but) the context would seem to demand that the family of Jesus is in view.[11]

Lane notes that there is also support in the papyri for the translation "family." Interestingly, by the second edition of his *Idiom Book*, Moule had, without comment, altered the reading which Lane had approvingly quoted to "his relatives."[12] Guelich states that the phrase can mean "adherents" and "envoys" (presumably this would be because the envoys one sends are chosen from among those at one's side). But, pointing to the "sandwich" structure and verse 31, Guelich finally opts for "relatives."[13]

Opting for a broader interpretation, McHugh refers to instances in the Septuagint where the phrase denotes "adherents" or "followers," and to refer to parents, other relatives, and to even broader senses in papyri, leading him to conclude that: "Mark denotes rather vaguely the 'family circle' at Nazareth, and can therefore best be rendered as 'his people.'"[14] I note that the idea of "relatives" is, in English, more general than that of "family." All family are relatives, but not all relatives are family.[15]

Consulting Louw and Nida's *Greek English Lexicon*, it is evident that the New Testament Greek literary language was not embarrassed by a deficit of words for "family" and "relatives." For "family," vol. 2 refers us to sections 10.8–13 and 24 of volume 1; and for "relatives," to 10.5–13. These are substantial entries.[16]

---

10. BDAG 756–57.

11. Lane, *Mark*, 138, n. 75.

12. Moule, *Idiom Book*, 52.

13. Guelich, *Mark*, 172. I prefer Kok's use of the term "intercalation," rather than "sandwiching": Kok, *Gospel on the Margin*, 76.

14. McHugh, *Mother of Jesus*, 238.

15. This raises a vexed question of translation which is tangential to our present purpose: when should one translate what the text *connotes* rather than what it *denotes*?

16. Louw and Nida *Greek English Lexicon*, vol. 2, 289 and 315. Louw and Nida

It follows from this discussion that the phrase *hoi par'autou* in Mark 3:21 was intentionally used as being general or even undefined: they were Jesus' "people," friends or relatives or both. But it is so vaguely put that one might wonder whether even the evangelist had a specific idea of who was encompassed. France properly observes that this is not "a normal Marcan term for the disciples or other associates of Jesus."[17] I would not agree, therefore, with Collins' suggestion, supported only by a reference to *BDAG*, that the phrase means "those who are intimately connected with someone."[18] They (*hoi*) need only be around him (*autou*), although they will, *ipso facto*, often be intimately connected. The point is that "family" is not the *meaning* of the phrase.

Many scholars point to Mark's "sandwiching" to argue that in 3:21 and 3:31, Mark must be referring to the same people.[19] Brown appeals to how Mark inserts the story of the hemorrhaging woman into that of Jairus, and concludes: "The comparison of the two scenes makes it likely that for Mark the 'mother and brothers' of 3:31 . . . are the same as the 'his own' of 3:21."[20] Collins asserts that *hoi par'autou* "is further defined in v. 31 as his mother and his brothers."[21] But there is no definition in verse 31. Both Brown and Collins beg the questions of how Mark's intercalation operates, and whether its operation is unvarying. So how does intercalation work in Mark? Marcus notes that the other Marcan "sandwiches" are:

1. The proclamation of John the Baptist in 1:4 and 1:7–8 framing vv. 5 and 6.[22]

2. The healing of a paralytic in 2:1–5 and 2:10b–12 framing vv. 6–10a.[23]

---

translate *hoi par'autou* as being "family" in Mark 3:21, but do not state their reasons: ibid., 1 10.9. I cite sections rather than pages of vol. 1 as more precise.

17. France, *The Gospel of Mark*, 166.

18. Collins, *Mark*, 226.

19. Marcus, *Mark* vol. I, 270; Brown, *Mary in the New Testament*, 54–55. This is also the view of the most recent substantial commentary on Mark known to me: Bock, *Mark*, 166–67.

20. Brown et al. *Mary in the New Testament*, 55.

21. Collins, *Mark*, 227. If Collins' references to vague passages in Plato and Philo on this same page are intended to show that the proffered interpretation is correct because it is "analogous" or "similar" (her words, *loc. cit.*), then this is to assume what should be demonstrated. Tan, *Mark*, 73 may make the same error with his reference to Apollonios. Tan thinks Apollonios' "*Epistles*," which Frede describes as "certainly not genuine," to be authentic: Frede, "Apollonios of Tyana," no page reference, accessed via internet on 11 July 2016.

22. Marcus, *Mark* vol. I, 154.

23. Ibid., vol. I, 219.

3. The request of Jairus in 5:21–24 and 5:35–43 framing the hemorrhaging woman in 5:25–34.[24]

4. The missionary journey of the Twelve in 6:7–13 and 6:30 framing the death of John the Baptist in 6:14–29.[25]

5. 11:11–25 provides two intercalations: 11:11 and 11:15, the entering into Jerusalem, frames the cursing of the fig tree, and that pericope together with the reference to the same tree in 11:20–25 frame the cleansing of the temple in 11:15–18, which itself follows Jesus' "possessive gaze" upon the temple in 11:11.[26]

6. The first intercalation in the passion account: Mark 14:1–11.[27]

7. The second intercalation in the passion account: Mark 14:53–72.[28]

I am here concerned only with the interpretive significance of this device. In instances 1, 4, 5, and 7, identity is not at all in question because the text can refer only to John the Baptist, the apostles, and to Jesus and the apostles, respectively: that is, Mark does not ask or require the reader to infer identity.

However, in instance 2, the first reference of the "sandwich bread" is to a paralytic and four men. The second reference, in 2:10b–12 is to the paralytic alone. In instance 3, Mark opens with a reference to Jairus, but 5:35 opens by referring to people from his house. Further, in instance 6, those seeking Jesus' death in 14:1 were "the chief priests and the scribes," while in 14:10, it is only "the chief priests" to whom Judas went. Here the context does not at all demand that we should understand "scribes" to be included in verse 10. If the two covering "slices" of the "sandwich" need not have identical referents in these three examples, they do not need to in the text from chapter 3 which we are examining, either.

This methodological issue is significant, as most scholars assume intercalation to inevitably point to an identity of both "slices" of the sandwich "bread." But based on an examination of how Mark actually uses intercalation, there is no stylistic convention to restrict the evangelist from taking people around Jesus in 3:21 and then moving to his mother and brethren in 3:31. The context must be determinative. The context indicates overlap, but not identity between the two "bread slices." Guelich, although he does

---

24. Ibid., vol. I, 364.
25. Ibid., vol. I, 385 and 397.
26. Ibid., vol. II, 776–77, 788 and 798–99.
27. Ibid., vol. I, 924–25.
28. Ibid., vol. I, 937–38.

not examine the stylistic device, nonetheless observes that *hoi par'autou* is ambiguous, and stands in contrast to the more precise words used in 3:31.[29]

Indeed, the difference between the terms of vv. 21 and 35 may even point to Mary and the brethren acting apart from, perhaps even to frustrate, *hoi par'autou*. On Brown's rather standard reading, Jesus' mother and brethren have set out to seize Jesus.[30] But this is an inference. Mark does not present the arrival of mother and brethren as a ruse to kidnap Jesus, and neither is it easily seen as such. Tan states that the brothers of Jesus must have accompanied Mary so that "if the situation becomes ugly, they can then help their mother."[31] I would respectfully suggest that the notion that they intended to bind or otherwise restrain Jesus by force, especially while an admiring crowd were in close vicinity, is implausible. To read Mark as attributing to named individuals an attitude which has been predicated of a vague group would defeat the very point of the generality of his chosen words.

It is equally possible to speculate that Mary and the brothers were concerned for Jesus' safety, perhaps because of the large crowds, or even that they intended to feed him. Luke 8:3 mentions Joanna and Susanna as being among those who provided for Jesus. Given the mention in Mark 3:20 that Jesus could not obtain food, the possibility that Mary intended to feed him cannot lightly be dismissed. But we do not know. It is not even clear that beyond seeing Jesus, Mary and the brethren (individually or collectively) had one and the same end in mind when making their request. We only know what the Gospel tells us, that is, that they sent a message to Jesus requesting him to come outside to them. Further, to believe that Mark intended readers or hearers to infer a reason for Mary's attendance is unjustified. Mark may not have any intention but to provide context for the teaching in 3:33–35.

From making an unjustified inference, it is easy to proceed to further speculations. For example, Brown and his colleagues begin by presenting *as a thesis* their interpretation that Mary and the brethren shared the critical view of Jesus referred to in 3:21, but then proceed to treat it as an established fact only a few pages later. There, they assert that Mark has "a reference to Jesus' family (including his mother) as thinking that Jesus is beside himself (3:21),"[32] when in fact this is an inference.

In Mark's presentation of Jesus' response to the presence of his mother and brethren, Jesus directs no comment to or against them. Yet Mark's

---

29. Guelich, *Mark*, 170.
30. Brown, *Mary in the New Testament*, 54–58.
31. Tan, *Mark*, 49.
32. Brown, *Mary in the New Testament*, 63.

depiction of Jesus is robust: Jesus expresses anger at the certain persons in the synagogue at 3:5, he calls Pharisees and scribes "hypocrites" at 7:6, addresses other sundry criticisms in 7:8–13, and overturns the tables in the temple in 11:15–19. In contradistinction, in Mark 3:31–35, Jesus breathes no criticism of his family. Rather, by saying that those who do the will of God are his family, Jesus *valorizes* family relations.

If Jesus meant that the family were to be seen in a negative light, he would not be paying his followers any compliment: the remark would be empty as "family" would be an empty term. But Jesus' point is that those who follow God's will are especially close to him, even perhaps united with him in the closest of human bonds.

Claims that the placing of Mary and the brethren outside of where Jesus is teaching are symbolic of their being among those "outside," as in Mark 4:10–11,[33] seem predicated upon the belief that Mark is not narrating testimony which has been passed down to him. This needs to be demonstrated, not assumed.[34] Further, if Jesus is surrounded by crowds while he is in a house, where else is Mark to place them? To read this as necessarily symbolic seems unwarranted.

3. Mark 6

We now come to the sole place in any of the Gospels where Jesus does seem to distance himself from his family: Mark 6:1–6. Noting that Jesus states: "A prophet is not without honor except in his native place and among his own kin and in his own house," Brown et al. ask:

> why does he have Jesus say obliquely that he is not honored by his own relatives? Such a negative attitude of Mary toward Jesus seems irreconcilable with Mary's having known that this was a miraculous child conceived without a human father. At least, the two authors who speak of a virginal conception did not find such a negative conception reconcilable with that tradition, for they omitted both the Marcan passages just cited.[35]

My first doubt is that Mary is depicted in the Gospel of Mark as having a "negative attitude" towards Jesus. The second question is what we can infer

---

33. Tan, *Mark*, 50; and Henderson, *Christology and Discipleship*, 100.

34. The testimony of Papias, Clement and Irenaeus is that Mark recorded the gospel taught by Peter, while Peter was alive. Papias states that Mark recorded it accurately. The "anti-Marcionite Prologue" supports most of this testimony. For an introduction, see Ellis, *Making of the New Testament Documents*, 358–62.

35. Brown, *Mary in the New Testament*, 63.

from the fact that Matthew and Luke omit this passage. The third question is whether the attitude displayed here is necessarily inconsistent with a belief in the virginal conception.

3.1 Does Mark's Mary have a "negative attitude" towards Jesus?

Even on the standard reading of this text, Jesus does not specifically embrace Mary in his comments about being a prophet without honor. That he does so include her can be maintained only upon an absolute reading of the terms "relatives" (*suggeneusin* from *suggenēs*, "belonging to the same extended family or clan")[36] and "family" (*oikia*),[37] so that they refer to each and every member of Jesus' family without exception. By the same token, the use of the Cretan Epimenides' famously paradoxical statement that all Cretans are liars, would involve the author of Titus 1:12–13 in an "irreconcilable" position. The most straightforward solution of the paradox is to see this as a manner of speaking, a *façon de parler*, not intended to be taken as categorically and literally true in all circumstances. I suggest that the same may be true of Mark 6:4.

Jesus' comment in Mark 6:4 is directed not against his relatives, but against the many who heard him and were skeptical of his authority *on the basis that they knew his family*. The skeptics who question Jesus here are clearly not his entire family, because they name his mother and brothers, and in 6:3 refer to his sisters as being "with us" (*pros hēmas*, the basic meaning of *pros* is "near").[38] It could be that his sisters shared in the stated skepticism, and if so, then the comments Jesus makes in 6:4 could have been intended to refer to them, rather than anyone else. Jesus effectively declares that their familiarity with him has blinded them to the reality before them. The comment is, I suggest, directed to those who expressed the doubts rather than being the occasion of a critique of all his family.

3.2 Mark and the Apostles

Mark's attitude to the family seems to be of a piece with his treatment of the apostles, and illuminates Mark's intent. For example, Evans states:

---

36. *BDAG*, 950.
37. Ibid., 694, offering the translation "family" for this appearance of the word.
38. Robertson, *Grammar of the New Testament*, 622.

> There are significant indications that Jesus' family did not endorse his ministry. The open hostility between Jesus and his family is barely masked in the Marcan account (Mark 3:20–35; cf. 6:1–6; John 7:5), which the Matthean and Lucan evangelists take pains to mitigate. Although it must be acknowledged that this hostile portrait may be due in part to Marcan theology, it was in all probability the resurrection (1 Cor 15:7) that altered his family's opinion.[39]

In referring refers to "Marcan theology," Evans may have in mind that it is distinctive of Mark to bring out the non-comprehension of those around Jesus. Mark extends this non-understanding of Jesus beyond the Pharisees and scribes to the disciples. Speaking of the portrayal of the apostles as fools if not knaves in the *Gospel of Judas*, de Conick states:

> This portrait of the Twelve, although queer to modern Christian sensibilities, is not an *ex nihilo* fabrication of anti-Christians. Rather it is an interpretation dependent upon a very literal reading of the *Gospel of Mark*. . . . It is in the *Gospel of Mark* that the demons are the entities who recognize Jesus and confess him, including Peter who is rebuked as Satan (1:34; 3:11; 5:6–7; 8:31–33). The twelve disciples never fare well. They are faithless and ignorant straight through to the end of the Gospel, even though they are handpicked by Jesus and given special teachings (3:13–19; 4:10–20; 4:37–41; 6:52; 8:15–21; 9:15–19; 9:33–35; 10:13–14). . . . The disciples' reputation is never redeemed, even in the longer ending of Mark where the disciples are chided by Jesus.[40]

Especially telling are the terms of 4:41 when, after the stilling of the storm, Mark writes that after Jesus had demanded of the twelve, "Do you not yet have faith?," they were "filled with great awe and said to one another: 'Who then is this whom even the wind and sea obey?'" Even after this lesson, they deserve the strong rebukes in the other passages de Conick refers to 9:19 ("O faithless generation, how long will I be with you? How long will I endure you?") with Jesus' criticisms of their lack of faith and prayer (9:19, and 28–29, and, implicitly, 9:23 although that is not directly addressed to them).

Mark's picture of the apostles is harsher than that of the other evangelists, for the comment in Mark 6:52 that their hearts were hardened is

---

39. Evans, "Context, Family and Formation," 14–15.
40. De Conick, "The *Gospel of Judas*," 104.

omitted from the other evangelists' accounts.[41] Marcus observes that this expresses:

> the typical Markan theme of apostolic misunderstanding. . . . Even more threatening to the disciples, in a story replete with exodus allusions, is the specific reference to their hardened heart. In this chapter of the story of the new exodus, Jesus' disciples not only appear thick-headed, faithless, and fearful, like Israel in the desert, but almost begin to approximate the image of Israel's hard-hearted opponent, Pharaoh.[42]

The logic of this type of argument is as follows:

1. Mark draws hostile portraits of Jesus' family and apostles.
2. This accords with his theology.
3. Therefore the hostile portrait may have been exaggerated to support his theology.

On this logic, any evidence cited in support of a belief is suspect precisely because it supports the belief. This cannot be a sound method of conducting scholarship. In Mark 3 and 6, rather than implying an unstated criticism of Jesus' mother and brethren, we could quite properly see a *selection* of material which ties in with Mark's theme of the non-comprehension of those around him, although as stated, Mary is not explicitly involved in this.

But even beyond this, Mark does not deny the central role of the apostles throughout Jesus' ministry. The importance of the apostles is so apparent as to make citation superfluous. Further, in both the longer and the shorter ending of the Gospel, the apostles are commissioned to preach by Jesus who therefore endorses them. If one reads the Gospel as a whole, the apostles are established as legitimate teachers of Jesus' message despite their failures to comprehend him and his teaching, at least prior to the resurrection. The overall picture of the apostles, then is not negative; it is positive.

Another issue is that Evans sees the passages in Mark to which he refers as attempting to *mask* a hostility, which, one is left to assume, was worse than what is explicitly stated. Why does he assume that the other Synoptics take pains to mitigate the depiction, rather than the opposite: i.e., that they may have been heirs to a tradition according to which Mark exaggerated the true situation? Any answer needs to consider the three Gospels as a whole, and to exercise caution when attributing motives to the evangelists.

---

41. Marcus, *Mark*, vol. I, 424-35. The pericope occurs in Mark, Matthew, and John.
42. Ibid., vol. I, 434.

4. Canonical Considerations

Although Mark's Gospel can be read in isolation from the other Gospels, this would be unreliable in that if the other evangelists did indeed have that text before them, then we may expect that the manner in which they wrote their Gospels reflects their understanding of Mark's. That is, one must read the Gospel of Mark with the benefit of considering how it was read in the ancient world. In this study, I shall consider only the most relevant portions of the other Gospels.

4.1 Why do Matthew and Luke omit Mark 6:4?

First, I shall take a well-developed and generally accepted argument that a reading of the Gospels of Matthew and Luke shows that they knew of and deliberately modified the picture of Mary found in Mark's Gospel.

Brown and his colleagues are hardly alone in arguing that when one compares Mark to Matthew and Luke who, by common but not unanimous consensus have the virginal conception,[43] one finds that just these two Gospels alter Mark's sayings about Jesus' family, as if they were embarrassing details.[44] This, Brown declares, is evidence that Mark's account should be read as critical of Mary and the brethren. The train of thought can be summarized like this:

A. Matthew and Luke could not believe that if Mary had experienced the conception and infancy of Jesus as depicted in their Gospels, she could ever have doubted Jesus as she is depicted doing in Mark 3 and 6.

B. Matthew and Luke therefore had to omit inconsistent details.

C. They do omit inconsistent details, specifically the depiction of a doubting Mary in Mark 3 and 6.

D. Therefore, Matthew and Luke omit those details because of the doctrine of the virginal conception.

E. Therefore, the pictures of Mary in Mark and in the other two Gospels are inconsistent.

F. Mark's picture is more historical since it is earlier, while the other two have been rewritten for doctrinal reasons.

---

43. The arguments of Schaberg, *Illegitimacy of Jesus* and others who see no virginal conception in Matthew and sometimes not even in Luke are not widely accepted.

44. Brown, *Mary in the New Testament*, 63 and 99.

If I am correct in my reading of Mark 3 and 6, then the entire argument fails because proposition A cannot be made out: that is, whoever else from the family may have doubted, there is no reason to believe that Mary was among their number. But for the sake of argument, let us grant that proposition A is sound. The argument at premises B and C is an example of a circular proof of the kind dealt with by Fischer in *Historians' Fallacies*.[45] My point may be easier to see if one takes a fictitious example which is blatantly fallacious:

- A. If Charles Dickens had denounced the monarch of England in any of his novels, his editors would have made him remove those references.
- B. None of Dickens' published novels include any denunciation of the monarch.
- C. Therefore the editor removed the denunciations before publishing Dickens' novels.

Proof that Dickens had ever submitted to his editor any denunciation of the monarch is missing. What is equally lacking, in the present instance, is evidence that Matthew and Luke saw any anomaly in Mary's experience of the conception and infancy of Jesus as depicted in their Gospels, and her attitude to Jesus as depicted in Mark 3 and 6.

Although Matthew and Luke do leave out the remarks in question, it is the merest assertion to affirm that they did so *because* of their belief in the virginal conception. That the proposed explanation is not the only one available follows from the fact that such a change in tone is also found in Matthew and Luke in a case where the virginal conception was not a factor: the parable of the sower. In Mark 4:13, Jesus is depicted as being incredulous when the apostles do not understand him. In Matthew, however, Jesus blesses their eyes and ears because they "see" and "hear," kindly replies to their query about its meaning, and when he asks whether they understand, they affirm that they do, and he seems to commend them (13:16, 36–37 and 51–52). Then, in Luke, Jesus is shown as treating the apostles kindly and patiently, although not to the same degree as in Matthew, and warns them to "take care" for "to anyone who has, more will be given and the from the one who has not, even what he seems to have will be taken away" (Luke 8:11–15 and 18).

Perhaps significantly, this passage in Luke is followed by the one where his mother and brothers attend for him (Luke 8:19–21). There it is made clear that they wished to join Jesus (*suntukhein aut ōi*, Luke 8:19). But this

---

45. Fischer, *Historians' Fallacies*, 49–51.

is not the relevant change, for Luke, rather than having Jesus unable to procure food, seems, by reference to the "many" who provided for him and those with him out of their resources (Luke 8:3), to indicate that he did have food. Therefore, the milder treatment of Mary and the family of Jesus in Matthew and Luke need not be understood solely by reference to the evangelists' belief in the virginal conception.

4.2 Luke 11:27–28

Next, the pericope Luke 11:27–28 is relevant, as it pertains to the question of why Luke omitted Mark 3:21:

> While he was speaking, a woman from the crowd called out and said to him: "Blessed is the womb that carried you and the breasts at which you nursed." He replied: "Rather (*menoun*), blessed are those who hear the word of God and observe it."

As Fitzmyer justly remarks, at first sight this seems even "more negative toward his mother" than the words of Luke 8:21 (paralleled in Mark 3), and some scholars do indeed so interpret the passage.[46] Fitzmyer, however, does not read it as excluding Mary in the blessing, although English translations cannot easily capture the appropriate sense of the Greek *menoun* without using additional words.[47] Significantly, to our sensibilities this might seem like a contradiction of the prophecy in Luke 1:48. However, Luke does not seem bothered by this. In other words, Luke sees nothing anomalous in retailing both the story of the virginal conception and this pericope. On what basis, then, would he have omitted 3:21 and altered 6:4 *because* of his belief in the virginal conception? This should serve as a further reminder of the futility of any wholesale projection of our attitudes upon the evangelists.

In addition, McHugh asks whether the very terms of Luke 1:48 might not imply that Mary was being hailed as blessed at the time Luke was writing.[48] If this is so, and without new evidence it would be impossible to claim certainty, then neither would the readers of Luke's Gospel have been concerned by the terms of 11:27–28.

---

46. Fitzmyer, *Luke*, vol. I, 927–28.
47. Ibid., vol. I, 926–28.
48. McHugh, *Mother of Jesus*, 71.

4.3 The Gospel of John

There is a steady tradition in the Gospels that Jesus' brethren are to be included among the skeptics. Given the terms of John 4:44 ("For Jesus himself testified that a prophet as no honor in his native place," *en tēi idiai patridi*), and 7:5 ("For his brothers did not believe in him"), I accept that tradition as historical. But there is no tradition of the same applying to Mary, and, nowhere in John is there any sign that the disbelief of his family was shared by Mary: rather, by depicting her at the opening and close of Jesus' ministry, John possibly associates her with the whole of Jesus' ministry.

This is significant for, as Bauckham demonstrates, John had available to him the Gospel of Mark. Bauckham notes that:

> On the assumption that Matthew and Luke used Mark . . . we can assume that Mark had circulated widely by the time John wrote, but not necessarily that Matthew and Luke had circulated widely. . . . The habit of regarding John as certainly the latest of the four Gospels is a relic of (1) the nineteenth-century view . . . that John is dependent on all three Synoptic Gospels, and (2) the view that John is more theologically advanced than Matthew and Luke and therefore also later (a non sequitur).[49]

Bauckham contends that the older view that John was intended to supplement the other Gospels must now again be entertained.[50] He also gives reasons for seeing that, in some cases at least (e.g., in the dating of the cleansing of the temple, and the anointing at Bethany), John corrects the chronology in Mark.[51] John drafted his text to allow readers and hearers of Mark to see the Gospels as dovetailing.[52] Bauckham thus concludes that John: "did not aim to replace Mark, but to write a different kind of Gospel: one which by selecting far fewer traditions, left space for the reflective interpretation that is the distinctive characteristic of the Fourth Gospel."[53]

A full treatment of John's Gospel and its portrait of Mary must await the promised fuller study. It suffices to say that on a cursory examination, John pre-eminently of the four evangelists presents a balanced and accurate picture of Jesus' relation to his family: i.e., the brethren did doubt Jesus, but Mary was closely associated with Jesus throughout his ministry.

---

49. Bauckham "John for Readers of Mark," 148 n.2.
50. Ibid., 149–50.
51. Ibid., 159.
52. Ibid., *passim*.
53. Ibid., 170.

4.4 The Family of Jesus in the Gospels

Once more, here this topic cannot be done justice, yet, briefly, if one took literally all Jesus' attested statements concerning the family, they would be violently contradictory. In Mark 7:10–12, Jesus rebuked the Pharisees and scribes: "For Moses said: "Honor your father and your mother," and "whoever curses father or mother shall die." Yet you say: "If a person says to father or mother, 'Any support you might have had from me is *qorban*' you allow him to do nothing more for his father or mother."

Further, in 10:19 Jesus reiterates the commandments for the rich man, including to honor one's father and mother. In 10:29–30 Jesus assumes the great value of these relations, because an ultimate increase in family is promised to those who first leave them for Jesus' sake:

> Amen I say to you, there is no one who has given up house or brothers or sisters or mother or father or children or lands, for my sake and for the sake of the gospel who will not receive a hundred times more now in this present age, houses and brothers and sisters and mothers and children and lands, with persecutions; and eternal life in the age to come.

These statements strongly endorse familial relations. As 10:29–30 demonstrates, Jesus taught a hierarchy of values where service and love of God came first, before all else. The logic here is that of Matthew 6:33: "seek first the kingdom and his righteousness, and all these things will be given you, besides."

The division between parents and children, and between members of the one household expressed in Matthew 10:35–37 and its parallel in Luke 14:26 (Jesus' follower must hate his father, mother, wife, children, brothers, sisters and even his own life), would seem to contradict the above teaching. If taken literally, and without reference to the hierarchy of values, the chances of making sense of these statements are nil. The commandment to hate would even contradict many texts such as the commandment to love even one's enemies in Luke 6:27–36. Yet, Luke apparently saw no anomaly in including both 14:26 and 6:27–36.

The pertinent verses in Mark 3 and 6 exemplify this picture of a hierarchy of values, and a demand that the love of Jesus and his teachings be the first priority, so much so that beside it all else may be dismissed. As noted above, to say that those who do the will of God are Jesus' family is to attribute positive value to being a member of his family.

Therefore, even if Mark's "attitude" to the family of Jesus and his apostles might be fairly described as "negative" in places, it would be an argument from modern sensibilities which are foreign to Mark, to say as Brown does, that it "seems irreconcilable" with knowledge of the virginal conception.

5. Conclusion

I contend, therefore, that a full consideration of the picture of Mary in Mark 3 and 6 leads to the conclusion that she is not depicted in a critical, negative or unfavorable light. There is no doubt that *hoi par'autou* do believe that Jesus is beside himself, but it is not at all clear that Mary is meant to be included among their number. It is wrong to read the general and vague terms of 3:21 as being defined by the more precise words in 3:35: even an examination of Mark's use of intercalation or "sandwiching"—something which, so far as I can see, has never been undertaken in respect of the identity of the parties at either end of the intercalations—shows that his method does not demand such a result.

Then, in Mark 6:4, the inclusion of Mary in the list of those who do not honor Jesus the prophet can be made only if the statement is taken literally and absolutely. There is no more warrant to do that than to take what is effectively the commandment to hate everyone but Jesus himself in Matthew 10:35–37 and Luke 14:26.

The fact that both the apostles and the family of Jesus are shown as not understanding him is no basis for seeing them as depicted in an unfavorable light: although Mark is silent as to the family, the apostles are shown as becoming enlightened after the resurrection. To see the family as being in a fundamentally different category is to project modern attitudes onto Mark.

Further, there is no basis to see Matthew and Luke modifying the scenes depicted in Mark 3 and 6 in order to accommodate their teaching on the virginal conception. They did not find anomalies in their texts so easily as modern scholars, perhaps hyper-critical modern scholars, do. A more balanced picture emerges in John's Gospel, and one which I would suggest John intended us to take as more accurate than the Synoptic account, whereby the brethren do indeed doubt, but Mary is associated with Jesus in his ministry. Finally, when one considers what is said in the Gospels as a whole concerning family, we see that there is a hierarchy of values: love of God and of Jesus transcends all else. To speak in disparagement of family is, then, a way of making a point not about the family, but about the surpassing greatness of the commandment to love God.

Bibliography

Bauckham, Richard, ed. "John for Readers of Mark." In *The Gospel for all Christians*, edited by Richard Bauckham, 147–71. Grand Rapids: Eerdmans, 1998.

Bock, Darrell. *Mark*. Cambridge: Cambridge University Press, 2015.

Bortone, Pietro. *Greek Prepositions from Antiquity to the Present*. Oxford: Oxford University Press, 2010.

Brown, Raymond E., et al. *Mary in the New Testament: A Collaborative Assessment by Protestant and Roman Catholic Scholars*. London: Chapman, 1978.

Choi, Jin Young. *Postcolonial Discipleship of Embodiment: An Asian and Asian American Feminist Reading of the Gospel of Mark*. New York: Palgrave Macmillan, 2015.

Collins, Adela Yarbro. *Mark*. Hermenia. Minneapolis: Fortress, 2007.

Conick, April de. "The *Gospel of Judas*: A Parody of Apostolic Christianity." In *The Non-canonical Gospels*, edited by Paul Foster, 96–109. London: T. & T. Clark, 2008.

Danker, Frederick William, et al. *A Greek-English Lexicon of the New Testament and Other Early Christian Literature*. 3rd ed. BDAG. Chicago: University of Chicago Press, 2000.

Donahue, John R., and Daniel J. Harrington. *The Gospel of Mark*. Collegeville, MN: Liturgical, 2002.

Ellis, E. Earle. *The Making of the New Testament Documents*. Leiden: Brill Academic, 2002.

Evans, Craig A. "Context, Family and Formation." In *The Cambridge Companion to Jesus*, edited by Marcus Bockmuehl, 11–24. Cambridge: Cambridge University Press, 2001.

Fenton, John. "The Mother of Jesus in Mark's Gospel and its Revisions." *Theology* 86 (1983) 433–37.

Fischer, David Hackett. *Historians' Fallacies*. New York: HarperPerennial, 1970.

Fitzmyer, Joseph A. *The Gospel according to Luke I–IX*. Anchor Bible 28a. New York: Doubleday, 1985.

France, R. T. *The Gospel of Mark*. NIGTC. Carlisle, UK: Paternoster, 2002.

Frede, Michael. "Apollonios (of Tyana)." In *Brill's New Pauly*. 2005–. Online: http://referenceworks.brillonline.com.ezproxy1.library.usyd.edu.au/entries/brill-s-new-pauly/apollonius-e128340#e128590

Gaventa, Beverly Roberts. "'All Generations Will Call Me Blessed': Mary in Biblical and Ecumenical Perspective." In *A Feminist Companion to Mariology*, edited by Amy-Jill Levine, 121–29. Cleveland, OH: Pilgrim, 2005.

Guelich, Robert A. *Mark 1–8:26*. Word Biblical Commentary 34A. Nashville: Thomas Nelson, 1989.

Henderson, Suzanne Watts. *Christology and Discipleship in the Gospel of Mark*. Cambridge: Cambridge University Press, 2006.

Kok, Michael J. *The Gospel on the Margin*. Minneapolis: Augsburg Fortress, 2015.

Lamarche, Paul. *Evangile de Marc*. Paris: Editions J. Gabalda et Cie, 1996.

Levenson, Jon D. *The Hebrew Bible, the Old Testament, and Historical Criticism*. Louisville: Westminster, 1993.

Louw, Johannes P. and Eugene A. Nida. *Greek English Lexicon of the New Testament based on Semantic Domains*. 2 vols. New York: United Bible Societies, 1988.

Marcus, Joel. *Mark 1–8*. Anchor-Yale Bible. New Haven: Yale University Press, 1999.

———. *Mark 9–16*. Anchor-Yale Bible. New Haven: Yale University Press, 1999.

McHugh, John. *The Mother of Jesus in the New Testament.* London: Darton, Longman & Todd, 1975.
Mitchell, Margaret M., and Frances M. Young, eds. *The Cambridge History of Christianity: Origins to Constantine.* Cambridge: Cambridge University Press, 2006.
Moule, C. F. D. *An Idiom Book of New Testament Greek.* 2nd ed. Cambridge: Cambridge University Press, 1959.
Robertson, A. T. *A Grammar of the New Testament in the Light of Historical Research.* 3rd ed. New York: Hodder & Stoughton, 1919.
Schaberg, Jane. *The Illegitimacy of Jesus: A Feminist Theological Interpretation of the Infancy Narratives.* Sheffield, UK: Sheffield Academic, 1990.
Tan, Kim Huat. *Mark: A New Covenant Commentary.* Cambridge: Lutterworth, 2016.
Young, Frances, Lewis Ayres, and Andrew Louth, eds. *The Cambridge History of Early Christian Literature.* Cambridge: Cambridge University Press, 2004.
Zervos, George. "Christmas with Salome." In *A Feminist Companion to Mariology,* edited by Amy-Jill Levine, 77–98. Cleveland, OH: Pilgrim, 2005.

3

Theotokoupoleis

The Mother of God as Protectress
of the Two Romes

—Mario Baghos

> Cities in late antique and medieval Christendom were often dedicated to the protection of a patron or matron saint, who, on account of their close proximity to God, could thus intercede to him on the behalf of citizens. Modern cities have lost this perception of reality, and, from a secular point of view, are bereft of intercessors. This chapter addresses the challenge presented by the latter phenomenon by turning to the medieval perception of Mary the Theotokos (Θεοτόκος, God-bearer) as protectress of and intercessor for the cities of Constantinople and Rome. I am undertaking this analysis in response to the replacement of saints from the public life of modern cities with the cult of the soldier, which is in fact a reversion of the paradigm that took place in the early Church, where the emphasis was shifted away from external, "flesh and blood" enemies to internal struggles against the passions. That the saints emerged victoriously from this struggle and, on account of their closeness to God, intercede to him on our behalf, will be presupposed by this chapter. It is one such intercessor that it will focus on, namely, the holy Mother of God, to whose protection the cities of Constantinople and Rome were ascribed.

This chapter addresses the challenge presented by the secularization of the city, and the concomitant loss of saints as protectors/intercessors to God for the salvation of the inhabitants of cities, by turning to the medieval perception of Mary the Theotokos as protectress of and intercessor for Constantinople and Rome. The title *Theotokoupoleis* (Θεοτοκούπολεις) means "cities of the Theotokos," and is meant to designate that these cities were dedicated to her. Both of these cities were organically connected by the fact that Constantinople was founded as New Rome by Constantine the Great, with the former Rome being under the political aegis of the Byzantine Empire, centered in Constantine's city, until at least the eighth century AD. Because of this historical connection, artistic representations of the Mother of God in Byzantium would condition those in Rome both before and even well after the Roman Catholic and Orthodox Churches, administratively centered in the two cities, drifted further apart from the eleventh century onwards. Hence, this chapter will address the role of the Mother of God as protectress of and intercessor for Constantinople and Rome by assessing the churches dedicated to her in both cities, the icons and mosaics depicting her, hymns extolling her, etc.

I am undertaking this analysis in response to the replacement of saints from the public life of cities with, in modern times, the cult of the soldier, which is in fact a reversion of the paradigm that operated in the early Church, where the emphasis was shifted away from the external, "flesh and blood" enemies conquered by militaristic heroes to the demonic forces and the internal passions that needed to be conquered by Christians by the grace of Christ.[1] It was those people who emerged successfully from this inner conflict—the saints—who became the heroes of Christendom and who took the place of the old gods as protectors of cities. The dissolution of traditional forms of Christianity in the public space in modernity meant that the saints were pushed into the background, and various war memorials and national days replaced the churches and Christian festivals that were at the center of public life in both West and East.

Herein I contend that this marginalization of the saints in the public space not only has had, in some cases, a negative effect on Christians—who might confuse the saints with national heroes, which in some cases, discussed below, led to the promotion of contradictory values by the

---

1. In other words, the ancient warrior motif that celebrated military exploits for country, family, the possession of wealth or land was inverted by the earliest Christians who applied militaristic language to the inner, spiritual warfare engaged by the saints. For examples, see Eph 6:12–18 and Rev 2:7, 11, 15, 17, 26; 3:12, 21.

Churches—but has deprived cities and the greater public sphere of those intercessors to God who entreat the Lord on our behalf for his mercy and for our salvation.² It is one such intercessor—perhaps the intercessor *par excellence*—that this chapter will focus on, the holy Mother of God, the Virgin Mary. Before turning to her representation and role in the two Romes, I shall consider the role of the saints as protectors/protectresses of and intercessors for cities, and address the critical challenge regarding the displacement of saints in the public space.

Saints, Cities, and the Critical Challenge

Unlike modern cities, which, in being constructed according to a secular and utilitarian paradigm reflect the corporate and commercial concerns of our age,³ ancient cities were by-and-large religious centers. From the earliest cities that emerged in Mesopotamia to late antique marvels such as Constantinople, the cities of the ancient world were full of symbols that reflected the religious conception of the world of the inhabitants.⁴ Indeed, scholars such as Jan Assmann have argued that the earliest cities, in Egypt for example, contained no characteristic structures apart from temples,⁵ so that religion conditioned the inhabitants more so than any other institution. The same could be said for Greece, where Delphi and Athens constituted veritable pilgrimage centers for the temples of Apollo and Athena, respectively.

A major characteristic of the religious conception of ancient cities concerns their dedication to one or more of the gods worshipped by the inhabitants. This can be discerned, in a general way, in ancient Babylon—where *Bāb-ilāni*, etymologically designated "the gateway of the gods"⁶—but more particularly in Ancient Egypt, where the city of Iunu was given the name of the sun god Ra or Helios by the Greeks in recognition that the city was dedicated to him.⁷ (Memphis is another example, dedicated to the god Ptah, and Amun to Thebes.)⁸ For the ancient Greeks it was Athens that had

---

2. That the saints continue to entreat God on behalf of those who revere them is presupposed in this chapter. By referring to the fact that the public space is deprived of saints, I mean the lack of public acknowledgment that can take many forms—artistic, processional, etc.

3. Mumford, *The City in History*, 445.

4. Eliade, *The Myth of the Eternal Return*, 15–16.

5. Assmann, *The Search for God in Ancient Egypt*, 1.

6. Eliade, *The Myth of the Eternal Return*, 14.

7. Cohn, *Cosmos, Chaos and the World to Come*, 7.

8. Bellah, *Religion in Human Evolution*, 652 fn. 106.

the honor of being named after the goddess of wisdom, Athena, and even in the case where cities were not named after gods or goddesses, they could receive the name of one of their attributes. This was the case with Delphi, which, on account of its association with Apollo, who according to Homer rode there on a dolphin before the construction of his temple, was named after the Greek word for dolphin, which is δελφίς (*delphis*).[9]

It is a truism that the temples in these cities were dedicated to their patrons or matrons. Hence, the Parthenon in the acropolis of Athens was dedicated to the virgin goddess, Athena,[10] and the Temple of Apollo in Delphi was famed for its oracle that was essentially the mouthpiece of the god.[11] In Rome, the temple of Jupiter Optimus Maximus on the Capitoline hill towered over the Forum, the sacred symbolic center, of the city.[12] The Romans in fact had a habit of constructing 'capitols' in the cities they conquered in order to demonstrate the "binding relationship between Rome and its dependent territories,"[13] and of their deities over those of the conquered peoples.[14] Thus, for the Romans, Jupiter ruled supreme.

With the spread of Christianity and the gradual substitution of polytheism for Christian worship in the major metropolises of the Roman Empire, a shift of emphasis was necessary in order to accommodate the new Christian worldview in the public space. It would be illogical to think that a habit that was essential to human beings since the dawn of civilization—that being, the infusion of cities with religious symbolism and their ascription to divine protectors—would dissipate. The early Church used various methods in order to shift the emphasis away from protector gods and goddesses to saints, who were not meant to be seen as gods *per se*, but as immediate participants in the grace of the Trinitarian God revealed through the God-man, Jesus Christ, and therefore able to entreat him on our behalf. Thus, cities throughout Christendom were ascribed saintly protectors who would shield

---

9. *The Homeric Hymns III–To Pythian Apollo*, in Hesiod, *The Homeric Hymns and Homerica*, 358–59.

10. It was dedicated to Athena Polias: "Athena worshipped specifically as the goddess of the city." Gates, *Ancient Cities*, 229.

11. Bellah, *Religion in Human Evolution*, 333, 372.

12. Gates, *Ancient Cities*, 342.

13. Bassett, *The Urban Image of Late Antique Constantinople*, 32.

14. The Romans could of course be very flexible, as the Roman pantheon was often extended to include the deities of the peoples they conquered. A manifest example of this expansion was the erection of temples to foreign deities in the city of Rome itself. Eric Onlin, "Urban Religion in the Middle and Late Republic," in Rüpke, ed., *A Companion to Roman Religion*, 62.

them from various disasters, both natural and human-made, and who were chiefly entreated to pray to God on behalf of the populace for their salvation.

It was in this capacity that the Theotokos was considered the chief intercessor on behalf of not just Constantinople and Rome, but of Paris and Aachen; St. Demetrios protected Thessalonike, St. Andrew protected Patras (the place of his martyrdom), St. George protected London, etc. In some places cities were even named after patron saints, such as Sfântu Gheorghe in the Romanian county of Covasna, and Giurgu in a county named after St. George, again in Romania.[15] A convenient example of how this shift of emphasis took place can be discerned in relation to Athens, where the Parthenon was, at least by the sixth century AD, converted into a church dedicated to the Virgin Mary, Parthenos Maria or the Theotokos Atheniotissa—the God-bearer of Athens—its main title after the twelfth century.[16]

This shift, from the old gods to the saints in Christ, was in fact part of a broader transference of emphasis from the external warrior motifs characterizing most ancient cultures to the internal spiritual warfare that characterized the Christian journey or the path of holiness.[17] Whilst aspects of the old warrior culture were difficult to shake off—especially from the reign of Constantine the Great (ostensibly the first Christian emperor) onwards[18]—and Christian symbols and saints were often, from an imperial point of view, construed militaristically, nevertheless the abiding perception of the Church in relation to the saints was that they had, firstly, undertaken the internal, spiritual struggle against the passions and demons and, by the grace of God, had conquered both, and, secondly, that they chiefly intercede on our behalf to the Trinitarian God for his mercy (and do not necessarily exact vengeance on behalf of believers).

Of course, the perception that the saints protected various cities from natural, human-made and spiritual evils, from Constantinople to Rome and beyond, was pervasive in the Middle Ages. However, the dismantling of Christianity in the public space since the eighteenth century in the West—accentuated by the Reformation, the separation between Church and state, the rise of deism, the spread of civil religion, and the growth of

15. I thank Protopresbyter Dr. Doru Costache for these details.

16. It was also known as "the Great Church of Athens." Kaldellis, *The Christian Parthenon*, 77–78.

17. This shift, from external conquests to internal ones, is pertinently illustrated by Eusebius of Caesarea in his *The History of the Church* 5, trans. G. A. Williamson, 138.

18. Constantine associated Christian motifs of victory over spiritual opponents with physical victories over his imperial rivals, such as Licinius. See Eusebius of Caesarea's *Life of Constantine* 2.46, trans. Averil Cameron and Stuart G. Hall, 111, and the same text, chapter 3.3, p. 122.

secularism—resulted in the gradual relegation of Christianity to the private sphere, meaning that the saints were no longer to be considered, at least on a public level in many secular countries, as protectors or protectresses of cities. Instead, beginning in France but extending also to America and throughout the world, civil religion—a religion of the state, marked by, but not necessarily dependent on, deism[19]—filled the vacuum left by Christianity.

Civil religion was characterized by the celebration of the military heroes and accomplishments of nation-states and witnessed a return to the former paradigm of the ancient warrior cultures, in a way that was not entirely bereft of religious connotations.[20] In some countries, such as France, the institution of civil religion involved a comprehensive supplanting of Christianity through the substitution of the Christian calendar and its heroes, namely Christ and his saints, with the birth of the state founded on the blood of revolutionaries, in other words, soldiers, who were commemorated instead of traditional Christian saints. Even Christmas was replaced by "the birth of the Republic."[21] In America, the Civil War produced an abundance of slain soldiers whose burial sites became "hallowed monument[s]," and thus Memorial Day grew out of the Civil War and gave "ritual expression" to the theme of the soldiers' sacrifice.[22]

These new heroes of country were to be annually remembered the way that, in Christendom, the saints were, and the proliferation of such memorial celebrations throughout the world in countries embroiled in both civil and international conflicts—such as World Wars I and II—led to the establishment of permanent war memorials in almost every capital city. War memorials thus acted as the ceremonial hubs of modern cities, pointing to an important phenomenon: that with the dissolution of Christianity in the public space the vacuum had to be filled, and the nation-states of modernity rehabilitated—and brought to the fore of public life—the cult of the hero that dominated pagan antiquity. This was done, in some cases quite consciously, at the expense of Christian saints, who were pushed more and more into the background.

The problem with the rehabilitation of the old warrior motifs in a more-or-less secular guise is that the militaristic paradigm, which involves external conquests and violence against our "flesh and blood" neighbors for whom Christ also died (1 Cor 8:11) is antithetical to the Christian message

---

19. Coleman, "Civil Religion," 70.

20. These memorials are treated as sacred spaces: silence is observed within them, obelisks mark them, they house perennial flames symbolizing eternal life and contain inscriptions outlining the campaigns and conflicts of a given nation.

21. Markoff and Regan, "The Rise and Fall of Civil Religion," 335.

22. Bellah, "Civil Religion in America," 269.

of loving self-sacrifice exemplified by the Savior for all people and reiterated by his saints. Its rehabilitation in traditionally Christian nations, for instance, has led to some confusion as to who should be venerated in the public space. In Greece, the beginning of the revolution against the Ottoman Turks on 25 March, 1821, coincided with the feast of the Annunciation, and attempts to create, within the ecclesial sphere, a connection between the national festival celebrating the revolution and the Christian Orthodox feast[23] have resulted in a tension between their respective messages, the former marked by ethnocentric militarism, and the latter honing in on the humility of the Virgin Mary and her conception—via the descent of the Holy Spirit—of the Lord of all, who loves and died for all people. Of course, the former, militaristic paradigm represents a mode of being that contradicts Christianity. The latter, however, prioritizes the saintly life in Christ above any nationalistic sentiments.[24] One need only remember St. Paul's exhortation that in Christ "there is neither Jew nor Greek" (Gal 3:28), not to mention the fact that the Annunciation—which declared the good news of the coming of the Savior of all—is simply incompatible with revolutionary struggles that are marked by behavior antithetical to Mary's humble submission to the will of God.

Moreover, and perhaps more problematic, is that civil religion represents an overarching framework for the public life of most cities (at least, in early modernity)[25] and can (a) inspire sentiments in the faithful that dwell in those cities that are incompatible with Christianity, and (b) does not offer the world intercessors to the Trinitarian God that can entreat him for the salvation of the entire human race. Soldiers cannot do this anymore than the pagan gods could: the latter are mythical and there is no guarantee that the former dwell in the company of the saints. That Christians can and should pray for the salvation of deceased soldiers—just as they should pray for everyone else—is an imperative, but there is a danger to Christians in most countries preoccupied with the cult of the dead soldier that they might either confuse these memorials—construed as sacred spaces—with the sacrality that proceeds from Christ alone (and, by his grace, through his

23. See Dimoula, "The Nation Between Utopia and Art," 206.

24. This is not at the expense of culture, including the Greek one, which is so rich. Indeed, cultures are the vehicles through which the Gospel is disseminated. Nevertheless, nationalism expressed in a militaristic sense is antithetical to the Christian message.

25. Whilst civil religion remains a principal framework, it was perhaps more popular in early modernity than it is today, rearing its head several times a year when a country undertakes its national celebrations. The cult of celebrities and the sportsmen and women seems to be more dominant in day-to-day life. I thank Protopresbyter Dr. Doru Costache for the latter nuance.

saints), or that the pervasive nature of these memorials will overshadow the significance of the saints who have traditionally been considered as intercessors to God on behalf of Christians, churches, cities, and the world.

It is this approach to the saints that this chapter seeks to bring to the fore by honing in on representations of the Mother of God in Constantinople and Rome. Both cities were dedicated to her and were full of images and churches that entreated her care, protection, and intercession to the God of the universe, her Son and our Lord Jesus Christ. For the sake of brevity, when turning to Rome this chapter will address the specifically Byzantine-inspired artistic representations of the Mother of God in that city up until the close of the Middle Ages. This organically connects Rome to Constantinople, which fell to the Ottoman Turks in 1453, at the close of the medieval period.

The Theotokos as Intercessor/Protectress of Constantinople

The role of the Virgin Mary as an intercessor to Christ in the cities of Constantinople and Rome was given impetus by the circumstances surrounding the third ecumenical council, where St. Cyril of Alexandria defended the use of the traditional title of the Virgin as Theotokos or God-bearer in opposition to the heresiarch Nestorius' downplaying of her role in the incarnation, and the incarnation itself.[26] The third ecumenical council canonized this traditional title[27]—used already by Origen in the mid-third century[28]—to refer to the Mother of God precisely as such. But interest in the Theotokos could arguably be traced, from a textual point of view, to much earlier: to the Gospel of Luke (chapters 1–2) and to second-century apocryphal texts such as the *Protoevangelium of James* that sought to flesh out the early life of the Virgin, such that it outlines her ancestry and nativity, entrance into the temple, and the Nativity of Christ in a cave instead of a manger.[29] All of these apocryphal themes were picked up in the liturgical tradition of the Orthodox Church[30] that flourished within Byzantium, the capital of which

26. Costache, "Fifth Century Christology between Soteriological Perspective and Metaphysical Concerns," 49–53.

27. "Council of Ephesus–431," 59.

28. Johnson, *Praying and Believing in Early Christianity*, 76.

29. *The Protoevangelium of James* 1–8, 426–29.

30. Indeed, the Mother of God's parents, Sts. Joachim and Anna, who are commemorated within the Orthodox Church on 9 September, are mentioned in this text, and the feasts of the Virgin's nativity (8 September), and entrance into the temple (21

was the city of Constantinople, founded, as we have seen, by the Roman emperor Constantine the Great.

Hence, from the inception of the Church we can discern an increase in interest and devotion to the Virgin that would undoubtedly affect the ecclesial and even public space of major cities such as Constantinople. This is emphatically evident in the sixth century, when the Byzantine emperor Maurice decided to inaugurate the feast of the Dormition of the Theotokos—in Constantinople and throughout the empire—on the fifteenth of August,[31] a feast that has textual antecedents in the apocrypha of the early fifth century, including *Transitus Mariae*, which describes the Virgin as having been resurrected by Christ;[32] a popular motif that was repeated by homilists for centuries. Maurice's decision to inaugurate the feast of the Dormition in the Great Church of Constantinople would resonate throughout Byzantium, and would lead to the adoption of the feast by Rome under Pope Sergius I in the seventh century.[33]

We will turn to Rome later. Suffice it to state for now that even before Maurice's inauguration of the Dormition feast, the civic space of Constantinople was already being populated with churches dedicated to the Virgin. After the council of Chalcedon in 451, or the fourth ecumenical council, which reiterated the Theotokos' title of God-bearer,[34] the empress Pulcheria, sister of the emperor Theodosius II, built three churches in Constantinople in her honor—the churches of Blachernae, Chalkoprateia, and the Hodegon.[35] These three churches all purportedly contained sacred relics associated with the Virgin: the Blachernae had her robe or funeral garb,[36] the Chalkoprateia, her girdle,[37] and the Hodegon the miraculous icon

---

November) could be said to have had textual precedents in it. See *The Protoevangelium of James* 2 (Cullman, 428) for the nativity, and the same text, chapter 7 (ibid., 429) for her entrance into the temple. The text also describes the birth of Christ in a cave, a favored motif in Orthodox iconography. *The Protoevangelium of James* 18–19 (ibid., 433–34).

31. Shoemaker, *Ancient Traditions on the Virgin Mary's Dormition and Assumption*, 73.

32. Beinert, "The Relatives of Jesus," 485.

33. Rubin, *The Mother of God*, 97.

34. "Council of Chalcedon–451," in *Decrees of the Ecumenical Councils*, 86.

35. Daley, trans., "Introduction," in *On the Dormition of Mary: Early Patristic Homilies*, 37 endnote 4.

36. The robe of the Virgin had been brought to Constantinople by two patricians from Palestine, and in 472 Emperor Leo I ordered it to be placed in a special reliquary and moved to the church of Blachernae. Klein, "Sacred Relics and Imperial Ceremonies at the Great Palace of Constantinople," 87.

37. Hennessey, "The Chapel of St. Jacob at the Church of the Theotokos

known as the Hodegitria, or "She who leads the way," which legend had attributed to the hand of St. Luke the Evangelist.[38] Obviously, the council of Chalcedon in 451 was a turning point. By the end of the fifth century the emperor Leo I had built the shrine of the "Virgin of the Spring, later called the Zoodochos Pege" or the Life-Giving Spring, above a spring on the outskirts of Constantinople.[39] According to later legend the emperor Justinian was healed of a urinary ailment by the water from the Pege, and commissioned the construction of a domed church on the site that survived until the fifteenth or sixteenth century.[40] The *Akathist hymn* dedicated to the Virgin Mary—"the oldest continuously performed Marian hymn used in the Eastern Orthodox Church"[41]—which is said to have been composed by the Constantinopolitan hymnographer St. Romanos the Melodist, dates from this period.

A generation after Justinian, when the Avars invaded and attacked Constantinople in 626 AD, the Patriarch Sergius, to whom defense of the city was entrusted whilst the emperor Heraclius was on campaign, each day made a circuit of the land walls whilst holding the icon of the Hodegitria, and it was to her that the victory against the Avars was ascribed.[42] After this event, a new proemium was added to the *Akathist hymn*, which entreats the Mother of God as follows:

> Unto you, O Theotokos, invincible champion,
> Your city, in thanksgiving ascribes the victory for the
> deliverance from sufferings.
> And having your might unassailable,
> Free me from all dangers, so that I may cry
> unto you: "Hail! O bride unwedded.[43]

Henceforth the Mother of God was considered Constantinople's special matron. More churches were built, such as a church dedicated to the Virgin of the Pharos within the precincts of the palace of Constantinople, and, as the name suggests, in close proximity to the "famous beacon or lantern" of the palace.[44] No longer extant, this church is mentioned for the first time

Chalkoprateia in Constantinople," 352.

38. McGuckin, "Hodegitria," 307.
39. Talbot and Johnson, "Introduction," xiv.
40. Ibid., xv.
41. Limberis, *Divine Heiress*, 90.
42. Pentcheva, *Icons and Power*, 57.
43. Limberis, *Divine Heiress*, 149.
44. Klein, "Sacred Relics and Imperial Ceremonies at the Great Palace of

in the eighth century and housed the "Byzantine empire's most sacred possessions: the relics of Christ's Passion and certain other important relics of Christendom."[45]

In the eleventh and twelfth centuries more churches were dedicated to the Virgin's honor: the church of the Theotokos Pammakaristos or "the All Blessed God-bearer,"[46] the church of the Theotokos Kyriotissa or of "Our Lady the God-bearer,"[47] the church of St. Mary of the Mongols (also known as Theotokos Panagiotissa or "All Holy God-bearer," and as Dormition of the Mother of God Mouchliotissa),[48] just to name a few. Some of these churches would become landmarks in various imperial processions. The church of Zoodochos Pege, for instance, "was the focus of an imperial procession on Ascension Day, when the emperor visited the church for the celebration of the liturgy and a ceremonial meal with the patriarch."[49] The tenth-century *Book of Ceremonies* records the procession undertaken by the emperor and patriarch to Hagia Sophia or Holy Wisdom on the feast of the Dormition, where the following *troparion* of the feast, still chanted in the Orthodox Church, was sung by all present as they entered the narthex:[50]

> In giving birth you kept your virginity,
> In falling asleep you did not abandon the world, O Theotokos.
> You passed over into life, you who are the Mother of Life,
> And through your intercessions, you redeem our souls from death.[51]

The Mother of God's intercessory role in Byzantium was also given an artistic expression in Hagia Sophia, where after the iconoclastic controversy a mosaic of her cradling the Christ-child was placed in the Eastern apse just beneath the church's massive dome.[52]

Constantinople," 79.

45. Ibid., 80.

46. Marinis, "Structure, Agency, Ritual, and the Byzantine Church," 351–52.

47. Krautheimer, *Early Christian and Byzantine Architecture*, 293.

48. Marinis, *Architecture and Ritual in the Churches of Constantinople: Ninth to Fifteenth Centuries*, 199.

49. Talbot and Johnson, "Introduction," xv.

50. Porphyrogennetos, *The Book of Ceremonies* 2.12, trans. Anne Moffat and Maxeme Tall, vol. 2, 554.

51. My translation of the Greek text from *The Divine Liturgy of our Father among the Saints John Chrysostom*, 134.

52. Beckwith, *Early Christian and Byzantine Art*, 186.

1. Ninth-century mosaic of the Mother of God cradling the Christ-child in the apse of the church of Holy Wisdom (Hagia Sophia), Constantinople. Photo by author.

In the fourteenth century, a mosaic of Christ Pantokrator or the "Master of All" was placed in Hagia Sophia's circular dome[53]—the circle designating the cosmos:[54] hence Christ's mastery over all things. We can thus contemplate the image of the Mother of God in the apse just below the Pantokrator as highlighting her role as intercessor to the Master, the God-man Christ. This representation would become standard in Byzantine and post-Byzantine churches, where it would be augmented by her depiction in the *orans* position, supplicating Christ as "Wider than the Heavens" because she contained the One who contains the universe in her womb.[55]

It is a shame that not many such images survive from medieval Constantinople itself. There are exquisite mosaics in Hagia Sophia of the Virgin

---

53. Gregoras, *Historiae Byzantinae* XXIX, 47f., in *The Art of the Byzantine Empire 312–1453*, trans. Mango, 249.

54. Tresidder, ed., *The Complete Dictionary of Symbols*, 108.

55. McGuckin, *The Orthodox Church*, 222.

holding the Christ-child being supplicated by various emperors and of her entreating Christ.[56] For instance, a mosaic tympanum which "was placed over the door leading from the south vestibule into the narthex" portrays the Virgin and Christ-child being supplicated by the emperor Justinian—who offers her the church of Hagia Sophia (depicted as a miniature in his hands) on her left—and Constantine the Great on her right, who offers her the city of Constantinople itself; an image that is indicative of her role as protectress of Constantinople, and which is still extant.[57] Such images were not restricted to Hagia Sophia. In the Monastery of the Holy Savior in Chora there are some beautiful mosaics of the Mother of God with the Christ-child in the center of the dome, as well as panel mosaics of her, either holding the Christ-child or entreating her Son. However, owing to conquest of the city by the Ottomans in 1453, many of these images have been damaged, and some of the figures effaced.[58]

2. Mosaic panel of the Mother of God supplicating Christ in the Church of the Holy Saviour, Chora (now **Kariye Müzesi**), Constantinople (est. 12th–14th century). Photo by Nicholas Sen.

Nevertheless, we can infer her intercessory role as expressed in art from churches in other territories of the Byzantine empire, such as in Greece where she appears in the apses of the churches of Panagia Pantanassa (or

---

56. Teteriatnikov, *Mosaics of Hagia Sophia, Istanbul*, 19, 50, 54.
57. Beckwith, *Early Christian and Byzantine Art*, 225.
58. Dursun et al., *Chora Museum*, 31, 37, 43, 51, 53.

"All Holy Queen of All") and Panagia Hodegitria in Mystra,[59] the Monastery of Hossios Loukas in Boetia,[60] etc. In fact, in Mystra—one of the last major Byzantine outposts before the fall of the city—there were several churches dedicated to the Virgin, including, amongst those mentioned, the church of Panagia Peribleptos, meaning the All Holy one who "Watches Over All."[61]

Returning to the feast of the Dormition as it was celebrated in Byzantium, an important insight for our present purposes can be derived from the fact that both emperor and patriarch, along with notables of Constantinople, chanted the Dormition hymn to our holy Mother in unison. This public acknowledgement, by representatives of both Church and State, that the Mother of God has not abandoned the world, but intercedes on our behalf to her Son and our God, is of tremendous existential importance for Christians and for society in general. In the ancient and medieval Church, the presence of God in the saints was considered a stabilizing force in a tumultuous world. Saints, on account of their close proximity to God, are often depicted as stabilizing the world—both human-made and natural—through their intercessions to him on our behalf.[62] The fact that the saints do this in cooperation with the grace of God, and not on their own accord, is attested to in the literature. Conversely, the absence of the grace dwelling in the saints and their intercessions could be catastrophic. The second exile of St. John Chrysostom from Constantinople, at the hands of the Empress Eudoxia, constitutes one such example: the ecclesiastical historian Sozomen records the hailstorm, and the death of the empress, that followed.[63] The Byzantines believed that the world functioned in just such a way. Thus, the Mother of God was entreated as the special protectress of the city precisely because they believed that her intercessions to the God of the universe—her Son and our God—were particularly effective for the stability of the world.

A striking example of their entreaties to her are reflected on the eve of Constantinople's collapse to the Ottoman Turks. The emperor Constantine Palaeologos, the last emperor of Byzantium,

> . . . commanded that the most venerable icon of the Mother of God, protectress of the city, should be brought out and carried

---

59. Emmanuel, "Religious Imagery in Mystra," 125.

60. Chatzidakis, *Hosios Loukas*, 21.

61. Emmanuel, "Religious Imagery in Mystra," 122.

62. For examples, see St. Serapion of Thmuis' depiction of St. Antony the Great in Serapion of Thmuis, *To the Disciples of Antony* 5–7, in *The Life of Antony*, 42. Also see *Letters from the Desert* 569, in *Barsanuphius and John*, 153.

63. *The Ecclesiastical History of Sozomen* 8.27, trans. Hartranft, in *Socrates, Sozomenus: Church Histories*, 417.

in procession round the streets. Suddenly the icon slipped off the frame on which it was being held aloft; and almost at once the streets were deluged with torrents of hail and rain. The procession was abandoned.[64]

Four days later, on May 28 1453, the Christian city of Constantinople was conquered by the Muslim Turks. This was of course difficult for the Byzantines to reconcile with the belief that the Theotokos protected their city, so a legend, recorded in one of the many laments for the city's fall, emerged that outlines that when the Turks broke into the city at the gate of St. Romanos, the emperor saw a Queen with her entourage of eunuchs enter a nearby church dedicated to the Virgin.[65] He followed her, and discovered that it was the Theotokos with a host of angels:

> She sat on the bishop's throne and looked very mournful. Then she opened her holy mouth and addressed the Emperor: 'This unhappy city was dedicated to me and many a time I have saved it from divine wrath. Now too I have entreated My Son and My God. But alas, he has decreed that this time you should be consigned to the hands of your enemies because the sins of your people have inflamed the anger of God. So leave your imperial crown here for me to look after until such time as God will permit another to come and take it.[66]

One might wonder as to the plausibility of this particular event. Granted, Christians believe in the literal existence of saints, in the fact that they are able to do what Christ did by the latter's grace (i.e., miracles, etc.), and that they entreat the Lord on our behalf, even on behalf of cities. But that the Mother of God should be so concerned in the affairs of a particular empire, with the intention of one day resurrecting it, seems incredulous, and can be relegated to the level of folklore or legend as opposed to authentic Church tradition. Nevertheless, this legend is telling of the Byzantine mentality regarding the empire of Constantinople—that it would forever continue by God's grace—that persisted even after the collapse of the city.

What is important for our purposes is that the perception concerning the Mother of God's care for God's people, reflected by the above story, lives on in the many Orthodox churches dedicated to the holy Theotokos. We have seen that this perception of the significance of the Virgin has antecedents in the New Testament and early apocryphal literature, in the third and fourth ecumenical councils, and in the institution of the feast of the

---

64. Nicol, *The Immortal Emperor*, 66.

65. Ibid., 89.

66. *Anonymi Monodia de capta Constantinopoli*, ed. Lambros (1908) in ibid., 89.

Dormition: that she was considered an intercessor to God—as reflected in the many churches dedicated to her in Constantinople—and that this intercessory capacity was accentuated after the Avar invasion in the seventh century and continued until the city's collapse (as it does in the Orthodox Church to this day). I will now turn to the city of Rome, which was (and still is) replete with images of the Mother of God and churches dedicated to her, in order to assess the extent to which she was considered protectress of and intercessor for that city. I will, of course, hone in especially on those churches influenced by Byzantine artistic motifs.

The Theotokos as Intercessor/Protectress of Rome

In the mid-fifth century a church on the Esquiline hill in Rome described as *ecclesia sanctae Dei Genetricis*, now known as Santa Maria Maggiore, was dedicated by Pope Sixtus III.[67] The church however was started by Pope Liberius, during whose episcopate, according to tradition, a childless patrician in the city named John, together with his wife, vowed to donate their possessions to the Virgin and prayed to her that she might make known to them the manner in which they should do so. On 5 August "during the night, snow fell on the summit of the Esquiline hill and, in obedience to a vision which they had the same night, they built a basilica, in honour of Our Lady, on the spot which was covered with snow."[68]

Thus the feast day of the church is known as *Dedicatio Sanctae Mariae ad Nives* or "Dedication of St. Mary of the Snows." The interior of the church mostly consists of the original basilica, which has of course been added to over time, but one of the most important additions for our purposes is the coronation of the Virgin mosaic in the apse, added by the artist Jacobo Torriti in the late thirteenth century.[69]

---

67. Brandenburg, *The Ancient Churches of Rome*, 176.
68. Ott, "Our Lady of the Snow," 361.
69. Paoletti and Radke, *Art in Renaissance Italy*, 61.

3. Apse mosaic of the Mother of God being crowned by Christ in Santa Maria Maggiore. Photo by author.

The mosaic, in the Byzantine style, depicts the Mother of God being enthroned and crowned by Christ in heaven. What I wish to hone in on is the close proximity of our holy Mother to her Son and our God in this mosaic, which, due to her supplicating him with hands outstretched, once again underlines her role as intercessor on our behalf. Beneath it is inscribed the following: *Maria virgo assumpta est ad aethereum thalamum, in quo rex regum stellato sedet solio* which translates into "the Virgin Mary is assumpted unto the heavenly chamber in which the king of kings sits upon his starry seat."[70] Beneath this is added: *Exaltata est sancta Dei Genitrix super choros angelorum ad celestia regna*, or "the holy Mother of God is exalted beyond the choir of angels to the heavenly kingdom."[71] The well-known ambiguity in relation to the assumption between Orthodox Christianity and Catholicism dates from a later period: the former believing that Mary died a physical death before being resurrected by her Son, and many of the latter believing the same thing, with some affirming that she did not in fact die but ascended into heaven.[72] This ambiguity, however, is not a problem in

---

70. Tosti-Croce, "La Basilica Tra Due E Trecento," 134. My translation.

71. Ibid.

72. Above we saw that the Dormition texts such as the *Transitus Mariae* dates from the early fifth century, whereas the texts describing the Virgin's assumption date from the first half of the sixth century. Panagopoulos, "The Byzantine Traditions of the

this mosaic, for below it appears a Byzantine image of the Dormition with the reposed Mother of God flanked by the Apostles,[73] who according to a tradition going as far back as *Transitus Mariae*, were transferred to the site of the Virgin's repose via bilocation.[74] Behind her is Christ cradling her departed soul, a role-reversal of images that usually depict her cradling the Christ-child.[75] This Dormition mosaic is flanked by other Byzantine mosaics and images depicting the Mother of God: the Annunciation, the Nativity in a cave (inspired by the *Protoevangelium of James*) and her Presentation of Christ in the Temple (with Sts. Joseph, Symeon and Anna).[76]

Another church in Rome with Byzantine inspired mosaics is Santa Maria in Trastevere, attributed to the papacy of Callixtus I in the third century, thus making it perhaps one of the oldest churches in Rome before it was rebuilt in the twelfth century.[77] The mosaics beneath the apse were installed by Pietro Cavallini in the late thirteenth century and include a Nativity cycle and Adoration scene inspired by Byzantine models: the Mother of God with midwives, the Annunciation, the Nativity, the Adoration of the Magi, the Presentation of Christ in the Temple, and the Dormition, which form a line beneath the apse that dates from over a century earlier.[78] The apse mosaic depicts the Mother of God seated next to Christ on a throne:[79] He is slightly above her, a nuance missing in the mosaic of Christ crowning the Virgin in Santa Maria Maggiore. In her hand, the Theotokos holds a scroll which says *Leva eius sub capite meo et dextera illius amplesabitur me* which translates to "His left hand is under my head, and his right hand shall embrace me" from the Song of Solomon 2:6 and 8:3. Likewise, Christ holds a scroll which affirms, *veni electa mea et ponam in te thronum meum*, meaning "Come, my chosen one, and I shall put you on my throne."[80] Just like the apse mosaic in Maria Maggiore, here too we can discern the close proximity of the Mother of God to her Son as intercessor.

Virgin Mary's Dormition and Assumption," 344.

73. Tosti-Croce, "La Basilica Tra Due E Trecento," 132–33, 148–49.

74. Shoemaker, *Ancient Traditions on the Virgin Mary's Dormition and Assumption*, 37.

75. Tosti-Croce, "La Basilica Tra Due E Trecento," 148–49.

76. Ibid., 145–47, 150.

77. Brandenburg, *The Ancient Churches of Rome*, 113.

78. Hetherington, "The Mosaics of Pietro Cavallini in Santa Maria in Trastevere," plates 21–22, 23–24.

79. Gunton, *Rome's Historic Churches*, plate 11.

80. These are the words Christ speaks to Mary in the *Golden Legend*. "The Assumption of the Blessed Virgin Mary," in de Voragine, *The Golden Legend*, 465.

4. Apse mosaic of the Mother of God being acclaimed by Christ in Santa Maria in Trastevere. Photo by author.

The question that we are left with is whether or not Maria Maggiore and Maria in Trastevere—selected because of their emphatically Byzantine representations of Mary—designated the Mother of God as a protectress of the city of Rome. Maria Maggiore hosts an icon, probably painted in the sixth century, which, since the Middle Ages, was considered a true representation of the Mother of God and the Christ-child insofar as it was widely believed that St. Luke the Evangelist had painted it.[81] Thus, the icon was an alternative to the Byzantine Hodegitria, and, according to Kirsten Noreen, was "used processionally . . . to protect Rome and its citizens from pestilence, famine and war."[82] The icon was therefore "defender of the city," or, rather, it was the Mother of God depicted in the icon who was considered

81. Noreen, "The Icon of Santa Maria Maggiore, Rome," 660.
82. Ibid.

the protectress of Rome, highlighted by the fact that in the nineteenth century the icon's epithet became "Salus Populi Romani, the 'Salvation of the Roman People.'"[83]

Maria in Trastevere does not, as far as I am aware contain any explicit references to Mary as the special protectress of Rome: but that Mary was accorded a general intercessory role in this church is evident from the apse mosaic. In fact, that the Mother of God was considered a special intercessor for the city can be discerned from the panoply of other churches in Rome. Some are dedicated to her, such as Santa Maria ad Martyres (St. Mary at the [church of] Martyrs), today better known by its ancient designation, the Pantheon, which was transformed into a church in AD 608 by Pope Boniface with the permission of the Byzantine emperor Phocas.[84] The substitution of the Pantheon, formerly dedicated to all the gods, for a church dedicated to all the saints, was interpreted by the venerable Bede and many medieval chroniclers as an attempt to substitute the ancient gods, considered to be demons, for saints: but the dedication to the Virgin specifically was only explicated in the eleventh century, when a canon of St. Peter's named Benedict described the dedication to her as a deliberate attempt to supplant its original ascription to the goddess Cybele.[85]

Echoing the transference of significance from paganism to Christianity that we saw took place in Athens in relation to the Parthenon, the dedication of the Pantheon to the Mother of God can be interpreted as an apologetic project, with Erik Thunø going a step further by asserting that since Rome had no church dedicated to the Mother of God with a centralized plan, then it appropriated the Pantheon precisely for such purposes. This was in fact undertaken in imitation of the Byzantine chapel of Holy Soros in Constantinople, which was full of Marian relics[86] (which was actually a chapel in the Blachernae church, mentioned above). Thunø continued that although the Pantheon could not boast any Marian relics, it did have, just like Santa Maria Maggiore, a miraculous icon.[87] This icon, which again looks very Byzantine,[88] "served as a cult image and virtually replaced pagan cult images," and is "venerated in the church to this day."[89]

---

83. Ibid.
84. Brandenburg, *The Ancient Churches of Rome*, 233.
85. Thunø, "The Pantheon in the Middle Ages," 235.
86. Ibid., 236.
87. Ibid.
88. Brandenburg, *The Ancient Churches of Rome*, 233.
89. Ibid., 234.

More examples of images of the Virgin as intercessor, undertaken in the Byzantine style, abound in the city. The ninth-century church of Santa Maria in Domnica depicts the Mother of God enthroned and holding the Christ-child in the apse, surrounded by angels. The Roman Pontiff who commissioned this church, Paschal I, is also depicted in the mosaic, kneeling at the Madonna's feet.[90] Beneath the existing church of San Clemente (built c. twelfth century), the first basilica from the fourth century, still extant, contains a fresco of the Ascension dating from the ninth century that depicts the Mother of God directly beneath the Lord Christ with her arms outstretched in the *orans* posture.[91] In the second basilica from the twelfth century—i.e. the existing church above—a Byzantine mosaic in the apse depicts Christ crucified on the cross as a living tree, with the Virgin and the beloved disciple John flanking the Lord's feet in a state of supplication. According to Mary Stroll, "[i]ssuing from the base of the cross are great whirls of acanthus and the four rivers, signifying the church as the body of Christ, which nourishes the faithful by the sacraments of baptism and the eucharist."[92] The four rivers in fact echo the paradisal state—the Church as Eden described in Genesis 2:10–14—and, in this mosaic, the Mother of God, ensconced by the paradisal vines, is framed by a branch on her left and by her Son on the right,[93] thus once again intimating her close proximity to him as intercessor.

Santa Maria Antiqua, located "at the foot of the Palatine hill from the northwest"[94] of the Roman Forum, the old symbolic center of the city, is thought to have been dedicated in the sixth century and contains frescos that have been painted over many times like a palimpsest. It is significant for us that the oldest layer contains a Byzantine image of the Mother of God enthroned.[95] The location of a church dedicated to the Virgin in the center of the Forum is important, for since Constantine's day the Forum—replete with pagan symbols designating Rome's privileged position at the center of the world—was populated with Christian images that shifted the attention to Christ and his saints. Finally, the papal cathedral church of Rome, St. John Lateran—considered by Roman Catholics to be the "Mother and

---

90. Gunton, *Rome's Historic Churches*, plate 9.

91. Ibid., plate 10.

92. Stroll, *Symbols as Power*, 118–19.

93. Brandenburg, *The Ancient Churches of Rome*, 150–51.

94. Monika Ożóg, "Traces of the History of the Roman Church of Santa Maria Antiqua," 62.

95. Lidova, "The Earliest Images of Maria Regina in Rome and the Byzantine Imperial Iconography," 233.

Head of the churches in the city and in the world"[96]—also contains mosaics indicating the Mother of God's privileged status in the city. Torriti, who I mentioned above executed the mosaics in Maria Maggiore, also worked on the original apse, which was remade in the nineteenth century,[97] with a bust of Christ hanging above a cosmic cross through which flow the waters of life dividing into four rivers—just like in San Clemente—but this time over the celestial Jerusalem. On the left, the Mother of God is depicted in blue and gold entreating her Son and our God,[98] which, if considered from the vantage point of this church constituting, for Roman Catholics, the *caput mundi* for all of their churches, symbolizes her intercessory capacity on behalf of not just the city, but of the world.

This representation of the Mother of God as intercessor for the whole world was, we have seen, reflected in Byzantium, since for the Byzantines, the *oikoumene*, or empire—which was recapitulated within the capital city—designated the inhabited Christian world, so that when Mary was depicted as protectress of the city, and hence the empire, the world is anyway implied (this would of course include the Church, since in Byzantium Church and state worked more-or-less in tandem). Moreover, Orthodox hymns on the feast of our holy Mother's Dormition—which are still chanted today— entreat her on behalf of the whole world,[99] and the Orthodox share with Roman Catholics the perception that the Mother of God entreats her Son on behalf of all peoples (reflected by the latter in *Lumen Gentium*, which has an entire section on the Virgin).[100] Hence, Our Lady can be considered as protectress of and intercessor for not just Constantinople and Rome in the distant past, but of the Churches that venerate her today, just as she can be considered the Mother of the whole world.

Concluding Remarks

We have seen that since ancient times cities were considered religious centers: they were conditioned by their temples and the gods worshipped

---

96. Gunton, *Rome's Historic Churches*, 20.

97. Murray, Murray, and Devonshire Jones, *The Oxford Dictionary of Christian Art and Architecture*, 521.

98. Brandenburg, *The Ancient Churches of Rome*, 23.

99. A line that concludes several *prosomia* in the Vespers of the Dormition extols the Mother of God as the one through whom the Lord grants mercy to the world. Although it is a truism that the Lord does not grant his grace to the world exclusively through the Virgin, nevertheless the hymns highlight her importance as intercessor for God's people. See *The Menaion*, vol. 12: *The Month of August*, 90.

100. Tanner, *The Church in Council*, 152–54.

within them, gods who acted as their special patrons or matrons. In the Christian era the external form of ascribing cities to the protection of deities was retained, but the content was radically altered. No longer would a city be ascribed to the protection of a god or goddess, but to the saints of Christ who were not considered divine in and of themselves, but who were revered for being filled with the grace of God and as having the ability—because of their close proximity to God—to entreat him to be merciful to us, and by his grace to stabilize the world. The cities of Constantinople and Rome are just two examples of cities filled with images of, and churches dedicated to, Christ and his saints, and in this chapter we have addressed the role of one of these saints—in many ways the saint *par excellence*—the Virgin Mary, who on account of her intimacy with her Son and our God as Theotokos, entreats him on our behalf. This was the perception of both the inhabitants of Constantinople and Rome, and we have addressed the cult of the Virgin and its impact on the two cities, the role of her relics, the churches dedicated to her, and the role of icons and mosaics in portraying her as our main intercessor to Christ.

Modern cities, however, are founded on very different principles. Influenced by civil religion, instead of churches at the center of cities conditioning the lives of their inhabitants, war memorials venerating deceased soldiers act as ceremonial hubs. But these memorials reflect a very different mentality to the programme initiated by the Church to shift the emphasis away from the pagan gods—who were in many cases belligerent—to the saints—who have overcome their passions and the demonic forces by God's grace—as protectors of and intercessors for cities. In fact, the institution of the cult of the soldier reflects a return to the former paradigm, though not completely, since the pagan gods were considered divine beings, which is not (at least consciously) the case with soldiers.

I chose the topic of the dissolution of the public representation of saints as intercessors to God on behalf of cities and their replacement by a more, although not thoroughly, secular alternative, that is, military heroes, in order to demonstrate that the former—for traditional Christians—is still beneficial insofar as the saints do continue to intercede to God for us, and that it is important to reflect upon examples of the way these intercessory roles were represented in the past, when the cityscape was conditioned by ecclesial rhythms, in order to be reminded to entreat them to pray for us. Moreover, the fact that many Christians confuse the new paradigm as compatible with the ecclesial one represents an existential problem, insofar as nationalistic militarism can inspire feelings of resentment and anger at one's enemy, whereas we have seen that for the Christian the only enemies are the spiritual forces (Eph 6:12) and the inner passions, and the saints—in having conquered these by the grace of God—show us the proper way to treat our neighbors—those for whom Christ died— irrespective of who they are or what they have done to us, that is, lovingly and altruistically, *in imitatio Christi*.

In any case, given the evidence I supplied above that, on a public level, human beings did (and in the traditional churches still do) venerate the saints as intercessors to Christ for their cities and their own lives, one might wonder whether or not some of the miraculous stories I outlined are plausible or not. I would like to affirm that this is beyond the point. The fact that the saints were acknowledged as being in close proximity to Christ and able to entreat him on our behalf is what is ultimately significant, since Orthodoxy and traditional trends in Catholicism have the following belief in common, that the saints are in direct communication with Christ, even in this very life. The fact that some saints, whilst living, could communicate with other members of the "Church triumphant," such as the Theotokos, is attested to in both the Orthodox and Catholic traditions: from St. Gregory the Wonderworker in the third century, to St. Dominic in the thirteenth century, and St. Seraphim of Sarov in the eighteenth, all purportedly communicated with her. The communication of these holy persons, whilst living, with our holy Mother therefore highlights the significance—in the traditions of Orthodoxy and Catholicism—of entreating her to pray to God for the common benefit of each and every city, of all Christians, and of all people.

Bibliography

Assmann, Jan. *The Search for God in Ancient Egypt*. Translated by D. Lorton. London: Cornell University Press, 2001.

"The Assumption of the Blessed Virgin Mary." In Jacobus de Voragine, *The Golden Legend: Readings on the Saints*, translated by William Granger Ryan, 464–83. Princeton: Princeton University Press, 2012.

Barsanuphius and John: A Selection of Questions and Responses. Translated by John Chryssavgis. Crestwood, NY: St Vladimir's Seminary Press, 2003.

Bassett, Sarah. *The Urban Image of Late Antique Constantinople*. Cambridge: Cambridge University Press, 2004.

Beckwith, John. *Early Christian and Byzantine Art*. New Haven, CT: Yale University Press, 1979.

Beinert, Wolfgang A. "The Relatives of Jesus." In *New Testament Apocrypha, Vol. 1: Gospels and Related Writings*, edited by Wilhelm Schneemelcher and R. McL. Wilson, 407–88. Louisville: Westminster John Knox, 1991.

Bellah, Robert. "Civil Religion in America." In *Culture and Society: Contemporary Debates*, edited by Jeffrey C. Alexander and Steven Seidman, 262–74. Cambridge: Cambridge University Press, 1990.

———. *Religion in Human Evolution: From the Paleolithic to the Axial Age*. Cambridge: Belknap, 2011.
Brandenburg, Hugo. *The Ancient Churches of Rome: From the Fourth to the Seventh Century*. Turnhout, Belgium: Brepols, 2004.
Chatzidakis, Nanno. *Hosios Loukas: Byzantine Art in Greece*. Athens: Melissa, 1997.
Cohn, Norman. *Cosmos, Chaos and the World to Come: The Ancient Roots of Apocalyptic Faith*. New Haven, CT: Yale Nota Bene, 2001.
Coleman, John A. "Civil Religion." *Sociological Analysis* 31:2 (1970) 67–77.
Costache, Doru. "Fifth Century Christology between Soteriological Perspective and Metaphysical Concerns: Notes on the Nestorian Controversy." *Phronema* 21 (2006) 47–59.
"Council of Chalcedon–451." In *Decrees of the Ecumenical Councils: Nicaea I–Lateran V*, edited by Norman P. Tanner, 86. Washington, DC: Georgetown University Press, 1989.
"Council of Ephesus–431." In *Decrees of the Ecumenical Councils: Nicaea I–Lateran V*, edited by Norman P. Tanner, 59. Washington, DC: Georgetown University Press, 1989.
Dimoula, Vassiliki. "The Nation between Utopia and Art: 'Canonizing' Dionysios Solomos as the 'National Poet' of Greece." In *The Making of Modern Greece: Nationalism, Romanticism, and the Uses of the Past (1797–1896)*, edited by Roderick Beaton and David Ricks, 201–10. Farnham, UK: Ashgate, 2009.
The Divine Liturgy of our Father among the Saints John Chrysostom. Sydney: St Andrew's Orthodox Press, 2005.
Dursun, A. Halûk, et al. *Chora Museum*. Istanbul: Bilkent Kültür Girişimi, 2013.
Eliade, Mircea. *The Myth of the Eternal Return*. Translated by Willard R. Trask. Princeton: Princeton University Press, 2005.
Emmanouil, Melita. "Religious Imagery in Mystra: Donors and Iconographic Programmes." In *Material Culture and Well-Being in Byzantium (400–1453)*. *Proceedings of the International Conference (Cambridge, 8–10 September 2001)*, edited by M. Grünbart et al., 119–27. Veröffentlichungen zur Byzanzforschung 11. Vienna: Österreichisce Akademie der Wissenschaften, 2007.
Eusebius of Caesarea. *The History of the Church*. Translated by G. A. Williamson. London: Penguin, 1989.
———. *Life of Constantine*. Translated by Averil Cameron and Stuart G. Hall. Oxford: Clarendon, 1999.
Gates, Charles. *Ancient Cities: The Archaeology of Urban Life in the Ancient Near East and Egypt, Greece, and Rome*. London: Routledge, 2011.
Gregoras, Nicephorus. *Historiae Byzantinae* XXIX.47. In *The Art of the Byzantine Empire 312–1453: Sources and Documents*, translated by Cyril Mango, 249. Toronto: University of Toronto Press, 2009.
Gunton, Lilian. *Rome's Historic Churches*. London: Allen & Unwin, 1969.
Hennessey, Cecily. "The Chapel of St Jacob at the Church of the Theotokos Chalkoprateia in Constantinople." In *Proceedings of the 7th International Congress on the Archaeology of the Ancient Near East, vol. 2*, edited by Roger Matthews, John Curtis et al., 351–66. Wiesbaden: Harrassowitz Verlag, 2012.
Hetherington, Paul. "The Mosaics of Pietro Cavallini in Santa Maria in Trastevere." *Journal of the Wauburg and Courtauld Institutes* 33 (1970) 84–106.

The Homeric Hymns III–To Pythian Apollo, in Hesiod, *The Homeric Hymns and Homerica*. Translated by Hugh G. Evelyn-White. London: Heinemann, 1914.

Johnson, Maxwell E. *Praying and Believing in Early Christianity: The Interplay between Christian Worship and Doctrine*. Collegeville, MN: Liturgical, 2013.

Kaldellis, Anthony. *The Christian Parthenon: Classicism and Pilgrimage in Byzantine Athens*. Cambridge: Cambridge University Press, 2009.

Klein, Holger A. "Sacred Relics and Imperial Ceremonies at the Great Palace of Constantinople." *BYZAS* 5 (2006) 77–99.

Krautheimer, Richard. *Early Christian and Byzantine Architecture*. New Haven, CT: Yale University Press, 1986.

Lidova, Maria. "The Earliest Images of Maria Regina in Rome and the Byzantine Imperial Iconography." *Niš and Byzantium: The Collection of Scientific Works* VIII (2010) 231–43.

The Life of Antony: The Coptic Life and the Greek Life. Translated by Tim Vivian and Apostolos N. Athanassakis. Kalamazoo, MI: Cistercian, 2003.

Limberis, Vasiliki. *Divine Heiress: The Virgin Mary and the Creation of Christian Constantinople*. New York: Routledge, 2002.

Marinis, Vasileios. *Architecture and Ritual in the Churches of Constantinople: Ninth to Fifteenth Centuries*. Cambridge: Cambridge University Press, 2014.

Markoff, John, and Daniel Regan. "The Rise and Fall of Civil Religion: Comparative Perspectives." *Sociological Analysis* 42.4 (1981) 333–52.

McGuckin, John A. "Hodegitria." In *The Encyclopedia of Eastern Orthodox Christianity*, vol. 1: *A–M*, edited by John McGuckin. Oxford: Wiley-Blackwell, 2011.

The Menaion, vol. 12: *The Month of August*. Translated by Holy Transfiguration Monastery. Boston: Holy Transfiguration Monastery, 2005.

Mumford, Lewis. *The City in History: Its Origins, Its Transformations, and Its Prospects*. London: Secker & Warburg, 1961.

Peter, Murray, Linda Murray, and Tom Devonshire Jones. *The Oxford Dictionary of Christian Art and Architecture*. Oxford: Oxford University Press, 2013.

Nicol, Donald M. *The Immortal Emperor: The Life and Legend of Constantine Palaiologos, Last Emperor of the Romans*. Cambridge: Cambridge University Press, 2002.

Noreen, Kirsten. "The icon of Santa Maria Maggiore, Rome: An Image and Its Afterlife." *Renaissance Studies* 19.5 (2005) 660–72.

Onlin, Eric. "Urban Religion in the Middle and Late Republic." In *A Companion to Roman Religion*, edited by Jörg Rüpke, 58–70. Oxford: Blackwell, 2007.

Ożóg, Monika. "Traces of the History of the Roman Church of Santa Maria Antiqua according to the Authors of *Liber Pontificalis*." *Christianitas Antiqua* 6 (2014) 61–70.

Ott, Michael. "Our Lady of the Snow." In *The Catholic Encyclopedia*, vol. 11: *New Mexico–Philip*, edited by Charles D. Herbermann et al., 361. New York: The Encyclopedia Press, 1913.

Panagopoulos, S. P. "The Byzantine Traditions of the Virgin Mary's Dormition and Assumption." *Studia Patristica* 63 (2013) 343–51.

Paoletti, John T., and Gary M. Radke. *Art in Renaissance Italy*. London: King, 2005.

Pentcheva, Bissera V. *Icons and Power: The Mother of God in Byzantium*. Philadelphia: Pennsylvania State University Press, 2006.

Porphyrogennetos, Constantine. *The Book of Ceremonies*, vol. 2. Translated by Anne Moffat and Maxeme Tall. Canberra: Australian Association for Byzantine Studies, 2012.

The Protoevangelium of James 1–8. Translated by Oscar Cullman, in *New Testament Apocrypha*, vol. 1: *Gospels and Related Writings*, edited by Wilhelm Schneemelcher and R. McL. Wilson, 426–29. Louisville: Westminster John Knox, 1991.

Rubin, Miri. *The Mother of God: A History of the Virgin Mary*. New Haven, CT: Yale University Press, 2009.

Serapion of Thmuis. *To the Disciples of Antony*. In *The Life of Antony: The Coptic Life and the Greek Life*. Translated by Tim Vivian and Apostolos N. Athanassakis. Kalamazoo, MI: Cistercian, 2003.

Shoemaker, Stephen J. *Ancient Traditions on the Virgin Mary's Dormition and Assumption*. Oxford: Oxford University Press, 2002.

Stroll, Mary. *Symbols as Power: The Papacy Following the Investiture Contest*. Leiden: Brill, 1991.

Talbot, Alice-Mary, and Scott Fitzgerald Johnson. "Introduction." In *Miracles Tales from Byzantium*, vii–xxiv. Cambridge, MA: Dumbarton Oaks Medieval Library, 2012.

Tanner, Norman P. *The Church in Council: Conciliar Movements, Religious Practice and the Papacy from Nicaea to Vatican II*. London: I. B. Tauris, 2011.

Thunø, Erik. "The Pantheon in the Middle Ages." In *The Pantheon: From Antiquity to the Present*, edited by Tod A. Marder and Mark Wilson Jones, 231–54. Cambridge: Cambridge University Press, 2015.

Tosti-Croce, Marina Righetti. "La Basilica Tra Due E Trecento." In *Santa Maria Maggiore a Roma*, edited by Carlo Pietrangeli, 129–70. Florence: Nardini Editore, 1988.

Tresidder, Jack, ed. *The Complete Dictionary of Symbols: In Myth, Art and Literature*. London: Baird, 2004.

4

Mariology of John Paul II: An Overview

—Mariusz Biliniewicz

Immediately after the Second Vatican Council (1962–65) Catholic Mariology suffered a period of decline. However, the long pontificate of Pope John Paul II (1978–2005) turned out to be a significant factor in the process of rediscovering the place and role of Mary in Catholic theology and piety. This chapter offers an overview of some important topics related to the teaching of John Paul II on Mary: the overall historical and theological context of his reflection, main inspirations and influences on his thought, and characteristic features of his Mariology. The chapter also highlights those aspects of John Paul II's Mariology which, in the author's judgment, need further reflection in the light of contemporary Mariological discussions.

The renewal of Catholic Mariology, like the liturgical, ecumenical, and theological renewal desired by the Second Vatican Council, turned out to be a slow and complicated process. As with these other areas, it is possible to distinguish a "first phase," often consisting of some distortions and not always successful experiments, from a "second phase," consisting of a more dispassionate, mature reflection, which attempted to regain the necessary balance between what preceded and what followed, with the right proportion of continuities and discontinuities. As in the case of other conciliar texts, there has been no one way of reading the text on the Blessed Virgin Mary (chapter 8 of *Lumen Gentium*). While some understood it as an encouragement to cultivate a widespread Marian piety in the Catholic world, albeit in the new "ecclesio-typical" style, others saw it as a significant demotion of Mariology, both in theology and in pastoral practice, finding support for this demotion not least in the Council's refusal to devote a separate document to Our Lady, as initially planned. The result of this understanding was a remarkable decrease of interest in Mary reaching its nadir in many parts of the Catholic world in the 1970s, which came to be known as "a decade without Mary."[1] Regarding this phenomenon, Avery Dulles quoted Wilhelm Beinert, who stated that:

> It is surprising that the conciliar innovation found no answering echo in the church. Mariology and Marian devotion are disturbingly close to nil. The choral praise of the Mother of God in the days of Pius XII has been succeeded by a deep silence.[2]

While Pope Paul VI, who presided over the Council, closed it, and ministered to the Church for thirteen years after its completion, attempted to somehow break this silence and bring the topic of Mary back into theological textbooks and the parish churches' pulpits in a balanced, nuanced, and renewed way, the results were not entirely successful.[3] In fact, many theologians welcomed this silence about Mary and were content that this topic was sidelined.[4]

However, at the end of "the decade without Mary," when Marian devotion was "at its lowest ebb since the Enlightenment,"[5] a considerable turning point took place. After Paul VI's death, and after the very short pontificate of John Paul I, the college of cardinals elected to the Chair of Peter Polish cardinal Karol Wojtyła, a man for whom Marian piety and devotion were not something of an addition to regular Catholic devotion, but were an integral

---

1. Dulles, "Mary since Vatican II," 12.

2. Originally quoted by De Fiores, "Mary in Postconciliar Theology," 474. See Dulles, "Mary Since Vatican II," 12.

3. See his proclamation of Mary as the Mother of the Church at the closing of the Third Session of the Council on 21 November 1964 (Rynne, *The Third Session*, 387) and the reiteration of this title in his encyclical letters *Mense maio* (29 April 1965) and *Christi Matri* (15 September 1966); also his direct and exclusive treatment of Mary in his apostolic exhortations *Signum Magnum* (13 May 1967), *Recurrens mensis october* (7 October 1969) and *Marialis Cultus* (2 February 1974).

4. See Küng, *On Being a Christian*, 461–62, in Dulles, "Mary Since Vatican II," 13.

5. O'Connor, "The Roots of Pope John Paul II's Devotion to Mary," 81.

and indispensable part of it.⁶ Brendan Leahy suggests that "Mariology has been a key reference point throughout these twenty five years"⁷ of his pontificate, and that "bringing Mary into everything that makes up one's inner life, into one's human and Christian 'I'" (Wojtyła's reading of John 19:27)⁸ proved to be "the most significant factor in his pontificate."⁹

In this short presentation it is not possible to go into great detail about John Paul II's teaching on Mary. In fact, it seems that a larger, more comprehensive study of John Paul II's Mariology is needed through an examination of his many works as a scholar, priest, bishop, and universal pastor.¹⁰ Nevertheless, what I will attempt here is to at least highlight the most important issues related to Mariology of John Paul II, such as: the sources of his Mariology, its main characteristic features, and the possible directions which could be taken in pursuing further reflection.

1. The sources of John Paul II's Mariology

John Paul II's successor on the Chair of Peter, Joseph Ratzinger (Pope Benedict XVI), confessed once that in the course of his theological endeavours he experienced a "Marian conversion,"¹¹ which meant for him rediscovering the proper place of Mary in Catholic theology and pastoral outlook. Without going into details of this matter,¹² what needs to be said here is that in the case of John Paul II, no such "conversion" was needed. The Pol-

---

6. Dulles, "Mary at the Dawn of the New Millennium," 9.

7. Leahy, "Totus Tuus," 91.

8. Cf. John Paul II, *Redemptoris Mater*, no. 45.

9. Leahy, "Totus Tuus," 91. Calkins, "Mary Co-Redemptrix," 392 believes that "the Marian magisterium of the late Pope John Paul II may well constitute his greatest single legacy to the Catholic Church."

10. In various works discussing either John Paul II or Mariology one can often find interesting and informative sections on aspects of the Mariology of John Paul II. However, these works seldom examine his overall Marian vision in the context of his thought in general. Rather, they often examine *particular aspects* of it or provide a general overview of some most important topics. Some most significant, more holistic contributions include: Nachef, *Mary's Pope*; Kushu-Solii, *The Relationship between Mariology and Ecclesiology in the Theological Thinking of John Paul II*; Kochaniewicz, *Wybrane zagadnienia z Mariologii Jana Pawła II*; Siudy, *Matka naszego zawierzenia*; and Ziegenaus *Mariologische Studien. Volume XVIII: Totus Tuus—Maria in Leben und Lehre Johannes Pauls II*.

11. Ratzinger and Messori, *The Ratzinger Report*, 105.

12. For a presentation of development of Ratzinger's Mariology, see McKenna, *Innovation Within Tradition*, 30–39, where she traces influences of Hugo Rahner, René Laurentin, and Karl Rahner on Ratzinger's thought on Mary.

ish Pope was raised in a country where Roman Catholicism was, and still is, the dominant Christian denomination, and where Marian piety is very strong, often embedded in a strong "Christo-typical" tradition.[13] As John Paul II himself suggested, in order to understand to what extent the Mother of God, the main patroness of Poland, is present in Polish piety, one probably would have to visit the country and experience the countless sanctuaries and magnificent basilicas dedicated to her, the walking pilgrimages to her shrines, the clerical and lay associations devoted to Marian piety, the roadside chapels, devotions, songs, litanies, holy images, statues, and so on. While it is true that one needs to be careful not to *over*estimate the influence of the historical and cultural context of the given theologian on his thought, it certainly is helpful to be aware of the *Sitz im Leben* in which their thought grew and matured.

The young Karol Wojtyła lost his own mother very early, one month before his First Communion, when he was nine years old. Some commentators argue that this painful loss played a significant role in developing his devotion to Our Lady.[14] However, the Pope himself was always rather reserved when talking about his mother.[15] When he was ten he received a scapular of Our Lady of Mount Carmel,[16] which he wore until he died.[17] The scapular reminded him of Mary's perpetual protection and of the fact that true devotion to Mary, rather than being an occasional event, should in fact be a "habit" which constantly shows Christians the right direction of their life, and reminds them of their covenant with God.[18] He was a member of

---

13. The expression "Christo-typical Mariology" is used to describe Mariology which focuses on analogies between Mary and Christ and her unique privileges, while "ecclesio-typical Mariology" focuses more on analogies between Mary and the Church and on her place within the community of believing disciples. Mauriello, *Venerable Pope Pius XII and the 1954 Marian Year*, 96, ascribes the first use of these expressions to Heinrich Koster in 1958.

14. Szulc, *Pope John Paul II*, 66, states that "cult of Mary flowered from his mother's death: the natural identification." However, Weigel, *Witness to Hope*, 29, argues that "such speculations, frequently based on amateur psychoanalysis conducted from afar, are of no use to serious students of Wojtyła's life" and that such "explanations can seem like evasions." Weigel also points to the fact that the Pope's "autobiographical writings are virtually silent on the subject of his mother." One might or might not agree with Weigel's judgment, yet his point that the *theological* value of such speculations is limited is a valid one.

15. John Paul II, *Gift and Mystery*, 20, wrote that due to his mother's death early in his life he did "not have a clear awareness of her contribution, which must have been great."

16. Ibid., 28.

17. Dziwisz, *Świętość Sługi Bożego Jana Pawła II*, II.2.

18. "In this way the Scapular becomes a sign of the 'covenant' and reciprocal

the "Living Rosary" group in Kraków, a regular pilgrim to the sanctuary in Kalwaria, and a pious devotee of Our Lady Help of Christians.[19]

While in Kraków, under the influence of his unofficial spiritual director, Jan Tyranowski, a lay man, the future Pope re-examined his Marian piety in the light of Louis-Marie Grignion de Montfort's work "True Devotion to Mary." He wrote:

> I was already convinced that Mary leads us to Christ, but at that time I began to realize also that Christ leads us to his Mother. At one point I began to question my devotion to Mary, believing that, if it became too great, it might end up compromising the supremacy of the worship owed to Christ.[20]

However, having read the works of the French priest, confessor, and preacher, Wojtyła came to the conclusion that the true devotion to the Blessed Virgin Mary does not overshadow devotion to Christ, but is in fact "the most perfect expression of giving oneself to Christ."[21] That is why this devotion, deeply rooted in his experience and personal piety, was one of the main characteristic marks of his ministry as bishop—both of Kraków and of Rome. We should recall his coat of arms—*Totus Tuus*, an abbreviated version of de Montfort's prayer: *Totus tuus ego sum, et omnia mea tua sunt.* ("I belong entirely to you, and all that I have is yours"). He said:

> I then realized that I could not exclude the Mother of the Lord from my life without disregarding the will of God-the-Trinity, who wanted to "begin and complete" the great mysteries of salvation history with the responsible and faithful collaboration of the humble Handmaid of Nazareth.[22]

---

communion between Mary and the faithful: indeed, it concretely translates the gift of his Mother, which Jesus gave on the Cross to John and, through him, to all of us, and the entrustment of the beloved Apostle and of us to her, who became our spiritual Mother." See John Paul II, "Message to the Carmelite Family" (25 March 2001).

19. John Paul II, *Gift and Mystery*, 28.

20. Ibid.

21. Moricová, "*Totus Tuus* odnowione," 164. See also the Pope's reiteration of this point in his Apostolic Letter *Rosarium Virginis Mariae*, no. 15, where he cites de Monfort's *Treatise on True Devotion to the Blessed Virgin Mary* and comments: "Our entire perfection consists in being conformed, united and consecrated to Jesus Christ. Hence the most perfect of all devotions is undoubtedly that which conforms, unites and consecrates us most perfectly to Jesus Christ. Now, since Mary is of all creatures the one most conformed to Jesus Christ, it follows that among all devotions that which most consecrates and conforms a soul to our Lord is devotion to Mary, his Holy Mother, and that the more a soul is consecrated to her the more will it be consecrated to Jesus Christ."

22. John Paul II, "Address to the Participants in the Eight Mariological Colloqium."

Thus, the personal devotion developing in the climate of the Polish Catholic church in the 1930s, 1940s, and 1950s, when "high Mariology" was at its peak, and the reading of Louis-Marie Grignion de Montfort's work, were at the background of his intellectual reflection.[23] What other sources of his Mariology can be found?

The Bible

Following the guidelines set by Vatican II, John Paul II's treatment of Our Lady is strongly rooted in the Sacred Scriptures, both of the Old and of the New Testaments. In the Old Testament the Pope points to the classical texts which are understood as Mary's pre-figuration:

> Zephaniah 3:14: "Sing aloud, O daughter Zion; shout, O Israel! Rejoice and exult with all your heart, O daughter Jerusalem!"[24]
>
> Zechariah 2:10: "Sing and rejoice, O daughter Zion! For lo, I will come and dwell in your midst, says the Lord."
>
> Genesis 3:15: "I will put enmity between you and the woman, and between your offspring and hers; he will strike your head, and you will strike his heel."
>
> Isaiah 7:14: "Look, the young woman is with child and shall bear a son, and you shall name him Immanuel."[25]

23. For his own account see *Gift and Mystery*, 27–31, also Frossard, *Be Not Afraid*, 124–27. For a more detailed analysis of de Monfort's influence on his Mariology see O'Connor, "The Roots of Pope John Paul II's Devotion to Mary," 85–87. Kochaniewicz, "Źródła Mariologii Jana Pawła II," 60–63, argues that John Paul II does not only repeat what de Montfort says, but also provides an original interpretation of the French writer. While de Montfort relies in his reflection on the mystery of Incarnation, John Paul II focuses more on the mystery of Redemption. While de Montfort develops the idea of being a "slave of Mary," John Paul II talks about the idea of "entrustment" and "welcoming" Mary in the Christian's life based on the new mother-son relationship between the Beloved Disciple and Mary. This argument of development of the ideas of the *Treatise on True Devotion to the Blessed Virgin* needs further exploration. The importance of the mystery of Redemption in John Paul II's Mariology was also noted by Tavard, *The Thousands Faces of the Virgin Mary*, 209–11. Nachef, *Mary's Pope*, 111, states that the influence of de Monfort's work on John Paul II consists also of the transmission to him of the ideas of Cardinal Pierre Bérulle (1575–1629) regarding "the doctrine of *status* (state)" as a way to explain the mysteries of Christ. For more see 111–12.

24. All biblical quotations are taken from New Revised Standard Version, unless stated otherwise.

25. For a more detailed analysis of the Pope's use of these texts see Mirosław S. Wróbel, "Rola Biblii w Mariologii Jana Pawła II," in *Mariologia Jana Pawła II*, 16–21, where, in the context of the Old Testament he also discusses the parallel between the

In the New Testament John Paul II first of all utilizes texts which mention Mary explicitly (cf. Gal 4:4–6; Luke 1:26–38, 39–45. 46–55; 2:1–7, 41–50, 51–52; John 2:1–12; 19:25–27; Acts 2:12–14), but also those which talk about her in an implicit manner (cf. Eph 1:4–7; Col 1:24; Matt 11:25; Luke 11:27–28; Rev 12:1–2). The Pope's biblical hermeneutics has certain characteristic features worth mentioning, and Mirosław Wróbel lists the following:[26]

- Drawing parallels between the New Testament and Old Testament passages (for example, comparing Mary's faith with that of Abraham's, between the power of the Almighty overshadowing Mary with Exodus 24:16, 40, 34–35 and 1 Kings 8:10–12, between Mary's presence at the foot of the cross and the Suffering Servant of God from Isa 53:3–5);

- Reading the New Testament as the fulfillment of the Old (Gen 3:15 fulfilled in the Incarnation and in Rev 12:1–2; Isa 7:14 in Matt 1:23);

- Interpreting Marian mysteries in the mystery of Christ (for example Eph 1:3–7 and Luke 1:26–38, 39–45; Luke 1:38 and Heb 10:5,7; Luke 1:48 and 11:27–28; John 19:25–27 and Phil 2:5–11);

- Reading Marian texts in the context of other Marian texts (for example Luke 1:45 and 1:28; Luke 2:34–35 with 1:26–38 and 2:19);

- Analyzing the same passages in different contexts (for example looking at Luke 1:45 in anthropological, ecclesiological, christological, and pneumatological keys).[27]

Also, the Pope often draws some far reaching analogies and interpretations of the biblical texts, analogies which might not be so readily accepted by contemporary biblical scholarship, but which, on the other hand, are very close to the stream of a spiritual reading of the Holy Scripture, sometimes bringing to mind the ancient School of Alexandria. While some authors call this more a devotional than historical reading,[28] or accuse the Pope's interpretation as being controlled by "dualistic anthropology,"[29] others argue that the extensive use of the *sensus plenior* of Scripture by John Paul II does

---

faith of Abraham and the faith of Mary in John Paul II's writings.

26. Wróbel, *Rola Biblii w Mariologii Jana Pawła II*, 24–28.

27. More on the Pope's biblical hermeneutics will be said in Part 2 of this chapter.

28. Taylor, "Redemptoris Mater," 133.

29. Johnson, *Truly Our Sister*, 62–63, criticizes the Pope's interpretation of the event of Pentecost. She says that, regarding the apostolic mission given only to men, the biblical text states the opposite to what John Paul II says. She also criticizes his reading of the account of the Last Supper, calling it an "idiosyncratic interpretation . . . unsupported by biblical scholarship."

not mean that his reading is only spiritual and devotional, or that it is devoid of historical value.³⁰

The Second Vatican Council

Bishop Wojtyła participated in the Council and was among the group of bishops who suggested that if the text devoted to the Blessed Virgin Mary was to be included in the Dogmatic Constitution on the Church, it would be better to include it as a second chapter of the document, not the last. The concern was that it might appear as a mere appendix and Mary's role might be sidelined. Although this did not happen,³¹ John Paul II never publicly criticized the structure of the document. Rather, he called the conciliar text on Mary the *magna carta* of Mariology for our times³² and stated that the implementation of the Council, also in its Mariological aspect, would be the main focus of his pontificate.³³

In his encyclical on Mary, *Redemptoris Mater*, John Paul II quotes the Council 103 times, not only the eighth chapter of *Lumen Gentium*, but also *Gaudium et Spes, Unitatis Redintegratio*, and *Dei Verbum*. He embraces the conciliar Mariology and its "ecclesio-typical" angle. Mary is not "above" the Church, but also "in" the Church. She is the Mother of the Church, but also the most noble member of it. Interestingly, the Pope does not only repeat and reiterate the teachings of Vatican II but takes "a deliberate step beyond the Mariology of the Council as found in the decree *Lumen Gentium*."³⁴³⁵

30. See Nachef, *Mary's Pope*, 34, 113–14, 125, 138, and 161. With regard to the fulfilment of the Old Testament prophecies in the New Testament, and the overall biblical hermeneutics of the Pope, Nachef writes (124): "The scholarly question—whether the New Testament could be foreshadowed by the Old Testament without the human author's specific knowledge—does not seem to constitute a problem for the Pope. This is also valid for the relationship between the books of the New Testament. In fact, it has been clear throughout the presentation of his thoughts that he accepts that one New Testament author can be interpreted through the information or theological outlook supplied by another."

31. For a brief history of these discussions see Bastero, *Mary, Mother of the Redeemer*, 54–56; also Jelly, "The Theological Context of and Introduction to chapter 8 of *Lumen Gentium*," 43–73.

32. John Paul II, "General Audience" (2 May 1979), 3.

33. John Paul II, "First Radio Message *Urbi et Orbi*" (17 October 1978).

34. Balthasar, "Commentary," 171. Tavard, *The Thousand Faces of the Virgin Mary*, 213–14 agrees that John Paul II develops the teaching of Vatican II (and Paul VI's). However, he takes a very critical stance on these developments, claiming that the Pope's interpretation "does not reflect the spirit of the text," and that his language is "dangerously unguarded." For extensive explanations of exactly how certain ideas present in *Lumen Gentium* are developed in the thought of John Paul II, see Nachef, *Mary's Pope*, xi, 12, 40–42, 45, 71–78, 100, 107, 130–38, 143–44, 162, and 165.

35. Kochaniewicz, "Źródła Mariologii Jana Pawła II," 48–49. For Pope Wojtyła's

St. John of the Cross' Teaching on Faith

The young scholar Karol Wojtyła wrote his doctorate in Rome in 1948 on the understanding of faith according to St. John of the Cross. The influence of the sixteenth-century Carmelite mystic on the Pope's Mariology can be found in his treatment of Mary's faith as both a dynamic reality (Mary's "pilgrimage of faith"),[36] and the experience of "the dark night of the soul," which is an indispensable element of this pilgrimage.[37] Wojtyła's discussions with some contemporary, neoscholastic interpretations of John of the Cross lead him to the inclusion of the category of experience into spiritual life: the human person's unique ability to being both the object and the subject of experience opens them to being transformed by it. In terms of the experience of God it transforms the person in a most radical fashion.[38] His treatment of Mary's development in faith, her growth in trust, and her continuing, inner transformation is also said to be related to his doctoral research and its findings.[39]

Anthropology

Wojtyła's first important work on anthropology was his book from 1969 titled *Osoba i czyn*, where he explains the structure of the human act. Kochaniewicz argues that the Pope's statement about Mary's "entrusting herself to God completely, with the 'full submission of intellect and will,' manifesting 'the obedience of faith,'" and responding "with all her human

---

own account of the importance of Mariology of Vatican II, see his "Inspiracja Maryjna Vaticanum II," 112–21. The Pope develops ideas contained not only in the Dogmatic Constitution on the Church but also in other documents. Kochaniewicz points also to the Pastoral Constitution *Gaudium et Spes* and the papal development of the notion that "only in the mystery of the incarnate Word does the mystery of man take on light," (no. 22) which he sometimes reads also in the Marian key.

36. In *Redemptoris Mater* alone this expression occurs nineteen times.

37. In no. 17 of *Redemptoris Mater* he refers to St. John of the Cross and the "night of faith" ("a kind of 'veil' through which one has to draw near to the Invisible One and to live in intimacy with the mystery") and to Mary's abandonment to God's decrees in "the dim light of faith" in (no. 14).

38. See Wojtyła, "O humaniźmie św. Jana od Krzyża," 14, in Kochaniewicz, "Źródła Mariologii Jana Pawła II," 51–52. See also Kushu-Solii, *Relationship between Mariology and Ecclesiology in the Theological Thinking of John Paul II*, 27.

39. Kochaniewicz, "Źródła Mariologii Jana Pawła II," 50–53. For a general overview of the history and the content of Wojtyła's doctoral dissertation and its history, see Weigel, *Witness to Hope*, 85–87.

and feminine 'I,'"⁴⁰ can be properly understood only in the context of his analysis of the human act.⁴¹ He explains that Wojtyła's understanding of the relationship between the human person's act (immanent dimension) and the reflection upon this act (transcendent dimension) leads him to state that the human act incorporates somehow the wholeness, the totality, of the person. Also, Wojtyła's phenomenological analysis of the relationship between the "I" and the "you" (the affirmation of separate identities with mutual inclination towards each other as the constitutive element of every "I"), and his personalistic understanding of "entrusting," meaning the ultimate realization of this relationship, arguably stand behind his elaboration on the true meaning of the "entrusting" of the Beloved Disciple to Mary at the foot of the cross, and generally of the act of "entrusting onself" to Mary.⁴² Among the most important philosophical notions derived from his personalism and present in his Marian thought Nachef lists the ideas of the person's self-consciousness⁴³ and self-fulfillment.⁴⁴

Theologians

Apart from the obvious marks which the works of De Montfort and of St. John of the Cross left on the Pope's Mariology, some authors point also to the influence of St. Thomas Aquinas, especially in his treatment of the topic of Mary's maternal mediation and its relationship with the only and complete mediation of Jesus (participation-inclusion).⁴⁵ Some also find resemblances with John Henry Newman's Mariology and anthropology in the Pope's thought.⁴⁶ Amongst more contemporary authors, commentators usually name Hans Urs von Balthasar, Karl Rahner, St. Maximilian Maria Kolbe (Polish Franciscan spiritual writer and martyr) and sometimes

40. An expression taken from *Redemptoris Mater*, no. 13.

41. Kochaniewicz, "Źródła Mariologii Jana Pawła II," 53.

42. Ibid., 53–55. Regarding the use of personalistic philosophy in the Pope's Marian thought, see Nachef, *Mary's Pope*, 130–33, 150, 171. Regarding Mary as an acting person, see Bulzacchelli, *Mary and The Acting Person, passim*. Peters, *Ecce Educatrix Tua*, 151–57. For a more detailed treatment of Wojtyła's/John Paul II's anthropology in general see Kupczak, *Destined for Liberty*; Schmitz, *At the Center of the Human Drama*; and Bransfield, *The Human Person*.

43. Nachef, *Mary's Pope*, 128–31, 135, 150.

44. Ibid., 79–81.

45. See Nachef, *Mary's Pope*, 154–55, 169–70. The importance of the category of "participation" in John Paul II's Mariology is also noted by Napiórkowski, "Doświadczenia i objawienia," 46, although he does not link this with Thomas.

46. See Gregoris, "John Henry Newman's Mariology," 99–138.

Wojtyła's doctoral supervisor Réginald Marie Garrigou-Lagrange as possible influences.⁴⁷

Rahner's influence on John Paul II is to be found in his concept of grace understood as God's self-communication and self-giving which reaches its climax in the event of Incarnation, in which Mary plays a pivotal role.⁴⁸ Von Balthasar's impact is primarily seen in the distinction between the Marian and the petrine dimensions of the Church, with the Marian having priority,⁴⁹ but also in his "vision of Mary as *tota pulchra*" and "his image of the rosary as the means by which the believer "sits at the school of Mary and is led to contemplate the beauty of the face of Christ and to experience the depths of his love."⁵⁰ Kolbe's influence can be traced in the Pope's treatment of the mystery of Mary's Immaculate Conception and in the overall importance of Marian piety and the Christian's entrustment to Mary.⁵¹

Fathers of the Church and Liturgy

John Paul II's use of the fathers of the Church in his reflections on Mary is one of the points of disagreement among his commentators. A. Nachef is of the opinion that the Pope, especially in *Redemptoris Mater*, "frequently alludes subtly to the fathers of the Church and analyses their understanding of the Marian doctrine,"⁵² and T. Siudy calls the Pope's use of the fathers "one of the three main pillars of the Pope's Mariology," the other

---

47. Kushu-Solii, *Relationship between Mariology and Ecclesiology in the Theological Thinking of John Paul II*, 45–46 mentions this last possibility, yet provides no clear evidence.

48. John Paul II, *Redemptoris Mater*, no. 9: "God's salvific giving of himself and his life, in some way to all creation but directly to man, reaches one of its high points in the mystery of the Incarnation. This is indeed a high point among all the gifts of grace conferred in the history of man and of the universe." See Kochaniewicz, "Źródła Mariologii Jana Pawła II," 53. This influence is to be found not only in the Pope's teaching on Mary but also on other areas. O'Collins, "Ressourcement and Vatican II," 382, traces it also in his *Dives in Misericordia* (1980) and *Dominum et Vivificantem* (1986).

49. Leahy, "John Paul II and Hans Urs Von Balthasar," 41–43; Dulles, "Mary Since Vatican II," 14–15; Kochaniewicz, "Źródła Mariologii Jana Pawła II," 67–68; Haffner, *The Mystery of Mary*, 243. The passages to which these comments refer to are *Mulieris Dignitatem*, 27 and John Paul II's Address to Roman Curia on 22 December 1987.

50. Murphy, "Immaculate Mary," 312, citing *Rosarium Virginis Mariae*, no. 1. On the petrine and Marian dimensions of the Church, yet without reference to Balthasar, see Leahy, *Totus Tuus*, 84–85.

51. Kochaniewicz, "Źródła Mariologii Jana Pawła II," 67–68; O'Connor, "The Roots of Pope John Paul II's Devotion to Mary," 86–87. See also the Pope's own remarks in his Homily in St. Mary's Major on 8 December 1982.

52. Nachef, *Mary's Pope*, 11.

two being the Bible and the teaching of Vatican II.[53] On the other hand, D. M. Montagna thinks that the Pope's use of the fathers is "rather partial and provisional,"[54] and B. Kochaniewicz argues that the references to the patristic sources are a later addition to the encyclical since the two most important parts of the document—Part I and Part II—do not have any direct references to the fathers, with the exception of St. Irenaeus and St. Augustine, whose presence in these parts of *Redemptoris Mater* can be explained by their presence in chapter 8 of *Lumen Gentium*, which is quoted by the Pope.[55] References to other ancient authors are usually made in an ecumenical context, and they most frequently include the parallel between Mary and Eve,[56] as well as the works of Leo the Great, St. John Damascene, and St. Bernard of Clairvaux. Kochaniewicz argues that the same method (bibliographical illustration and explanation, most often in the ecumenical context, yet without any significant influence on the text itself), is adopted in the Pope's use of liturgical texts.[57]

Other sources

Apart from some more obvious sources listed above, there are other less obvious ones which also contribute to the Pope's distinctive Marian thought. These include his understanding of the category of experience in religious life, including experiences both of communities (such as the belief that the Polish nation has always been delivered from the hands of oppressors due to Mary's maternal protection), and of individuals including, to certain extent, private revelations);[58] poetry (he makes numerous

---

53. Siudy, *Matka naszego zawierzenia*, 35.

54. Montgana, "Reminiscenze patristiche medioevalli nell' enciclica Redemptoris Mater," 383, cited in Nachef, *Mary's Pope*, 11.

55. Kochaniewicz, "Źródła Mariologii Jana Pawła II," 55–57.

56. Not only in the context of Annunciation, as is the case in St. Irenaeus (the first author who used this parallel), but also in the context of John 19:25–27, which is a certain novelty brought by the Pope. See Siudy, *Matka naszego zawierzenia*, 24.

57. Ibid., 57–58, also 72.

58. Napiórkowski, "Doświadczenie osób i wspólnot chrześcijańskich jako źródło teologii," 41–56; Agaciński, "Znaczenie doświadczenia jako faktu poznania Boga w pobożności maryjnej według Karola Wojtyły," 54–60; Kochaniewicz, "Źródła Mariologii Jana Pawła II," 64–67. Tavard, *The Thousand Faces of the Virgin Mary*, 215 takes a critical stance towards the Pope's affection for private revelations and is particularly uncomfortable with his statements about Mary's "presence" in various Marian shrines around the world, which he finds "theologically hazardous." This critique, however, is not very convincing, since John Paul II never talks about Mary's physical presence (as Tavard seems to suggest), but rather about "the radius of the maternal presence" of

references to such authors as Dante Alghieri, Polish Poet Cyprian Kamil Norwid, and Russian writer Fiodor Dostojewski);[59] works of art (iconography—see *Redemptoris Mater*, 33);[60] testimonies of the saints (especially martyrs); and the history of the Church.[61]

2. Some characteristic features of Mariology of John Paul II

The first obvious feature of John Paul II's Mariology is that it is very biblical. Leaving aside discussions about his hermeneutics, it needs to be said that it is evident from the Pope's works on Mary that he took seriously Vatican II's wish that "the Bible be the soul of theology," and moved beyond a neo-scholastic "Mariology of privileges" based mainly on recent papal writings, with little reference to Scripture and the earliest Tradition. His contribution consists also of the fact that he does not only re-read the classical Marian scriptural texts, but also uses other ones in a novel way, interpreting them in Mariological key (for example, Eph 1:4–6; Col 1:24).

Second, the teaching of John Paul II on Our Lady bears the features of both Christo-typical and ecclesio-typical Mariologies.[62] On the one hand, the Pope does not refrain from using titles such as Mediatrix, Advocate, or even occasionally Co-Redemptrix, especially in his speeches, audiences, homilies, and interventions, which have a more devotional character and reflect his personal piety.[63] On the other hand, in his official documents he attempts to place Mary and Mariology in the context of Christology, trinitarian theology, the theology of God, and ecclesiology. This tension can be illustrated by the way in which he uses the traditional, rather Christo-typical axiom *per Mariam ad Iesum* (through Mary to Jesus), but also *per Iesum ad Mariam* (through Jesus to Mary), which, when properly understood, can be a very effective illustration of the contemporary, ecclesio-typical approach.[64]

Mary (see *Redemptoris Mater*, 28) which suggests spiritual presence.

59. Kochaniewicz, "Źródła Mariologii Jana Pawła II," 68–69.
60. Ibid., 69–70.
61. Ibid., 70–72.
62. Calloway, "Preface," 2.
63. See Dulles, *The Splendor of Faith*, 53.
64. The *per Iesum ad Mariam* formula was used to at the conclusion of the homily given by the Pope at the closing of the Twentieth International Mariological Conference in Rome on 24 September 2000. Interestingly, it seems that this formula was the Pope's spontaneous addition to the written text, since the official text of the homily in *L'Osservatore Romano* was concluded by the traditional formula per *ad Iesum per Mariam*, without the addition of *per Iesum ad Mariam* (this version remains on the official Vatican web-page to this day). On the significance of using this formula (the first

Third, it can be argued that the Mariology of John Paul II bears features of dynamism and development. When analyzing, for example, his interventions from the 1980s and his later addresses, some authors notice a shift of emphasis from the *person* of Mary to the *role* of Mary in the Church, from who Mary *is* to what Mary *does*, although this issue needs further study.[65]

Fourth, the main context within which John Paul II makes his Mariological reflections seems to be the event of Incarnation and Mary's Divine Motherhood.[66] While, obviously, the Pope is not silent on Mary's other privileges and mysteries, such as the Assumption or the Immaculate Conception, it seems that his point of departure is always located in the event of God becoming man. Mary's motherhood, in the Pope's thought, is not limited to being the Mother of the Son of God, but also of the whole of humankind.[67] This seems to correspond well with one of the most important and influential intuitions of his whole pontificate, expressed already in his first encyclical *Redemptor hominis*, that is, that through Incarnation Christ has somehow united himself with every human being.[68] Apart from the concept of maternal "mediation," the Pope develops also that of maternal "presence," and Nachef argues that it is the central theme of *Redemptoris Mater*.[69]

Finally, an important contribution of Pope Wojtyła in the area of Mariology is his understanding of Mary as the example to be followed not only by women, but also by men. It has been asked, especially by feminist theologians, how contemporary women can identify and relate to Mary, an immaculately conceived Virgin and Mother?[70] By pointing to Mary as a pattern of existence for everyone, not just women, as John Paul II did in

---

time ever by any pope), see Nadbrzeżny, "*Per Iesum ad Mariam*," 151–61. The author goes as far as to say that this formula is a summary and final conclusion of the Pope's developing Marian thought (152). For more on this see the published proceedings of the symposium devoted specifically to this topic: *Materiały z sympozjum Mariologicznego zorganizowanego przez Polskie Towarzystwo Mariologiczne*.

65. Czaja, "Rozwój papieskiej Mariologii," 97–98, he argues that there is a "significant shift" in the Pope's Mariology, a "significant evolution" from a Mariology which is "quite autonomous" to a Mariology which is not only seen in the context of Christology, but also is "at its service." He does not, however, provide any particular evidence of this (his intervention is short and is a part of a panel discussion).

66. See Dulles, *The Splendor of Faith*, 50–51.

67. McNamara, "Foreword," 5–6. Tavard, *The Thousand Faces of the Virgin Mary*, 212, criticizes the Pope, however, for "isolating Mary's motherhood from her daughterhood and sisterhood" (in her relation to the Church).

68. *Gaudium et spes*, no. 22.

69. Nachef, *Mary's Pope*, 75–76, following B. Billet. He mentions that the term "presence" is used in the encyclical fourteen times, and the term "present" twenty-one times.

70. See Johnson, *Truly Our Sister*, 8–17, and *passim*.

Mulieris Dignitatem (the apostolic letter on the dignity of a woman), the Pope moves this discussion onto another level, from outside Mary's unique theological, historical, and cultural circumstances to a more universal dimension.[71] Instead of being only the model of *woman*, Mary becomes the model of a *human person*.[72]

3. Areas for further study

Having listed, although not exhausted, some of the most important sources and characteristic features of John Paul II's Mariology, I shall very briefly outline some of the areas which, in my judgment, need more academic exploration.

First, there is a need to read John Paul II's Mariology in the wider context of not only the historical and theological "external" circumstances surrounding his ministry, but also within the framework of his own thought as such. I am referring here to placing his teaching on Our Lady within the context of his general teaching and understanding of Christology and anthropology, his personalistic philosophy, his theology of the family, his theology of the body, and so on. Understanding the basic presuppositions which his theology has in general will be helpful in identifying and exploring them in his Mariology in particular.[73]

---

71. Anna Kulczycka, "Z niewiast najsławniejsza," *passim*.

72. This shift, although recognized by feminist theologians, is not considered by some of them as sufficient. Johnson, *Truly Our Sister*, 63, argues that John Paul II's "affirmation of spiritual and metaphysical equality . . . is compromised in practice by the pope's commitment to gender dualism," and that assigning certain qualities (such as "self-offering totality of love, the strength that is capable of bearing the greatest sorrows, limitless fidelity and tireless devotion to work, the ability to combine penetrating intuition with words of support and encouragement," see *Redemptoris Mater*, 46) to women and not to men might "challenge women to develop a spiritual life" but also "block their mature growth as active subjects of their own history" and "deny them opportunities for equal partnership in society." Carr, "Mary: Model of Faith," 14, also accuses the Pope of "androcentrism" and of holding a "stereotypical view of women" in his *Redemptoris Mater* (she refers to paragraphs 7–23 and 46). In similar fashion speaks Cunneen, *In Search of Mary*, 289–90. Dulles seem to agree with the opinion that despite developments in understanding Mary as a model for all Christians, in John Paul II's thought "Mary is pre-eminently a model for women" (*The Splendor of Faith*, 55).

73. Nachef, *Mary's Pope*, 6, comes to a similar conclusion and lists also areas such as: "human person, devotion in general, discipline, drama, intellectualism, isolation, mysticism, suffering, mystery and fascination." The most important contributions in this area include Calloway, *The Virgin Mary and Theology of the Body*; Kushu-Solii, *Relationship between Mariology and Ecclesiology in the Theological Thinking of John Paul II*, especially chapters III, IV, and V; sections of Siudy, *Matka naszego zawierzenia* (31–42, 43–47, 51–63, 85–96); Peters, *Ecce Educatrix Tua*, Part I, especially chapter VI.

Second, there is a need to look more closely at the issue of development in the Pope's thought about Mary. A study of his pre-papal works,[74] and of the many interventions which he made during his long pontificate, could be helpful in determining if there have been shifts in his reflections, what kind of shifts in emphasis these might be, how these shifts could be traced in his reflections, and to what they could be attributed (simply to different contexts or perhaps to other reasons).[75]

Third, since John Paul II insists that: "It is necessary to emphasize that Marian teaching and devotion are not the fruit of sentimentality," and that "the mystery of Mary is a revealed truth which imposes itself on the intellect of believers and requires of those in the church who have the task of studying and teaching a method of doctrinal reflection no less rigorous than that used in all theology,"[76] it is necessary to study his Mariological thought in the light of critical voices which are raised in some theological circles.[77]

Finally, there remains the question of the impact of John Paul II's Mariology on contemporary Marian theology, and on pastoral practice. This impact will, of course, be different in countries where Marian piety has a long tradition, with its bright and dark sides, than it will be in post-Catholic countries where it disappeared nearly completely in the post-conciliar years, and in missionary countries where it is still maturing and developing.

John Paul II was one of the most prolific papal writers in history. The Church after this pontificate has been left with many written works to digest and ponder upon.[78] Pope Benedict XVI, shortly after his election, stated that rather than producing new documents, he saw his role being that of helping the Church to absorb the existing ones, especially the ones left by

---

74. Such as Abramek, "'Jasnogórska' Mariologia kardynała Karola Wojtyły Papieża Jana Pawła II," 7–39.

75. Nachef also argues that "a comparative analysis of the terminology and content of *Redemptoris Mater* with all other documents will help to realize the historical development of the Pope's Marian thought between 1978 and 1999" (his book was published in 2000). However, in his otherwise very thorough and detailed study (*Mary's Pope*) he does not provide such an analysis.

76. John Paul II, *General Audience* (3 January 1996), no. 2.

77. These include, but are not limited to, authors mentioned here, such as Johnson, Carr, Cunneen and Tavard.

78. With regard to his teaching on Mary alone, apart from his major documents devoted to Mary directly (*Redemptoris Mater, Rosarium Virginis Mariae*) or indirectly (*Mulieris Dignitatem*), "all of his encyclicals and nearly all of his major talks as well as countless minor addresses and letters contain an invocation of Mary or at least a brief and incisive exhortation about her" (Leahy, *Totus Tuus*, 70). John Paul II also devoted seventy weekly audiences specifically to teaching about Mary (September 1995–November 1997).

his predecessor.[79] At the beginning of the Third Millennium of the Incarnation, the teaching of St. John Paul II on the Mother of the Incarnate Word certainly gives us a lot to absorb.

Bibliography

Abramek, Rufin Józef. "'Jasnogórska' Mariologia kardynała Karola Wojtyły Papieża Jana Pawła II." *Studia Claromontana* 1 (1981) 7–39.

Agaciński, Jarosław. "Znaczenie doświadczenia jako faktu poznania Boga w pobożności maryjnej według Karola Wojtyły." In *Matka Boska ludowa i polska (Materiały do studium Mariologii ludowej w Polsce)*, edited by Stanisław Celestyn Napiórkowski and Wojciech Życiński, 54–60. Lublin-Łódź-Łagiewniki: Wyższe Seminarium Duchowne OO. Franciszkanów, 1991.

At the Center of the Human Drama: The Philosophy of Karol Wojtyla/Pope John Paul II. Edited by Kenneth L. Schmitz. Washington, DC: Catholic University of America Press, 1993.

Balthasar, Hans Urs von. "Commentary." In *Mary: God's Yes to Man. John Paul's Encyclical Redemptoris Mater. Introduction by Joseph Cardinal Ratzinger. Commentary by Hans Urs von Balthasar*, 161–179. San Francisco: Ignatius, 1988.

Bastero, Juan L. *Mary, Mother of the Redeemer: A Mariology Textbook*. Dublin: Four Courts, 2006.

Bransfield, J. Brian. *The Human Person: According to John Paul II*. Boston: Pauline Books and Media, 2010.

Bulzacchelli, Richard H. *Mary and the Acting Person: An Anthropology of Participatory Redemption in the Personalism of Karol Wojtyła/Pope John Paul II*. Dayton, OH: Marian Library/International Marian Research Institute, 2012.

Calloway, Donald H. "Foreword." In *The Virgin Mary and Theology of the Body*, edited by Donald H. Calloway, 1–4. West Chester, PA: Ascension, 2007.

Calkins, Arthur Burton. "Mary Co-Redemptrix: The Beloved Associate of Christ." In *Mariology. A Guide for Priests, Deacons, Seminarians, and Consecrated Persons*, edited by Mark I. Miravalle, 349–409. Goleta, CA: Queenship, 2007.

Carr, Anne. "Mary: Model of Faith." In *Mary, Woman of Nazareth: Biblical and Theological Perspectives*, edited by Doris Donnelly, 7–24. Mahwah, NJ: Paulist, 1989.

Cunneen, Sally. *In Search of Mary: The Woman and the Symbol*. New York: Ballantine, 1996.

Czaja, Andrzej. "Rozwój papieskiej Mariologii." In *Mariologia Jana Pawła II. Problem interpretacji—sposób recepcji*, edited by Karol Klauza and Kazimierz Pek, 97–98. Lublin: Wydawnictwo KUL, 2007.

Dulles, Avery. "Mary at the Dawn of the New Millennium." *America* 178 (1998) 8–19.

———. "Mary since Vatican II: Decline and Recovery." *Marian Studies* LIII (2002) 9–22.

———. *The Splendor of Faith: The Theological Vision of Pope John Paul II*. New York: The Crossroad, 2003.

---

79. Gibson, *The Rule of Benedict*, 248.

Dziwisz, Stanisław. Świętość Sługi Bożego Jana Pawła II. Speech at the Official Opening of the Rogatory Inquiry on the Life and Work of Pope John Paul II. Online: http://www.opoka.org.pl/biblioteka/W/WE/dziwisz/swietosc_jp_04112005.html

Frossard, André. *Be Not Afraid: John Paul II Speaks Out on His Life, His Beliefs, and His Vision for Humanity*. New York: St. Martin's, 1984.

Gibson, David. *The Rule of Benedict: Pope Benedict XVI and His Battle with the Modern World*. New York: HarperCollins, 2006.

Gregoris, Nicholas L. "John Henry Newman's Mariology: A Key to Unlocking John Paul II's Theology of the Body." In *The Virgin Mary and Theology of the Body*, edited by Donald H. Calloway, 99–138. West Chester, PA: Ascension, 2007.

Haffner, Paul. *The Mystery of Mary*. Leominster, UK: Gracewing, 2004.

Jelly, Frederick. "The Theological Context of and Introduction to Chapter 8 of Lumen Gentium." *Marian Studies* 37 (1986) 43–73.

John Paul II. "Address to the Participants in the Eight Mariological Colloqium." Online: https://w2.vatican.va/content/john-paul-ii/en/speeches/2000/oct-dec/documents/hf_jp-ii_spe_20001013_8-colloquio-mariologia.html.

———. "First Radio Message *Urbi et Orbi*." 17 October 1978. Online: https://w2.vatican.va/content/john-paul-ii/en/speeches/1978/documents/hf_jpii_spe_19781017_primo-radiomessaggio.html

———. "General Audience." 2 May 1979, 3. *L'Osservatore Romano. Weekly Edition in English*, 10 January 1996, 11.

———. "Homily in St. Mary's Major." 8 December 1982. Online: https://w2.vatican.va/content/john-paul-ii/it/homilies/1982/documents/hf_jp-ii_hom_19821208_immacolata.html

———. "Message to the Carmelite Family." 25 March 2001. Online: https://w2.vatican.va/content/john-paul-ii/en/speeches/2001/march/documents/hf_jp-ii_spe_20010326_ordine-carmelo.html

———. Apostolic Letter *Mulieris Dignitatem*. 15 August 1988. Online: https://w2.vatican.va/content/john-paul-ii/en/apost_letters/1988/documents/hf_jp-ii_apl_19880815_mulieris-dignitatem.html

———. Apostolic Letter *Rosarium Virginis Mariae*. 16 October 2002. Online: https://w2.vatican.va/content/john-paul-ii/en/apost_letters/2002/documents/hf_jp-ii_apl_20021016_rosarium-virginis-mariae.html

———. Encyclical Letter *Redemptoris Mater*. 25 March 1987. Online: http://w2.vatican.va/content/john-paul-ii/en/encyclicals/documents/hf_jp-ii_enc_25031987_redemptoris-mater.html

———. *Gift and Mystery. On the Fiftieth Anniversary on My Priestly Ordination*. New York: Doubleday, 1996.

Johnson, Elizabeth A. *Truly Our Sister. A Theology of Mary in the Communion of Saints*. New York: Continuum, 2003.

Klauza, Karol, and Kazimierz Pek, eds. *Mariologia Jana Pawła II. Problem interpretacji—sposób recepcji*. Lublin: Wydawnictwo KUL, 2007.

Kochaniewicz, Bogusław. *Wybrane zagadnienia z Mariologii Jana Pawła II*. Niepokalanów: Wydawnictwo Ojców Franciszkanów, 2007.

Kulczycka, Anna. "Z niewiast najsławniejsza." In *Mariologia Jana Pawła II. Problem interpretacji—sposób recepcji*, edited by Karol Klauza and Kazimierz Pek, 133–49. Lublin: Wydawnictwo KUL, 2007.

Kushu-Solii, Ngah Andrew. *The Relationship between Mariology and Ecclesiology in the Theological Thinking of John Paul II.* Bern: Lang, 2012.

Leahy, Brendan. "John Paul II and Hans Urs Von Balthasar." In *The Legacy of John Paul II*, edited by Gerald O'Collins and Michael Hayes, 31–50. London: Burns & Oates, 2008.

———. "Totus Tuus: The Mariology of John Paul II." In *John Paul the Great. Maker of the Post-conciliar Church*, edited by William Oddie, 69–93. London: Catholic Truth Society & The Catholic Herald, 2003.

Mariologische Studien. Volume XVIII: Totus Tuus—Maria in Leben und Lehre Johannes Pauls II. Edited by Anton Ziegenaus. Regensburg: Pustet Verlag, 2004.

McKenna, Mary Frances. *Innovation within Tradition: Joseph Ratzinger and Reading the Women of Scripture.* Augsburg, MN: Fortress, 2015.

McNamara, Kevin. "Foreword." In *Pope John Paul II. Mother of the Church*, edited by Seamus O'Byrne, 5–7. Cork, Ireland: Mercier, 1987.

Moricová, Jana. "Totus Tuus odnowione." In *Mariologia Jana Pawła II. Problem interpretacji—sposób recepcji*, edited by Karol Klauza and Kazimierz Pek, 163–73. Lublin: Wydawnictwo KUL, 2007.

Mauriello Matthew Rocco. *Venerable Pope Pius XII and the 1954 Marian Year: A Study of His Writings within the Context of the Marian Devotion and Mariology in the 1950s.* University of Dayton: Marian Library/International Marian Research Institute, 2010.

Murphy, Francesca. "Immaculate Mary: The Ecclesial Mariology of Hans Urs Von Baltasar." In *Mary: The Complete Resource*, edited by Sarah Jane Boss, 300–312. New York: Continuum, 2007.

Nachef, Antoine. *Mary's Pope: John Paul II, Mary and the Church since Vatican II.* Franklin, WI: Sheed & Ward, 2000.

Nadbrzeżny, Antoni. "Per Iesum ad Mariam. Hasło, które stało się programem." In *Mariologia Jana Pawła II. Problem interpretacji—sposób recepcji*, edited by Karol Klauza and Kazimierz Pek, 151–61. Lublin: Wydawnictwo KUL, 2007.

Napiórkowski, Stanisław Celestyn. "Doświadczenia i objawienia." In *Mariologia Jana Pawła II. Problem interpretacji—sposób recepcji*, edited by Karol Klauza and Kazimierz Pek, 29–46. Lublin: Wydawnictwo KUL, 2007.

Napiórkowski, Celestyn Stanisław. "Doświadczenie osób i wspólnot chrześcijańskich jako źródło teologii (Mariologia św. Maksymiliana a Redemptoris Mater)." *Roczniki Teologiczne* 44 (1997/2) 41–56.

O'Collins, Gerald. "Ressourecement and Vatican II." In *Ressourcement. A Movement for Renewal in Twentieth-Cantury Catholic Theology*, edited by Gabriel Flyn and Paul D. Murray, 372–91. Oxford: Oxford University Press, 2012.

O'Connor, Edward D. "The Roots of Pope John Paul II's Devotion to Mary." *Marian Studies* 39 (1988) 78–114.

Peters, Danielle M. *Ecce Educatrix Tua. The Role of the Blessed Virgin Mary for a Pedagogy of Holiness in the Thought of John Paul II and Father Joseph Kentenich.* Lanham, MD: University Press of America, 2010.

Ratzinger, Joseph, and Vittorio Messori. *The Ratzinger Report. An Exclusive Interview on the State of the Church.* Translated by Salvator Attanasio and Graham Harrison. San Francisco: Ignatius, 1985.

Rynne, Xavier. *The Third Session: The Debates and Decrees of Vatican Council II. September 14 to November 21, 1964.* London: Faber and Faber, 1964–65.

Siudy, Teofil. *Matka naszego zawierzenia. Maryja w nauczaniu błogosławionego Jana Pawła II*. Warszawa: Wydawnictwo Sióstr Loretanek, 2013.

Szulc, Tad. *Pope John Paul II: The Biography*. New York: Scribner, 1995.

Tavard, George H. *The Thousands Faces of the Virgin Mary*. Collegeville, MN: Liturgical, 1996.

Taylor, Richard J. "Redemptoris Mater. Pope John Paul's Encyclical for the Marian Year: Some Reflections." *Priests & People* 2 (1988) 133–36.

Weigel, George. *Witness to Hope. The Biography of Pope John Paul II, 1920–2005*. New York: Harper Collins, 2001.

Wojtyła, Karol. *The Acting Person (Analecta Husserliana)*. Translated by Andrzej Potocki. Dordrecht: Reidel, 1979.

———. *Faith According to Saint John of the Cross*. Translated by Jordan Aumann. San Francisco: Ignatius, 1981.

———. "Inspiracja Maryjna Vaticanum II." In *W kierunku prawdy*, edited by Bohdan Bejze, 112–21. Warszawa: ATK, 1976.

———. "O humaniźmie św. Jana od Krzyża." *Znak* 5.27 (1951) 6–20.

Wróbel, Mirosław S. "Rola Biblii w Mariologii Jana Pawła II." In *Mariologia Jana Pawła II. Problem interpretacji—sposób recepcji*, edited by Karol Klauza and Kazimierz Pek, 15–28. Lublin: Wydawnictwo KUL, 2007.

5

Marian Arks Cut Adrift
The Post-Roman Catholic Development of Two Australian Marian Apparitional Movements

—Bernard Doherty

In an important recent sociological study on the organizational development of Marian apparitional movements, David G. Bromley and Rachel S. Bobbitt (2011) outlined a model to account for how Marian apparitional movements develop in interaction with their surrounding culture and the institutional Roman Catholic Church, charting some of the alternative trajectories that such movements can take during this development. This chapter seeks to develop aspects of Bromley and Bobbitt's model to illuminate the strategies deployed by apparitional movements which are rejected by the institutional Roman Catholic Church and continue to resist attempts to curtail their activities, and to clarify some of the ways in which movement careers develop in their post-Roman Catholic phase. This chapter demonstrates how post-Catholic apparitional movements develop through the interplay of at least five distinct strategies: (1) denial and reinvigoration; (2) individual reintegration; (3) regularization/normalization; (4) alternative legitimation; and (5) hereticization. This chapter concludes by examining how these strategies have been deployed by two controversial and highly publicized Marian apparitional movements in Australia: the Magnificat Meal Movement International and the Order of Saint Charbel, both of which ultimately split from the Church to found sectarian religious communities organized around the visions of their respective charismatic leaders, Debra Burslem (b. 1953) and William Kamm (b. 1950), better known as "The Little Pebble."

In a famous 1985 interview with Italian journalist Vittorio Messori in which he candidly discussed the challenges faced by the Roman Catholic Church during his lifetime, Pope Emeritus Benedict XVI noted that:

> By inserting the mystery of Mary into the mystery of the Church Vatican II made an important decision which should have given a new impetus to theological research. Instead, in the early post-conciliar period, there has been a sudden decline in this respect—almost a collapse, even though there are now signs of a new vitality.[1]

Here, and in the pages that followed, then Cardinal Ratzinger alluded to two closely related trends which had emerged following the epoch-making and at times controversial reforms in the Church which came on the coattails of the Second Vatican Council held between 1962 and 1965: the conservative reaction and the marked increase in the number of alleged appearances of the Virgin Mary across the globe.

Cardinal Ratzinger and many other early supporters of the Council's reformist agenda had come to believe that some aspects of the subsequent implementation of the Council's teachings had ultimately proved detrimental to the long-term viability of the Catholic faith—particularly in the immediate euphoria amongst some priests, religious, and an emboldened laity following the Council.[2] Such allegedly detrimental effects were felt acutely, at least for a time, in the respect accorded to the Virgin Mary—who some conservative Catholics felt had been slighted by reform oriented theologians who sought to avoid causing offence to "separated brethren" by embracing a form of Marian minimalism (or an ecclesio-typical Mariology) and who saw Marian devotion as at best a medieval anachronism, at worst superstition bordering on idolatry.[3] Despite what he viewed as the neglect of some theologians, Cardinal Ratzinger pointed to a number of areas where reflection on the place of the Virgin Mary in the Catholic tradition could provide a new impetus for theological reflection and Church renewal. Among these,

---

1. Ratzinger with Messori, *Ratzinger Report*, 104.
2. Greeley, *The Catholic Revolution*, 82.
3. See Laurentin, *Mary's Place in the Church*, 53–81.

he cautiously noted, could be included the burgeoning number of alleged Marian apparitions.

Since the end of the Second World War the number of claimed apparitions of the Virgin Mary has proliferated across the world—with a recent cover-story in *National Geographic* and numerous journalistic books by Vaticanologists and others bearing witness to the massive upsurge in alleged sightings.[4] While a few of these apparitions have received a degree of Church approbation—notably those at Kibeho in Rwanda between 1981–89 and Akita in Japan in 1973—in the vast majority of cases the Church has refrained from passing judgment regarding their supernatural origins. In general, the Church continues to follow a set of guidelines first established by Pope Benedict XIV in his eighteenth century work *De Servorum Dei Beatificatione et Canonizatione* ("On the Beatification and Canonization of the Servants of God") and most recently codified in 1978 as the *Normae de modo procedendi in diudicandis praesumptis apparitionibus ac revelationibus* (Norms regarding the manner of proceedings in the discernment of presumed apparitions or revelations).[5] These guidelines pertain to how such visionary experiences, and their often accompanying prophetic messages (or private revelations) and supernatural manifestations, should be assessed. Usually this results in one of three outcomes: (1) the supernatural nature of the apparition is established (*constat de supernaturalitate*); (2) the supernatural nature of the event has not been established (*non constat de supernaturalitate*); or (3) the non-supernatural nature of the event has been established (*constat de non supernaturalitate*).[6]

In a very small number of cases, usually the most controversial or widely publicized, a diocesan bishop will establish what is best described as an *ad hoc* canonical commission of investigation modeled on nineteenth-century precedents and conclude on grounds usually not made privy to the wider public that no supernatural significance can be attached to a particular apparition.[7] Historically, such inquires have roughly approximated the general form described by David Blackbourn:

---

4. Orth, "Most Powerful," 40–41; for various estimates as to the exact number see Apolito, *Madonna*, 25–26 and Matter, "Apparitions," 125. For a selection of journalistic works see Cornwell, *Powers of Darkness*; Garvey, *Searching for Mary*; O'Neill, *Exploring the Miraculous*; and Thavis, *Vatican Prophecies*.

5. These norms were only made public in 2011, having previously only been available in Latin to diocesan bishops. See O'Neill, *Exploring*, 38–59; Thavis, *Vatican Prophecies*, 75–76.

6. Maunder, *Our Lady*, 40–49; Zimdars-Swartz, *Encountering Mary*, 9–12.

7. Such investigations see Jelly, "Canonical Considerations," 142–44.

The most rigorous canonical commissions deliberated for years. Generally organized by the bishop's vicar-general, they typically consisted of members of the cathedral chapter and theologians from a local seminary. They took detailed statements from the visionaries themselves, usually the result of repeated questioning; they considered evidence from hundreds of witnesses; and they took into account medical evidence, both on the state of mind of the visionaries, and on the precise status of any miraculous cures that had been claimed. Cases were officially recognized by the church only after the commission of enquiry had satisfied itself that deception, vanity, collusion between the persons involved, auto-suggestion, hallucination, and diabolical influences could be excluded from consideration.[8]

Negative judgments by diocesan commissions, however, have rarely led to the complete disappearance of devotions or pilgrimages to non-sanctioned apparition sites, as the still unresolved cases of Medjugorje in Bosnia-Hercegovina and Garabandal in Spain aptly demonstrate.

While the contemporary Marian revival's relationship to Vatican II is far more complex than has often been stated,[9] the vast majority of Marian apparitional groups to have emerged in the wake of the Council can be classified as, at the very least, what the Swiss scholar of religion Jean-François Mayer has called "selective traditionalists"[10] whose relationship to many aspects of the conciliar reforms has been, at best, ambiguous, at worst antagonistic.[11] For many in this broad group, certain liturgical changes, such as the moving of the tabernacle from its central place on the altar to the side of the Church, the reception of communion in the hand rather than kneeling and on the tongue, and the shift from the "Tridentine" Latin Mass to the *Novus Ordo Missae* in the vernacular, have proven scandalous. However, for the same groups post-conciliar reforms involving the increased role accorded to the laity within the life of the Church and the encouragement of charis-

---

8. Blackbourn, *Marpingen*, 50. For another historical perspective Kselman, *Miracles and Prophecies*, 148f. writes: "The pattern in these cases was elaborated and extended throughout the century, but the basic elements remained constant: clergy hand-picked by the bishop were given the responsibility for investigating and reporting on the miracle; an attempt was made to limit publicity on the miraculous to official sanctioned accounts; medical experts were called on for advice, but real authority remained with the clergy and ultimately the bishop."

9. On this see the discussion in Kane, "Marian Devotion," 89–129, especially 114–19; and Krebs, "Transposing Devotion," 37.

10. Mayer, "There Will Follow," 201.

11. See also Kohle, "Fundamentalistische Marienbewegungen," 60–106; Krebs, "Transposing Devotion," 37; and Margry, "Marian Interventions," 246–48.

matic gifts through movements like the Catholic Charismatic Renewal, have proven more amenable.

This wider visionary milieu, sometimes referred to as Marian or Catholic Apocalyptic,[12] occupies a particular sociological niche on the wider spectrum of conservative Catholic groups to have emerged in the wake of the Council; often straddling the boundaries between canonically approved conservative groups like Opus Dei and canonically suppressed groups like the Society of St. Pius X (SSPX). While space does not permit an outline of a detailed ideal-type,[13] in essence Marian Apocalyptic is usually characterized by a loose-knit devotional subculture centered on a series of private revelations (often referred to as "messages from heaven") received by various alleged seers. This subculture places a strong emphasis on various seers's alleged experiences of thaumaturgical, supernatural, and preternatural phenomena ranging from cardiognosis, hierognosis, and bilocation, to stigmata and bleeding or weeping statues.

Marian Apocalyptic is largely promoted through a shared communication structure of periodicals and the Internet and in private Marian prayer groups found on the fringes of parochial Catholic life. Owing to the often apocalyptic nature of these private revelations, a number of the more organized groups which have formed from this milieu American anthropologist Miguel Leatham has referred to as "Marian Arks"[14] reflecting a commonly held belief that they represent a remnant of the true Church which will be preserved during a fast encroaching period of divine chastisement, if not the Second Coming. Moreover, historically this subculture has also given birth to a number of breakaway Catholic sects and "Adventist"[15] religious orders, though characterizing the entire subculture in terms of canonical status or theological orthodoxy remains difficult. While some groups like the Spanish Palmarian Catholic Church and the Canadian Army of Mary have been declared schismatic and heretical under Canon Law, other groups, particularly many associated with Fatima (e.g., the Blue Army), or those associated with the charism of what might be called clerical prophets and saints (e.g., Louis-Marie Grignion de Montfort),[16] remain accepted within the wider Church and incline closely to the theological positions held by

---

12. Cuneo, "Vengeful Virgin," 175–94; and Luebbers, "Remnant Faithful," 221–41.

13. For a good outline see Cuneo, "Vengeful Virgin," 178–80; and Luebbers, "Remnant Faithful," 221–41.

14. Leatham, "Shaking Out the Mat," 177.

15. Séguy, "Apocalyptic Theme," 203–21.

16. Ibid., 206–7; and Séguy, "Millénarismes," 23–48.

other (usually more conservative) Catholic groups, though often holding potentially suspect beliefs about eschatology.

Theologically Marian Apocalyptic groups run the entire gamut from sedevacantists to conservatives and thus some would be classified in a formal canonical sense as either heretical or schismatic (or both).[17] In terms of ethics these groups hold similar views to other Catholic conservatives, indeed many of the private revelations of visionaries outline traditional conservative Catholic moral concerns over issues ranging from abortion to immodesty in dress and homosexuality. Politically Marian Apocalyptic groups have traditionally been strongly anti-communist and embrace many of the conspiracy theories found more broadly among traditionalist and sedevacantist groups, as well as the political far-right. However, such groups are devotional rather than activist in their primary orientation and aims. In organizational terms these groups tend to follow some kind of charismatic leadership structure centered on a primary lay visionary; however, some might also be founded by clergy or attract dissident clergy who provide a façade of institutional legitimacy.

With this particular sociological niche in mind, this chapter seeks to examine the developmental dynamics of these groups and how these apply to the post-Catholic development of two specific Australian Marian Apocalyptic groups which emerged from this wider subculture and which, along with their respective visionaries, William Kamm (better known as "The Little Pebble") and Debra Burslem, have been publicly censured by the institutional Church in Australia. Both these religious groups—the Order of Saint Charbel and the Magnificat Meal Movement—have been the topic of often intense Church and media scrutiny between the 1980s and today. Following diocesan investigations held into the claims of both visionaries and—with the express approval of the Congregation for the Doctrine of the Faith—official decrees were issued censuring both movements and declaring them canonically schismatic and heretical. While space does not permit me to trace the complex organizational development of these groups prior to this negative ecclesiastical judgment, it suffices to say here that both groups approximate the developmental model proposed by David Bromley and Rachel Bobbitt in their 2011 study.[18]

---

17. See *The Code of Canon Law*, Can.751. This canon reads: "Heresy is the obstinate denial or doubt, after baptism, of a truth which must be believed by divine and catholic faith. Apostasy is the total repudiation of the Christian faith. Schism is the withdrawal of submission to the Supreme Pontiff or from communion with members of the Church subject to him."

18. Bromley and Bobbitt, "Visions."

What this chapter seeks to address is how Marian Apparitional Movements respond when censured by the institutional Church. As such, this chapter builds on the final part of Bromley and Bobbitt's model which they have dubbed "alternative movement trajectories" in further elaborating on the processes of "rejection and resistance" and the kinds of strategies adopted by Marian apparitional movements who have found themselves under Church censure.[19] While Bromley and Bobbitt's model provides an excellent analysis of the dynamics of the origins and early development of such groups, of necessity it only provides preliminary analysis of the significant number of "rejected" groups and some of the forms their resistance to ecclesiastical censure might take. This chapter seeks to build on this and other earlier studies by outlining various strategies adopted by Marian Apparitional Movements and their individual members when confronted by ecclesiastical censure, as well as suggesting some of the factors which might influence various responses.

In order to address the dynamics and strategies utilized by various Marian Apparitional Movements, the history of a preliminary sample of twenty well documented groups or individual visionaries from the wider Marian Apocalyptic subculture has been analyzed. Included in this sample are a number of groups—ranging chronologically from nineteenth-century breakaway sects like the Vintrasian Carmelites (better known as the Work of Mercy) to the Mexican sedevacantist colony of Nueva Jerusalén, as well as those associated with individual visionaries like Saint Faustina Kowalska and Saint Padre Pio—that have attracted a significant following and which have at one time or another encountered some degree of censure from the institutional Church. From this sample five broad strategies adopted by such groups—or individual members of these groups—following their rejection by the mainstream Church have been identified: (1) denial and reinvigoration; (2) individual reintegration; (3) regularization/normalization; (4) alternative legitimation; and (5) hereticization. While by no means exhausting the ways in which such groups have responded to Church censure, what follows will firstly delineate each of these strategies before a concluding discussion of how they help to illuminate how the Order of Saint Charbel and the Magnificat Meal Movement have reacted in similar circumstances.

Denial and Reinvigoration

Denial and reinvigoration can be defined as *the intransigent denial by those associated with an unapproved apparition to accept or recognize the validity*

19. Ibid., 25–28.

of a Church censure and the redoubling of promotional efforts. Unsurprisingly this is a very common occurrence, especially amongst those who are heavily committed to an apparition, and is often akin in certain ways to the much debated social psychological phenomenon of disconfirmed prophecy, whereby, paradoxically, one witnesses "increased fervor following disconfirmation of a belief."[20] In the case of rejected apparitions, denial and reinvigoration will usually take the form of a semi-official protest or appeal of a decision to a higher jurisdiction accompanied by heavy publicity and increased promotion whereby a group makes clear that it does not accept the decision of a local bishop and will only recognize that of the Holy See (or even that of God). Groups engaging in this strategy will often seek to query the procedural fairness of diocesan inquiry or to posit a human or demonic conspiracy behind a negative decision.

Almost every post-World War II unapproved apparition has witnessed this strategy, often accompanied by reams of literature and tortuous and at times highly spurious argumentation from Canon Law as to why an original Church decision is incorrect. A good example of denial and reinvigoration, however, is the case of Fr. Nicholas Gruner and his Fatima Crusader Network, whose controversial ministry surrounding claims about the otherwise approved apparition of Fatima has caused controversy for decades.[21] In the face of numerous official Church censures regarding their claims, Gruner and his followers have fastidiously continued to make various claims (among other things) about the content of the so-called "Third Secret of Fatima" and what they consider its unparalleled importance for humanity's future. Indeed, even after the official text of Sister Lucia's vision was publicly released by the Congregation for the Doctrine of the Faith in June 2000, the Fatima Crusader Network refused (along with various other rejected apparitional movements) to acknowledge its authenticity, accompanying their allegations that it was a forgery with a combination of spurious theological arguments and conspiratorial claims.[22]

Individual Reintegration

Individual reintegration can be defined as *the abandonment of devotion to an unapproved apparition by an individual follower and their reentry into mainstream diocesan parish life*. In essence this involves members ceasing involvement in a group or devotion to a particular apparition and returning

---

20. Festinger et al., *When Prophecy Fails*, 3.
21. On Gruner see Alban, *Fatima Priest*; and Cuneo, *Smoke of Satan*, 134–52.
22. Bertone, *Last Secret of Fatima*; see also Thavis, *Vatican Prophecies*, 7.

to regular life within the canonical Church. Several factors might support or mitigate the adoption of this strategy.

With regard to individual reintegration the length of time a group has existed and the degree of its organizational development and whether or not they have set up alternative ecclesiastical structures similar to canonical religious orders will often be key to whether individual followers adopt this strategy. To use a distinction drawn from the study of political extremist groups, Marian Apparitional Movements can be divided into *bounded* groups, whose membership "involves trust, obligations, commitment and—very significantly—being initiated into some of the group's secrets," and *unbounded* groups, whose "boundaries are relatively fuzzy, and, who is inside and who is outside is not clearly defined."[23] Bounded apparitional groups will tend to be more difficult to exit than is the case for unbounded groups. Moreover, the older and more organized a group has become, the less likely members will leave the group after having already invested considerable resources both financial and human and having been heavily socialized into the alternative theological worldview and community life offered by a particular apparition or group, as Rosabeth Moss Kanter has noted in her classic study of commitment mechanisms, "[when a member] commits his resources to it [a group]: time, energy, money, property, and reputation all become bound up with the movement, so that leaving it means leaving all that behind."[24]

For individual reintegration to be successful a number of preconditions must usually be present. First, given the high intensity and devotional focus of these groups there need to be alternative spiritual outlets to which exiting members can be redirected. A good example of this is the fostering of approved forms of Marian pilgrimage and devotional activities at either a parish or diocesan level. Second, such a strategy will tend to only emerge in places where local clergy or the Church hierarchy are sympathetic and willing to facilitate the re-entry of censured devotees; particularly if the group has been officially declared schismatic or heretical. As Krebs has observed in her recent study, "while the agency of lay Catholics cannot be denied, the decisions and actions of priests sometimes cause tension within local communities resulting in the marginalization of visionaries and their supporters."[25] Other preconditions which will facilitate individual reintegration are matters of disillusionment and malfeasance. For example,

---

23. Bjørgo, "Entry, Bridge-Burning, and Exit Options," 232.

24. Kanter, "Commitment and Internal Organization," 228; see also Beit-Hallahmi and Argyle, *Psychology of Religious Behaviour*, 135–36.

25. Krebs, "Transposing Devotion," 38.

the discovery that a charismatic leader or visionary is engaged in morally reprehensible conduct often leads to a large number of members departing from a group or a believer begins to doubt the veracity or theological content of a visionary's private revelations.

The process of individual reintegration, however, can be complicated, especially when serious canonical impediments exist—for instance in the case of dissident clergy who have involved themselves with censured groups, or members who have obtained illicit forms of ordination or episcopal consecration. Other factors which can mitigate individual reintegration might also include positive aspects found within a censured group, for instance, a strong sense of community amongst members (particularly in the cases which have instituted communal living arrangements) or a situation where a potential exiting member has nowhere to go, as might be the case again if a member has staked all on their commitment to a group and burned their bridges with their family, the Church, or former associates, as can be the case with the more sociologically sectarian apparitional movements.

Despite such caveats, individual reintegration is by far the most regular strategy adopted by individual members of censured groups. If certain preconditions like those outlined above are met the majority of individuals involved in censured groups are likely to be reconciled with the mainstream Church, provided that few or no mitigating factors are present. It is also the most damaging response to the long-term viability of many of these groups, for not only do they lose members but it also creates ideal conditions for the emergence of "apostate" ex-members who will work to put further pressure on their former coreligionists through campaigning against their former group either by contacting Church authorities or going to the media.[26] Two good historical examples of this are the French Work of Mercy and the Polish Mariavite Church, both of whom lost key members who subsequently rejoined the mainstream Church at various stages following their censure by Rome. In both these cases these highly placed ex-members subsequently recounted tales of sexual malfeasance within these groups, in the case of the Mariavites the polygamy of the group's leader Jan Kowalski, in the case of the Work of Mercy the allegedly (though still debated) sexual nature of certain of the group's liturgical practices.[27]

---

26. For the reasons for this see Bromley, "Linking Social Structure."
27. See Garçon, *Vintras*, 143–60; and Peterkiewicz, *Third Adam*, 99–118,

Regularization/Normalization

Regularization or normalization can be defined as *the re-entry of an entire censured group (or large part of a group) into diocesan life as a canonically recognized entity.* Like individual reintegration, in terms of preconditions, this process is assisted by the presence of alternative spiritual outlets, sympathetic local hierarchy, and the presence of disillusionment and/or malfeasance within the group's leadership (though usually not amongst other tiers of membership). However, unlike individual reintegration this is a more realistic option for groups that have undergone a greater level of organizational development or routinization, for example, in cases where a group has developed a form of a religious rule and a structured ecclesial life and developed a hierarchy of religious within the group (e.g., priests and religious). Regularization/normalization can also take place with regard to private prayer groups—like those associated with the Divine Mercy Devotion and Padre Pio—which while previously treated with a degree of caution are integrated into the mainstream Church following a reversal or clarification of the status of their devotional practices[28]; this has also been the case with a series of originally unapproved European shrines which have remained popular (including with clergy) but not crystallized into discrete apparitional movements and have eventually "converged" with the institutional Church.[29]

Regularization/Normalization is historically the least likely outcome for a censured group, largely owing to mitigating factors such as irregular spiritual practices or the formation of dissident religious and the general reluctance of most local diocesan bishops—to whom most canonical responsibilities relating to apparitions ultimately devolve—to risk the potential embarrassment or scandal which such groups may attract. This is particularly the case when a visionary is still alive and claiming to receive new private revelations. Here the potential exists for conflict between the charismatic authority of a group's leader and the legal authority of the local hierarchy, as Introvigne has noted in reference to the "domestication of charisma" which takes place when a visionary's followers are regularized by the Church, "since a living prophet is, by definition, unpredictable, the domestication often takes place after his or her death."[30]

Regularization/normalization is, however, not entirely unknown. While not strictly a Marian Apparitional Movement, the Society of St. Pius

---

28. See Margry, "Merchandising and Sanctity."
29. See Margry, "Marian Interventions," 256–57.
30. Introvigne, "Modern Catholic Millennialism," 563.

X (SSPX), formed by the traditionalist former missionary Archbishop Marcel Lefebvre following Vatican II does have some quite strong connections to this wider milieu owing largely to its shared disquiet regarding the direction of the post-conciliar Church—these connections include a seldom spoken belief among some followers that Archbishop Lefebvre's self-appointed mission to save the Church from the apostasy of Vatican II was prophesied by an earlier visionary and strong historical links between the group and the San Damiano apparition in Italy.[31] When SSPX became formerly schismatic in 1988, following Archbishop Lefebvre's illicit joint consecration of four of his followers as bishops without a papal mandate, a significant rump of the movement, not wishing to follow Lefebvre into schism, were regularized and went on to form the Priestly Fraternity of St. Peter (FSSP) and were granted the canonical status of a Clerical Society of Apostolic Life of Pontifical Right. FSSP parishes now exist as small Latin Mass enclaves in many dioceses, are answerable only to the local bishop with regard to certain pastoral matters, and are otherwise given wide ambit for their activities.

Other groups formerly associated with SSPX have also been regularized since with similar conditions—such as the French Institute of the Good Shepherd. Indeed, the pontificate of Benedict XVI, and his commitment to rapprochement with SSPX in particular, created the ideal conditions for a number of formerly schismatic traditionalist groups to be regularized through the auspices of the Pontifical Commission Ecclesia Dei or through the work of sympathetic local diocesan bishops. Perhaps the most notable example of a local bishop regularizing a rejected group is that of a convent of American nuns formerly associated with the sedevacantist Congregation of Mary Immaculate Queen (CMRI) who were slowly reconciled with the Diocese of Spokane in Washington and eventually formed the Sisters of Mary, Mother of the Church.[32] It is important to note, however, that most of the groups which have been regularized have been far less reliant on a charismatic leaders or have invested far less authority in private revelations than other groups within this wider subculture.

Alternative Legitimation

Without delving heavily into the complexities of the sociology of institutional legitimation,[33] alternative legitimation can be defined as *the*

---

31. See Maunder, *Our Lady*, 142–47; Tissier de Mallerais, *Marcel Lefebvre*, 534; White, *Horn of the Unicorn*, 194; and Zimdars-Swartz, *Encountering Mary*, 110–11.

32. Graves, "Return to Rome."

33. This section draws on Lewis, *Legitimating New Religions*.

attempt of a group to circumvent a Church censure through seeking an alternative source of ecclesiastical legitimation; either canonical or irregular. This can be further divided into three subtypes: (a) *jurisdictional legitimation*; (b) *irregular episcopal legitimation*; and finally (c) *mystical legitimation*.

Jurisdictional legitimation can be defined as *the attempt to circumvent a local ordinary by seeking legitimation and approval elsewhere; for example in a neighboring diocese, seeking to appeal to Rome over a diocesan bishop's head, seeking to align with one of the Eastern Rite Churches in communion with Rome, or in the case of dissident clergy seeking alternative incardination.* Rarely is this strategy successful, though it does provide a façade of legitimation to many groups which have been censured as well as a time delaying tactic. For instance, many groups will maintain that while their appeals have not been answered by Rome they are still able to operate and use the lack of a definitive decision by Rome (or the Pope) as justification. Given that Rome rarely answers appeals by such groups, and when it does it often takes a significant period of time and is less than forthcoming with procedural details, this allows groups breathing space in which to continue operating even after an initial censure.

A good example of this is the case of Fr. Nicholas Gruner who was originally incardinated in Italy, but who operated his para-church Fatima ministry in the U.S. and Canada.[34] When Gruner's ideas became increasingly outré and conspiracy driven during the early 1980s his incardination was revoked and local bishops in the U.S. and Canada began to strongly discourage the laity and clergy from offering him any kind of support. Gruner sought to circumvent this by having a sympathetic Indian bishop incardinate him, which allowed him to continue to claim legitimacy. This, however, was eventually quashed when he was suspended *a divinis* in 1996. Gruner, predictably, appealed to Rome and in the interim was able to continue operating for another five years before the Congregation for the Clergy—after consulting the Apostolic Signatura—rejected Gruner's appeal. This, of course, did not stop Gruner's ministry which continued until his death in 2015, though notably Fr. Gruner's Requiem Mass was conducted by the Superior General of the SSPX Bishop Bernard Fellay.

Irregular episcopal legitimation can be defined as the seeking by clerical (and sometimes lay) members of censured groups to *attempt to provide a semblance of legitimacy through canonically illicit priestly ordinations or episcopal consecrations*. This leads into the often eccentric world of *episcopi vagantes* ("wandering bishops") who through various episcopal

---

34. On Gruner see Alban, *Fatima Priest*; and Cuneo, *The Smoke of Satan*, 134–52.

lineages can claim some degree of apostolic succession.[35] While numerous apostolic lines of succession exist through the Anglican, the Eastern Orthodox, and the Old Catholic churches, the most important contemporary example for understanding Marian Apparitional Movements is that of the bishops associated with a number of sedevacantist groups, such as CMRI and the Society of St. Pius V (SSPV), who had themselves consecrated by the aged Vietnamese exiled Archbishop Pierre Martin Ngô Đình Thục over the course of the 1970s and early 1980s. These consecrations led to a burgeoning of additional consecrations—all of which have resulted in excommunication *latae sententiae*[36]—meaning that now the number of so-called "Thục Line" bishops could be reckoned in the dozens.[37] Most notable among Thục's consecrations was that of the Spanish visionary Clement Domínguez y Gómez in 1976, founder of the censured Holy Apostolic Catholic Palmarian Church.[38]

The other way in which groups have sought to do this, as in the case of some of the Polish Mariavite churches—which were censured by Pope Pius X in 1906—was to seek recognition from various Old Catholic groups and even the Eastern Orthodox. In 1909 the Mariavites briefly achieved recognition and consecration by Old Catholic bishops from the Union of Utrecht. However, in 1924 the Old Catholics severed relations with the Mariavites following a scandal pertaining to "mystical marriage" and ordination of women. After this some of the remaining Mariavites sought legitimation from the Eastern Orthodox through the Ecumenical Patriarch—it suffices to say here that this was unsuccessful. Similarly, following the death of their founder Eugene Vintras, the remaining members of the French Work of Mercy became involved with various Neo-Gnostic churches which emerged in France in tandem with the late nineteenth-century French Occult revival.

The third subtype of alternative legitimation is mystical legitimation. This strategy can be defined as *a visionary invokes a private revelation which bestows upon them or another individual of their designation a mystical episcopal consecration or in some cases papal office*. The two best Marian Apparitional Movement examples of this are the Quebecoise Apostles of Infinite Love, whose initial leader, a French priest named Michel Collin

---

35. For a very dated look at this subculture and its many contours see Anson, *Bishops at Large*.

36. See *Code of Canon Law*, Can. 1382, this reads: "Both the Bishop who, without a pontifical mandate, consecrates a person a Bishop, and the one who receives the consecration from him, incur a *latae sententiae* excommunication reserved to the Apostolic See."

37. Introvigne and Zoccatelli, "Sedevacantists and Antipopes," 2563–64.

38. Lundberg, "Fighting the Modern."

claimed in 1936 that he had been ordained a bishop by Christ himself. In 1950, however, Christ allegedly promoted Collin to the office of pope and he subsequently styled himself Pope Clement XV.[39] A more flamboyant example is that of the aforementioned Spanish visionary Clemente Domínguez y Gómez from Palmar de Troya. Clemente had himself first consecrated as one of the first Thuc-Line bishops in 1976, after a since defrocked Swiss priest had convinced the arguably senile Archbishop Thuc that Clemente's visions were valid. When Pope Paul VI died in 1978 Clemente claimed that he had been crowned Pope by Jesus in a vision he received while on holiday in Colombia, subsequently styling himself Pope Gregory XVII.[40]

Hereticization

The final strategy adopted by censured Marian apparitional movements discussed in this chapter is hereticization, which can be defined as *the development of heterodox doctrines or practices which ensure a group's continual institutional alienation from the wider Church*. This is a tricky area, particularly from a religious studies perspective, but when dealing with Roman Catholicism it is less problematic as the Church is quite clear on what constitutes heresy and in most cases in which a group is considered heretical this will be publicly declared, as in the recent case of the Army of Mary.[41]

It is worth noting, however, that in general few visionary groups have developed anything approaching systematic theologies, but rather the private revelations of visionaries tend to be bland and repetitive, and while quite theologically old fashioned and marked by a high Mariology (or Marian Maximalism) generally orthodox. However, some groups have developed doctrines based on private revelations which diverged significantly enough from Church teaching to be considered heretical, this is particularly the case with regard to eschatology with various groups adopting or modifying alternative millennialist scenarios long present in the Catholic tradition or, as in recent cases such as that of the infamous Bayside apparition in the U.S., the adoption of eschatological ideas clearly borrowed from Protestant fundamentalism such as the Rapture.[42]

39. On the Apostles of Infinite Love see Cuneo, *Smoke of Satan*, 121–34.

40. Lundberg, "Fighting the Modern," 47 writes, "at the death of Pope Paul VI on 6 August 1978, Domínguez, then in Bogotá, claimed to have become pope not by conclave election but by divine intervention. Christ himself had placed the tiara on his head in the presence of St. Peter, St. Paul and the recently deceased Pope Paul VI."

41. Fastiggi, "Rise and Fall," 150.

42. For an overview of these systems see McGinn, "Forms of Catholic Millenarianism," 1–13. On the adoption of Rapture doctrines by Marian apocalypticists see Cuneo,

Two good examples of hereticization are again the nineteenth-century French Work of Mercy, which developed a complex theological system that combined ideas from the French Occult revival, Neo-Gnosticism, and a variant of the medieval tripartite eschatological ideas associated with the Franciscan visionary Joachim of Fiore. The group's visionary Eugene Vintras believed that he was the reincarnation of the Prophet Elijah who would herald in a new age of the Paraclete. Together with this, Vintras developed an alternative Marian centered form of the liturgy as well as curious ideas about the atonement. Vintras' successor, the defrocked Abbé Joseph-Antoine Boullan, went one step further and mixed in a combination of late nineteenth century French occultism and *possibly* Satanism.[43] Another example was the Mariavite bishop Jan Kowalski who, following the group's rejection by Rome, developed a complex amalgam of doctrines surrounding mystical marriage, eventually becoming a polygamist and fathering numerous children who he held would form a new holy race. Unsurprisingly, this also led to a criminal conviction and prison term. A similar situation has emerged more recently with the Army of Mary who have declared their founding visionary, Marie-Paule Giguère, to be the reincarnated Virgin Mary and one person in an alternative Marian Trinity.[44]

The strategy of hereticization, however, is complicated for chronological reasons. Heretical teachings (or the suspicion of such teachings) are often the chief reason that a group is censured by the Church in the first place, rather than strictly a response to such a censure. That a visionary will develop heretical doctrines as a result of Church opposition, however, is not an uncommon occurrence amongst religious founders more generally. Most rejected Marian visionaries began their careers as devoted Catholics who were struggling with both social and ecclesial change and felt that the mainstream Church was either powerless, reluctant, or ineffective in its response.[45] Bearing this in mind, sociologist Rodney Stark's theory of revelations is suggestive. Stark notes that "novel (heretical) revelations will most likely come to persons of deep religious concerns who perceive shortcomings in the conventional faith(s)," and that "the probability that individuals will perceive shortcomings in the conventional faith(s) increases during periods of social crisis."[46] In such a situation, when a visionary is rejected by the mainstream Church, but followers maintain their commitment and sup-

---

"Vengeful Virgin,"189; and Luebbers, "Remnant Faithful," 225.
    43. On Vintras see Ziegler, *Satanism*, 116–81.
    44. On this see Margry, "Mary's Reincarnation," 496–505.
    45. Maunder, *Our Lady*, 3.
    46. Stark, "A Theory of Revelations," 308.

port, a situation emerges where former institutional controls and threats of censure are no longer considered to be binding or valid, opening the door to theological novelty. This has increasingly been the case in the post-Vatican II era where the authority structure of the Church has increasingly come into question and individual Catholics have become increasingly willing to exercise their autonomy.[47]

Conclusion

In conclusio—having briefly outlined these organizational strategies and some historical examples of each—how do they help to explicate the career trajectory of the two Australian Marian Apparitional Movements introduced earlier?[48]

Over the course of their controverted relationships with their respective diocesan bishops both the MMM and Charbelites have, at various times, utilized most of these strategies in coping with ecclesiastical censures of varying severity. Throughout their history the Charbelites have regularly adopted a strategy of denial and reinvigoration, called into question the credibility of Church censure, and continued a massive, and at times quite successful, international program of promoting the visions of William Kamm in spite of ongoing issues with successive bishops. Most notable in this regard was their response to the diocesan investigation instituted under Bishop Philip Wilson which resulted in an official degree against them by his successor Bishop Peter Ingham in 2005. For the Charbelites this process did not meet their historical expectations of how an investigation should take place—only Kamm was ever formerly interviewed—and they immediately sought to appeal to Rome (who have still not answered—at least publicly). For the MMM the group frequently ignored any attempts by their Bishop William Morris to establish any oversight of their activities, and when Morris first publicly noted that the group had no standing within the Roman Catholic Church in 1996, he found himself being accused of Freemasonry. When the official diocesan commission was established a year later, Burslem refused to appear or acknowledge its legitimacy and continued promoting her visions. When an official decree was made by Bishop Morris in 1999,

---

47. See Barkun, *Culture of Conspiracy*, 20–21 and Krebs, "Transposing Devotion," 41–42.

48. Much of the information in the following section was obtained through confidential records and informal interviews conducted by the author. For published details see Doherty, "Mourning"; Hartney, "More Catholic"; Kahl and Doherty, "Channelling"; and Wickham and Hartney, "Rockchopping."

Burslem told reporters the entire commission had been biased and that "the end result was pretty obvious."[49]

Most members of both the MMM and the Charbelites have been reintegrated into the mainstream Church following their respective episcopal censure(s). This was facilitated, as with earlier cases, by the presence of sympathetic local clergy and bishops who in many cases created opportunities for members to return to mainstream parochial life. In some cases local clergy were also able to re-administer arguably invalid sacraments members had received during their time within the censured groups. In both cases, alleged or established malfeasance by the leaders of both groups, in the case of Kamm that of his conviction and imprisonment on child sex offences, and in the case of Burslem ongoing investigations into financial irregularities, influenced a significant number of members of these groups to seek reintegration into the wider Church, often bringing with them additional allegations about the less-savory internal operations of each group. Others were drawn away after starting to doubt the direction in which the group was travelling or doubts concerning the leader's orthodoxy. As one former MMM member put it:

> Things started to change; Debra got more and more powerful and started to move more clearly away from the Catholic Church, replacing herself as Christ and the Church's authority. . . . She was starting to proclaim that the teaching of the Church had been tampered with and could not be trusted. . . . People in MMM were encouraged to renounce marriage and baptismal vows, and eventually husbands or wives not accepting MMM were asked to leave.[50]

In some cases, however, individual reintegration was stalled or problematized. Among the Charbelites a number of members had received illicit ordinations at the hands of their (Thuc-line) bishop Malcolm Broussard and were thus required to go through a canonical process with the Congregation for the Doctrine of the Faith. Moreover a small number of members have chosen to remain. Most of the remaining Charbelites are either committed members of the group's sociologically bounded "inner circle," or elderly members who are heavily financially invested in the group's community and who have assumed the role of religious within the group's alternative ecclesiastical structure and thus have little incentive or opportunity to exit the group without a degree of difficulty. Moreover, after decades of shared communal life most who remain within the Charbelites have experienced

49. Gearing, "Vatican."
50. Dobbyn, "Cunning Psychology."

positive communal life and emotional support within the group, retain their faith in the group's leadership, and thus see no reason to leave.

With regard to regularization/normalization the Magnificat Meal Movement appears to have never seriously contemplated this option. From the group's inception its charismatic leader, Debra Burslem, displayed resistance to any form of ecclesiastical oversight, especially regarding financial matters, even when the group was just a series of private prayer groups similar to those found in the Catholic Charismatic Renewal. Indeed the group's lack of docility to appropriate ecclesiastical oversight was arguably the chief reason for the group's censure. In the case of the Charbelites the group has made approaches to the Pontifical Commission Ecclesia Dei and various other Vatican dicasteries over a number of years seeking to clarify or normalize their position. However, the likelihood of the group making any headway here is small; no Thuc-line bishop has yet been regularized by this commission and, for reasons discussed below, as with other organized groups like the Army of Mary it would be virtually impossible to regularize this group *en masse* without entirely dismantling the group's alternative ecclesiastical structure and removing its current leadership, many of whom are the subject of serious canonical penalties including excommunication.

The possibility of regularization/normalization for the Charbelites, moreover, has been complicated by what the Church perceives as irregular spiritual practices within the group and concerns about the formation of its religious, who were formed under a rule and constitution which was found to be very problematic by canon lawyers during the diocesan investigation into the group held under Bishop Wilson. The concern of the local clergy and the hierarchy here appears to be that some of the group's devotional practices may become (as they have in the past) a divisive and disruptive presence in diocesan and parochial life.

In terms of alternative legitimation, both groups have sought, at various times to circumvent episcopal censure in various ways. As early as the mid-1980s the Charbelites, then known as the Marian Work of Atonement, attempted to bypass their original 1984 censure by Bishop William Murray of Wollongong by establishing another community in the Diocese of Bathurst, appealing to Bishop Patrick Dougherty who subsequently had a report written on the group and decided against any form of recognition, concluding that the group was disruptive to parish life. Around the same time the group made front page news when a number of photographs emerged of William Kamm and key followers in an audience with Pope John Paul II in which they claimed the pontiff had blessed the group's activities. It was later established through the Apostolic Nunciature in Australia that the Pope denied this claim.

Moreover, the adoption of the name of Charbel Makhlouf, a Maronite saint, for the Order in 1986 was perhaps an attempt to seek alternative legitimation under the Maronite Eparchy, as well as to win sympathy within the devout and strongly Marian Maronite community. In this instance, both former Bishop Joseph Hitti and most recently Bishop Antonie-Charbel Tarabay have been forced to issue public statements noting that the Order of Saint Charbel has no association with the Maronite Church and to discourage their parishioners from any involvement with the group.

Furthermore, the Charbelites have sought to win sympathy by charitable donations for, or the establishment of prayer houses in, various dioceses in Asia, Africa, and India. Following such donations, the letters of thanks sent by local bishops have been utilized by the Charbelites as purported evidence for their legitimacy, the most notably example being an attempt in the Philippines to claim the approval of the late Cardinal Jaime Sin. This is a strategy which may have borrowed from the late Fr. Nicholas Gruner, whose Fatima ministry sought to take advantage of the intense Marian devotion found in some Indian and African diocese and Eastern Rite churches. However, it is also worth noting that support for Marian apparitional movements has often been strong in these regions—as the infamous example of the Movement for the Restoration of the Ten Commandments of God (MRTCG) in Uganda amply demonstrates[51]—and one should not discount the degree of active support which groups like the Charbelites have received in such countries from both priests and laity. Over his career Kamm has travelled extensively to promote his visions and has attracted significant crowds in a number of countries.

In terms of illicit episcopal legitimation the Charbelites current superior, Bishop Malcolm Broussard, a defrocked Texan priest, was consecrated by an alleged Thuc-line bishop in 2003, thus incurring a *latae sententiae* excommunication. Broussard has gone on to consecrate a number of the group's followers as bishops, and to ordain a number of others, including Kamm, to either the diaconate or the priesthood, thus resulting in their automatic excommunication. Finally, in terms of mystical legitimation, from nearly the outset of the movement, William Kamm has claimed that he is prophesied to be the next and final Pope (*Petrus Romanus*). However, to this date, Kamm has not sought to set himself up as Pope Peter I.

The Magnificat Meal Movement, sought to win support by making false claims regarding support within the Melkite Catholic Church, introducing a

---

51. However, bearing this in mind it is important to note that press claims of a link between the MRTCG and the Charbelites were overblown and any links between the two groups were likely ephemeral and linked to the loose-knit nature of much of the Marian apocalyptic subculture.

series of Melkite prayers into their liturgies and attending Melkite services. When this proved unsuccessful and Bishop Morris censured the group, the MMM made a *volte face* from their earlier support of Vatican II and sought to align itself with the Society of St. Pius X. This proved, given theological aspects of Debra's private revelations, to be a mistake, with SSPX rejecting the movement in even harsher terms than Bishop Morris, labeling its beliefs Protestant.

In terms of hereticization this is clearly shown in the development of aspects within the private revelations of both visionaries. Following the rejection of SSPX Debra's private revelations have become increasingly idiosyncratic and are now largely concerned with a variety of themes associated with what political scientist Michael Barkun have dubbed "improvisational millennialism."[52] While space does not permit detailed analysis here it suffices to say that the MMM has now wholly rejected any Catholic identity, labelled Pope Francis an antipope, and now appears more concerned with a combination of alternative medicine, New Age spirituality, and right-wing conspiracy theory.[53]

The Charbelites case is more complex. In the early 1990s the group began to augment its eschatological ideas to include a concept of a "New Holy Era" following a period of divine chastisement which would see most of the human race wiped out and during which Kamm would lead the remnant church from his papal castle in Germany. The subtleties of this millennialist belief system are quite complex, and are drawn from an amalgam of Catholic apocalyptic ideas dating back to at least the Middle Ages. However, in essence Kamm believed that his prophetic mission, aside from being Pope, was to marry seventy-two princesses and twelve queens, who would immaculately conceive children for him for the breeding of a new holy race during the New Holy Era. It suffices to say here that it was this belief which he used to justify his subsequent "mystical marriages" to a series of teenage female followers, a development which in turn led to his conviction and imprisonment for a series of child sex offences. Kamm claims, however, that this aspect of his mission has since been suspended by divine fiat and Bishop Broussard in particular has vigorously defended the group's belief in its theological orthodoxy and Catholic identity.

52. Barkun, *Culture of Conspiracy*, 15–38.

53. For a detailed discussion of this transformation see Kahl and Doherty, "Channelling."

Bibliography

Alban, Francis. *Fatima Priest: Priest, Prophecy and Peril. . . . The Vatican Key to Peace or Terror.* Pound Ridge, NY: Good Counsel, 1997.
Anson, Peter. *Bishops at Large.* London: Faber and Faber, 1964.
Apolito, Paolo. *The Internet and the Madonna: Religious Visionary Experience on the Web.* Chicago: University of Chicago Press, 2005.
Barkun, Michael. *A Culture of Conspiracy: Apocalyptic Visions in Contemporary America.* Berkeley: University of California Press, 2003.
Beit-Hallahmi, Benjamin, and Michael Argyle. *The Psychology of Religious Behaviour, Belief & Experience.* London: Routledge, 1997.
Bertone, Tarcisio. *The Last Secret of Fatima: The Revelation of One of the Most Controversial Events in Catholic History.* New York: Image, 2008.
Bjørgo, Tore. "Entry, Bridge-Burning, and Exit Options: What Happens to Young People Who Join Racist Groups—and Want to Leave?" In *Nation and Race: The Developing Euro-American Racist Subculture,* edited by Jeffrey Kaplan and Tore Bjørgo, 231–58. Boston: Northeastern University Press, 1998.
Blackbourn, David. *Marpingen: Apparitions of the Virgin Mary in Nineteenth-Century Germany.* New York: Knopf, 1994.
Bromley, David G. "Linking Social Structure and the Exit Process in Religious Organizations: Defectors, Whistle-Blowers, and Apostates." *JSSR* 37 (1998) 145–60.
Bromley, David G., and Rachel S. Bobbitt. "The Organizational Development of Marian Apparitional Movements." *Nova Religio* 14 (2011) 5–41.
Cornwell, John. *Powers of Darkness Powers of Light: Travels in Search of the Miraculous and the Demonic.* New York: Viking, 1991.
Cuneo, Michael. *The Smoke of Satan: Conservative and Traditionalist Dissent in Contemporary American Catholicism.* New York: Oxford University Press, 1997.
———. "The Vengeful Virgin: Case Studies in Contemporary American Catholic Apocalypticism." In *Millennium, Messiahs, and Mayhem: Contemporary Apocalyptic Movements,* edited by Thomas Robbins and Susan J. Palmer, 175–94. New York: Routledge, 1997.
Dobbyn, Paul. "The Cunning Psychology of a Cult." *The Catholic Leader* May 5, 2015. Online: http://catholicleader.com.au/people/the-cunning-psychology-of-a-cult.
Doherty, Bernard. "'Mourning the Death of Our Faith': The Little Pebble and the Marian Work of Atonement 1950–1984." *Journal of the Australian Catholic Historical Society* 36 (2015) 231–73.
Fastiggi, Robert. "The Rise and Fall of the Army of Mary (L'Armée de Marie)." *Marian Studies* 63 (2012) 124–55.
Festinger, Leon et al. *When Prophecy Fails: A Social and Psychological Study of a Modern Group that Predicted the Destruction of the World.* New York: Harper Torchbooks, 1957.
Garçon, Maurice. *Vintras: Hérésiarque et Prophète.* Paris: Librairie Critique Émile Nourry, 1928.
Garvey, Mark. *Searching for Mary: An Exploration of Marian Apparitions across the U.S.* New York: Plume, 1998.
Gearing, Amanda. "Vatican Sees through Visions." *The Courier-Mail,* February 17, 1999.

Greeley, Andrew. *The Catholic Revolution: New Wine, Old Wineskins, and the Second Vatican Council*. Berkeley: University of California Press, 2004.

Graves, Jim. "The Return to Rome, Five Years Later." *The Catholic World Report*, October 19, 2012. Online: http://www.catholicworldreport.com/Item/1677/the_return_to_rome_five_years_later.aspx.

Hartney, Christopher. "More Catholic Than the Pope: The 'Catholic' Career of William Kamm, and the Rise of the Order of St. Charbel." *Alternative Spirituality and Religion Review* 7 (forthcoming).

Introvigne, Massimo. "Modern Catholic Millennialism." In *The Oxford Handbook of Millennialism*, edited by Catherine Wessinger, 549–66. Oxford: Oxford University Press, 2011.

Introvigne, Massimo, and PierLuigi Zoccatelli. "Sedevacantism and Antipopes." In *Religions of the World: A Comprehensive Encyclopedia of Beliefs and Practices*, edited by Martin Baumann and J. Gordon Melton, 2562–66. San Francisco: ABC-CLIO, 2010.

Jelly, Frederick M. "Discerning the Miraculous: Norms for Judging Apparitions and Private Revelations." *Marian Studies* 44 (1993) 41–55.

Kahl, Janet, and Bernard Doherty. "Channelling Mary in the New Age: The Magnificat Meal Movement." *Alternative Spirituality and Religion Review* 7 (forthcoming).

Kane, Paula M. "Marian Devotionalism since 1940: Continuity or Casualty?" In *Habits of Devotion: Catholic Religious Practice in Twentieth-Century America*, edited by James M. O'Toole, 89–130. Ithaca, NY: Cornell University Press, 2004.

Kanter, Rosabeth Moss. "Commitment and the Internal Organization of Millennial Movements." *American Behavioural Scientist* 16 (1972) 219–43.

Kohle, Hubert, "Fundamentalistische Marienbewegungen." In *Handbuch der Marienkunde*, edited by Wolfgang Beinert and Henrich Petri, 60–106. Regensberg: Verlag Friedrich Pustet, 1997.

Krebs, Jill. "Transposing Devotion: Tradition and Innovation in Marian Apparitions." *Nova Religio* 19 (2016) 31–53.

Kselman, Thomas A. *Miracles and Prophecies in Nineteenth-Century France*. New Brunswick: Rutgers University Press, 1983.

Laurentin, René. *Mary's Place in the Church*. London: Burns & Oates, 1963.

Leatham, Miguel C. "'Shaking Out the Mat': Schism and Organizational Transformation at a Mexican Ark of the Virgin." *JSSR* 42 (2003) 175–87.

Lewis, James R. *Legitimating New Religions*. New Brunswick: Rutgers University Press, 2003.

Luebbers, Amy. "The Remnant Faithful: A Case Study of Contemporary Apocalyptic Catholicism." *Sociology of Religion* 62 (2001) 221–41.

Lundberg, Magnus. "Fighting the Modern with the Virgin Mary: The Palmarian Church." *Nova Religio* 17 (2013) 40–60.

Margry, Peter Jan. "Marian Interventions in the Wars of Ideology: The Elastic Politics of the Roman Catholic Church on Modern Apparitions." *History and Anthropology* 20 (2009) 243–63.

———. "Mary's Reincarnation and the Banality of Salvation: The Millennialist Cultus of the Lady of All Nations/Peoples." *Numen* 59 (2012) 486–508.

———. "Merchandising and Sanctity: The Invasive Cult of Padre Pio." *Journal of Modern Italian Studies* 7 (2002) 88–115.

Matter, E. Ann. "Apparitions of the Virgin Mary in the Late Twentieth Century: Apocalyptic, Representation, Politics." *Religion* 31 (2001) 125–53.

Maunder, Chris. *Our Lady of the Nations: Apparitions of Mary in 20th-Century Catholic Europe*. Oxford: Oxford University Press, 2016.

Mayer, Jean-François. "'There Will Follow a New Generation and a New Earth': From Apocalyptic Hopes to Destruction in the Movement for the Restoration of the Ten Commandments of God." In *Violence and New Religious Movements*, edited by James L. Lewis, 191–214. Oxford: Oxford University Press, 2011.

McGinn, Bernard. "Forms of Catholic Millenarianism: A Brief Overview." In *Millenarianism and Messianism in Early Modern European Culture. Vol. 2 Catholic Millenarianism from Savonarola to the Abbé Grégoire*, 1–13. Dordrecht: Kluwer, 2001.

O'Neill, Michael. *Exploring the Miraculous*. Huntington, IN: Our Sunday Visitor, 2015.

Orth, Maureen, "The World's Most Powerful Woman." *National Geographic* 228 (2015) 30–59.

Peterkiewicz, Jerzy. *The Third Adam*. London: Oxford University Press, 1975.

Ratzinger, Joseph, with Vittorio Messori. *The Ratzinger Report: An Exclusive Interview on the State of the Church*. Leominster, UK: Fowler Wright, 1985.

Séguy, Jean. "The Apocalyptic Theme in Religious Orders." In *Secularization, Rationalism, and Sectarianism: Essays in Honour of Bryan R. Wilson*, edited by Eileen Barker et al., 203–21. Oxford: Clarendon, 1993.

———. "Millénarismes et "orders adventistes": Grignion de Montfort et les Apôtres des Derniers Temps." *Archives de sciences sociales des religions* 53 (1982) 23–48.

Stark, Rodney. "A Theory of Revelations." *JSSR* 38 (1999) 287–308.

Thavis, John. *The Vatican Prophecies: Investigating Supernatural Signs, Apparitions, and Miracles in the Modern Age*. New York: Viking, 2015.

Tissier de Mallerais, Bernard. *Marcel Lefebvre: The Biography*. Kansas City: Angelus, 2004.

White, David Allen. *The Horn of the Unicorn: A Mosaic of the Life of Archbishop Marcel Lefebvre*. Kansas City: Angelus, 2006.

Wickham, Shelly, and Christopher Hartney. "Rockchopping with the Little Pebble: Mainstream, Fringe and Criminal." In *Through the Glass Darkly: Reflections on the Sacred*, edited by Frances Di Lauro, 288–301. Sydney: Sydney University Press, 2006.

Ziegler, Robert. *Satanism, Magic and Mysticism in Fine-de-siècle France*. London: Palgrave Macmillan, 2012.

Zimdars-Swartz, Sandra L. *Encountering Mary: From La Salette to Medjugorje*. Princeton: Princeton University Press, 1991.

6

How Is Mary a Seat of Wisdom?
A Spatial Exploration

—Renée Köhler-Ryan

> *In his encyclical* Fides et Ratio, *Pope John Paul II reflects on the nature of the human person as someone who seeks for truth specifically by loving wisdom. That is to say, to be human is to be a philosopher. At the very end of that document, the late pope presents Our Lady as the model for how to synthesize faith and reason in response to a love of the divine Wisdom. In doing so, he takes an epithet from the Litany of Loreto and calls her "Seat of Wisdom." This chapter explores some of the medieval iconography of Mary as Seat of Wisdom. By considering images of Mary contained by God (as* theotokos*) as well as being contained by him (held by Christ in an* aureola*), the discussion considers how Mary both bears the divine Wisdom and at the same time presents wisdom by becoming its model for all humans.*

Mary is our model of human wisdom because of her unique participation in the Wisdom of God. Considering her as the Seat of Wisdom, several artworks in the twelfth century enable us to contemplate her under this guise, such that a tantalizing paradox arises: Mary is identified both as a seat for wisdom (as *theotokos*), but also as quintessentially wise.

She may not be divine Wisdom—one cannot elevate Mary so high as to displace God; nonetheless, Mary is the greatest human model of wisdom. As such, she is an exemplar for the philosopher.

Artworks depicting Mary as the seat of wisdom dwell especially on the mystery of the Incarnation. Along with this, they subtly accentuate the generative power of responsiveness to God's law. Here John Paul II's reflections on the freedom of the human person, and the importance of philosophy's relationship to theology, are significantly helpful. He argues in *Veritatis Splendor* that humans are capable of recognizing and responding to *theonomy*.[1] That is, our free response to God's law lends our obedience its ability to be creative and beautiful. At no point in history is this more profoundly seen than at the moment of Mary's *fiat*, which is differently accentuated as she sits enthroned, presenting to us her divine Son, Wisdom itself, to be known, loved and worshiped.

John Paul II explains *theonomy*, or *participated theonomy*, saying that

> man's free obedience to God's law effectively implies that human reason and human will participate in God's wisdom and providence. By forbidding man to "eat of the tree of the knowledge of good and evil," God makes it clear that man does not originally possess such "knowledge" as something properly his own, but only participates in it by the light of natural reason and of Divine Revelation, which manifest to him the requirements and the promptings of eternal wisdom. Law must therefore be considered an expression of divine wisdom: by submitting to the law, freedom submits to the truth of creation. Consequently one must acknowledge in the freedom of the human person the image and the nearness of God.[2]

True human wisdom, then, participates in divine knowledge. Such knowledge is not produced by humans; instead, it is discovered. Such a discovery is a personal response to what the human person ultimately desires: the truth of reality itself which both creation and Revelation disclose as the lawful regularity of God's eternal wisdom. While John Paul II talks about submitting to the law and to truth, such submission in no way detracts from personal freedom. Instead, when one freely submits to the truth, by acknowledging it as such, one becomes freer. Such liberty transcends the antinomy that modern philosophy sets up between autonomy and heteronomy. Instead of one aspect of creation imposing upon another, with the human person as nexus point, he or she responds to a divine call already

---

1. John Paul II, *Veritatis Splendor*, no. 41.
2. Ibid.

written into creation. As will be argued below, Mary is the person most able to do this; and so she is the wisest created human person. Thus we can think of her as the place where true wisdom is to be found. This is the wisdom of a reasoning human person finding truth in the world. Mary is at the same time the person who points us to divine Wisdom, and makes possible the incarnate presence of that Wisdom in the world, in the Person of Christ.

Veneration of Mary as "Seat of Wisdom," taken together with this idea of *theonomy*, makes this better known. Images of Our Lady under this title flourished in the twelfth century in a variety of ways. This philosophical enquiry will take three instances of such images as the basis for reflection upon what it means for Mary, and then for us, to be wise. A throne in Santa Maria in Cosmedin calls attention to the idea that Mary is wise like her son. This similarity of mother and child will need to be clarified. The second depiction will be the "Enthroned Virgin and Child" from Auvergne in France, which is one of many examples of a *sedes sapientiae* to be found in Europe in the twelfth century. The third example, again from that century, is the arrangement of mosaics in the church of Santa Maria in Trastevere in Rome. There, Innocent II commissioned a mosaic of Christ and Mary enthroned in the apse calotte, together with mosaics of Isaiah and Jeremiah to each side on the apidisal arch. Later, in the thirteenth century, Pietro Cavallini composed six more mosaics in the same church. These depictions of scenes from the life of Mary subtly emphasize the spatial dimensions of Mary's life on earth and the Incarnation of her divine Son. The profound ambiguity of thinking of Mary as the seat of wisdom thus comes to light as a mystery to be pondered. She is both a throne and enthroned; just as she is the place where wisdom is to be found and at the same time the lover of Wisdom—the true philosopher.

Seated or a Seat: the Litany of Loreto in Image?

Before embarking in earnest on this spatial exploration, it is important to develop the relationship between the Litany of Loreto, where we first find the name "Seat of Wisdom," and the idea of Mary as enthroned. This link can be made when one considers that it is because of Mary's relationship to Wisdom that she is enthroned. In his encyclical *Fides et Ratio*, a resource for philosophers and theologians alike, Pope John Paul II reflects on the nature of the human person as someone who seeks for truth specifically by loving wisdom.[3] In what follows I will argue that such love, when directed toward what one believes by faith, is a type of obedience that frees. Thus, obedi-

---

3. See especially John Paul II, *Fides et Ratio*, nos. 1–6.

ence to what is true is the attitude of the one who is truly wise. The human person, through love of Eternal Wisdom, is called to become obedient to what is; to the contours of reality both as they are found through reason and as they are revealed. According to John Paul II, each one of us has the vocation of a philosopher, and the model for living out that vocation is Mary the Mother of God. In the last paragraph of the encyclical, the late pope writes:

> I turn in the end to the woman whom the prayer of the Church invokes as *Seat of Wisdom* and whose life itself is a true parable illuminating the reflection contained in these pages. For between the vocation of the Blessed Virgin and the vocation of true philosophy there is a deep harmony. Just as the Virgin was called to offer herself entirely as a human being and as woman that God's Word might take flesh and come among us, so too philosophy is called to offer its rational and critical resources that theology, as the understanding of faith, may be fruitful and creative.[4]

Here, Mary is explicitly linked to the figure of the philosopher.[5] Like Mary, the philosopher attends to what can be known, through reason, of the world. It is not too much to say that John Paul II thinks of Mary as the quintessential metaphysical realist. Her ability to recognize in the message of an angel the truth for which every person in salvation history longed was preconditioned by her ability to know what is real. The richness of Mary's ability to know the truth relies on its deeply personal nature: she responds out of freedom, to what is intrinsically fulfilling to the human person. That is, when Mary agrees to be the mother of God, she accepts that while her knowledge of what this means has some limitations, more will be revealed to her as she trusts in God—bringing her "rational and critical resources" to the decision to accept God's invitation, she becomes literally "fruitful and creative."

In this invocation of Mary at the end of an encyclical concerned with the fruitful dialogue between faith and reason, John Paul II refers directly to the Litany of Loreto in calling her the Seat of Wisdom. That name in the Litany is situated within a hierarchy of invocations that follow the logic of Mary's role in salvation history. First come prayers to Our Lord, to God, and then, after Our Lady has been invoked as Mary, Mother, and Virgin, she

---

4. Ibid., no. 108.

5. Prudence Allen, R.S.M. and David Vincent Meconi, S.J. have each contributed to a discussion of how Mary can be considered a philosopher. This chapter takes a different approach, by considering how Mary's representation in works of veneration and art can enable us to understand her as both wise and the lover of Wisdom. See Allen, "Mary and the Vocation of Philosophers," and Meconi, "*Philosophari in Maria.*"

is called "Mirror of Justice" and next: "Seat of wisdom, / Cause of our joy, / Spiritual vessel, / Vessel of honor, / Singular vessel of devotion, / Mystical rose, / Tower of David (cf. Song 4:4), / Tower of ivory (cf. Song 7:4), / House of gold, / Ark of the covenant, / Gate of heaven, / Morning star (cf. Song 6:10; Rev 2:28), / Health of the sick, / Refuge of sinners, / Comfort of the afflicted, / Help of Christians."[6] A final series invokes her as Queen, and then we return to Christ, as the Lamb of God, before a closing prayer. Images build on each other, so that Mary's enthronement relies first on the way that she imitates, or mirrors, God's justice, and finally makes way for her Queenship. The strangeness of some of the intervening images used here to invoke Mary is striking. How, exactly, is Mary a rose, tower, house, ark, gate, or star? Each of these metaphors needs some knowledge of an aspect of Mary not so readily available to reason. Mary's regal status, however, and her participation in divine justice—her wisdom—are more clearly discernible.

Considering the image of a seat enables one to see more clearly what is at stake here. The seat, or throne, evokes a sense of majesty, but also more specifically the personhood of the one who is enthroned. Wisdom is a personal attribute in a way that a rose, tower, house, ark, gate, or star is not. As noted, the pursuit of wisdom defines what it means to be a human person, and is exemplified by Mary. Thinking through Mary's wisdom in terms of a seat, or throne, gives a double key to appreciating her prototypical human vocation. For, to say that *someone* is a seat or a throne could mean several things. A seat is, of course, where someone sits. However, as *sedes*, it can also refer to a person with authority in the church. Then again, a seat is simply where something is—I go to the seat of wisdom to find it there. Furthermore, a throne connotes monarchical authority. When one approaches a throne, one comes to a person, usually in supplication and with humility. In each case, wisdom is situated. It can be found, in a person who occupies a throne and thereby has a certain status.

Further to this, Kingship and Queenship in the period of the twelfth century, when the kinds of images I will discuss momentarily were made, brought with them ideas of divinely ordained power and authority. To approach a royal person was to come before one who was divinely anointed and appointed. The power of a queen, then, is hers, but only because she has received it. Her influence in the world is derived from an authority that she has been given, and for which she takes responsibility. This already gives some insight into the Queenship of Mary. Mary's regal status follows the contours of a very Christian argument: that the humblest person becomes

---

6. "The Loreto Litanies," http://www.vatican.va/special/rosary/documents/litanie-lauretane_en.html.

the greatest; while the proud are cast down. As Mary declares in her *Magnificat*, the Lord has the high and the lowly exchange places when she becomes the Mother of God. The lowly handmaiden has exchanged places with princes on their thrones.[7] In Mary's case, she actively makes herself humble, by acknowledging that the Lord and his law are above her. This makes her *the* Christian Queen, the seat and lover of wisdom.

To highlight Mary's wisdom, depictions of her as the Seat of Wisdom in the twelfth century used imagery from the throne of Solomon—the king rewarded with the gift of wisdom for his humility and righteousness. Examples of the *sedes* that we will consider shortly have emblematic details of Solomon's throne. The throne in the twelfth-century renovation of Santa Maria in Cosmedin in Rome shares some of these and articulates this point. Standing in the apse, the throne makes direct reference both to Solomon and to Mary. 1 Kings 10:18–20 describes Solomon's throne as made of ivory and gold, round at the back and with six steps. Two lions stood beside the seat and twelve were on the steps. The throne in Santa Maria in Cosmedin has only three steps and two lions, but it features a decorated circle set into the wall behind, and its inscription reminds immediately of Solomon by referring to wisdom: "Alfanus made this for you, Mary, Virgin and Mother of the King, nurturing wisdom (*alma sophya*) of the supreme Father." Dale Kinney comments that "*Alma Sophia* alludes to another metaphorical throne, the seat of wisdom (*sedes sapientiae*), in which Wisdom was understood as Christ and his seat—the throne—as the womb of Mary."[8] At the same time he notes that the grammar of the inscription "equat[es] Wisdom with Mary rather than with Christ."[9] The main argument of Kinney's article does not lend itself to dwelling on the provocative nature of such an inversion. However, his focus on the intimate way in which Alfanus invokes Mary provides a certain insight into that slight deviation of attention from the Father to Mary, Mother of the King. Alfanus seems to feel much closer to Mary; he can make something for her, perhaps because he feels a kind of closeness to the regal mother. Alfanus is attracted specifically by Mary's wisdom, which truly nurtures the life of Christ, divine Wisdom, in the world.

This first example of an art work that reflects openly on Mary as the seat of wisdom brings to the fore a vital and fertile tension. Greater than Solomon, Mary is the Mother of God the Son, who is Divine Wisdom. Thought of only and simply as a kind of Solomon, sitting on a throne that identifies the one seated as being wise, would not so precisely coincide with the idea

---

7. Luke 1:52
8. Kinney, "Rome in the Twelfth Century," 209.
9. Ibid.

that Mary is herself the throne, or seat, wherefrom Christ reigns. Alfanus's throne and inscription muses on Mary both as throne and as wisdom. This presents a different problem, which is that Mary as wisdom would then seem to be vying with her Son. Such a representation might elevate Mary too high, with the attendant danger that she could usurp Christ's place in the imagination of the worshiper. In proceeding, one must attend to an important philosophical distinction: for Mary to be the seat of wisdom, participating in divine Wisdom, does not mean that she is divine. Only when we recognize how her participation operates, according to the *theonomy* identified by John Paul II, can the humanity of her wisdom be accentuated; and with this her importance as a model philosopher. Her exemplary function in this respect is grounded in her appreciation of the order of reality: Mary constantly shows us that everything comes from God—and that we can find this in every aspect of our lives.

The *Sedes* as Throne

In the Middle Ages, wooden depictions of Mary as seat of wisdom revealed her as a model for humanity and for philosophers in particular.[10] Unmistakably majestic, these images of Mary and her Son were usually encased in precious metals and jewels, and sometimes functioning also as reliquaries.[11] Nonetheless, these statues were so lifelike as to make palpable both the Incarnation of Christ and the humanity of his mother. Ilene Forsyth argues that *sedes* depictions were prevalent throughout Europe, and offered cult objects in which "divine presence seemed more fully concentrated. The mystery of the incarnation with its implicit fusion of God and Man was made manifestly visible."[12] Previously, depictions of Mary had not been carved into three dimensions. Now, this presentation of Our Lady in the round brought her closer, within the lived space of the onlooker, while at the same time giving the impression that, with their gleaming ornamentation, the onlooker experienced a glimpse into another world. Forsyth argues that the *sedes* was able to bridge what would be otherwise an "abyss between the visible and the invisible," while still maintaining the appropriate link between "image and prototype."[13] To see one of these objects of veneration

---

10. It should also be noted that Mary figures as a throne in the thought of the early Church. See Forsyth, *Thrones of Wisdom*, 24–30.
11. Forsyth, *Thrones of Wisdom*, chapter II.
12. Ibid, 23.
13. Ibid, 60.

was not exactly to see Mary; but in another very profound way it was to know her in the richness of her role as *theotokos* and as queen.

The relationship between image and prototype is significant both for knowing Mary, and for seeing how she, and we, can participate in God's eternal wisdom. The mystery of the Incarnation, on which medieval images of the *sedes* provide a powerful visual meditation, makes that participation even more evident. Effectively, the one who can navigate between the divine and its imitations in the world, along the paths of thought and worship, is wise. That is to say, to truly recognize the significance of Christ's time on earth, from the moment of the Annunciation through to his Ascension and as he now reigns from heaven, is to have insight into the great intimacy between God and humanity present in the Incarnation. The motherhood of Mary enables that closeness. Her presentation of the Son as sovereign places him immediately within his human family, as well as his divine context. Mary, the *theotokos*, bears Christ now not as a mother cradling an infant, but as a queen revealing her Son's majesty—and thereby her own regal status. A particular image is helpful here, to define more precisely the impact that the *sedes* can make on one's appreciation of Mary as the seat of wisdom.

The "Enthroned Virgin and Child," crafted in Auvergne France, sometime between 1150 and 1200, is typical of the *sedes* depictions in the period under consideration.[14] The statue is made from walnut wood and gesso, and we can still find on her traces of paint and linen. Mary sits on a simple throne, which in comparison with the seat she forms for her son is rather unremarkable. Her garments cascade from her shoulders, and her gown extends to the floor, with two slippered feet protruding from the skirt at the front. Her arms, parallel to the ground, are encased in sleeves that flow from the lengths of her arms and are parallel to the ground. Everything about Mary serves to enclose the Christ-king. Her face is rounded, and her demeanor serene. Most prominent are her hands, which are both oversized. The left encases Christ's knee, while the right encloses his waist. He, meanwhile, has the dimensions of a child but the features and comportment of an adult. Dressed in priestly vestments, also falling in elaborate folds, he holds up his right hand in benediction, while his left supports a book signifying his wisdom. Mary here is Christ's mother, his throne, and the one who presents him to us. She is also, though, one who shares in his majesty, through a relationship that, while unrepeatable in its essence, might still be considered a prototype for our mimetic action. The philosopher cannot actually be Mary, but can still imitate her relationship with Christ, not least by offering

---

14. For a picture of this *sedes*, see New York Metropolitan Art Museum. http://www.metmuseum.org/art/collection/search/471853.

material for reflection, so that our appreciation of the Incarnation might benefit. This though, can only be understood once we have considered Mary as the personification of Wisdom, and then as *theotokos*. These two ways of understanding her are united by the mystery of her Son's Incarnation.

In his encyclical *Redemptoris Mater*, John Paul II explains that Mary enters definitively into salvation history with her *fiat* at the Annunciation. At that point, Gabriel calls her "full of grace," thereby speaking in a "Gospel context, which mingles revelations and ancient promises."[15] This "enables us to understand that among all the 'spiritual blessings in Christ' this is a special 'blessing.' In the mystery of Christ she is present even 'before the creation of the world,' as the one whom the Father 'has chosen' as Mother of his Son in the Incarnation."[16] Mary is "united to Christ," eternally loved by Him, and "at the same time, she is and remains perfectly open to this 'gift from above.'"[17] Here John Paul II reflects not only on Mary's presence in the plan of creation and salvation from the beginning of time itself, but also on her free obedience. Each of these aspects refers to a space of fertility—to the generative Word of God in the beginning of the world, and to the life-giving work of the Spirit, by whom Mary conceives. Cosmos and womb here mirror each other, in each case because of a free and loving act. Such action calls for the quintessentially human response: both reasonable and free.

However, a hierarchy between such acts is immediately evident. God creates, while the creature participates in creation. Mary's unique place in salvation history has to do with her graced position in the divine plan; her power is in her free choice for what John Paul II speaks of as the *theonomos*. John Paul II maintains that Mary has a unique place in history, present even before there was a world for the Word to enter. In keeping with this, Louis Bouyer argues that Mary can indeed be found in the history of salvation, when we look at the Old Testament.[18] Understanding her role there, where she is identified as wisdom, brings us closer to knowing her as Seat of Wisdom, but also in her personal dimensions. Bouyer maintains that we actually know relatively little about Mary from the Gospels; in the New Testament she receives only a few (albeit significant) lines. When these are read in light of the Old Testament, however, the case for Our Lady as Wisdom becomes clearer. In the Old Testament, Bouyer says, "Divine Wisdom makes its appearance as a mysterious female personality in the immediate neighborhood

---

15. John Paul II, *Redemptoris Mater*, no. 8.
16. Ibid.
17. Ibid.
18. Bouyer, *Seat of Wisdom*. This is the argument of chapters 1 and 2 of the book.

of the Creator and associated with his work."[19] That the significance of the feminine character of wisdom should not be underestimated is supported by Joseph Ratzinger, who highlights that:

> In both Hebrew and Greek, "wisdom" is a feminine noun, and this is no empty grammatical phenomenon in antiquity's vivid awareness of language. "Sophia," a feminine noun, stands on that side of reality which is represented by the woman, by what is purely and simply feminine. It signifies the answer which emerges from the divine call of creation and election. It expresses precisely this: that there is a pure answer and that God's love finds its irrevocable dwelling place within it.[20]

That pure answer is best understood in terms of Mary's obedience, or free submission, which is a fulfillment of her human nature. Strikingly, this obedience is something that she teaches to her divine Son. They share an obedience to the Father, and it is precisely in this attitude that they also participate in Wisdom. The person who becomes like Mary practices the philosophical act that we have seen John Paul II refers to in *Veritatis Splendor* as a *participated theonomy*.[21] In other words, in obeying the divine law, one participates in it. One truly imitates God, mirroring the ordered way in which he has created the world. Such obedience does not deny anything of the freedom and powers of self-determination of the human person.[22] Instead, it opens up a space of freedom to inquire, to know, and to love. Bouyer speaks of Wisdom as

> essentially, architectonic; it is the art whereby man comes to such a knowledge of the world, and so to adapt himself to it by an experience, manifold but unified on a superior plane, that he is enabled to mould history to his own purposes, and, ultimately, to give the world itself its final form.[23]

In other words, Wisdom involves an obedience to what exists, as given, which then empowers. Freedom and creativity, including human fertility in all its dimensions, presupposes that obedience which first and foremost freely acknowledges what is real.

19. Ibid, 2.
20. Ratzinger, *Daughter of Zion*, 26.
21. John Paul II, *Veritatis Splendor*, no. 41
22. Such self-determination is central to John Paul II's understanding of the human person and personal freedom. See Wojtyla, "The Personal Structure of Self-Determination" and Wilk, "The Human Person and Freedom."
23. Bouyer, *Seat of Wisdom*, 191.

The relationship between wisdom and obedience is emphasized by Fulton Sheen, who remarks in *The World's First Love: Mary, Mother of God*, that Christ's subjection, as a boy and young man, to his Mother, "is associated with growth in wisdom and favor with God. It is in His human nature that our Blessed Lord gives us a perfect example of obedience."[24] More importantly for our purposes, Sheen adds that this "leads us to a forgotten aspect of obedience to law, namely, that intelligence is related to obedience. . . . The more we obey the inherent laws of anything, the more that thing reveals to us."[25] Here, then, says Sheen, "Two great miracles of humility and exaltation are involved—God obeying a woman, and a woman obeying her God. The very fact that He makes Himself subject endows her with power."[26] We are, in other words, dealing with two persons who are wise, specifically by being obedient. Their wisdom enables them to be obedient, and their obedience allows them to grow in wisdom. One could include Joseph in this family of philosophers—for Joseph is also known for his obedience to wisdom; he too is wise. Love of wisdom (which the term "philosophy" refers to directly) characterizes the holy family, and sustains their regal elevation.

The preconditions of that elevation are again mysterious. Louis Bouyer enables one to make this point, before considering Mary's Wisdom through images of her as throne and enthroned. Bouyer says that "the divine word borrows [the images of Wisdom literature] from the experience of man, but transfigures it by its own intervention."[27] Only when the images are gathered together do they give a clear outline of this female personification, which simultaneously elaborates some of the most fundamental aspects of Mary. Bouyer explores images taken from Revelation. What though, might the philosopher find through examining spatial images familiar to us from simply living in the created order? How can we find, through reason and imagination, the contours along which creation is already *theonomous*? Several ways of thinking about space are particularly important here. Firstly, one can consider creation as a space: the divinely fashioned cosmos operates according to an eternal law; and that cosmos facilitates the freedom of the human person to dwell with creation and to make his or her way in the world.[28] Secondly, that same cosmos can be thought of as a porous contain-

24. Sheen, *The World's First Love*, 107.
25. Ibid.
26. Ibid., 109.
27. Bouyer, *Seat of Wisdom*, 2.
28. I am aware of contemporary debates which give predominance to place over space. I am speaking of space more as it would be aligned with Augustine's understanding of cosmic space. See Casey, *The Fate of Place* and Fiedrowicz, "General Introduction." See also Ryan, "An Archaeological Ethics."

er, in the way that Augustine speaks of the world as capable of containing, but not of containing God.[29] Thirdly, one can think of the interior space of the human person. All of these ways of contemplating space are magnified when one turns to Mary as *theotokos* and as a philosopher.

Effectively, Mary's royalty, which is symbolized by her enthronement, relies upon these spatial considerations. Within the world, she is obedient to its laws and to God who transcends it; and due to this she responds freely to truth and becomes the queen of heaven and earth. Mary's royalty is only possible because first she is an obedient handmaid, and only then a mother who gives birth to and receives obedience from her son. This pattern of divine grace given, received, and transforming, finds its correlate in events of salvation history. The world is created with and through Christ, and within that world Christ is born: Mary is in the space of Christ. Then, Mary agrees to be the Mother of God. She freely consents and at that moment conceives by the Holy Spirit: Christ is within the space of Mary. Throughout their earthly relationship, Mother and Son continue to cooperate, with Mary's authority coming from her submission to the divine will. In the fullness of time, the earthly relationship between Mother and Son begins, but its deeply personal origins are to be found in the beginning of creation. So it is that the female personification of wisdom in the Old Testament is fulfilled in the New. Later, Christ ascends and Mary is assumed into heaven. Crowned queen of heaven, Our Lady is finally enthroned, giving a heavenly way to think of her as Seat of Wisdom. Another image, or set of images, advances thinking of Mary in this way. Strikingly, the interior space of Mary is where Christ places his throne.

Santa Maria in Trastevere: A Narrative of Enthronement

From a philosophical perspective, it is becoming more and more apparent that one of the most intriguing aspects of Christ's Incarnation can be described in spatial terms. Somehow, the womb and then the arms and lap of a young woman are able to contain the uncontainable; she becomes the Godbearer and thereby reveals something about the Godhead, suddenly and unexpectedly, and all because of her willingness to listen and then assent to the question contained in the message of an angel. At that moment, God becomes flesh, sharing in the life and taking on the nourishment, physical and then spiritual too, of his mother. The shape of God's incarnate presence in Mary's life now become more pronounced. In the church of Santa Maria in Trastevere in Rome, a scene with Christ and Mary enthroned together is

---

29. Augustine, *Confessions*, Book I, 2.

later articulated by mosaics that show an interplay between Son and mother in the narrative of her life. Considering these images together, in light of the way that containment can be known, offers a final way to understand Our Lady as Seat of Wisdom, due to her lived *participated theonomy*.

Special use of the mandorla shape in the series of scenes from Mary's life accentuates what we have already thought about regarding space. The mandorla shape, used in medieval depictions of Christ and of Mary, stresses the mystery of how God could be spatially contained. Mandorla comes from the word for "almond" in Italian, and its use stresses how the persons of Our Lord and Our Lady are in this world, and thereby offer a glimpse of the eternal world beyond. The shape is made by overlapping two circles, thus symbolizing the merging of two aspects of reality—the space of the world and the eternal ream of the Godhead. The name mandorla, rather than aureole (which can also simply mean halo) is more helpful here because it retains a reference to the almond, which I would like to argue gives us another key to understanding how divine Wisdom enters and lives in the world. References in the Old Testament within the book of Jeremiah and the book of Numbers make apparent the significance of the almond. A rod of almond signifies both being watchful and alert—an almond looks like nothing more than a stick, and then suddenly bursts into bloom, eventually yielding an almond fruit. Jeremiah sees a vision of an almond rod immediately after God has put his words into the prophet's mouth (cf. Jer 1:11). In the book of Numbers, Aaron's staff bursts into flower and then immediately bears ripened almonds. This miracle makes his staff a warning to any who would rebel against Yahweh (cf. Num 17). The place from which the almond comes follows laws that are hidden, but nourishing—like the workings of Yahweh's mind, they must be attended to by those who wish to be truly wise. Iconography of Saint Joseph has in past times included him holding an almond staff, signifying his own participating in kingship, but also his *theonomy*. A powerful analogy seems to be here at work: as the mandorla signifies where God and human person meet, so does *theonomy* indicate a free response to that interaction. Each member of the Holy Family has been represented in some way with the mandorla. One instance of this is present in the series of mosaics in Santa Maria in Trastevere; but all that the mandorla signifies—the meeting of heaven and earth, and the human ability to be *theonomous*, resounds in each of the scenes depicted.

Arguably, through the sparse employment of the mandorla, Pietro Cavallini's series of mosaics in the Church of Santa Maria in Trastevere illustrates that Christ and Mary exchange roles in containing and being contained. This mutual substitution, itself a kind of submission, mirrors the way that during their earthly lives they were in turn obedient and wise.

Thus, Christ and Mary manifest what is otherwise hidden: they reveal to us the Wisdom inherent in every aspect of the world and the self. Through each of them, Wisdom is incarnate. The mosaic series runs under an apse mosaic, the focal point of which is a throne, on which Christ and Mary are both seated. The throne depiction comes from 1140–43, while Cavallini's mosaics are from between 1296 and 1300. In other words, the throne was there first and Cavallini's sequence offers a way to interpret Christ and his Mother's sharing of the Seat of Wisdom.[30] Keeping in mind the notion of *theonomy*, with its attendant ideas of obedience and freedom, bolsters this point. The central figures in the enthronement scene will first be discussed, and then Cavallini's sequence.

Mary and Christ are unmistakably majestic as they share a throne. They are flanked by saints and the patron of the church, Pope Innocent II. Three of these figures (including Innocent II) stand on the side of Mary and four next to Christ. This arrangement places Christ in the center, in the main axis and directly above the paschal lamb in the center of a row of sheep below. The sheep surrounding the paschal lamb are twelve in number, replacing the lions of the throne of Solomon. In the *sedes* depictions, Mary embraces and presents her Son. This time, Christ has his arm around Mary and she points toward him. Each holds a text. As Ernst Kitzinger describes:

> The texts inscribed on the book held by Christ and on the scroll held by the Virgin are both taken from [the liturgy of the Feast of the Assumption of the Virgin]. Christ's text reads: "Veni electa mea et ponam in te thronum meum." . . . The text held by the Virgin reads: "Leva eius sub capite meo et dex(t)era illius amplesabit(ur) me."[31]

The texts are at the same time paraphrases from the Song of Songs. In the first, most significantly, Christ declares, "in you I will place my throne;" while the second refers to Song of Songs 2:6 and 8:3, where the bride says that her head rests on her beloved's left arm, while his right arm embraces her. In this depiction, Mary is crowned, enthroned, and apparently acknowledged as both mother and bride. Much more could be said about this glorious depiction, but the most salient point rests on the association between the image and the mystery of the Assumption.[32]

---

30. Pictures of the mosaics can be found here: Web Gallery of Art, http://www.wga.hu/html_m/zgothic/mosaics/2trastev/index.html.

31. Kitzinger, "A Virgin's Face," 8.

32. The history of the relationship between the church of Santa Maria in Trastevere and the feast of the Assumption is developed in detail in Kitzinger. He relates how in the middle ages, on the feast of the Assumption, a procession would carry "the icon of

The ancient Feast of the Assumption focuses very much on the embodied Mary, whose womb is the place where Christ first came to dwell in the world. That contained space, sanctified by his presence, is now visibly glorified in the depiction of Mary as enthroned, body and soul, in heaven at the right hand of her Son. Kitzinger speaks at length about the origins of the *synthronos* motif, where Mary shares Christ's throne. "[R]eckless tampering with venerable sources," he argues, have had the bridegroom placing his bride on the throne, rather than taking in the stranger idea that he is placing his throne *in* her.[33] Kitzinger hypothesizes that perhaps such a coronation scene arises from listening to a bowdlerized, more logical version of the verse in question, whereby *te* and *in* are inverted, and Mary is "placed on Christ's throne."[34] Arguably though, remaining true to the text unlocks the meaning of this scene. Mary is the seat of wisdom in keeping with our discussion of her in relation to Wisdom itself. Namely, as the mother of Christ she is the space where he takes up his kingship over the cosmos. On the basis of this she can be enthroned. And, as herself enthroned she is the one to whom we go in order to see what human wisdom looks like; in her we find how a creature can live according to the laws that God has written into creation and our history of salvation.

The scenes composed by Cavallini reiterate some of these spatial themes, in particular by emphasizing the embodied reality of Mary and of Christ through the use of shapes that enclose the respective bodies of mother and Son. Six scenes extend in a row beneath the enthronement mosaic. They are, in turn: the birth of the Virgin; the Annunciation; the Nativity; the Adoration of the Magi; the Presentation; and the death of the Virgin. In the first four scenes, Mary is either seated in an enthroned position, or else reclining. She sits on the lap of a nurse after her birth—looking very much like her infant son in other depictions; on a simple throne that references the throne of Solomon when hailed by the angel Gabriel; she reclines on a mandorla-shaped bed with her Son happily in a very angular manger beside her after his birth; enthroned as the Magi approach, she presents her Son as the kings bow before the royal pair. At the presentation this changes. Everyone stands except for Christ who, this time enthroned in the arms of Simeon, points downward, questioningly, toward the altar. His mother, separated from him by the canopied altar, indicates in the direction both of her Son and the sign of his future sacrifice. Here containment is both referenced and interrupted. Mother and Son are separated by the altar, but that same altar will bring

---

Christ of the Lateran" to visit Santa Maria in Trastevere. Ibid, 16.

33. Ibid, 11.
34. Ibid.

them together. Through Christ's passion and resurrection, his mother, the new Eve, can join him in heaven. Mary's distinctively active role in her Son's education in obedience on earth, and her presence with him on the cross, are underlined with her changed posture.

The final scene brings us back to containment and the mystery of the Assumption, this time with a portrayal of the Dormition that at the same time brings heaven and earth together. Here, in short, we find a striking use of the mandorla, with Christ holding Mary as though she were now the baby. Even seeming to wear swaddling clothes, his arms are now her throne; and he presents her to us. In this inversion of depictions of mother and child, now, in the arms of Christ who brings together heaven and earth through the Incarnation, rests the Virgin Mother. This end point of her earthly life serves as a commentary on the main mosaic above, as well as the Old Testament, the presence of which is remembered in the figures of Isaiah and Jeremiah, who prophesy the Virgin birth and comment on Christ's redemptive action on either side of the entire series of mosaic. Reaching back further than these prophets, the imagery in the enthronement scene reminds us of the Garden of Eden, as grass, flowers, birds, trees surround Mary and her Son.

At that point, Eve and Adam refused to be wise, by thinking that obedience would disempower them, denying them real freedom. This, finally, is where Mary the true philosopher becomes our model. In accepting God's invitation, and remaining obedient to his will, she became truly free. This, the most astonishing moment of her life, is the action that every philosopher might hope to emulate. Mary was at that moment philosophical, for here love of wisdom is at its keenest point. Mary as seat of wisdom is not only the place where divine Wisdom resides. Her obedience and her love are never wholly passive. She offers to philosophers a model for how to make wisdom real—incarnate—in the world. We can love wisdom in its most personal form, because Mary first responded and grew wiser in the company of her Son. In her he has set his throne; in her heaven and earth meet.

Conclusion: Mary and theonomy

These reflections on various twelfth century depictions of Mary as the Seat of Wisdom bring us closer to understanding the mystery of the relationship between Mary and her Son. In each example, it is the physical presentation, each of the other, that signifies how Mary is both the place where divine Wisdom comes into the world, and the person to whom we can look for guidance in becoming wise. The throne in Santa Maria in Cosmedin indicates some of the difficulties of thinking through the implications of Our Lady as Seat of Wisdom. The *sedes* emphasizes some of these points, but reminds emphatically that Mary's role as *theotokos* means that she is both enthroned and throne. The mosaics in Santa Maria in Trastevere offer various ways of thinking about Mary again as the Seat of Wisdom. They draw attention to her own physicality, fittingly as this depiction was the focus of a pilgrimage to celebrate the feast of the Assumption.[35] They also illuminate one of the most intriguing aspects of the relationship between Mother and Son. Occasionally these two seem to change places. At one moment Mary submits, but because of that she rules. While Christ rules, he also submits to his parents. Nonetheless, Mary's wisdom is in her *participated theonomy*. The one who writes the laws, her Son, prepared a space for her from the beginning of time. Into that space he then entered, because she freely assented to God's law. Thinking of Our Lady through depictions of her as the Seat of Wisdom enables one to understand these mysteries more deeply.

Bibliography

Allen, Prudence. "Mary and the Vocation of Philosophers." *New Blackfriars* 90 (1025) (2009) 50–71.

Augustine. *The Confessions*. Translated by Maria Boulding, O.S.B. *The Works of Saint Augustine: A Translation for the 21st Century*. Hyde Park, NY: New City, 1997.

Bagley, C. H. "Litany of Loreto." In *New Catholic Encyclopedia*, Volume 8, edited by Erin Bealmear, 602–3. Detroit: Gale, 2003.

Borsook, Eve. "Rhetoric or Reality: Mosaics as Expressions of a Metaphysical Idea." In *Mitteilungen des Kunsthistorischen Institutes in Florenz* 44 (2000) 2–18.

Bouyer, Louis. *The Seat of Wisdom: An Essay on the Place of the Virgin Mary in Christian Theology*. Translated by Fr. A.V. Littledale. New York: Pantheon, 1962.

Casey, Edward S. *The Fate of Place: A Philosophical History*. Los Angeles: University of California, 1997.

Coor-Achenbach, Gertrude. "The Earliest Italian Representation of the Coronation of the Virgin." *The Burlington Magazine* 99.655 (1957) 328–32.

Fiedrowicz, Michael. "General Introduction." In *On Genesis. The Works of Saint Augustine: A Translation for the 21st Century*, 13–22. Hyde Park, NY: New City, 2002.

Forsyth, Ilene H. *The Thrones of Wisdom: Wood Sculptures of the Madonna in Romanesque France*. Princeton: Princeton University Press, 1972.

Gardner, Julian. "Pope Nicholas IV and the Decoration of Santa Maria Maggiore." *Zeitschrift für Kunstgeschichte* 36 (1973) 1–50.

Hetherington, Paul. "The Mosaics of Pietro Cavallini in Santa Maria in Trastevere." *Journal of the Warburg and Courtauld Institutes* 33 (1970) 84–106.

John Paul II. *Fides et Ratio*. Encyclical Letter. Vatican Website. September 14, 1998.

———. *Redemptoris Mater*. Encyclical Letter. Vatican Website. March 26, 1987.

---

35. See the reference to Numbers 17 above.

———. *Veritatis Splendor*. Encyclical Letter. Vatican Website. August 6, 1993.
Kinney, Dale. "Rome in the Twelfth Century: Urbs Fracta and Renovatio." *Gesta* 45.2 (2006) 199–220.
Kitzinger, Ernst. "A Virgin's Face: Antiquarianism in Twelfth-Century Art." *The Art Bulletin* 62.1 (1980) 6–19.
Koterski, Joseph W., S.J. "*Fides et Ratio* and Biblical Wisdom Literature." In *The Two Wings of Catholic Thought: Essays on* Fides et Ratio, edited by David Ruel Foster and Joseph W. Koterski, S.J., 129–63. Washington DC: Catholic University of America Press, 2003.
"The Loreto Litanies." Online: http://www.vatican.va/special/rosary/documents/litanie-lauretane_en.html.
Meconi, David Vincent, S.J. "*Philosophari in Maria: Fides et ratio* and Mary as the Model of Created Wisdom." In *The Two Wings of Catholic Thought: Essays on* Fides et Ratio, edited by David Ruel Foster and Joseph W. Koterski, S.J., 69–90. Washington DC: Catholic University or America Press, 2003.
Meyendorff, John. "Wisdom-Sophia: Contrasting Approaches to a Complex Theme." *Dumbarton Oaks Papers* 41. *Studies on Art and Archeology in Honor of Ernst Kitzinger on His Seventy-Fifth Birthday* (1987) 391–401.
Ratzinger, Joseph. *Daughter Zion: Meditations on the Church's Marian Belief*. Translated by John. M. McDermott, S.J. San Francisco: Ignatius, 1983.
Rubin, Miri. *Mother of God: A History of the Virgin Mary*. London: Penguin, 2010.
Ryan, Renée. "An Archaeological Ethics: Augustine, Desmond, and Digging Back to the Agapeic Origin." In *Between System and Poetics: Themes in the Work of William Desmond*, edited by Thomas Kelly, 163–81. Aldershot, UK: Ashgate, 2006.
Sheen, Fulton J. *The World's First Love: Mary, Mother of God*. 2nd ed. San Francisco: Ignatius, 2010.
Sweeney, Kathleen Curran. "The Perfection of Women as Maternal and the Anthropology of Karol Wojtyla." *Logos: A Journal of Catholic Thought and Culture* 9 (2006) 129–53.
Wilk, Rafal K. "Human Person and Freedom According to Karol Wojtyla." *International Philosophical Quarterly* 47.3 (2007) 265–78.
Wojtyla, Karol. "The Personal Structure of Self-Determination." In *Person and Community: Selected Essays*. Translated by Theresa Sandok. 187–96. New York: Lang, 1993.

7

Revisiting the Marian Dimension of Ignatian Spirituality

—Robin Koning SJ

In Ignatius' own spiritual experience, Our Lady has a prominent place, one which carries over into the dual role she plays in the Spiritual Exercises he composed. Narratively, Mary features in a number of the scenes proposed for contemplation; functionally, Ignatius invites us to engage with her as an agent in various prayer exercises. The most significant of these functional roles appears in the Triple Colloquy, a prayer form in which Mary is a key intercessor. Some contemporary presentations of the Exercises downplay this functional role of Mary, especially when they are offered to people from Christian traditions not comfortable with praying to Mary. Directors may suggest removing Mary from the Triple Colloquy and replacing her with the Holy Spirit. This suggestion is justified as authentically Ignatian and even what Ignatius would have hoped for had the Church in his age not been so suspicious of appeals to the Spirit. These claims, though, are ungrounded, as a proper understanding of the Triple Colloquy and of Ignatius' own practice testify. Moreover, a Triple Colloquy involving the Spirit in place of Mary as intercessor with Christ presents a subordinationist view of the Trinity.

In a paper originally presented in 1988, the then Jesuit Superior General, Fr Peter-Hans Kolvenbach, wrote of Mary as being "at the very heart of the *Spiritual Exercises*." At the same time, he lamented the fact that "not seldom does one come across excellent commentaries on the *Exercises* today with no reference whatever to Our Lady, or at best a quick mention in passing."[1] Almost thirty years later, Kolvenbach's evaluation remains largely true. Indeed, as Ignatian spirituality has become more and more available to and adapted for non-Catholic audiences, the understandable concern for Protestant sensibilities has led to a further downplaying of Mary's significant place in that spirituality, so that it is seen as virtually dispensable except insofar as she may appear in some of the Gospel scenes which one might contemplate in the Exercises.

In this chapter I will examine various aspects of Our Lady's role in Ignatian spirituality. My starting point is necessarily her place in the life of Ignatius himself, as revealed especially in his *Autobiography*. From there, I move to the ways in which Ignatius presents Mary to others in his Spiritual Exercises. Finally, I will engage with the current practice whereby Mary's functional role as an agent within the dynamic of the Exercises, particularly as mediator in the Triple Colloquy, is sidelined in some presentations of the Exercises, especially for non-Catholics. Here I will point to some issues raised by this practice—both those to do with a proper understanding of what Ignatius is up to in this significant element in the Exercises, and those to do with trinitarian theology.

Ignatius' Own Marian Experiences

Ignatius was born, it is believed, in 1491. His *Autobiography* takes up his story from the time just before his conversion experience, in 1521, up to the early 1540s, soon after the Society of Jesus was founded. What we know of his childhood and youth come from other sources. He grew up as the youngest of thirteen children in a Basque noble family. They were a people of strong, traditional faith and piety, their identity firmly grounded in their being proudly Catholic with an undoubting fidelity. Ignatius was brought up in a religious milieu, and would often pray before the image of the Annunciation in the chapel of the family castle in Loyola.[2] His schooling, too, was in a religious milieu.[3] Like some forms of pious Catholicism in any

---

1. Kolvenbach, *Road from La Storta*, 33.
2. Rahner, *Spirituality*, 18.
3. Ibid., 21.

generation, this did not mean that Ignatius' moral life kept step with his ingrained sense of devotion. He himself admits as much in his autobiography in which, speaking of himself in the third person, he says: "Until the age of twenty-six he was a man given up to the vanities of the world, and his chief delight used to be in the exercise of arms, with a great and vain desire to gain honour."[4] This is filled out by one of his early companions who noted: "Like all the young men who live at court and dream of military exploits, he was rather free in affairs of the heart, in games of chance and in matters of honor."[5] At the same time, Ignatius can speak about his "regular devotion to St. Peter."[6] His cousin confirms this picture of the co-existence of religious inclinations and a worldly spirit: "Just before engaging in a duel, he used to compose verses in honor of our Lady."[7]

As is well known, the occasion of Ignatius' conversion to a more personal encounter with Christ and a radical commitment to following his way was a serious injury sustained in the battle of Pamplona in 1521, during which his right leg was smashed by a cannon ball. During his long convalescence, he pined for reading material suited to his taste for tales of chivalry and knightly adventure. But none of these was at hand. Instead, he was offered Spanish translations of a life of Christ by Ludolph of Saxony and a collection of saints' lives known as the *Golden Legend (Flos Sanctorum)* compiled by the thirteenth-century Dominican Archbishop of Genoa, Jacopo of Varazze. This reading matter awakened Ignatius' desire to do even greater things for Christ than the saints had done.[8]

During this time of convalescence, Ignatius had the first of numerous mystical experiences involving the Blessed Virgin. He recounts it in these words:

> [B]eing awake one night, he saw clearly a likeness of Our Lady with the Holy Child Jesus, at the sight of which, for an appreciable time, he received a very extraordinary consolation. He was left so sickened at his whole past life and especially at matters of the flesh, that it seemed to him that there had been removed from his soul all the likenesses that he had previously had painted in it. Thus, from that hour until August 1553, when

---

4. Ignatius, *Autobiography*, no. 1. References to the Autobiography of St. Ignatius use the standardized paragraph numbering. The translation used is that of Munitiz and Endean found in Saint Ignatius, *Personal Writings*, 13–64.
5. Polanco, quoted in Meissner, *Ignatius of Loyola*, 22.
6. Ignatius, *Autobiography*, no. 3.
7. Rahner. *Spirituality*, 21.
8. Ignatius, *Autobiography*, nos. 1–2, 5.

this is being written, he never again had even the slightest complicity in matters of the flesh.⁹

During that same period of convalescence, Ignatius began to keep a book in which he would write things that particularly struck him in whatever he was reading. He would write the words of Christ in red ink and those of Our Lady in blue.¹⁰ Noting such things was part of the process which would culminate in the book of the *Spiritual Exercises*.

When Ignatius was well enough, he set out on his new way of life as a pilgrim with the Benedictine monastery of Montserrat as his immediate goal. On the way, his devotion to Our Lady was manifest in three events. He kept an all-night vigil at the shrine of Our Lady of Aránzazu,¹¹ which some consider to be the occasion on which he made the vow of perpetual chastity to Our Lady, a vow he mentioned later in life, saying that he had made it on the journey to Montserrat.¹² He would admit at that point that making a vow to Mary was theologically incorrect—that he should have made it to God.¹³ He was still very much a student in the ways of God. On the journey Ignatius also distributed some of his last monies for the repair and adornment of a damaged image of Our Lady at Navarette.¹⁴

The third event, elaborated at greater length, reveals both Ignatius' instinctive devotion to Our Lady and how young he still was in the ways of discernment. Riding towards Montserrat on his donkey, he traveled part of the way alongside a Moor. Their conversation at one point turned to Our Lady. The Moor said he had no problem accepting the virginal conception of Jesus but that he could not believe that Mary remained a virgin in giving birth to Jesus. Though Ignatius tried to argue the point, the Moor was still unconvinced by the time he travelled on ahead of Ignatius. After they parted company, Ignatius began to feel disturbed, wondering if he had properly exercised his duty of defending Our Lady's honor. The idea came to him that he should find the Moor and stab him, but he was not sure if this was the right thing to do, and remained conflicted for some time. In the end, having reached no resolution, he decided to allow his donkey to make the decision. As he approached a fork in the road, he gave the animal a loose rein. If it followed the path the Moor had taken, then he would look for him and stab

---

9. Ibid., no. 10.
10. Ibid., no. 11.
11. Ibid., no. 13.
12. Dalmases, *Ignatius of Loyola*, 49.
13. Coleman, *Walking with Inigo*, 29–30.
14. Ignatius, *Autobiography*, no. 13.

him; if not, he would leave him be. Thankfully, the mule chose wisely and Ignatius continued his pilgrimage.[15]

Having reached Montserrat, Ignatius spent three days preparing for and then making a general confession of his whole life. Having made his confession, he spent a night in vigil before the Black Madonna, kneeling or standing the whole time, and leaving his sword and dagger before Our Lady while he took up a pilgrim's staff. After this, he made his way to a small town called Manresa where he lodged in an almshouse.[16]

During this time at Manresa, Ignatius had a clear sense that God was "dealing with him in the same way as a schoolteacher deals with a child."[17] In particular, he had a number of mystical experiences which gave him some understanding of various truths of the faith—concerning the Trinity, creation and the Eucharist.[18] He also speaks of an inner vision of the humanity of Christ, appearing to him "like a white body" in which "he did not see any distinction of limbs." Then he goes on to say: "Our Lady too he has seen in a similar form, without distinguishing the parts."[19] All of these visions, including that of Our Lady, were strongly confirming of the faith for Ignatius, so much so that he commented: "if there weren't Scripture to teach us these matters of the faith, he would be resolved to die for them solely on the basis of what he has seen."[20] While Ignatius does not go into the details of these visions or their frequency, at the time of his canonization the postulator of his cause noted that Our Lady appeared to Ignatius more than thirty times during those eight months that he spent at Manresa.[21]

A major moment in the eventual movement towards the foundation of the Society of Jesus was the commitment Ignatius and the various companions he had gathered around him at the University of Paris made in 1534. Few details are given by Ignatius in the *Autobiography*,[22] but others of his companions fill out the picture. They had decided to commit themselves to vows of poverty and chastity, to go together to Jerusalem and, if they could not remain there, to travel to Rome and offer themselves to the Pope

---

15. Ibid., nos. 15–16.
16. Ibid., nos. 17–18.
17. Ibid., no. 27.
18. Ibid., nos. 28–29. The vision of the Trinity Ignatius describes here occurs while he was praying the office of Our Lady.
19. Ibid., no. 29.
20. Ibid., no. 29.
21. Hardon, *All My Liberty*, 113–14.
22. Ignatius, *Autobiography*, no. 85.

to send them wherever he felt they were needed.[23] For our purposes, what is of interest is that they chose to make these commitments on the Feast of the Assumption, and to take Our Lady as their "helper and protector and special intercessor before her Son Jesus Christ our Lord."[24] This was highlighted by the fact that, while the chapel on Montmartre in which they made their vows was dedicated to St. Denis, the church housing the chapel was called St. Mary.[25]

Soon after this, Ignatius returned to Spain for a period, his doctors having advised him that his native air might help with some medical problems he was facing. While in his home province, he embarked on a program of moral reform (challenging the entrenched gambling and concubinage, for example) as well as social reform (public provision for the poor) while also adding a religious dimension—arranging that the Angelus should be rung at morning, midday and evening, so that the people could pray.[26]

A few years later, in 1537, we find a further reference to Our Lady in which Ignatius sought her intercession for a significant grace that he desired. Though he had already been ordained, out of reverence for the Eucharist, he "had resolved to remain a year . . . without saying mass, preparing himself and praying Our Lady to be pleased to place him with her Son."[27] This prayer was answered bountifully in a key mystical vision Ignatius had in a chapel at La Storta outside of Rome where he saw God the Father himself placing him with Jesus.[28] Diego Lainez, one of his companions on that journey, recounts what Ignatius said of this vision in this way: "[H]e seemed to see Christ with the cross on his shoulder. And the eternal Father was close by, saying, 'I want you to take this person as your servant'. And thus Jesus took him, and said, 'I want you to serve us.'"[29] Here, through the intercession of Our Lady, Ignatius received a great grace, one with "a clear repercussion upon the foundation of the Society of Jesus. With deep feeling Ignatius perceived himself as one intimately united with Christ; and he also desired that the society which was soon to be founded should be totally dedicated to Him and bear His name."[30]

---

23. Rodrigues, *A Brief and Exact Account*, 13–15.
24. Ibid., 15.
25. Conwell, "Commentary," in ibid., 16.
26. Ignatius, *Autobiography*, no. 88.
27. Ibid., no. 96.
28. Ibid.
29. Quoted in Ignatius, *Personal Writings*, 376.
30. Dalmases, *Ignatius of Loyola*, 153.

The final reference to Our Lady in the *Autobiography* occurs where Ignatius speaks of the process by which he wrote the Jesuit Constitutions in the years after the Society had been approved by the Pope in 1540. Each day he would pray over the particular point he was considering and offer Mass for clarity on that matter. During this time, he experienced many visions. As he puts it, he would see "sometimes God the Father, at other times all the three persons of the Trinity, at other times Our Lady interceding, at other times her confirming" the choices he was making.[31] We get a fuller picture of the sorts of experiences Ignatius is referring to from his spiritual diary, of which we have extant his notes from the period 2 February 1544 to 17 February 1545.[32] In the first part of the diary especially, we find that Ignatius regularly seeks Mary's intercession, often along with that of her Son, sometimes grouped together simply as "the two mediators." On one occasion he sees "the Mother and the Son ready and willing to intercede with the Father."[33] On another he senses "that the two mediators had made supplication."[34] Again, he "desired to make this offering to the Father through the mediation and prayers of the Mother and the Son" and, having done this, he feels within himself that he "approached, or was taken before, the Father."[35] Another time Ignatius found himself sobbing as "could feel the Mother and the Son to be interceding" and so "felt a complete security that the Eternal Father" would grant what he asked.[36] Two days later, he wrote:

> I seemed to feel the Heavenly Father showed himself propitious and kind—to the point of making it clear to me that he would be pleased if Our Lady . . . would intercede. . . . I felt and saw that Our Lady was very propitious, pleading before the Father.[37]

Here in his spiritual diary we find filled out the image we are left with of Ignatius at the end of his autobiography, summed up by Coleman in this way:

> The final picture we have of Inigo as he finished his Autobiography is of a person absorbed by God the Father and the Trinity. A person who could find God at any moment of the day and was always ready to hear what we being asked of him. A person who

---

31. Ignatius, *Autobiography*, no. 100.
32. Ignatius, "Spiritual Diary," in Ignatius, *Personal Writings*, 73–109. Here, as is customary, references will be made to the dates of the entries in the diary.
33. Ibid., 5 Feb 1544.
34. Ibid., 7 Feb 1544.
35. Ibid., 8 Feb 1544.
36. Ibid., 13 Feb 1544.
37. Ibid., 15 Feb 1544.

not only served Christ but had a deep sense of His presence. A person who never forgot that he had Mary interceding on his behalf.[38]

Mary in the Spiritual Exercises

Having noted the various ways in which Our Lady played an important role in Ignatius' own spiritual journey, we turn now to her place in the various prayer exercises and meditations he offered to others. The main source for this material is, of course, the Spiritual Exercises of St. Ignatius. When we speak of the Spiritual Exercises, it is helpful to be clear what we mean by this term. In its broadest sense, the term "spiritual exercises" refers to any form of spiritual activity, as Ignatius notes in the very first paragraph his book of the Exercises:

> [B]y this name of Spiritual Exercises is meant every way of examining one's conscience, of meditating, of contemplating, of praying vocally and mentally, and of performing other spiritual actions, as will be said later. For as strolling, walking and running are bodily exercises, so every way of preparing and disposing the soul to rid itself of all the disordered tendencies, and, after it is rid, to seek and find the Divine Will as to the management of one's life for the salvation of the soul, is called a Spiritual Exercise.[39]

When we speak of *the* Spiritual Exercises, though, we generally mean one of two things. Firstly, it can mean the whole book put together by St. Ignatius, which comprises a range of ways of praying and examining one's conscience, various recommendations for spiritual directors, and a series of rules or guidelines. There are rules for eating, for dealing with scruples, for giving alms, and the two most well-known ones—Ignatius' rules for the discernment of spirits and his rules for thinking and feeling with the Church (*sentire cum Ecclesia*). The major part of this book, though, comprises a program for a retreat in which one moves through a structured series of meditations and contemplations in four stages which Ignatius calls "weeks," though he makes clear these are not to be taken strictly as calendar

---

38. Coleman, *Walking with Inigo*, 208. Inigo was Ignatius' baptismal name. It is not clear when he started using Ignatius or precisely why he did so.

39. Ignatius, *Spiritual Exercises*, no. 1. References to the Exercises use the standardized numbering. The translation used here is that of Elder Mullan.

weeks.[40] The first week involves a deep reflection on one's sinfulness in the light of God's mercy, seeking the grace of coming to know oneself as a loved sinner. With that grounding, one enters into exercises aimed at a deeper communion with Christ, contemplating his incarnation, infancy and public ministry in the second week, his passion and death in the third, and his resurrection appearances in the fourth. Often, the term *the* Spiritual Exercises is used to refer, not to the whole book of the Exercises, but to this program, also known as the full Spiritual Exercises.

Before turning to the text of the Exercises, it is perhaps worth noting a particular discussion of Mary's role in the composition of the Exercises. From the early seventeenth century at least, a belief existed that the Exercises were dictated to Ignatius by Our Lady. Some have held this in a very strong sense of Mary's direct involvement and literal dictation to Ignatius as he wrote this work. Others have suggested that there is no reason to doubt a similar dynamic in the composition of the Exercises to that noted above in relation to the composition of the Constitutions—that the Exercises would have been composed in a context of prayerful consideration by Ignatius, involving regular recourse to Mary's intercession and experiences of her presence, including mystical visions. This view also allows for the range of other evident sources for the Exercises such as the life of Christ Ignatius had read during his convalescence, his own spiritual experiences, and what he gleaned from his spiritual conversations with others.[41]

Whatever of this discussion, it does not affect our aim which is to review what role Mary plays in the text of the Exercises, independent of any theory of how they were composed. I would, however, note the idiosyncratic view of one person concerning the composition of the Exercises. A certain Benedictine, Constantin Cajetan—not to be confused with the famous Dominican Cajetan—had a great zeal for the honor of his order. One manifestation of this zeal was his view that a Benedictine had written the *Summa Theologica*, as also the *Imitation of Christ*. In similar vein, he believed that the Exercises were no more than an adaptation from the *Exercitatoria* of a Benedictine, Garcia de Cisnernos. Because of this belief, he felt there was no need to posit any special interaction between Our Lady and St. Ignatius in writing the Exercises.[42]

---

40. Ibid., no. 4.

41. For a helpful, detailed discussion of this matter, see Bonacci, "The Marian Presence," 157–233.

42. Marien, "Our Lady and the Exercises," 227.

Narrative Element

So we turn to the text of the Exercises themselves. Here the Marian dimension can helpfully be divided, as Fr. Kolvenbach proposed, into the narrative element, in which Mary is one of the objects of contemplation in a scene, and the functional element, in which Mary is an agent within the prayer exercise.[43] In terms of the narrative element, this first comes into play in the second week of the Exercises, when the exercitant is invited to contemplate the mysteries of Christ's life from the Incarnation through his public ministry. Many of the earlier contemplations are from the infancy narratives and so inevitably involve Mary as one of the key characters. Throughout the Exercises, though, Ignatius' interest is not in Mary in isolation, but always in connection to Jesus, nor in her feelings or inner life except in relation to "her role in the work of our salvation."[44] In the points Ignatius gives for contemplation of those mysteries in which Mary is present, we find a number of interpretive additions to the biblical text. Hence, in relation to the circumcision of Jesus, the third point is: "They gave back the Child to His Mother, who had compassion for the Blood which came from her Son,"[45] while in the contemplation of Christ's baptism, Ignatius notes that Jesus goes to the Jordan "after having taken leave of His Blessed Mother."[46]

In the third week, in which one contemplates the passion of Christ, Mary is less a part of the narrative, in accord with the scriptural texts. Still, there are three telling details where Ignatius moves beyond the text. In the contemplation of Jesus' deposition from the cross, the points refer to Mary's presence,[47] which is not recorded in Scripture, though it is very much part of the tradition, as in the various Pietà images. After the deposition, Ignatius would have us contemplate the movement from the tomb "to the house where Our Lady was, after her Son was buried."[48] And then, at the end of the third week, Ignatius invites us to contemplate the entire passion, including a consideration of "the loneliness of Our Lady, whose grief and fatigue were so great."[49]

---

43. Kolvenbach, *Road from La Storta*, 34–35. Kolvenbach draws this distinction between these two elements from Giuliani, "Le mystère de Notre Dame," though Giuliani himself does not name them "narrative" and "functional."

44. Ibid., 39.

45. Ignatius, *Spiritual Exercises*, no. 266.

46. Ibid., no. 273.

47. Ibid., no. 298.

48. Ibid., no. 208.

49. Ibid.

In the Fourth Week, we find the most significant extra-biblical Marian element in the Exercises. Here Ignatius invites us to contemplate "the first apparition" of the Risen Christ, by which he means Jesus' appearance to his mother.[50] While the scene is not recorded in the Gospels, it is part of an ancient tradition attested at least as far back as the fourth century by John Chrysostom and Ephrem the Syrian, and accepted by such writers as Sedulius, Paulinus of Nola, Albert the Great, Bernardino da Siena, Maldonatus, and Benedict XIV, among others.[51] For them, as for Ignatius, it is unimaginable that Our Lord should not make his Risen presence known to the one who had said "Yes" to his Incarnation, who had borne him in her womb, under whose authority he had lived as a child, and who had suffered with him throughout his agony on the cross. Ignatius is well aware that some will question the inclusion of this scene in the Exercises, and he responds with a polemical tone that is absent elsewhere in the Exercises:[52] "This, although it is not said in Scripture, is included in saying that He appeared to so many others, because Scripture supposes that we have understanding, as it is written: 'Are you also without understanding?'"[53]

What are we to make of this appearance of Christ to his Mother in a theological sense, given the testimony of Scripture which states clearly that he appeared first to Mary Magdalene (Mark 16:9) and of the tradition, grounded in that scriptural testimony, that speaks of the Magdalene as the first witness of the Resurrection, the apostle of the apostles? Commentators on the Exercises speak of this appearance as being of a very different kind to that of the other Resurrection appearances. Hardon, for example, notes that the scriptural affirmation about the Magdalene should be understood to mean "either that she was the first amongst those whom the Gospels describe as witnesses of the resurrection or among those to whom Christ appeared in order to confirm their faith."[54] This is not to say, though, that the apparition to Our Lady is not without an ecclesial character. In fact, Our Lady, the only one capable of doing so at this point, receives the new risen life for the Church. "The Risen Lord appears in the faith of Our Lady: she is the fountainhead and icon of the faith of the Church, ... which is then hierarchically and sacramentally articulated."[55] Likewise, Cusson speaks of Mary offering the "consent of redeemed humanity, which was now free to

---

50. Ibid., nos. 218–25, 299.
51. Decloux, "Mary in the Exercises," 303–4.
52. Kolvenbach, *Road from La Storta*, 48; Coathelem, *Ignatian Insights*, 217.
53. Ignatius, *Spiritual Exercises*, no. 299.
54. Hardon, *All My Liberty*, 117.
55. Kolvenbach, *Road from La Storta*, 60.

receive Love and to respond to Love"—that is, the risen Love who is Christ.[56] In Mary, "the new 'Mother of the living,' the risen Christ appeared to all of the new creation, to the universal Church born on that day."[57]

Functional Element

Beyond these narrative Marian elements of the Exercises are the functional elements—how Ignatius invites us to engage with Mary at various points along the way even when she is not present in the narrative being contemplated, or where there is no narrative being contemplated. Outside of the four weeks of the program of the full Exercises, Ignatius proposes three methods of prayer in each of which Mary is mentioned. In the first method, one of the exercises involves reflection on the bodily senses. Here Ignatius offers guidance for those wishing to imitate Christ in the use of their senses and also for those who wish to imitate Our Lady.[58] In the second and third methods, where Ignatius presents two ways of reflecting on common prayers word by word, the Hail Mary and the Hail, Holy Queen are two of the prayers he suggests.[59] The Hail Mary is, in fact, also used as a measure of time, alongside the Our Father. Hence we are invited at times to reflect "the space of time one says the Our Father and the Hail Mary three times."[60] Moreover, the crucial oblation to Christ we are invited to make after meditating on the Call of the King is made in the presence of Christ's mother and all the heavenly court.[61]

The most significant functional Marian element in the Exercises, though, is Mary's place in the colloquies that arise at key moments of the Exercises. For Ignatius, a colloquy is, at its simplest, a conversation. Having spent time in each prayer period either meditating or contemplating, attentive to the movements of consolation and desolation within, Ignatius would have us end, if we have not already spontaneously done so during the prayer, with a time of colloquy. He understands this as follows: "The Colloquy is made, properly speaking, as one friend speaks to another, or as a servant to his master; now asking some grace, now blaming oneself for some misdeed,

---

56. Cusson, *Biblical Theology and the Exercises*, 305.
57. Ibid., 306.
58. Ignatius, *Spiritual Exercises*, no. 248.
59. Ibid., nos. 256, 259.
60. Ibid., no. 241. See also no. 73.
61. Ibid., no. 98.

now communicating one's affairs, and asking advice in them."[62] Later in the Exercises, he returns to a discussion of the nature of the colloquy:

> [I]n the Colloquies I ought to discuss and ask according to the subject matter, that is, according as I find myself tempted or consoled, and according as I desire to have one virtue or another, as I want to dispose of myself in one direction or another, as I want to grieve or rejoice at the thing which I am contemplating; in fine, asking that which I more efficaciously desire as to any particular things.[63]

So while there is often an element of petition in a colloquy, it is always a petition set within a conversation, a speaking and listening, in which I reveal what is in my heart. It is well-captured in the motto of Cardinal Newman—*Cor ad cor loquitur*—heart speaks unto heart. For Ignatius, this heart to heart conversation can take place not just with the Divine Persons but also with the saints, especially Our Lady.[64]

The Triple Colloquy

Mary is particularly prominent in that form of Colloquy known as the Triple Colloquy. This form of prayer first appears on the very first day of the First Week of the Exercises, when the exercitant is reflecting on sin. The basic structure, excluding the particular graces being sought, is simple. The first Colloquy is to Our Lady, "that she may get me grace from Her Son and Lord" with the particular grace then being named. This is followed by a Hail Mary. The second Colloquy is to the Son, asking for the same grace, "begging him to get it for me from the Father." This is followed by the Soul of Christ (*Anima Christi*) prayer. Finally, the third Colloquy is to the Father "that the Eternal Lord Himself may grant it to me." This is followed by the Our Father.[65]

The Triple Colloquy, here and elsewhere, is suggested by Ignatius at points where a particular seriousness of prayer is called for—where we are seeking a grace which is crucially important for our growth in Christ and yet is one to which we naturally find strong resistance. Here in the First Week, the crucial but difficult grace relates to our knowledge of sin: "first, that I may feel an interior knowledge of my sins, and hatred of them; second, that

---

62. Ibid., no. 54.
63. Ibid., no. 199.
64. Ibid., no. 109.
65. Ibid., no. 63.

I may feel the disorder of my actions, so that, hating them, I may correct myself and put myself in order; third, to ask knowledge of the world, in order that, hating it, I may put away from me worldly and vain things."[66]

Given this mix of significance and resistance, Ignatius has us call firstly on the two persons to whom, at some points of his Spiritual Diary, as noted earlier, he refers simply as "the two Mediators"—Mary and Jesus. So important is this notion of mediation for Ignatius that Egan can refer to his "mediator mysticism" by which he is particularly sensitive to the role of mediators in our relationship with God, knowing which ones to call upon at particular times.[67] Not that all mediators are equal, of course. Rather, Jesus the Incarnate Word is first in order of importance, the principal source of all grace, while Mary, exalted as she may be above all other humans, remains in a subordinate position in relation to and dependent on her Son.[68]

In light of what Ignatius says about the nature of colloquies, our requests for the intercession of Mary and of Jesus should be set within a conversation, perhaps naming what we might be experiencing as we ask for these graces—the desires we might feel, on the one hand, along with any resistance. But more than this, Ignatius points us to these two not simply because they are key mediators but because they embody these graces perfectly—Mary, the human one who, by God's grace, is not marred by sin, and Jesus, the divine-human One, like unto us in all things but sin. As Endean notes, "When, in the Triple Colloquies, we pray through Mary and Jesus to the Father, we are remembering that the new creation is a guaranteed reality, and invoking their 'intercession' in order to stimulate it within ourselves."[69] In Mary "is found the fullness of imitation and of understanding of the 'true life and teaching' of Christ"[70] that it is possible to find in any human person.

In the second week, the Triple Colloquy comes into play once more, and again it arises when there is a difficult yet supremely significant grace to be sought. Thus in the meditation on the Two Standards in which the exercitant considers the opposed methods of the evil one and of Christ, Lucifer leads all the forces ranged against us and our spiritual growth, enticing us to attachment to riches, honor and pride, from which he "draws on to all other vices."[71] Ranged against Lucifer and his strategy is Christ, "the supreme Commander-in-chief of the good." His strategy is the complete

---

66. Ibid.
67. Egan, "Spiritual Exercises," 113.
68. Coathelem, *Ignatian Insights*, 109.
69. Endean, "Our Lady," 53.
70. Ivens, *Understanding the Exercises*, 112.
71. Ignatius, *Spiritual Exercises*, nos. 140–42.

opposite—to attract people to "the highest spiritual poverty" (and, if so chosen, to actual poverty); then, to insults and contempt; and then flowing from these two, humility. Poverty, insults, humility—"from these three steps let them induce to all other virtues."[72]

Having meditated on these two leaders vying for our souls and their opposed strategies, we again are invited to make a Triple Colloquy. The grace sought here is "that I may be received under [Christ's] standard" which means following in the way he follows—the highest spiritual poverty, including openness to actual poverty, and insults and contempt.[73] Again, it is not simply a matter of having Mary as our intercessor, but also as someone who has received the graces we seek and lived according to them, so that we can converse with her about them and be inspired to imitate her. Hence the Triple Colloquy is a carefully structured prayer involving both intercession and imitation. So important are these graces of the Two Standards meditation for an authentic life in Christ and for making a good election that Ignatius invites us to pray for them, using the Triple Colloquy, for the remainder of the Second Week,[74] and even, if we so desire, into the Third Week.[75]

Contemporary Adaptation of the Triple Colloquy

Having noted the significance of the Triple Colloquy in the Exercises, we now turn to a particular aspect of current practice concerning this prayer in the giving the Exercises. More and more, Ignatian spirituality has been of interest to members of those churches arising from the Reformation who are attracted to it particularly by its strong christological focus, with its capacity to lead people into a vibrant living relationship with Christ, and by the biblical emphasis in the contemplation of Gospel passages into which one is invited to enter.[76]

More problematic for Protestants, of course, is the Marian dimension we have been examining, though not all its aspects. Mary's narrative presence, based on the whole on Gospel scenes in which she appears, is generally

---

72. Ibid., nos. 143–46.
73. Ibid., no. 147.
74. Ibid., nos. 148, 156–57, 159, 164, 168.
75. Ibid., no. 199.
76. See, for example, Wakefield, *Sacred Listening*; Chadwick, "Giving the Exercises in Ecumenical Context"; Heiding, "Exercises at Ecclesial Frontiers"; Huggett, "Ignatian Spirituality Hooks Protestants"; Reiser, "The Exercises in a Pluralistic World"; Anderson, "Reflections."

not the issue. It is when we come to the more functional Marian dimension of the Exercises that problems often arise for Protestants. This is most an issue when Ignatius asks us to pray the Triple Colloquy, in which the first step is to converse with Our Lady, a practice with which many Protestants are at best uncomfortable, since it is unfamiliar, and to which at worst they are passionately opposed because of their understanding of what it means for Christ to be the "one mediator between God and humankind" (1 Tim 2:5).

Directors have often dealt with this sensibility by encouraging the Protestant retreatant to make the first colloquy to the Holy Spirit, rather than Our Lady, and then to move on to Jesus and finally to the Father—that is, to make it an explicitly trinitarian prayer.[77] I will come back to this, but would note first that it is not the only alternative suggested. One Protestant making the Exercises in daily life spoke to his director about his unease about conversing with Mary in the Triple Colloquy. He was told he could "choose someone besides Mary for this part of the exercise." And so he chose to speak to a deceased Catholic friend of his, which to him seemed to be less problematic than speaking to Our Lady![78]

The idea of replacing Mary with the Holy Spirit in the first colloquy would, *prima facie*, seem to be justified for at least two good reasons. Firstly, the Exercises are nothing if not open to adaptation. Ignatius himself notes that they "have to be adapted to the dispositions of the persons who wish to receive them, that is, to their age, education or ability."[79] In keeping with this principle, Ignatius mentions a range of ways that such adaptation might happen. There are two ways of giving someone the full Exercises—in a month-long silent retreat, or in daily life over longer period.[80] Ignatius also notes that some people will benefit from the exercises of the first week even without the other weeks.[81] For the full Exercises, the four weeks will be of different lengths, depending on how the retreatant is responding to the material and how quickly or slowly he or she receives the main graces being sought in each week.[82] Likewise, the number of prayer periods each day may be varied at times, depending on how the person is being graced and is responding.[83] The choice of particular Gospel scenes to contemplate is also

---

77. Huggett, "Ignatian Spirituality Hooks Protestants," 32; Chadwick, "Giving the Exercises in Ecumenical Context," 38; Veltri, *Orientations*, vol. 2, ch. 8; Anderson, "Reflections," 18.

78. Nelson, "The Triple Colloquy."

79. Ignatius, *Spiritual Exercises*, no. 18.

80. Ibid., nos. 19–20.

81. Ibid., no. 18.

82. Ibid., nos. 4, 162, 209, 226.

83. Ibid., nos. 133, 205, 227.

variable, once again depending on the retreatant's needs,[84] as is the number of points the person might consider within the prayer period.[85] Adaptation is certainly possible and necessary for the Exercises to be of most benefit to people; indeed one key role of the director is to discern what adaptations might be most helpful for the directee.

Secondly, there seems to be an innate logic in suggesting that a prayer involving three interlocutors, two of whom are persons of the Blessed Trinity, is really meant to be Trinitarian, involving the third person as well. As one commentator puts it, "It is particularly in the triple colloquies that the mediatory role of the Son vis-à-vis the Father is made explicit; but, strangely enough, where we would have expected a mention of the Holy Spirit, it is our Lady who appears to complete the triad."[86] This seems to receive further validation when we recognize there were good reasons for downplaying the place of the Holy Spirit in the period in which the Exercises were composed. The Spanish Inquisition was showing great interest in the *Alumbrados*—the illuminated ones—a loose movement whose major features included an emphasis on God's direct dealing with the believer, often expressed in terms of the action of the Holy Spirit, to the extent that a dismissive attitude was taken to authority and to the external rituals of the Church.[87]

It is certainly true that there were concerns that Ignatius was tainted with the spirit of the *Alumbrados*, and at least two investigations of his teaching and way of life by the Inquisition were because of such suspicions. The first was in Alcala, and was resolved fairly simply.[88] The second arose when he was invited to dine with the Dominicans of Salamanca who began to question him during the conversation after dinner. They asked what he would speak about in the spiritual conversations for which he was noted as he sought to "help souls," as Ignatius put it. He said he would speak to them of a number of things, including virtue and vice. They then asked on what basis he would speak of such issues of morality, so important to people's growth in faith: either he must be speaking on the basis of a study of theology, of which he had admitted he knew little, or by the direct guidance of the Holy Spirit. Ignatius realized the danger of this line of questioning, and chose not to answer. It was at this point that they locked him up and brought him before the Inquisition.[89]

84. Ibid., nos. 162, 209.
85. Ibid., no. 228.
86. Martín-Moreno, "The Gift of the Holy Spirit," 19.
87. Egan, "Spiritual Exercises," 120; O'Leary, "Consoler," 64–65; Sachs, "Spirit," 22.
88. Ignatius, *Autobiography*, no. 58.
89. Ibid., nos. 64–66.

These sorts of experiences did have an impact on the text of the Exercises. There, in that very public document, Ignatius shows great restraint in his explicit references to the Holy Spirit. In fact, there are only six such references and five of these are in quotations from scriptural stories which refer to the Spirit, and so could hardly be faulted. The final reference is in the famous thirteenth rule of the Rules *Sentire Cum Ecclesia*—Rules for Thinking with the Church:

> To be right in everything, we ought always to hold that the white which I see, is black, if the Hierarchical Church so decides it, believing that between Christ our Lord, the Bridegroom, and the Church, His Bride, there is *the same Spirit* which governs and directs us for the salvation of our souls. Because by *the same Spirit* and our Lord Who gave the ten Commandments, our holy Mother the Church is directed and governed.[90]

The solid ecclesial context of this statement ensured that even the Inquisition would have trouble construing the reference to the Holy Spirit in a problematic way.

To deduce from this analysis, though, that Ignatius really wanted a trinitarian Triple Colloquy falters on a number of counts.

Firstly, this prayer was not original to Ignatius. Luther preached a sermon in which he drew on an example from St. Bernard of Clairvaux which speaks about praying to Mary, who will pray to her Son, who will in turn pray to the Father.[91] Hence the basic structure of the Triple Colloquy predates the *Alumbrado* controversy.

Secondly, there is the evidence of Ignatius' own practice as seen in his Spiritual Diary. There, in an essentially private journal which he never expected to be seen by others, Ignatius is quite happy to refer to the Holy Spirit without restraint as he recounts his inner experiences. In fact, on at least one occasion, he makes a colloquy with the Spirit.[92] Yet, even in this private forum away from the glare of the Inquisition, Ignatius often takes Mary as an intercessor, as we have already noted, or Mary and Jesus together as his "two mediators." Most significantly, on two occasions he makes a Triple Colloquy in the precise manner in which he has given it to us in the Exercises—from Mary to Jesus to the Father.[93] Furthermore, on one of those occasions, the grace Ignatius asks for in this Triple Colloquy is precisely related to the Spirit—that the Father might give him the Spirit. Here, in the freedom of his

---

90. Ignatius, *Spiritual Exercises,* no. 365 (emphasis added).
91. Kolvenbach, *Road from La Storta,* 42.
92. Ignatius, "Spiritual Diary," 11 Feb 1544.
93. Ibid., 8 Feb 1544, 11 Feb 1544.

own personal prayer, where he could have made use of a trinitarian Triple Colloquy if he so desired, there is no record of such a thing.[94]

Thirdly, there is no evidence that the adaptation Ignatius allows at various points in the Exercises applies to the structure of the Triple Colloquy. We have seen that Ignatius himself, as witnessed in his spiritual diary, is very free in choosing with whom he makes colloquies. Moreover, he encourages such freedom in relation to colloquies at some points in the Exercises.[95] But when it comes to the Triple Colloquy, there is no hint of the adaptation allowed in other parts of the Exercises, or of multiple options being put before us. Rather a very clearly articulated structure is given us. It is not simply three independent colloquies, but a prayer involving a twofold mediation. We do not just speak with Mary, and then Jesus, and then the Father, independent of each other. We ask Mary to intercede for us with Jesus and we then ask Jesus to intercede for us before the Father. Moreover, as we have seen, the dynamic of the Triple Colloquy also involves imitation in that we can see in Mary a human existence which is already blessed by the graces we seek, and in the humanity of Jesus a human existence embodying these graces. This element of imitation is lost if we converse with the Holy Spirit instead.

Fourthly, precisely because of the mediatory structure of the Triple Colloquy as proposed in the Exercises, the suggestion that the Spirit might replace Mary is theologically problematic. If the retreatant was simply to have a conversation with the Spirit, asking for the grace he or she seeks, and then one with the Son, and then one with the Father, there would be no theological problem. But to have the Spirit seeking a grace from Jesus makes no theological sense and smacks of subordinationism. The Spirit is God, consubstantial with the Father and the Son, and so is capable of giving any grace at all without needing to seek it from the Son.

Some might object to this argument on the basis that St. Paul speaks of the Spirit interceding for us. "Likewise the Spirit helps us in our weakness; for we do not know how to pray as we ought, but that very Spirit intercedes with sighs too deep for words. And God, who searches the heart, knows what is the mind of the Spirit, because the Spirit intercedes for the saints according to the will of God" (Rom 8:26–27). This is not the place to enter into the various interpretations of this passage in detail. But I would note two points for our purposes. Firstly, the situation of the Triple Colloquy as proposed by Ignatius is hardly one in which "we do not know how to pray as we ought," nor one in which we do not know "what we ought to pray for," as

---

94. Ibid., 11 Feb 1544.
95. Ignatius, *Spiritual Exercises*, nos. 109, 199.

some translations render the Greek. Ignatius gives us clear guidelines both for how to pray and what to pray for. Secondly, the Spirit's intercession in Romans, whatever it might mean precisely, is with God—that is, in the context of the passage, with the Father. It is not a matter of the Spirit interceding with the Son.

Others might object that the Spirit interceding with the Son makes no less sense than Jesus interceding before the Father. But with Jesus we are dealing with the incarnate Son, so that we can validly speak of Christ interceding for us before God *in his humanity*. Indeed, Scripture speaks of such a role as a major function of the ascended Christ who "always lives to make intercession" (Heb 7:25) on the basis of the merits won for us by all he suffered in his humanity. In fact, one of the early directories of the Spiritual Exercises—notes which directors put together to offer further guidance on giving these retreats—deals precisely with this point:

> [A]s regards the second colloquy of the 3rd and 4th exercises, where Christ is addressed as mediator to obtain from the Father the graces mentioned there, an explanation ought to be given to less well educated persons. They should be told that while it is true that in his divine nature, by which he is equal to the Father, it is Christ's role to bestow grace and not to ask for it, nevertheless in his human nature, by which he is less than the Father, he can ask graces from the Father, from himself in his own divine nature, and from the Holy Spirit. This is evident in the prayer *Anima Christi* ("Soul of Christ") given in the exercise: it is addressed to Christ according to the human nature he has assumed.[96]

This Directory, along with at least two others,[97] points to the theological sensitivity of the early Jesuits to any notion that one Person of the Trinity could be considered as interceding before another, with the only exception being that the Son, having assumed a human nature, can truly be said to be interceding before the Father, but only by virtue of his humanity.

Conclusion

The analysis of the last section shows the problematic nature of any simplistic solution to the difficulties non-Catholic retreatants might have with praying to Mary. Apart from misunderstanding Ignatius' intention, there

---

96. Palmer, *On Giving the Exercises*, 128.
97. Ibid., 213, 247.

are significant theological issues with a simple interchange of Mary and the Holy Spirit in the Triple Colloquy. This is not to say that retreatants whose prayer experience and/or theological persuasions mean they feel unable to engage with Mary should be forced to do so. It does mean, though, that such retreatants cannot practice the Triple Colloquy in the full sense that Ignatius intends—that is, as a structure involving both mediation and engagement with models of the graces being sought. Furthermore, removing Mary from her role as mediator and model reduces her place within the Exercises largely to the narrative element. This raises the larger question of the bounds of legitimate adaptation—when does any adaptation of Ignatian spirituality reach the point that it is no longer authentically Ignatian in the fullest sense? We cannot address this question here, either in general or in relation to this spirituality's Marian dimension.[98] I would simply note that a merely narrative role for Mary in the Exercises makes it difficult to speak with Kolvenbach of Mary as having a place "at the very heart of the *Spiritual Exercises*,"[99] and does not do justice to the significant place we have shown Our Lady to have played both in Ignatius' own journey and in the journey he set out for others in the Exercises he bequeathed the Church.

Bibliography

Anderson, Susan. "Reflections on the Experience of Making and Giving the Exercises." *The Way Supplement* 68 (1990) 13–21.

Bonacci, Louis A. "The Marian Presence in the Life and Works of Saint Ignatius Loyola: From Private Revelation to Spiritual Exercises—The Cloth of Loyola's Allegiance." STD diss., University of Dayton, International Marian Research Institute, 2002.

Chadwick, Geoffrey. "Giving the Exercises and Training Directors in an Ecumenical Context." *The Way Supplement* 68 (1990) 35–41.

Coathelem, Hervé. *Ignatian Insights: A Guide to the Complete Spiritual Exercises.* Translated by Charles J. McCarthy. Taichung, Taiwan: Kuangchi, 1961.

Coleman, Gerald. *Walking with Inigo: A Commentary on the Autobiography of St. Ignatius.* Anand, India: Gujarat Sahitya Prakash, 2001.

Cusson, Gilles. *Biblical Theology and the Spiritual Exercises: A Method toward a Personal Experience of God as Accomplishing within Us His Plan of Salvation.* Translated by Mary Angela Roduit and George E. Ganss. St. Louis. MO: The Institute of Jesuit Sources, 1988.

Dalmases, Cándido de. *Ignatius of Loyola: Founder of the Jesuits: His Life and Work.* Translated by Jerome Aixalá. St. Louis: The Institute of Jesuit Sources, 1985.

---

98. Closely related to the Marian dimension is the larger issue of the ecclesial dimension of Ignatian spirituality, an issue I have examined in Koning, "Ignatian Spirituality as Ecclesial Spirituality."

99. Kolvenbach, *Road from La Storta*, 33.

Decloux, Simon. "Mary in the Spiritual Exercises of Saint Ignatius." *Review of Ignatian Spirituality* 19 (1988) 100–44.

Egan, Harvey D. *The Spiritual Exercises and the Ignatian Mystical Horizon*. St. Louis, MO: The Institute of Jesuit Sources, 1976.

Endean, Philip. "'Our Lady' and the Graces of the Fourth Week." *The Way Supplement* 99 (2000) 44–60.

Giuliani, Maurice. "Le mystère de Notre Dame dans les Exercises." *Christus* 3 (1954) 32–49.

Hardon, John A. *All My Liberty: Theology of the Spiritual Exercises*. Westminster, MD: Newman, 1959.

Heiding, Sven Fredrik. "Giving Ignatian Exercises at Ecclesial Frontiers." DPhil diss., University of Oxford, 2011.

Huggett, Joyce. "Why Ignatian Spirituality Hooks Protestants." *The Way Supplement* 68 (1980) 22–34.

Ivens, Michael. *Understanding the Spiritual Exercises: Text and Commentary: A Handbook for Retreat Directors*. Leominster, UK: Gracewing, 1998.

Kolvenbach, Peter-Hans. *The Road from La Storta: Peter-Hans Kolvenbach, S.J., on Ignatian Spirituality*. Saint Louis, MO: The Institute of Jesuit Sources, 2000.

Koning, Robin. "Ignatian Spirituality as Ecclesial Spirituality." In *Exploring Contemporary Spirituality and its Impact on the Practice of Spiritual Direction: Proceedings of the Inaugural National Symposium of the Australian Ecumenical Council for Spiritual Direction held in Parkville, Victoria, Australia, 29–30 October 2010*, 5–13. Australia: Australian Ecumenical Council for Spiritual Direction, 2010.

Marien, Francis J. "Our Lady and the Exercises." *The Woodstock Letters* 82 (1953) 224–37.

Martín-Moreno, Juan Manuel. "The Gift of the Holy Spirit in the Spiritual Exercises." *Review of Ignatian Spirituality* 20 (1989) 17–33.

Meissner, W. W. *Ignatius of Loyola: The Psychology of a Saint*. New Haven, CT: Yale University Press, 1992.

Nelson, "The Triple Colloquy." Online: http://www.coffeehousecontemplative.com/2011/12/triple-colloquy.html.

O'Leary, Brian. "Consoler and Consolation." *The Way Supplement* 99 (2000) 61–69.

Palmer, Martin E., trans. and ed. *On Giving the Spiritual Exercises: The Early Jesuit Manuscript Directories and the Official Directory of 1599*. St. Louis, MO: The Institute of Jesuit Sources, 1996.

Rahner, Hugo. *The Spirituality of St. Ignatius Loyola: An Account of its Historical Development*. Translated by Francis John Smith. Westminster, MD: Newman, 1953.

Reiser, William. "The *Spiritual Exercises* in a Religiously Pluralistic World." *Spiritus* 10 (2010) 135–57.

Rodrigues, Simão. *A Brief and Exact Account: The Recollections of Simão Rodrigues on the Origin and Progress of the Society of Jesus*. Translated by Joseph F. Conwell. St. Louis, MO: The Institute of Jesuit Sources, 2004.

Sachs, John R. "The Spirit of the Risen Lord." *The Way Supplement* 99 (2000) 22–34.

Saint Ignatius of Loyola. *Personal Writings: Reminiscences, Spiritual Diary, Select Letters including the Text of the Spiritual Exercises*. Translated by Joseph A. Munitiz and Philip Endean. London: Penguin, 1996.

———. *The Spiritual Exercises of St. Ignatius of Loyola.* Translated by Elder Mullan. New York: Kennedy & Sons, 1914.

Veltri, John. "Chapter 8." *Orientations*, Vol 2. Guelph, ON: Loyola House, 1998. Online: http://orientations.jesuits.ca/or2ch8.html.

Wakefield, James L. *Sacred Listening: Discovering the Spiritual Exercises of St. Ignatius Loyola.* Grand Rapids: Baker, 2006.

8

Mary as Priest, Prophet, and King

—Peter John McGregor

In Lumen Gentium *Mary is identified as a member of the Church. In the same document one finds some significant reflections on how members of the Church can participate in the priestly, prophetic, and kingly mission of Christ. Since Mary is a member of Christ's body, it is valid to ask how she participates in this three-fold mission. An analysis of the three-fold mission in* Lumen Gentium *reveals some discrepancies in its presentation. However, a more integrated understanding of the three-fold mission can be discerned in the* Catechism of the Catholic Church *and in Sacred Scripture. Looking at Mary's words and actions in Sacred Scripture can help us see how she participates in the three-fold mission. Mary can also help us see how the three aspects of this mission are integrated into a single mission. She can help us understand how all Christians can participate more fruitfully in this mission of the Church.*

At Vatican II a decision was made not to produce a document specifically devoted to Mary, but to include a section on her in *Lumen Gentium*, thereby emphasizing the relationship between her and the Church.[1] Therein, while Mary is acknowledged as the Mother of God

---

1. Jelly, "The Theological Context of and Introduction to Chapter 8 of *Lumen Gentium*," 56.

and Mother of the Redeemer, it is also acknowledged that she is "a preeminent and singular member of the Church."[2] In Sacred Scripture we see Mary presented as one of the disciples in the Cenacle, since she is united in prayer with all the rest (cf. Acts 1:12–14). Given this, what can Mary reveal to us about the nature of discipleship?

In *Lumen Gentium* the mission of a disciple was defined as a sharing in the priestly, prophetic, and royal offices of Christ.[3] In the estimation of Pope John Paul II the Second Vatican Council linked the "salvific mission of God . . . with the threefold power of Christ as priest, prophet and king, while also showing that participation in that power determines the reality of the Christian life." Indeed, for John Paul II, participation in this salvific mission through sharing in this three-fold power of Christ was "a central theme of the Conciliar doctrine concerning the People of God."[4] If Mary is a pre-eminent and singular disciple, what light can she shed upon our participation in this three-fold office of Christ? Also, can she help us see if and how these three aspects form a single integrated mission?[5] If reflecting on Mary's participation in these three offices can help us in these ways, we should be able to advance in our understanding, and hopefully our application, of the teaching of *Lumen Gentium* on our participation in the salvific mission of Christ.

The Three-fold Mission according to *Lumen Gentium*, the *Catechism of the Catholic Church*, and Sacred Scripture

Before attempting to answer these questions it will be necessary to analyze briefly the teaching of *Lumen Gentium*, the *Catechism of the Catholic Church*, and Sacred Scripture on the three-fold office. In *Lumen Gentium* this teaching is presented in chapter 2, which is on the Church as the people of God, and chapter 4, which is on the laity. At first glance this teaching seems to present us with some difficulties. For one thing the teaching as a whole is

---

2. *Lumen Gentium*, no. 53.
3. Ibid., nos. 10–12 and 34–36.
4. Wojtyła, *Sources of Renewal*, 219.
5. In *Sources of Renewal*, Karol Wojtyła claimed that the "attitudes" arising from sharing in the three-fold mission of Christ are interrelated. He stated that, "It should be noted at the outset that these attitudes inter-penetrate and in a certain sense determine one another. They form, so to speak, an organic complex within the fundamental attitude of testimony." However, he did not specify how these attitudes interpenetrate. Rather, he stated that they are difficult to "separate and distinguish with precision (221)." For John Paul II's understanding of the three-fold mission, see McGregor, "Priests, Prophets and Kings," 61–78.

not presented in an integrated way. That in the chapter on the people of God is "asymmetrical," since it only explicitly mentions the priestly and prophetic offices, while that in the chapter on the laity explicitly deals with all three offices, the priestly, prophetic, and royal. Yet *Lumen Gentium* also states that: "Everything that has been said ... concerning the People of God is intended for the laity, religious and clergy alike."[6] Does this mean that all the baptized share in the priestly and prophetic offices of Christ, but only the laity share in his royal office? Or is this discrepancy simply an oversight by the commission responsible for the final draft of the Dogmatic Constitution, an oversight not detected by the Council fathers? For reasons which hopefully will become clear, in order to help overcome these difficulties, the teaching as it applies to the laity will be addressed first.

In the chapter on the laity, the explanation of how lay people participate in the three offices is clear and orderly. First Christ, the supreme and eternal Priest, gives lay people

> a sharing in His priestly function of offering spiritual worship for the glory of God and the salvation of men. . . . For all their works, prayers and apostolic endeavors, their ordinary married and family life, their daily occupations, their physical and mental relaxation, if carried out in the Spirit, and even the hardships of life, if patiently borne—all these become "spiritual sacrifices acceptable to God through Jesus Christ" (1 Pet 2:5). Together with the offering of the Lord's body, they are most fittingly offered in the celebration of the Eucharist. Thus, as those everywhere who adore in holy activity, the laity consecrate the world itself to God.[7]

As the great Prophet, Christ continues to fulfill his prophetic office through the laity. They

> go forth as powerful proclaimers of a faith in things to be hoped for (cf. Heb. 11:1), when they courageously join to their profession of faith a life springing from faith. This evangelization, that is, this announcing of Christ by a living testimony as well as by the spoken word, takes on a specific quality and a special force in that it is carried out in the ordinary surroundings of the world.[8]

---

6. *Lumen Gentium*, no. 30.
7. Ibid., no. 34.
8. Ibid., no. 35.

Finally, Christ the King shares his royal power, his royal freedom, with the faithful, so that "they might conquer the reign of sin in themselves (cf. Rom. 6:12). Further, He has shared this power so that serving Christ in their fellow men they might by humility and patience lead their brethren to that King for whom to serve is to reign."[9] Since the Lord

> wishes to spread His kingdom also by means of the laity, namely, a kingdom of truth and life, a kingdom of holiness and grace, a kingdom of justice, love and peace.... The faithful... must assist each other to live holier lives even in their daily occupations. In this way the world may be permeated by the spirit of Christ and it may more effectively fulfill its purpose in justice, charity and peace.[10]

The above is all neatly cut and dried. The reader is presented with a description of three distinct offices. Yet when we look at the earlier teaching on the participation of the People of God in the mission of Christ we do not find the same "orderliness." The reason for this is the scriptural passage chosen to orientate this teaching—1 Peter 2:9–10: "For those who believe in Christ . . . are finally established as 'a chosen race, a royal priesthood, a holy nation, a purchased people . . . who in times past were not a people, but are now the people of God.'"[11] This passage substantially determines how the teaching on Christians' participation in the mission of Christ is presented. With this in mind a brief commentary shall be given on this teaching in *Lumen Gentium* 10–12.

> Christ the Lord, High Priest taken from among men (cf. Heb. 5:1–5), made the new people "a kingdom and priests to God the Father" (Apoc. 1:6; cf. 5:9–10). The baptized, by regeneration and the anointing of the Holy Spirit, are consecrated as a spiritual house and a holy priesthood, in order that through all those works which are those of the Christian man they may offer spiritual sacrifices and proclaim the power of Him who has called them out of darkness into His marvelous light (cf. 1 Pet. 2:4–10). Therefore all the disciples of Christ, persevering in prayer and praising God (cf. Acts 2:42–47), should present themselves as a living sacrifice, holy and pleasing to God (cf. Rom. 12:1). Everywhere on earth they must bear witness to Christ and give an answer to those who seek an account of that hope of eternal life which is in them (cf. 1 Pet. 3:15) . . . in virtue of their royal

---

9. Ibid., no. 36.
10. Ibid.
11. Ibid., no. 9.

> priesthood [they] join in the offering of the Eucharist. They likewise exercise that priesthood in receiving the sacraments, in the witness of a holy life, and by self-denial and active charity.[12]

Although, ostensibly, this paragraph concerns Christians' participation in the priesthood of Christ, in fact, participation in all three offices is addressed. It is addressed, one could say, from a priestly perspective. Not only are Christians to offer "spiritual sacrifices," they must also carry out the prophetic task of proclaiming the power of God, and giving an account of the hope that is in them. They carry out a royal task by virtue of the fact that they are not just priests, but "royal priests" and "holy kings." They are a "kingdom," a "spiritual house," and a "holy priesthood." They have been called out of darkness into to the "royal freedom" of the marvelous light of God. The people of God exercise their priesthood not only by their participation in the Eucharist and other sacraments, but by the prophetic witness of a kingly holy life, sacrificial self-denial, and a prophetic and royal active charity.

> The holy people of God shares also in Christ's prophetic office; it spreads abroad a living witness to Him, especially by means of a life of faith and charity and by offering to God a sacrifice of praise, the tribute of lips which give praise to His name (cf. Heb. 13:15). The entire body of the faithful, anointed as they are by the Holy One (cf. John. 2:20, 27), cannot err in matters of belief. They manifest this special property by means of the whole peoples' supernatural discernment in matters of faith when "from the Bishops down to the last of the lay faithful" they show universal agreement in matters of faith and morals. That discernment in matters of faith is aroused and sustained by the Spirit of truth. It is exercised under the guidance of the sacred teaching authority, in faithful and respectful obedience to which the people of God accepts that which is not just the word of men but truly the word of God (cf. 1 Thess. 2:13). Through it, the people of God adheres unwaveringly to the faith given once and for all to the saints (cf. Jude 3), penetrates it more deeply with right thinking, and applies it more fully in its life.[13]

This teaching on Christians' participation in the prophetic office of Christ also demonstrates an understanding which is not limited to what one may think of as being strictly prophetic. It addresses all three offices from a prophetic perspective. The prophetic office involves more than a "supernatural discernment of matters of faith," and a verbal witness to this faith in Christ.

12. Ibid., no. 10.
13. Ibid., no. 12.

It includes a "living witness" to Christ which is carried out especially by a royal "life of faith and charity," as well as by the priestly offering to God of "a sacrifice of praise, the tribute of lips which give praise to His name."

Although the teaching of *Lumen Gentium* on the People of God offers us no complete triptych, no explicit exposition of the royal office of Christians, we should regard this as a casualty of composition by committee. The implicit attention given to explaining how the priestly and prophetic offices can be carried out in a kingly way is enough to show us that baptized Christians also participate in that office.

There is at least one further question which arises from the teaching of *Lumen Gentium* on the three-fold office. Why is the priestly office the first to be expounded? An answer is given by Karol Wojtyła/John Paul II. While Archbishop of Kraków he looked at the mission of the Church in some detail in a work entitled *Sources of Renewal*. There he drew upon the teaching of *Lumen Gentium* that the Church's mission is a sharing in the priestly, prophetic, and royal mission of Christ.[14] For Wojtyła, Christ's priesthood and our share in it were central to the teaching of Vatican II about the Church, mankind, and the world.[15] Moreover, according to him, it is the priestly mission of Christ and of Christians which most fully and simply expresses who they are.

> There is . . . good reason to consider participation in the priesthood of Christ and the attitude that derives therefrom, before turning to the prophetic and kingly aspects. While all these aspects indicate the orientation of the Conciliar enrichment of faith in respect of the attitudes of every Christian, it is participation in the priesthood of Christ which denotes the simplest and most complete attitude.[16]

However, Wojtyła did not go beyond this assertion. Exactly *why* this is so, what this *good reason* is, was not addressed by him. In *Sources of Renewal* Wojtyła made this point without any preparation or development.[17] Yet, according to him, *Lumen Gentium* placed participation in the prophetic mission of Christ on a par with participation in Christ's priesthood.[18] What did he mean by this? If *Lumen Gentium* placed participation in the prophetic mission of Christ, and by implication also the royal mission, on a par with

---

14. Wojtyła, *Sources of Renewal*, 91–100.

15. Ibid., 225.

16. Ibid., 224.

17. Ibid., 245. I am not aware of any place wherein Wojtyła/Pope John Paul II developed this thought further.

18. Ibid.

participation in Christ's priesthood, as Wojtyła claimed, in what sense can participation in the priestly mission of Christ most fully and simply express the identity of a Christian?[19] The two positions seem contradictory. Or is it a case of participation in the priestly office of Christ being foundational for the other two? Is it prior to but not superior to them?

Fortunately, in the *Catechism of the Catholic Church*, some indication is given as to why the priestly office should be considered first. Unlike *Lumen Gentium* itself, the *Catechism* addresses the three-fold office in three places rather than two. The section on the laity parallels *Lumen Gentium* 34–36. It too looks at these three offices as discrete missions.[20] Also, the section on the Church as the people of God, unlike *Lumen Gentium* 10–12, looks at the three missions in the same, more discrete manner to be found in *Lumen Gentium* 34–36.[21] However, at the beginning of Part Two of the *Catechism*, "The Celebration of the Christian Mystery," in addressing the question "What does the word liturgy mean," liturgy is presented as the activity which unites the three-fold office.

> The word "liturgy" originally meant a "public work" or a "service in the name of/on behalf of the people." In Christian tradition it means the participation of the People of God in "the work of God" [cf. Jn 17:4]. Through the liturgy Christ, our redeemer and high priest, continues the work of our redemption in, with, and through his Church. In the New Testament the word "liturgy" refers not only to the celebration of divine worship but also to the proclamation of the Gospel and to active charity [cf. Lk 1:23; Acts 13:2, Rom 15:16, 27; 2 Cor 9:12; Phil 2:14–17, 25, 30]. In all of these situations it is a question of the service of God and neighbor. In a liturgical celebration the Church is servant in the image of her Lord, the one "leitourgos" [cf. Heb 8:2, 6]; she shares in Christ's priesthood (worship), which is both prophetic (proclamation) and kingly (service of charity).[22]

What is revealing about this passage is that it recognizes that the primary Christological meaning of *leitourgos* and *leitourgia* is priestly, and then recognizes that all other Christian ministry, be it prophetic proclamation or kingly service of charity, is also *leitourgia*, carried out by one acting as a *leitourgos*, a priestly service carried out by a priest. In short, the priesthood

---

19. Ibid.
20. *Catechism of the Catholic Church*, nos. 901–13.
21. Ibid., nos. 783–86.
22. Ibid., nos. 1069–70.

of Christ is expressed in two ways. It is simultaneously an act of prophetic proclamation and a kingly service of charity.

Is this a valid reading of what Scripture reveals about "ministry"? In the Scriptural passages referred to we certainly see a priestly service indicated. Zechariah returns home when his time of service in the temple is ended (cf. Luke 1:23), and it is while the prophets and teachers of the church at Antioch are ministering to the Lord and fasting that the Holy Spirit commands the setting aside of Paul and Barnabas for the prophetic ministry of proclaiming the gospel to new hearers (cf. Acts 13:1–2). The proclamation of the gospel is even explicitly presented as a priestly, and indeed, sacrificial act. Thus Paul justifies his writing to the Christians of Rome to remind them of some important doctrines on the grounds that he is "a minister of Christ Jesus to the Gentiles in the priestly service of the gospel of God, so that the offering of the Gentiles may be acceptable, sanctified by the Holy Spirit" (Rom 15:16). Finally, the kingly service of charity is regularly spoken of liturgically (cf. Phil 2:25 and 30). This royal ministry is occasionally linked with the other two offices. Thus, like the link between worship and proclamation presented in Acts 13, it is because the Gentiles have shared in the spiritual blessings given to the Jewish Christians, blessings which have come through the liturgical action of Christ, that "they [the Gentiles] ought to be of service to them in material blessings" (Rom 15:27). Also, regarding the offering for the saints in Jerusalem, "the rendering of this service not only supplies the wants of the saints but also overflows in many thanksgivings [*eucharistion*] to God" (2 Cor 9:12), charity leading to worship. This kingly service is even spoken of in sacrificial terms. Thus, when Paul exhorts the Christians of Philippi to live holy lives (cf. Phil 2:12–16), he is willing "to be poured out as a libation upon the sacrificial offering of [their] faith" (Phil 2:17), that is to say, the faith that they live out, shining "as lights in the world [and] holding fast the word of life" (Phil 2:15–16).

Contemplating Mary as a Liturgical Priest, Prophet, King

How can our contemplation of Mary in the New Testament help us to answer the questions which have been raised above? What light can she shed upon our participation in the three-fold office of Christ? Can she help to show us if and how these three aspects form a single, integrated mission? Can she enlighten us further as to why the priestly office is the first to be expounded? To begin with we can see that *Lumen Gentium* offers us two ways to approach these questions, one which focuses on the three offices individually, and the other which looks at them as interrelated. Furthermore, we can see that any contemplation of the three-fold ministry of Mary must also look upon her as participating in the *leitourgia* of Christ. Like all Christians, Mary participates in the ministry of Christ the *leitourgos*.

Our first task is to identify Mary's Christological status vis-à-vis the threefold office. If we apply St. Augustine's definition, seconded by John Paul II, to Mary, then she is most definitely a "christ," an "anointed one." In *Christifideles Laici* John Paul II linked the threefold mission with the fact that Jesus is the Christ, the "Anointed One," and Christians are in union with him.[23] Of all human persons, Mary is the "anointed one" par excellence. She is addressed by the angel Gabriel as *kecharitōmenē*—"having been graced" (Luke 1:28, my translation). Her anointing by the Holy Spirit at the moment of her conception, renewed at the conception of Jesus in her womb, can be seen as a "type" of the anointing received by everyone who becomes a Christian.

Having established her *bona fides* as an anointed one, we can ask how Mary exercises the three offices? Following the explicit method of *Lumen Gentium* 34–36, one could say that Mary engages in a priestly ministry most obviously in her sacrificial union with Jesus as she stands at the foot of the cross, a union foretold by Simeon—"and a sword will pierce through your own soul also" (Luke 2:35). Another example would be her intercession in the Upper Room for the outpouring of the Holy Spirit (cf. Acts 1:14). Her exercise of a prophetic ministry can be seen in the Magnificat: "My soul magnifies the Lord, and my spirit rejoices in God my Savior" (Luke 1:46–47). Finally, her exercise of a kingly ministry can be observed in her response to the word of the angel that her cousin Elizabeth has conceived a son. Mary arises and goes "with haste" to her cousin, and stays with her for the remaining three months of her confinement (cf. Luke 1:39 and 56). We may confidently assume that these three months were spent in serving her cousin.[24] However, what is the result if one follows the method of *Lumen Gentium* 10–12? In what follows this method shall be applied to some scriptural passages which concern Mary.

---

23. John Paul II, *Christifideles Laici*, no. 14., where he refers the reader to St. Augustine, *Ennar. In Ps XXVI*, II, 2: CCL 38, 154ff.

24. The decision to speak of Mary as a king rather than a queen has been quite deliberate. To address Mary's royal ministry through the title "queen" would conjure up all kinds of ideas and images—Mary as the Queen Mother, and as *Regina caeli*, "taken up body and soul into heavenly glory, and exalted by the Lord as Queen over all things," as we are told in *Lumen Gentium*, no. 59, something which could distract us from Mary as the exemplar of the earthly disciples, and something which could emphasize her distinction from Christ rather than her participation in his mission.

The Annunciation (Luke 1:28–38)

"Rejoice, having been graced. The Lord is with you" (my translation). The angel brings the word of God to Mary. "But she was greatly troubled by his saying, and considered what kind of greeting this might be" (my translation). Why is Mary greatly troubled by this greeting, and why does she need to deliberate about its meaning? For one thing, it is a very unusual greeting. Mary is not addressed by name, but rather, by a title, the having-been-graced one. She is not being granted a grace. The grace has already been given. And the Lord is not being given to her. He is already with her.[25] By her Immaculate Conception, Mary, the having-been-graced-one, shares in the "royal freedom" of Christ from sin.

"And the angel said to her, 'Fear not, Mary, for you have found favor with God'" (my translation). The angel identifies the emotion which greatly troubles Mary as fear. What could this fear be of? It could not be a fear of something which Mary perceives as evil. Rather, it can only be a holy fear of an incomprehensible and awe inspiring revelation from God, the revelation of who she is before him, and of his presence with her.[26] For Mary, even before the conception of Jesus, God truly is Emmanuel, God with her (cf. Matt 1:23).

After allaying Mary's fear the angel reveals to her the will of God for her. The annunciation is not presented as a request, but as something that will happen, something which God commands. Notwithstanding Mary's *fiat* we are presented with the election of Mary by God. The great mystery of God's predestination of Mary as the mother of the Word made flesh (cf. Rom 8:28–30), and Mary's freedom, is presented to us. "And Mary said to the angel, 'How can this be, since I know not man'" (my translation). Unlike Zechariah's, Mary's question does not spring from doubts about God's power to do what he promises, but from a desire to understand God's will for her, hence the very different response of the angel. Rather than being struck dumb, she receives an explanation. "And the angel answered her, 'The Holy Spirit shall come upon you, and the power of the Most High shall overshadow you. Therefore the holy one born of you shall be called Son of God'" (my translation).

---

25. Ratzinger makes the point that "grace is a relational term: it does not predicate something about an I, but something about the connection between an I and a Thou, between God and man. 'Full of grace' could therefore also be translated as: 'You are full of the Holy Spirit; your life is intimately connected with God.'" See Balthasar and Ratzinger, *Mary*, 67.

26. Cf. Ibid., 70.

Further, the angel reveals even more to Mary. "And behold, your cousin Elizabeth has conceived a son in her old age, and this is the sixth month with her who was called barren. For with God nothing shall be impossible" (my translation). Why does the angel give Mary this extra revelation? Since Mary does not doubt God's power to do what he says he will, the reason for this revelation about Elizabeth must have another purpose. We shall see what that purpose is when we attend to the Visitation. "And Mary said, 'Behold the handmaid of the Lord. Let it be to me according to your word'" (my translation). Mary does not present herself as a generic servant, but as a particular kind of servant, a female slave or bond-servant (*doule*) of the Lord (*kuriou*). The relationship is not one of a hired servant to an employer, but one of a slave to a master. In other words, she declares her total subservience to God and his will for her. Mary acts as an obedient servant who thereby shares in the obedient kingly ministry of Christ.

What can be gleaned from this meditation on the Annunciation vis-à-vis Mary's identify as a *leitourgos* and her participation in a *leitourgia* which is priestly, prophetic, and kingly? To begin with, before one can be a prophet (speaker) for God, one must be a hearer of his word, and not just a hearer, but a listener. As we shall see Mary will soon exercise a prophetic ministry, but for now she listens to, considers, and questions the word of God. She is the elected vessel of God, chosen by him. As a disciple she exemplifies Peter's identification of the People of God as a "chosen race" (cf. 1 Pet 2:9). As elected by God, her ultimate response to the word of God is to declare her absolute acceptance of it as a slave of the Lord. This acceptance is not just passive. In a special way it fulfills the instruction given by St. Paul to the Christians of Rome: ". . . present your bodies as a living sacrifice, holy and well-pleasing to God, your worship according to the word (*logiken latreian*)" (Rom 12:1, my translation).[27] Through her word, Mary the *leitourgos*, Mary the priest, presents her whole psycho-somatic self for divine impregnation; a living sacrifice, a holy, consecrated sacrifice to God. Now she conceives Emmanuel. But even more, now having Emmanuel, the light of the world,

---

27. The *logike latreia* of St. Paul is a key concept in Ratzinger's liturgical theology. As he states in *A New Song for the Lord*: "Paul coined the expression *logike latreia* (Rom 12:1), which is quite difficult to translate into our modern languages because we do not have a real equivalent for the concept of logos. One could translate it 'spiritual worship' and so refer at the same time to the saying of Jesus about worshiping in spirit and truth (John 4:23). One could, however, translate it 'divine worship shaped by the word,' but would then of course have to add that 'word' in the biblical sense (and also in the Greek sense) is more than language and speech, namely, creative reality. It is also certainly more than mere thought and mere spirit. It is self-interpreting, self-communicating spirit (152)." See also McGregor, *Heart to Heart*, 165.

her own mind is enlightened by the Holy Spirit, and she is able to discover and act upon the good, well-pleasing and perfect will of God (cf. Rom 12:2).

The Visitation (Luke 1:39–56)

The first good, well-pleasing and perfect act which Mary undertakes is to go "with haste into the hill country, to a city of Judah," to the house of Zechariah, where she enters the house and greets Elizabeth. Although this three month sojourn can validly be seen as a service to her cousin in her confinement, it is much more than that. Mary's going "with haste" is the right response to the revelation of God's will. We find the same "haste" exercised by the shepherds in response to the angelic revelation given to them (cf. Luke 2:16).

Now, rather than being the greeted, Mary is the greeter. She is the angel of God to Elizabeth. Not only does Mary greet Elizabeth. Even before Christ is born, Mary is the *Theotokos*, the God-bearer. Elizabeth calls her the "mother of my Lord." Mary is already the God-bearer, and she bears Christ the Lord to Elizabeth and the babe in *her* womb, who, like David before the Ark of God, leaps for joy. Here Mary acts as a priestly mediator. She has offered her body as a living sacrifice to God, who, in accepting that offering through his Incarnation in her womb, now comes to others through her. This bringing Jesus to others is a priestly offering of the fruit of Mary's sacrifice, the fruit of her womb. It is also an evangelistic act which calls forth joyful praise and worship in the ones to whom Jesus is brought. The babe leaps for joy, and Elizabeth blesses God, who is present as the fruit of Mary's womb. It is also an act of royal service, for by what greater way can one serve others than by bringing Jesus to them?

As has been said, before a prophet can speak the word of God, the prophet must hear the word of God. Elizabeth is filled with the Holy Spirit, and prophetically proclaims that both Mary and the fruit of her womb are blessed. Mary is blessed among women because she believed what was spoken to her from the Lord would be fulfilled. Mary listens to the prophetic word of Elizabeth, and responds with her own prophetic proclamation, her own "gospel" (cf. 1:46–56), wherein she declares the marvelous deeds of God for her and for her people, Israel. Mary begins by describing the effect which these marvelous deeds have had upon her. "My soul magnifies that Lord, and my spirit exults in God my Savior" (1:46–47). Mary's prophesying flows out of her offering of worship to God. Her prophesying recounts the reasons for her worship. Here, Mary becomes a type of the chosen race, the royal priesthood, the holy nation, the people procured by God, and consequently, she proclaims the virtues of the one who has called her into his marvelous light (cf. 1 Pet 2:9). Furthermore, the fundamental act of God which Mary proclaims in her Magnificat is his mercy to his people (cf. 1 Pet 2:10).

The "Pondering" of Mary in Her Heart

We have already seen how Mary responded to the initial message of the angel. She "considered" (*dielogizeto*) what kind of greeting this might be (cf. 1:29). Joseph Ratzinger points out that the word used for "consider" "derives from the Greek root 'dialogue'. In other words, Mary enters into an interior dialogue with the Word . . . she speaks to it and lets it speak to her, in order to fathom its meaning."[28]

This "consideration" continues for Mary. When the shepherds make known to Mary, Joseph, and others what they had been told by the angel concerning her child, all who hear it marvel at what they are told. Yet Mary does more than "marvel." She kept all the sayings she had heard, pondering them in her heart (cf. 2:19). This verse employs the same kind of parallelism (magnify and exult) found at the beginning of the Magnificat. The verb normally translated as "kept" (*synēteri*) here means "kept together."[29] The second verb, normally translated as "pondering" (*symballousa*), presents us with a difficulty—exactly what the term means in 2:19 is not clear from the context.[30] The verb *symballō*, in its transitive sense, means to "throw together" or "bring together." In its intransitive sense it means to "meet." This verb only occurs in Lukan writings, twice in the Gospel and four times in the Acts of the Apostles.

Otfried Hofius suggests that the context of 2:19 is the extraordinary and mysterious occurrence reported by the shepherds to Mary and others. According to Hofius, the verb "might mean *grasp the true sense, hit upon the right meaning*. . . . In contrast to the [all] of v. 18, Mary knows the true significance 'of all these things.' . . . She recognizes in the miraculous appearance of the angel and its message (vv. 9–14) a confirmation of the promise she herself has already received from the angel (1:26ff)."[31] Here Hofius presents us with a monologic activity. However, if one looks at the other five uses of the verb by Luke, one finds that every single one involves an interaction with another person. In Luke 14:31 it refers to waging war with

---

28. Ibid.
29. See Balthasar and Ratzinger, *Mary*, 71–72.
30. Hofius, "*symballō*" 286. Cf. Brown and Reumann, "Mary in the Gospel of Luke and the Acts of the Apostles," 149.
31. Ibid.

someone, in Acts 4:15 it means to confer with someone, in Acts 17:18 it means to converse or argue with someone, in Acts 18:27 it means to be of use to or help someone, and in Acts 20:14 it means to meet with someone.[32] Given that every other use by Luke has a "dialogic" meaning, and given the dialogic meaning of 1:29, should we not read 2:19 in the same way, that it indicates an interior dialogue with the Word?[33]

A third time we find Mary "considering/pondering." Although both Jesus' mother and putative father "marvel" at the prophecy of Simeon that in Jesus he has seen the salvation of God, and although neither Mary and Joseph understand what Jesus says to them in the temple regarding his presence in his Father's house, we are told that it is Mary who "kept together" (*dietērei*) all that she has heard in her heart (cf. Luke 2:51). As Ratzinger points out, this verb is not the same as that used in Luke 2:19. Rather, in that earlier verse it "emphasizes more the aspect of 'together,' of unifying contemplation, [while in Luke 2:51 the verb] stresses the element of 'through,' of carrying the word to term and holding it fast."[34]

The phrase *symballousa en tē kardia autēs* is normally translated into English as "pondering them in her heart."[35] In order to come to a more thorough understanding of Mary's "pondering" we must also give our attention to the place wherein this *symballousa* of Mary takes place, her *kardia*. In Sacred Scripture we find that "heart" is used in many different senses.[36] If we look at the New Testament specifically, we find that the term *kardia* is sometimes used in contradistinction to the mind, to the soul, to the soul and mind, and to the conscience.[37] However, it is more often used in the

32. Ibid.

33. Further support for a dialogic reading of Luke 2:19 comes from Raymond Brown and John Reumann: "Drawing on a study of the use of *symballein* in Hellenistic literature from passages assembled by Wettstein over two hundred years ago, W. C. van Unnik understands *symballein* to refer to an interpretation of dark or difficult matters, the right meaning of which is often ascertained only by means of divine help (sometimes given in oracles, dreams, or signs). Thus, Josephus describes Joseph as 'having interpreted by reflection [*syllabōn tō logismō*]' the dream of the baker in prison (Gen 40:16)." See Brown and Reumann, "Mary in the Gospel of Luke and the Acts of the Apostles," 149–50. For the original quotation in Josephus, see his *Ant*. 2.5.3. no. 72. However, Joseph Fitzmyer, although he alludes to the passage in Josephus, thinks that the meaning of *symballein* in the other five Lukan passages do not suit the context of Luke 2:19. See Fitzmyer, *The Gospel According to Luke (I–IX)*, 413.

34. Balthasar and Ratzinger, *Mary*, 71–72.

35. The Douay-Rheims, Authorized, Revised Standard, New Revised Standard, New English, Jerusalem, New Jerusalem, New American Standard, and New International versions of the Bible all translate this phrase as "pondering/pondered in her heart."

36. See McGregor, *Heart to Heart*, 280–82.

37. For *kardia* in contradistinction to the mind, cf. 2 Cor 3:14–15; Phil 4:7; Heb 8:10

following senses. As the affective center of the human person it is the locus of the passions. As the intellectual center of the human person it is the locus of thought, understanding, doubt and questioning, deception and belief. As the volitional center of the human person it is the locus of intention and decision. The heart is also the locus of imagination and memory. As the moral center of the human person it is the locus of virtue, including theological virtue. It is the locus of conscience. It is the locus of that holiness which is normally called singleness or purity of heart. It is the locus of relation with other human persons.[38]

According to Sacred Scripture, the heart thinks, chooses, feels, imagines, and remembers. If it does all these things it cannot simply be any one of these things, but must be the union of all these things. As it happens, this is Ratzinger's understanding of the heart. For him, the heart is not to be identified simply with the intellect, or the will, or the passions, or the senses, or the body, or the soul. Nor is it to be identified with the *ego*. The heart is not identical with the person. Rather, for Ratzinger, it is the "place" of the integration of the intellect, will, passions, and senses, of the body and the soul. One could say that, for him, the human heart *is* the personal integration, the integration by the person, of these aspects of their human nature.[39]

The heart is also the locus of relation with God. It is the place which God searches and knows. It is the locus of revelation, as well as that refusal of revelation which is often called "hardness of heart." It is also the locus of God's indwelling, in Christ.[40] Ratzinger also agrees with this aspect of the

---

and 10:16; Rev 2:23. To the soul, cf. 1 Pet 1:22. To the soul and mind, cf. cf. Matt 22:37. To the conscience, cf. 1 Tim 1:5.

38. For *kardia* as the locus of the passions, cf. Matt 5:28 and 6:21; John 14:1, 14:27, 16:6 and 16:22; Acts 2:26, 7:54, 14:17 and 21:13; Rom 1:24, 9:2 and 10:1; 2 Cor 2:4; Jas 3:14; 2 Pet 2:14. For thought, cf. Matt 9:4 and 24:48; Mark 7:21 and 11:23; Luke 2:35 and 9:47; Rom 10:6; Rev 18:7. For understanding, cf. Matt 13:15 and 24:48; John 12:40; Acts 28:27; Rom 1:21; 1 Cor 2:9; Heb 4:12. For doubt and questioning, cf. Mark 11:23; Luke 24:38; Rom 10:6. For deception and belief, cf. Luke 24:25; Heb 3:12; Jas 1:26. For intention and decision, cf. Luke 6:45 and 21:14; Acts 5:3–4, 7:39, 8:22, and 11:23; 1 Cor 4:5, 7:37 and 14:25; 2 Cor 9:7. For imagination and memory, cf. Luke 1:51 and 66, 2:19, and 2:51. For virtue, cf. Luke 8:15; Acts 2:46 and 15:9; Rom 6:17 and 10:9; 2 Thess 3:5. For conscience, cf. 1 John 3:20. For purity of heart, cf. Matt 5:8; Acts 15:9; Eph 6:5; Col 3:22; 1 Thess 3:13; 2 Tim 2:22; Heb 10:22. For relation with other human persons, cf. Matt 18:35; Acts 16:14; 2 Cor 6:11–13 and 7:2–3; Phil 1:7.

39. See Ratzinger, *Behold the Pierced One*, 55–56; and *Jesus of Nazareth: From the Baptism*, 92–93. For Ratzinger's understanding of the human heart, see McGregor, *Heart to Heart*, 58–61, 85–93, 122–23, and 279–310.

40. For *kardia* as the locus of which God searches and knows, cf. cf. Luke 16:15; Rom 8:27; 1 Thess 2:4. Of revelation, cf. Luke 24:32; Acts 2:37; Rom 2:15; 2 Cor 3:3 and 4:6; Eph 1:18. Of the refusal of revelation, cf. Mark 3:5; 6:52 and 8:17; Matt 13:19; John 12:40; Acts 8:21; Rom 2:5; Eph 4:18. Of God's indwelling, in Christ, cf. Gal 4:6;

biblical understanding of the heart. Combining this insight with his concept of the heart as the integration of the human person, he holds that:

> The organ for seeing God is the heart. The intellect alone is not enough. In order for man to become capable of perceiving God, the energies of his existence have to work in harmony. His will must be pure and so too must the underlying affective dimension of his soul, which gives intelligence and will their direction. Speaking of the *heart* in this way means precisely that man's perceptive powers play in concert, which also requires the proper interplay of body and soul, since this is essential for the totality of the creature we call "man." Man's fundamental affective disposition actually depends on just this unity of body and soul and on man's acceptance of being both body and spirit. This means he places the body under the discipline of the spirit, yet does not isolate intellect or will. Rather, he accepts himself as coming from God, and thereby also acknowledges and lives out the bodiliness of his existence as an enrichment for the spirit. The heart—the wholeness of man—must be pure, interiorly open and free, in order for man to be able to see God.[41]

How is God revealed in the heart? The Acts of the Apostles consistently speaks of Christians being "filled with the Holy Spirit," or being "full of the Spirit." Christians become the dwelling place of the Spirit. Yet, although the Holy Spirit is presented as enlightening and renewing the minds of Christians, and inspiring peace and joy in Christians, neither the mind nor the passions are presented as the dwelling place of the Spirit.[42] The place which is thus presented is the heart. "God has sent the Spirit of his Son into our hearts, crying, '*Abba*! Father!'" (Gal 4:6). It is by searching the hearts of Christians when they pray in the Spirit that God "knows what is the mind of the Spirit" (Rom 8:27). Furthermore: "[God] has set his seal upon us and given us his Spirit in our hearts as a guarantee" (2 Cor 1:22). This guarantee is the love of God which "has been poured into our hearts through the Holy Spirit who has been given to us" (Rom 5:5).[43]

Eph 3:17; 2 Pet 1:19.

41. Ratzinger, *Jesus of Nazareth: From the Baptism*, 92–93.

42. For Christians being filled with the Holy Spirit, cf. Acts 2:4, 6:3, 7:55, 9:17, 11:24, 13:9, and 13:52. For Christians as the dwelling place of the Holy Spirit, cf. Rom 8:9; 1 Cor 3:16 and 6:19; Eph 2:22; 2 Tim 1:14. For the Holy Spirit enlightening and renewing the minds of Christians, cf. Rom 8:5–6; 1 Cor 2:13; Eph 4:23. For the Holy Spirit inspiring peace and joy in Christians, cf. Rom 12:11 and 14:17; 1 Thess 1:6.

43. The only alternative dwelling place of the Spirit which is given is the body of the Christian, in the particular context of sexual immorality (cf. 1 Cor 6:12–19).

The analysis given above on the biblical understanding of the heart has been necessary, since the scholarly attention given to Mary's "keeping" and "pondering" has not been matched by scholarly analysis of what might be meant by her "heart." All this being so, what does it mean to say that "Mary kept all these things, pondering them in her heart" (Luke 2:19)? If one accepts a dialogic reading of this verse, combined with the biblical understanding of the heart and Ratzinger's insights, then this verse would refer to an interior conversation between Mary and the Word of God, through the Holy Spirit dwelling in her heart, regarding the words and events which she has witnessed. Hence, Mary's pondering would be a prayerful pondering. Unlike the proud who have the comprehension of their hearts scattered by God (cf. Luke 1:51), it is Mary's encounter with God in her heart which enables her to grasp the true sense of what God has revealed to her. Moreover, we could say that Mary's heart is the place wherein all that has happened to her with regard to Jesus is brought together in this prayerful pondering—her memory of all the events pertaining to Jesus, and all the thoughts and feelings attendant upon those events, are made present and grow together into one coherent whole in the pure heart of Mary. Ratzinger sums up this meaning of Luke 2:19 as follows.

> The Evangelist here ascribes to Mary the insightful, meditative remembrance that in the Gospel of John will play such an important role in the unfolding of the message of Jesus in the Church under the working of the Spirit. Mary sees the events as "words," as happenings full of meaning because they come from God's meaning-creating will. She translates the events into words and penetrates them, bringing them into her "heart"—into that interior dimension of understanding where sense and spirit, reason and feeling, interior and exterior perception interpenetrate circumincessively.[44]

The Wedding at Cana (John 2:1–12)

Herein, considerable attention has been devoted to the nature of keeping and pondering in Mary's heart because it provides us with the example *par excellence* of an indispensible prerequisite for knowing *how* to participate in the priestly, prophetic, and kingly mission of Jesus Christ. Indeed, the very fact that Mary demonstrates an inability to immediately grasp the meaning of God's word to her (cf. Luke 1:29; 2:18, 33 and 50) shows us how vital it

---

44. Balthasar and Ratzinger, *Mary*, 70–71.

is, if we wish to exercise this three-fold mission, to enter into a dialogic encounter with the Word of God in the Spirit before we dare to participate in this priestly, prophetic, and kingly mission. We shall conclude by looking at an instance of Mary living this mission.

The wedding at Cana is a remarkable pericope. It is the only place in the New Testament where Jesus does not receive top billing: "On the third day there was a marriage at Cana in Galilee, and the mother of Jesus was there; Jesus also was invited to the marriage, with his disciples" (2:1–2). After the focus of the prologue of John on the Word made flesh (cf. 1:1–18), and the explicit demarcation of four separate days (cf. 1:29, 35 and 43), a further three day period occurs before the wedding (cf. 2:1). The enumeration of seven days is meant to remind us of the new creation (cf. 1:1–5).[45] The phrase, "on the third day," specifically draws our attention to the "hour" of Jesus (cf. 2:4).

At the wedding Mary has the attitude of a servant. She is aware that the wine has run out. Her response is to engage in an act of royal priesthood: "They have no wine" (2:3). It is royal intercession because it is a service to the newlyweds and their guests. The meaning of Jesus' reply has been the subject of much debate. In the first creation "woman" was the name which Adam gave to Eve. Here the New Adam is addressing the New Eve. We could even say that they are the true spousal couple in this wedding vignette. Calling Mary "woman" on the seventh day points to an anticipation of the "wedding of the Lamb" (Rev 19:7) with his Bride, a "sign" of the new covenant, as the Sabbath was a sign of the original covenant with creation.

Jesus' semitic reply, "what to me and to you," can be understood in three ways. The first two are an expression of displeasure at being unjustly bothered (cf. Judg 11:12; 2 Chr 35:21; 1 Kgs 17:18), or a denial of responsibility for the matter (cf. 2 Kgs 3:13; Hos 14:8).[46] However, the presentation of Mary as the "woman," the fact that she is otherwise only identified in this story as "the mother" of Jesus (cf. 2:1, 3, 5, and 12), thereby stressing the intimacy of their relationship, her response to the reply of Jesus, "Do whatever he tells you (2:5)," and the whole covenantal context of the verse, indicates a third meaning. "What to me and to you" is meant to indicate a covenantal agreement. For example, when Abraham wishes to bury Sarah in land belonging to Ephron the Hittite (cf. Gen 23:1–20), the phrase, "what is that between you and me" (Gen 23:15), seals the covenant between them. Thus Jesus' reply to Mary indicates covenantal agreement to fulfill her re-

---

45. Carson, *The Gospel according to John*, 167–68.

46. Donfried and Krodel, "The Mother of Jesus in the Gospel of John," 191. The standard reading of John 2:4 only recognizes these two ways. For instance, see Brown, *The Gospel according to John (I-XII)*, 99.

quest, an agreement which Mary comprehends, for she then prophetically instructs the servants to follow Jesus' instructions.[47]

Conclusion

Mary's ministry takes place within her dialogic relationship with Jesus in the Spirit. All her actions spring from her oneness with the Word in the Spirit. All three missions, the priestly, prophetic, and kingly, are united in Mary's actions. Through meditating upon Mary's exercise of the three-fold mission, we can see that these missions are one mission. Although one can analytically dissect this mission, it must be exercised synthetically. From the mysteries of Mary's life we can learn how offering priestly worship in the Spirit can prophetically evangelize, how kingly service to others can prophetically proclaim the gospel, how prophetic evangelization can be kingly service to others, how kingly service to others can be an act of priestly worship, how priestly sacrifice can proclaim the gospel, and how prophetically evangelizing can be a priestly magnification of God. Mary can show us how to be a "minister (*leitourgon*) of Christ Jesus to the Gentiles in the priestly service (*hierourgounta*) of the gospel (*euangelion*) of God, so that the offering (*prosphora*] of the Gentiles may be acceptable, sanctified (*hēgiasmenē*) by the Holy Spirit" (Rom 15:16).

Bibliography

Balthasar, Hans Urs von, and Joseph Ratzinger. *Mary: The Church at the Source*. Translated by Adrian Walker. San Francisco: Ignatius, 1997.
Brown, Raymond E. *The Gospel according to John (I-XII)*. London: Chapman, 1971.
Brown, Raymond E., and John Reumann. "Mary in the Gospel of Luke and the Acts of the Apostles." In *Mary in the New Testament*, edited by Raymond E. Brown et al., 105–77. Philadelphia: Fortress, 1978.
Carnazzo, Hezekias. "The Wedding at Cana." In *The Luminous Mysteries*, Part Three. Online: https://instituteofcatholicculture.org/the-luminous-mysteries-part-three/
Catechism of the Catholic Church. Homebush, NSW: St. Pauls, 1994.
Donfried, Karl P., and Gerhard Krodel. "The Mother of Jesus in the Gospel of John." In *Mary in the New Testament*, edited by Raymond E. Brown et al., 179–218. Philadelphia: Fortress, 1978.
Fitzmyer, Joseph A. *The Gospel according to Luke (I-IX)*. Garden City, NY: Doubleday, 1981.
Hofius, Otfried. "*symballō*." In *Exegetical Dictionary of the New Testament*, edited by Horst Balz and Gerhard Schneider, 3:285–86. Grand Rapids: Eerdmans, 1993.

---

47. For an illuminating commentary on the covenantal significance of John 1–2, see Carnazzo, "The Wedding at Cana."

Jelly, Frederick M. "The Theological Context of and Introduction to Chapter 8 of *Lumen Gentium.*" *Marian Studies* 37 (1986) 43–73.

"Lumen Gentium." In *The Documents of Vatican II with Notes and Index: Vatican Translation.* Australian ed. Strathfield, NSW: St. Pauls, 2009.

McGregor, Peter John. *Heart to Heart: The Spiritual Christology of Joseph Ratzinger.* Eugene, OR: Pickwick, 2016.

———. "Priests, Prophets and Kings: The Mission of the Church according to John Paul II." *Irish Theological Quarterly* 78 (2013) 61–78.

Pope John Paul II. *Christifideles Laici.* Homebush, NSW: St. Paul, 1989.

Ratzinger, Joseph. *A New Song for the Lord: Faith in Christ and Liturgy Today.* Translated by Martha M. Matesich. New York: Crossroad, 1996.

———. *Behold the Pierced One: An Approach to a Spiritual Christology.* Translated by Graham Harrison. San Francisco: Ignatius, 1986.

———. *Jesus of Nazareth: From the Baptism in the Jordan to the Transfiguration.* Translated by Adrian J. Walker. New York: Doubleday, 2007.

———. *Jesus of Nazareth: Holy Week: From the Entrance into Jerusalem to the Resurrection.* Translated by Philip J. Whitmore. San Francisco: Ignatius, 2011.

Wojtyła, Karol. *Sources of Renewal: The Implementation of the Second Vatican Council.* Translated by P. S. Falla. London: Collins, 1980.

9

Luke 1:26–38 as a Model of Dialogue[1]

—M. Isabell Naumann ISSM

> *The human person is called and gifted to participate profoundly in an ongoing dialogue with God. The principle of dialogue, evident throughout Sacred Scripture, for example, in the covenant stories of the Old Testament, is particularly evident in an exemplary mode at the beginning of the New Testament when God calls Mary to her distinguished active role at the center of the history of salvation, in the mystery of the Incarnation and the Redemption. A central text to illustrate the dialogic God-human relationship and cooperation is Luke's account of the Annunciation to Mary, Luke 1:26–38. In an archetypal fashion, Mary, in her response to God in the dialogic event—Trinitarian freedom and Mary's human freedom—emerges as the theological person, the person with God.*

Introduction

The human person is called and gifted to participate profoundly in an *ongoing dialogue with God*. This dialogic relationship is exemplified in the covenant stories of the Old Testament, for example, "Abraham," where God calls a single person and when through God's love for the

---

1. Revised edition of a paper given at the First Asia-Oceania Mariological Conference (12–16 September 2009) in Cavite, Philippines.

person the individual is liberated from his/her solitude,"² and is eminently evident at the beginning of the New Testament, when God calls Mary. ³

A central text to illustrate the God-human relationship and cooperation is Luke's account of the Annunciation to Mary, Luke 1:26–38. It is in this narrative where an anthropology—based on the creature's exercise of free will in the reception of grace, situated in an *I-Thou* relationship—is revealed. It reflects an intimate, personal relationship in which God and Mary (representing all creatures) are free partners. In an archetypal fashion, Mary, in her response to God in the dialogic event—Trinitarian freedom and Mary's human freedom—emerges as the *theological* person,⁴ the person *with* God. ⁵

The dialogue-relationship, as mentioned above, is established by divine initiative and human response. God's word to Mary "is pure *Yes*, just as she herself stands before him as a pure *Yes*" [freedom from original sin]. "This correspondence of God's *Yes* with Mary's *Yes* . . . denotes that Mary reserves no area of being, life, and will for herself as a private possession: instead, precisely in the total dispossession of self, in giving herself to God, she comes to the true possession of self."⁶ Through the progressive emptying-assimilation of her mission, she reaches her ultimate vocation. On the basis of these considerations some aspects of the actual Annunciation Narrative of Luke 1:26–38 shall be considered here.⁷

---

2. Novotny, "Making Mary's Yes Our Own," 104–5.

3. Rosenzweig expresses this pertinently when he writes: "With the call of the proper name the word of revelation steps into real dialogue." Rosenzweig, *The Star of Redemption*, cited in Novotny, "Making Mary's Yes Our Own," 105.

4. Novotny, "Making Mary's Yes Our Own," 101–3.

5. Roten succinctly illustrates this when he distinguishes Mary not only as "actor in the event and process of salvation history" but also as the "recipient of salvation, and thus a redeemed creature. This fully graced person is indeed both a 'fully and perfectly redeemed person' and the 'ideal of faith,' and thus is justly acclaimed as the 'personal summit of the faithful.' . . . Redeeming grace was given to her in abundance, but it needed to be received in faith and lived out in obedience patterned on the Fiat of the Annunciation." Roten, "Marian Devotion for the New Millennium," 61–62. See also: Rahner, "The Immaculate Conception," *Theological Investigations* I, 201–13; Naumann, "Mary as the Anthropological Model in the Thought of J. Kentenich," 31–47.

6. Ratzinger, *Daughter Zion* 70. See in this context also: Lohfink and Weimer, *Maria—nicht ohne Israel*.

7. In the scope of this presentation, I am not concerned with a comprehensive exegetical analysis of this passage which has been and still is the subject of considerable scholarly debate. For an extensive treatment of this Lukan account, see: Naumann, *The Annunciation Narrative of Luke 1:26–38 and its Interpretation for a Theology of Discipleship*.

Luke 1: 26–38: Divine Initiative and Human Response

The passage of Luke 1:26–38, with its five elemental characteristics of Old Testament annunciation narratives, parallels the episode in Luke 1:5–25.[8] The basic structure of the narrative is that of a dialogue with a proper opening scene where the two main characters are introduced. The dialogue then develops in three parts (cf. v. 28, vv. 30–33, v. 35), each part revealing more and more the divine message. The dialogue finishes with Mary's consent.

The opening of the episode makes reference to the time (the sixth month) which provides a link with the previous episode (cf. Luke 1:24) and prepares for the forthcoming announcement to Mary referring to Elizabeth's pregnancy (cf. Luke 1:36). The heavenly messenger[9] Gabriel, who was also involved in the announcement of John reappears. This provides a link between the passage announcing John (cf. Luke 1:19) and the one which follows the present text, Mary meeting Elizabeth (cf. Luke 1:39–56). "From God," indicates that God is the initiator in sending the angel.[10]

In order to appreciate the importance of Mary's calling into a covenanted relationship, established through this dialogue, the greeting (cf. Luke 1:28)—*Hail, O favored one, the Lord is with you* (*chairè, kecharitōmenē ho Kurios meta sou*) shall be considered in some detail.

For centuries, *chairè* was regarded as a common everyday greeting as the Greek equivalent of the Hebrew *shalom* or the Aramaic *shelam*. In the Latin translation it is also seen as an everyday greeting and therefore rendered as *Ave* and in English as *Hail*. In 1939 Lyonnet objected to this classical interpretation, concluding that Gabriel's *chairè* must be more than just an everyday greeting because the Septuagint usage of *chairè* refers to "the joy attendant on the deliverance of Israel"[11] carrying the meaning

---

8. The five-element pattern of the Old Testament annunciation narratives are: Appearance (1:26–28); Reaction (1:29); Announcement (1:30–33); Objection (1:34); Sign (1:35–38). Both the introduction and the conclusion of the narrative are set in the context of an angelophany (vv. 26a and 38b).

9. On the significance of OT angelology: Fitzmyer, *The Gospel according to Luke I–IX and X–XXIV*, 316, 324, 327–28; O'Toole, "The Unity of Luke's Theology," 23–32; Jeremias, *Die Sprache des Lukasevangeliums*; Hahn, *Kristisch-Exegetischer Kommentar über das Neue Testament*, 54–55; Radl, *Das Lukas-Evangelium*, 63.

10. While Zechariah is instantly addressed, Mary is first greeted by the angel before the message is imparted. For the custom in Israel to greet a woman, see: Grundmann, *Das Evangelium nach Lukas*, 55.

11. Lyonnet mentions Luke 10:5 and 24:36 where Luke expresses a greeting against a Semitic background in the customary Semitic term "peace." *Chairè* as a greeting occurs in the Lucan Gospel only in 1:28 and it is only used in this manner in Acts 15:23 and 23:26. Lyonnet "*Chairè kecharitōmenē*," 131–41; McHugh, *The Mother of Jesus in the New Testament*, 39.

"rejoice greatly."[12] The *Daughter of Zion* is called to rejoice at the coming of her king and savior.[13]

Luke 1:28 seems to render the same message: Mary shall rejoice, not fear, because the Lord is with her and the son of her womb will be the king of Israel and its savior.[14] In this, Mary is the personification of the *Daughter of Zion* in the day of eschatological salvation.[15] Thus, the angel's salutation, with its implicit reference to the messianic prophecies concerning the *Daughter of Zion*, is an invitation to Mary to rejoice greatly at the beginning of the messianic era that should come about by her active listening to the Word and acting upon it, that is, through her total obedience to God.

Chairè is immediately followed by the angel's assurance that Mary is the *recipient of God's favor—kecharitōmenē*.[16] Laurentin translated *kecharitōmenē* as "object-of-the-favor-of-God"—not just to look upon with favor but being *transformed by this favor or grace*,[17] hence *kecharitōmenē* in Luke 1:28 should not be reduced to a lesser sense but be rendered the meaning of: *You who were and remain the object of the grace of God*. It is a

---

12. Brown, *The Birth of the Messiah*, 321–24. Nolland, "Luke's Use of Charis," 614–20; Cambe, "La charis chez saint Luc," 192–207. Further references to "the rejoicing of Israel" are to be found in Jer 31:13, (38:13 in LXX), Bar 4:37; Hab 3:13; Zech 4:10; 10:7. The present imperative *chairè* in only found in Zeph 3:14; Joel 2:21; and Zech 9:9. Here the "rejoicing" refers to the deliverance of Israel.

13. In the Septuagint the imperative *chairè* is (with the exception of Lam 4:21) always addressed to the "Daughter of Zion" as an invitation to "rejoice greatly" because "the Lord is with her" as king and savior. For "Daughter of Zion" see Cazelles, "Fille de Sion et théologie Mariale dans la Bible," 51–71.

14. Lyonnet concludes that "rejoice" is a better translation than "hail" because it would do justice to the Old Testament language and background of the context and to Gabriel's opening word as he announces the end of the entire Old Testament and, therefore, its fulfilment. Lyonnet, "*Chairè kecharitōmenē*," 136–39. For the criticism of Lyonnet's thesis, see in particular Strobel, "Der Gruss an Maria (Lk 1:28)," 86–110.

15. McHugh, *The Mother of Jesus*, 44; Laurentin, *The Truth of Christmas*, 50–60; Audet, "L'annonce a Marie," 346–74.

16. The precise meaning of *kecharitōmenē* is explained by the angel in verse 30, where the phrase "you have been favored by God" shows that Mary is designated as the recipient of divine favor (*kecharitōmenē* being the perfect passive participle of *charitoo*). Fitzmyer points out that this "favor" is to be understood in the context of the unique role which Mary is to play in conceiving God's Messiah—*gratia gratis data* (a grace freely given), Fitzmyer, *Gospel According to Luke I–IX*, 345–46. Apart from the reference in Luke 1:28 the word occurs in the New Testament in Eph 1:6, a meaning that Luke seems to apply here, "that Mary was endowed with divine graces freely bestowed." McHugh, *The Mother of Jesus*, 47.

17. For a full exposition of *kecharitōmenē*, see Laurentin, *Truth of Christmas*, 18–19.

new name given to Mary (cf. Judg 6:12)—her actual name—revealed to her by God through his messenger.

The name establishes an eschatological context in reference to Zephaniah 3. As such this name which has been given to Mary "stands at the height of the fulfilment of salvation history. The name prefaces the vocation given to Mary to be the Mother of the Messiah, the Son of God."[18] Mary's name reveals a new dimension of her relationship with God. The person who is called to receive the Word becomes bearer of the Word and thus can be called by a new name, Christ-bearer.

Considering Laurentin's suggestion, it follows that in Christ the era of grace has come and Mary, "the chosen one," is already endowed with that fullness of grace which is not only offered to her in order to fulfill her unique role as the first adherent to Christ in the history of salvation but which God will also bestow on humankind. Mary is favored by God. She is to be the Mother of the descendant of David and the Son of the Most High. This state or condition of divine favor as expressed in the *kecharitōmenē* is to be understood in relation to the unique role that she is to perform in conceiving God's Messiah[19] and God is the one who will sustain her in her task on her journey of faith. Such is God's offer to every person: to freely accept God's favor, to act upon it and to walk life's journey in this light.

The Old Testament phrase *ho kurios meta sou* (the Lord is with you), intended to prepare the person for divine service with the assurance "the Lord will help you,"[20] never refers to a person in ordinary circumstances but is always addressed to someone for whom God has great plans. It gives the assurance that he will be constantly at the person's side in all difficulties on his/her journey of faith, helping the person to accomplish his/her mission, for example, Israel, Moses, Gideon, and Jeremiah.[21] These passages all bear the same message: "they are all concerned with Israel's destiny; the person called by God is called to a high vocation and entrusted with a momentous mission; the destiny of Israel is dependent on the person's response to God's call."[22] The same may be applied to Mary when Gabriel greets her thus. The statement assures her that she would get every assistance but everything depends on her free response.

---

18. Laurentin, *Truth of Christmas*, 19. See also Miguens, *Mary, the Servant of the Lord*.

19. Fitzmyer, *Gospel according to Luke I–IX*, 345–46; De la Potterie, "Kecharitōmenē en Lc 1, 28," 357–82, 480–508.

20. Grundmann, *Das Evangelium nach Lukas*, 56; Moloney, *Mary, Woman and Mother*, 19.

21. Gen 26:24; 28:15; Exod 3:12; Judg 6:16; Jer 1:4–8.

22. Grundmann, *Das Evangelium nach Lukas*, 56.

Gabriel's greeting was very *perplexing*.[23] Luke shows clearly that Mary's disturbance was caused by the angel's words, for she pondered[24] the meaning of these words (the greeting) and, entering "interiorly into dialogue with the Word, she addressed the Word and allowed herself to be addressed by it in order to arrive at its basic meaning."[25]

In verse 30 the angel reassured Mary of "God's favor." The Hebrew idiom "to win someone's favor" with its equivalent Greek translation (to find favor with), as it occurs in the Old Testament,[26] carries the concept of election for some given purpose or mission and it also indicates the free choice of God who, totally independent of the human acceptability or worth of the one to be chosen, chooses whom he wants. Judging from the description of the *calling* of the chosen people in the Old Testament, and Luke's possible appropriation of Mary as (in Old Testament language) "the Daughter of Zion at the end of time,"[27] the destiny of Israel (and therefore ultimately of the Church as new Israel) is dependent on Mary's response in this crucial moment of divine-human encounter.

The significant salutation to Mary opened the dialogue and prepared for the next movement, the actual messianic message with the actual birth announcement of the messianic king, and the virginal conception of Jesus with the sign of assurance.

Luke's understanding was obviously that of the early Church, where there was a close association between the reign of Jesus and his resurrection and exaltation. The latter linked Jesus' reign with the Davidic promises (cf. Acts 2:30–36). The association also expresses that the kingdom of God is already present in Jesus' ministry and that his exaltation is an open recognition of the One who already acted in his earthly life with kingly power as the representative of God.[28]

Mary's question (v. 34), first, as a literary device, leading to verse 35 in order to prepare for the central message of that verse, is intended by the evangelist to show the reader that the conception through the Holy Spirit causes the virginal birth and that Mary gave birth to the Messiah as a

---

23. For a detailed exposition see Marshall, *The Gospel of Luke: A Commentary on the Greek Text*, 66.

24. *Dialogizomai* (*dielogizeto*—she stood there wondering), see: Jeremias, *Sprache des Lukasevangeliums*, 47–48.

25. Ratzinger, "'You are full of grace': Elements of Biblical Devotion to Mary," 54–68.

26. For example, Gideon: Judg 6:17; Moses: Exod 33:12–17.

27. McHugh, *The Mother of Jesus*, 52.

28. Schürmann, *Lukasevangelium* I, 48, 49.

virgin.²⁹ Further important instances stress that the messianic era would be characterized by the outpouring of the Spirit (cf. Joel 3:1–5), and that the messianic king will possess God's Spirit (Isa 11:1–2). The word *episkiazo* (to overshadow) is rarely used in the Septuagint, and when it is, it occurs in passages which speak of the presence of God; in the Gospels it appears only when referring to the cloud of the transfiguration symbolizing the divine presence³⁰—as did the *Shekinah* imagery of the Old Testament.³¹

Because of this implication commentators suggest that the word in Luke 1:35 resembles the meaning of Exodus 40:34–45, that is, that God's Holy Spirit will descend upon Mary as the "glory of God once descended upon the tent of witness and filled it with a divine presence."³² Accordingly, one may surmise that Yahweh visits his people when he comes to Mary. God does so by what he creates in her womb "without the intervention of a human father. This is why the holy child is called God's Son."³³

It could follow then that the temple is no longer the place where God dwells. Rather, Mary, through her virginal conception, becomes the new dwelling place of God, and this holy child, Jesus, is the Son of God, as revealed in the two theophanies in the early part of his ministry—the Transfiguration and the Baptism.³⁴

Though Mary requests no sign (in contrast to Zechariah), she receives a confirmation in the sign of Elizabeth's pregnancy, indicating that God can also bring about the virginal conception in her.

Mary, in saying *"behold I am the handmaid of the Lord; let it be to me according to your word,"* identifies herself as a slave or servant³⁵ and believes the word (*rema*) of the angel. In so doing she stands in the great tradition of her people, for example, David is referred to as the servant of

---

29. Gewiss, "Marienfrage, Lk 1:34," 253; Schürmann, *Lukasevangelium* I, 51. For a detailed discussion regarding Mary's question, see for example: Harnack, "Zu Lk 1:34–35," 53–57; Rahner, *Mary, Mother of the Lord*; McHugh, *The Mother of Jesus*, 196–97; De Satge, *Mary and the Christian Gospel*, 112–14; Ratzinger, *Daughter of Sion*, 47–61.

30. Mark 9:7; Matt 17:5; Luke 9:34.

31. For example, Num 9:17–18; Wis 19:7–8; Exod 25:20; 40:34–35; Isa 4:2–6.

32. Benoit, *Exegese et Theologie*, 206–8.

33. McHugh, *The Mother of Jesus*, 58. For a different opinion on this issue, see Brown et al., *Mary in the New Testament*, 133–34; Brown, *Messiah*, 311–16.

34. Matt 17:5; Mark 9:7; Luke 9:35, and Matt 3:17; Mark 1:11; Luke 3:22.

35. In this verse the use of *idou* (behold) with the following nominative is an expression of the readiness to serve or to listen (cf. 1 Sam 3:5, 6, 8). For the Old Testament use of *doule* (female slave and the masculine equivalent), see: Rengstorf, "δοῦλος," in Kittel and Friedrich, *Theological Dictionary of the New Testament*. II, 268, 273. See also 1 Sam 1:11; 25:41; 2 Sam 9:6; 2 Kgs 4:16.

the Lord,[36] and the nation as such is identified as the servant of the Lord.[37] Therefore, it is quite probable that in the phrase "the handmaid of the Lord" Luke intended a double reference, "on the one hand a reference to Mary and on the other a reference to the nation she represents."[38] Mary's description of herself is characteristic for the new community in Christ.[39]

The final word of Mary *genoito moi* (let it be to me),[40] often interpreted in terms of a humble (passive) submission to God's will, is understood by McHugh as an expression of joy and prayer in that it resembles more convincingly the Lucan presentation of what is about to come: the messianic era with its characteristic features of the outpouring of the Spirit and messianic joy (cf. Ezek 36:37).[41]

Taking into account that according to Luke, the infancy of Jesus is marked by the outpouring of the Spirit upon the "poor of Yahweh," those who waited for the eschatological coming of the Savior, Mary is the first recipient of this Spirit who enables her, after she has carefully considered and deliberated (cf. Luke 1:29, 34), to make a Christological commitment (cf. Luke 1:38), a commitment which reflects messianic joy. In this she is from the very outset the first adherent to Christ, the prototype of the Church.[42]

The Theological Intention of Luke 1: 26–38

The whole of the Annunciation story is "an extremely fundamental Christological statement, spelling out Jesus' divine identity in terms of his conception."[43] The theological intention of Luke 1:26–38 is the affirmation

---

36. Pss 78:70, 89:3, 20; 132:10.

37. Isa 42:1; 48:20; 49:3, 5.

38. Leaney, "The Birth Narratives in St. Luke and St. Matthew," 159.

39. Acts 2:18; 4:29; 1 Cor 7:22; 1 Pet 2:16.

40. Zerwick and Grosvenor, *A Grammatical Analysis of the Greek New Testament*, 172; Jeremias, *Die Sprache des Lukasevangeliums*, 54–55.

41. Coming from the Greek text where the phrase is in the aorist optative, thus expressing a wish or prayer, McHugh notes a difference to the submissive tone in, for example, Jesus' prayer in Gethsemane (cf. Luke 22:42) where it has the aorist imperative. The Latin rendering Fiat does not accurately bring out the distinction. Therefore McHugh comes to the conclusion that the correct translation of Luke 1:38 would be a cry of joy—"O, may it be so for me, according to thy word." Luke's choice of this mood means that Mary's words are both a prayer and an expression of joy, not just a declaration of humble submission. McHugh, *The Mother of Jesus*, 65.

42. Laurentin, "Mary: Model of the Charismatic as seen in Acts 1–2, Luke 1–2, and John," 28–43.

43. La Verdiere, *Luke*, 20.

that Jesus was the Son of God through his virginal conception. Besides this Christological confirmation which is certainly the primary import of the passage under consideration, there is also a significant Mariological indication. "Mary's highly personalized dialogue with God, through Gabriel, will also be the archetype of the God-human relation, not only because it includes all of the dialogic elements but also because of her uniqueness."[44]

She, in contrast to Zechariah, is greeted by the angel as the one who "found favor with God" and who, by her free virginal response to God's initiative, cooperates as "the handmaid of the Lord" in the plan of God. Committing herself wholly to him she becomes the most perfect example of the "poor of Yahweh," resembling the image of the eschatological "Daughter of Zion," whose spiritual poverty finds its expression in the fruitfulness of her womb. She becomes the mother of the Messiah and the first adherer to the Word.[45]

Balthasar, in his estimation of Mary, is not content with seeing her as model and prototype for all persons, but refers to her interaction with God, as fulfilled in the Annunciation event, as the *exemplary event of the God-human relationship*—encouraging every person to creatively participate fully in the glorious liberty of the children of God.[46] Undoubtedly, the creature finds its truth in Mary: to be called into existence as one whose being is to welcome and to respond to God's call and to become fruitful in that gratuitous response. Mary then guarantees the ontological independence of creation, but she does so as woman. To deny or reject this feminine-Marian aspect of creatureliness would entail "the negation of creation and the invalidation of grace and would lead to a picture of God's omnipotence that reduces the creature to a mere masquerade and that also completely fails to understand the God of the Bible."[47]

Conclusion

In conclusion it can be said that the centrality of "Mary's *fiat* reveals what is at stake in man's dialogue with God: what it is to be a person, that is, 'to be a fit habitation for God.'"[48] It is a gradual discovering of the dialogue of love

---

44. Novotny, "Making Mary's Yes Our Own," 101–3.

45. Luke 2:11. Ratzinger, "'You are full of grace,'" 54–68; Laurentin "Mary, Model of the Charismatic as seen in Ac 1-2, Lk1-2," 36–39.

46. Rom 8:21. Balthasar, *Theo-Drama*, Vol. III, 298–99; Balthasar, *You Crown the Year: Radio Sermons*, 191.

47. Ratzinger, *Daughter Zion*, 28; López, "Mary, Certainty of our Hope," 197.

48. López "Mary, Certainty of our Hope," 178–79.

that constitutes the very divine nature and God's continuous *gift* of entering into a dialogic covenanted relationship with the human creature.[49]

Bibliography

Audet, Jean Paul. "L'annonce a Marie." *Revue Biblique* 63 (1986) 346–74.
Balthasar, Hans Urs von. *Theo-Drama: Theological Dramatic Theory.* Vol. III. *Dramatis Personae: Persons in Christ.* San Francisco: Ignatius, 1992.
———. *You Crown the Year: Radio Sermons.* San Francisco: Ignatius, 1989.
Benoit, Pierre. *Exegese et Theologie.* 3 vols. Vol. III. Paris: Cerf, 1961–68.
Brown, Raymond. *The Birth of the Messiah: A Commentary on the Infancy Narratives in Matthew and Luke.* New York: Doubleday, 1979.
Brown, Raymond, et. al. *Mary in the New Testament.* London: Chapman, 1978.
Cambe, Michel. "La charis chez saint Luc: Remarques sur quelques textes, notamment le *kecharitōmenē*." *Revue Biblique* 2 (1963) 192–207.
Cazelles, Henri. "Fille de Sion et théologie Mariale dans la Bible." *Bulletin de la Société Francaise d'Etudes Mariales* 21 (1964) 51–71.
De la Potterie, Ignace. "*Kecharitōmenē* en Lc 1,28: Etude exegetique et theologique." *Biblica* 68 (1987) 357–82, 480–508.
De Satge, John. *Mary and the Christian Gospel.* London: SPCK, 1976.
Fitzmyer, Joseph A. *The Gospel according to Luke I–IX and X–XXIV. A New Translation with Introduction and Commentary.* The Anchor Bible. Vols. 28 & 28A. New York: Doubleday, 1986.
Gewiss, Josef. "Marienfrage, Lk 1:34," *Biblische Zeitschrift,* Neue Folge 5 (1961) 221–54.
Grundmann, Walter, *Das Evangelium nach Lukas, Theologischer Hand-Kommentar zum Neuen Testament* 3. Berlin: Evangelischer Verlag, 1966.
Harnack, Adolf. "Zu Lk 1:34–35." *Zeitschrift für die Neutestamentliche Wissenschaft* 2 (1901) 53–57.
Jeremias, Joachim. *Die Sprache des Lukasevangeliums.* Sonderband. Kritisch-Exegetischer Kommentar über das Neue Testament. Göttingen: Vandenbhoeck & Ruprecht, 1980.
Laurentin, Renee. "Mary: Model of the Charismatic as Seen in Acts 1-2, Luke 1-2, and John." In *Mary, the Spirit and the Church,* edited by Vincent Branick, 28–43. New York: Ramsey, 1980.
———. *The Truth of Christmas. Beyond the Myths: The Gospels of the Infancy of Christ.* Petersham, MA: St. Bede's, 1986.
La Verdiere, Eugene. *Luke.* Dublin: Veritas, 1980.
Leaney, Robert."The Birth Narratives in St. Luke and St. Matthew." *New Testament Studies* 8 (1961–62) 158–66.
López, Antonio. "Mary, Certainty of our Hope." *Communio* 35 (2008) 174–99.
Lohfink, Gerhard and Ludwid Weimer. *Maria—nicht ohne Israel: Eine neue Sicht der Lehre von der Unbefleckten Empfängnis.* Freiburg: Herder, 2008.
Lyonnet, Stanislaus. "*Chairè kecharitōmenē.*" *Biblica* 20 (1939) 131–41.
Marshall, Howard. *The Gospel of Luke: A Commentary on the Greek Text.* NIGTC. Exeter, UK: Paternoster, 1978.

---

49. Novotny, "Making Mary's Yes Our Own," 101–22.

McHugh, John. *The Mother of Jesus in the New Testament.* London: Darton, Longman & Todd, 1975.

Miguens, Manuel. *Mary, the Servant of the Lord.* Boston: St. Paul, 1978.

Moloney, Francis. *Mary, Woman and Mother.* Homebush, Australia: St. Paul, 1988.

Naumann, Isabell. "The Annunciation Narrative of Luke 1:26–38 and its Interpretation for a Theology of Discipleship." MTh thesis, Sydney College of Divinity, 1990.

———. "Mary as the Anthropological Model in the Thought of J. Kentenich," *Ephemerides Mariologicae* LIX, I (2009) 31–47.

Nolland, John L. "Luke's Use of Charis." *New Testament Studies* 32 (1986) 614–20.

Novotny, Ronald. "Making Mary's Yes Our Own: A Study of Theological Personhood." *Marian Studies* LVI (2005) 101–22.

O'Toole, Robert F. "The Unity of Luke's Theology: An Analysis of Luke-Acts." *Good News Studies* 9 (1984) 23–32.

Ratzinger, Joseph. *Daughter Zion.* San Francisco: Ignatius, 1983.

———. "'You are full of grace': Elements of Biblical Devotion to Mary." *Communio* 16 (1989) 54–68.

Radl, Walter. *Das Lukas-Evangelium.* Erträge der Forschung. Band 261. Darmstadt: Wissenschaftliche Buchgesellschaft, 1988.

Rahner, Karl. "The Immaculate Conception." In *Theological Investigations.* Vol I. 201–13. London: Darton, Longman & Todd, 1974.

———. *Mary, Mother of the Lord.* Glasgow: Glasgow University Press, 1974.

Rengstorf, Karl. "δοῦλος." In *Theological Dictionary of the New Testament.* Vol. II, edited by Gerhard Kittel and Gerhard Friedrich, 261–80. Grand Rapids: Eerdmans, 1964–76.

Rosenzweig, Franz. *The Star of Redemption.* Notre Dame, IN: Notre Dame, 1985.

Roten, Johann. "Marian Devotion for the New Millennium." *Marian Studies* LI (2000) 52–95.

Schürmann, Heinz. *Das Lukasevangelium.* Teil 1. Kommentar zu Kapiteln 1,1–9,50. Freiburg: Herder, 1969.

Strobel, August. "Der Gruss an Maria (Lk 1:28). Eine philologische Betrachtung zu seinem Sinngehalt." *Zeitschrift für Neutestamentliche Wissenschaft* 53 (1962) 86–110.

Zerwick, Max and Mary Grosvenor. *A Grammatical Analysis of the Greek New Testament.* Rome: Biblical Institute, 1981.

10

Marian Epistemology

—Matthew John Paul Tan

This chapter will argue that being a creature in the Body of Christ entails knowing in the same manner as Mary did as the icon of the Church. It will argue that Mary's embodying the life of the disciple extends to the way in which she embodies an epistemology, one that runs counter to many modern forms of epistemology by those within many parts of the Church, which in turn has aligned the Church with institutions, practices, and premises whose evangelical value can only be described as questionable. With reference to the Marian narratives in Scripture, this chapter will suggest the beginnings of a Marian epistemology, grounded in what Paul in 1 Corinthians 13 calls "knowing in part." This is a way of knowing grounded not in triumphalistic comprehension of an object but in inquiry, prophetic utterance, hopeful commitment, and embodied service. Before concluding, the chapter will explore possibilities for a Marian epistemology to not only correct modern presumptions of knowledge but also speak to and engage postmodern theories such as standpoint feminism.

Introduction

This chapter will begin with the question: what does being a creature in the Body of Christ entail in terms of discipleship? Catholics, Orthodox, and Anglicans at least are aware that the Church proposes an important part of the answer to this question is the person of Mary the mother of Jesus. At least in the context of the three aforementioned traditions, it is a longstanding tradition in the Church that Mary is not just the Mother of God, but also something more. Though mentioned elsewhere, this additional element was most explicitly articulated in a 2004 joint international Mariological statement between the Anglican and Catholic Church entitled *Mary Grace and Hope in Christ*.[1] That statement reminds us that Mary's significance for Christians is due to the fact that Mary is "the one who, of all believers, is closest to our Lord and Savior Jesus Christ." Mary is thus an icon of the Church, Mary stands as *the* exemplar of the life of a believer in the Church.

This chapter will be but a fragment in the much larger inquiry on how we in our discipleship can follow Mary as the icon of discipleship. It will do so by tentatively proposing that the iconography of Mary's life of a disciple is not just expressed merely in terms of a template of patterns of action. For underlying these patterns of action is also a unique, Marian contribution to the study of epistemology. What this chapter proposes, in other words, is that Mary's path to discipleship is also a way of knowing, a way of knowing that, as icon of the Church, Christian disciples are called to imitate but rarely put into practice.

It is submitted that the epistemological slant of this chapter is necessary, due to the patterns of institutional practice in the life of the contemporary Church which are often taken for granted. Attention is being drawn to these patterns because they imply an epistemology that has moved away from the Marian icon of discipleship towards essentially modern alternatives, which manifest themselves in forms of bureaucratic or instrumental reason. This has often been unintentional, and is the result of a presumption that the institutional forms of a practice are inherently neutral, free from any ideational burden, and can be made to bend in accordance to the intentions of the practitioner, which get infused into the form without complication. The basis of this chapter's main argument, however, is that such a presumption of the ideational neutrality of institutions is problematic. It is problematic because, at one level, institutional forms and practices *do* come with ideational weight, and that ideational weight resists any bending by a practitioner's intentions—indeed that very solidity could very well mean that the political, social, philosophical, and even theological presumptions built into the institutional form could infuse the intentions of the practitioner.[2]

1. Anglican-Roman Catholic International Commission, in *Mary, Grace and Hope in Christ*, 7–88.

2. For a more thorough investigation of the problematique of the impact of

What this means is that, coupled with the Church's adoption of modern institutional forms into its lifeworld, there is also an ecclesial buying into the modern presumptions that have been built into those forms, key to which are the modern forms of epistemology. This has facilitated alignments of the Church with certain institutions, practices, and premises that embody modern modes of knowing. This in turn has underpinned evangelical practices whose evangelical value is questionable, or even worse fallen short of the Marian icon.

At a second, more strategic level, the Church's falling short of the Marian ideal through its alignment with modern institutions and concomitant adoption of modern presumptions is problematic because it has allowed the Church to be culturally sideswiped by our contemporary postmodern condition. As shall be demonstrated below, the mismatch between the Church's modern alignments and postmodern culture is particularly acute in the area of epistemology, which forms the basis of expressing certain types of truth claims publicly. Put more specifically, the Church would find its evangelical mission hampered by its adoption of a modern epistemology defined here as full comprehension, apprehended exclusively in the mind of a solitary individual. Put conversely, this chapter proposes that Mary embodies an alternative way of knowing, an icon of knowing that is more in keeping with the Church's status as pilgrim, as articulated in the Dogmatic Constitution on the Church in the Second Vatican Council. Such an epistemology would also be more in keeping with the cultural anthropology defined by Josef Pieper as "being on the way"—being *status viatoris*.[3] Going further still, it will be submitted in the paragraphs that follow that Mary's way of knowing would enable better traction between the Church and postmodern culture as the former's pilgrimage to the last things enters into the lands of the latter.

In order to dispense with this burden, this chapter will divide its case into three sections, each of which is headed by a guiding question. The first question—*what* did Mary know?—will look to Scripture to show the extent of Mary's comprehension of truth claims when such claims were communicated to her and apprehended by her. The second question—*how* did Mary know?—looks to Scripture again and also to the Christological anthropology of Graham Ward to explain the process by which Mary's knowledge is demonstrated once it is apprehended. It will highlight the way in which the icon of the Church eschewed both knowledge defined as full comprehension, but also the notion of knowledge as exclusively cognitive and atomistic. The

---

institutional forms and their presumptions on Christian practice, see Tan, *Justice, Unity and the Hidden Christ*.

3. Pieper, *Faith, Hope, Love*.

final question—what can Mary's knowing say to postmodern culture?—will demonstrate the traction that can be gained with the Church's postmodern context via recourse to the Marian ideal of knowledge with reference to the epistemology of standpoint feminism. More particularly, it will highlight the way the latter's notion of the "achievement" of standpoints finds premodern echoes in the former's path towards purification and perfection of all things, including knowledge.

What Did Mary Know?

To answer the question of *what* Mary knew, it is necessary to turn to the primary text that records her biography, namely Scripture. The Gospels, in particular, constitute the most reliable source pertaining to the life of the Mother of God. What readers might notice upon a first reading of the Gospels is that they do not seem to convey very much material to answer the specific question of what she knew. Certainly, there are specific items of knowledge conveyed to Mary that were conveyed in the Gospels, such as the annunciation of the Incarnation by the angel Gabriel (cf. Luke 1:26–38), the prophecy of Simeon to Mary (cf. Luke 2:25–35), and the lack of wine at the wedding at Cana in the Gospel of John (cf. John 2:1–11). This, however, does not make for a very extensive list. The situation changes, however, when one shifts the focus of the answer away from the items of data acquired, to focus instead on the *certainty* that came with Mary's apprehension of the data that was acquired, and her response in the face of that lack of certainty. It is submitted that when this rubric of certainty and response is used to answer this question, the Gospels suddenly possess a richness and fecundity, because this rubric would cause other biographical data recorded in the Gospels to take on great epistemological significance, layering the recognizable knowledge claims in the biblical texts to create a highly nuanced, bodily textured epistemological tract.

Certainty is important to consider because it has become one of the focal points of epistemological debate in recent decades. Since Descartes, modern epistemology has insisted that the trustworthiness of a knowledge claim rests on its ability to furnish absolute certainty to the mind of the one doing the knowing unaided by anything other than his or her own reason, what James K. A. Smith calls knowledge grounded in comprehension.[4] Cartesians found this mode of knowing to be an ostensibly attractive way to furnish a reliable grounding in establishing valid knowledge claims, as well as a means to insulate the knower from manipulation by outside forces. Be

---

4. Smith, *Speech and Theology*, 28.

that as it may, thinkers in the early twentieth century coming from different standpoints, such as those in the traditions of Martin Heidegger, Hans Georg Gadamer, and Emmanuel Levinas, expressed doubt in the confidence in the certainty that can be obtained in any act of knowing. Whilst the ground for this doubt was laid by the collective shock in the aftermath of the First World War, the blowback against this insistence on certainty really came to a head following the end of the Second World War. This second war capped off a first half-century marked by experiments in warfare, totalitarianisms on both left and right, mass killings of combatants and mass extermination of civilians at the hands of governments, all of which were assured by the firm ground of comprehension—of histories, of politics, of *poloi*, and of peoples. Heidegger questioned certainty in knowledge by claiming that knowledge is never without an object that circumscribes my knowledge.[5] Similarly, Gadamer claimed that no one can claim to see beyond those horizons with the rhetorical question concerning whether "all human existence, even the freest, [are] limited and qualified in various ways."[6] Emmanuel Levinas furnished an ethical imperative for questioning the possibility and desirability for full comprehension—what he called "totality" as the basis of knowledge, warning his readers that the act of knowing as certain comprehension reduces what is known to something less than it truly is, excluding the fullness of its own existence while forcing—often violently—the object of our knowledge into a framework that produces knowledge as "more of the same."[7] Rather than being a triumph of humanism, knowledge as full comprehension has given rise to lifeworlds that were anything but humanizing.

Understandably, a question arises here. If knowledge as comprehension in the individual mind has yielded adverse results, what then is the alternative? What follows is the elaboration of an alternative knowing, one defined as incomplete yet growing understanding in an economy. It is submitted that this first century Palestinian woman named Mary speaks directly to the apprehension about certainty expressed by the twentieth century Jewish philosopher, Levinas. In addition, it is submitted that Mary also demonstrates how knowing can operate within the framework of care and within the horizons of epistemological limitation highlighted by

---

5. Heidegger's linking of knowledge to the object is the result of his conception of our existence as something we are fundamentally being thrown into, rather than something from which we are detached and enter only through our willing engagement. This means that our knowledge is similarly "swimming" within the world into which we are thrown. For a summary of this Heideggerian mode of knowing as intentional care, see Smith, *Desiring the Kingdom*, 47–49.

6. Gadamer, *Truth and Method*, 276.

7. Levinas, *Totality and Infinity*.

Heidegger and Gadamer. As the paragraphs below hope to demonstrate, the biography of Mary recorded in the canonical Gospels is a tale of encounters with knowledge claims whose certainty is not established in Mary's mind. Indeed, her mode of knowing embodies the recognition that, in the words of Paul in 1 Corinthians 13:9, that we "know in part" and await for one to make whole what now exists in only parts (cf. 1 Cor 13:9–11).

Mary's lack of absolute certainty can be demonstrated by several episodes in the Gospels of Luke and John. First, there is the annunciation of the incarnation by Gabriel in the first chapter of Luke's Gospel, where the greeting and announcement by Gabriel was greeted by Mary's response, which can at least be classed as less than comprehending. An indicator of this can be found in her initial response was to be "deeply disturbed" in the face of this knowledge claim, a very far cry from the static detached center of the knowing subject in Descartes. Knowledge claims are not calmly received into this center, but constitute instead a disturbance to that calm, a cause to shift from a static center, as shall be demonstrated below. The other indicator for Mary's less than comprehending status can be seen with her next response to Gabriel's greeting, as she "wondered what this greeting could mean" (cf. Luke 1:29) and responded to the announcement of the incarnation with "but how can this come about?" (cf. Luke 1:34). At this point it could be argued that her lack of comprehension could arise from the supernatural nature of the episode, both in terms of the source of the greeting and the content of the annunciation. Any normal human being might not be predisposed to full comprehension of knowledge claims if put in the same position as Mary. This counterargument, however, is blunted once the annunciation by Gabriel is placed alongside other, less extraterrestrial, episodes in the biography of Mary where she manifests the same response.

Consider, for instance, the prophecy of Simeon in the second chapter of Luke's Gospel, where Simeon, at the sight of the infant Jesus at his presentation in the temple proclaims his praise to God for both being able to see in the child Jesus the salvation of all the nations and his own release from his earthly life (cf. Luke 2:29). Simeon also announces to Mary that her son will be "destined for the rise and fall of many in Israel," with a sword destined to pierce her soul, "so that the secret thoughts of many may be laid bare" (cf. Luke 2:34-35). While the parents of the Lord will certainly have noticed what Simeon said—it is hard not to notice someone declaring that a sword will pierce one's soul—what is fascinating about the Gospel is that it records the only response of Mary as well as Joseph as their "wondering at the things that were being said" (cf. Luke 2:33). Once again, there is demonstrated by Mary a less than full comprehension of the knowledge claims that are relayed to her. An even less dramatic episode can be seen in the finding of Jesus in the temple after Mary's searching for him for three days. Having been found, Jesus questioned the need for the search for him, declaring his need to "be in his father's house." Once again we see recorded in Scripture Mary's and Joseph's response as a failure to understand (cf. Luke 2:50). Once again we see a knowledge claim being met by a knower with less than full comprehension, and while there are indeed other episodes with similar responses by other people, the ones above provide the most direct and explicit record of such responses by Mary, all of which precede these similar responses by others, and can thus be said to form the archetype of such responses.

How Did Mary Know?

Taken in isolation, the above sample of biographical events might make Marian modes of knowing seem like passive bewilderment. This impression might be accentuated if one were to confine Mary's knowing to what goes on in her mind. This chapter suggests, however, that a very different picture emerges if one were to shift the focus of the analysis of Mary's epistemological responses from the thoughts in her mind and to the fullness of her person, a shift which will incorporate the practices of Mary's body. In other words, this chapter will focus on bodily practices as part of Mary's epistemological response, for bodies are as much epistemological elements as the mind. This attention to bodily practices as epistemological categories takes as its starting point the writing of the Anglican theologian Graham Ward.

In his *Christ and Culture*, Ward talks about the acknowledgement in postmodern epistemology that the acquisition of knowledge has less to do with cognitive apprehension than what he calls corporeal "performance," or what Maurice Merleau-Ponty calls *praktognosia*—knowledge through practice—in the same way that a batsman acquires knowledge via a disciplined regimen of swinging a bat, rather than thinking of or reading about how to hit a ball.[8] This attention to practice as a locus of knowledge is crucial because, according to Merleau-Ponty, the locus of practice is the site of a lifeworld—what Merleau-Ponty calls the *lebenswelt*—a "world prior to [cognitive] knowledge" and a world that is lived in before it is reflected upon.[9] The nexus between the *lebenswelt* and the body that lives in it is so tightly bound—Merleau-Ponty uses the word "intervolved" to describe the body's interconnectedness with the world that is so intimate that any separation is

8. Ward, *Christ and Culture*.
9. Merleau-Ponty, *Phenomenology of Perception*, lxxii, 49.

treated like a harmful tear rather than a medicinal excising—that every instance of the body's living in the world constitutes an act of knowing, albeit in a pre-reflective phase. For Merleau-Ponty, mental reflection is not the primary engine of knowledge as it is a secondary construction upon this primordial nexus of the intervolved body and world.[10] The intervolved body then is constantly engaged in acts of receiving knowledge without the comprehension that comes with analysis—it should be noted that analysis may not necessarily yield the full comprehension necessary for more Cartesian forms of knowing.

Conversely, this intervolvement of the body and world also means that the body is not merely a passive recipient of knowledge, but is responding to it through what Merleau-Ponty calls a "haunting" of the world,[11] responding to its entanglement in the world via a series of engagements with "situated tasks." Intervolvement with the body thus does not render the body inert, but renders it a "potency," a deposit of response in symphony with the world.[12] In light of this corporeal mode of knowing, with corporeality understood in terms of a body that is primordially connected to a world of pre-reflective knowledge and not separated from it, the locus of knowledge thereby shifts from an individual mind to an economy consisting of the self, the world and its other inhabitants.

Drawing upon the insights of Merleau-Ponty, Ward goes a step further, elaborating upon the intervolved body as a locus of knowledge. If Merleau-Ponty is correct, Ward says, then "I am not some monadic centre of my knowing and my knowledge." Knowledge is "a performance demonstrating that one knows how to," a kind of knowing that is "only relational," in terms of a body's relation with other bodies, and more primarily in terms of a practice's relation with other practices to which it is a response. Knowledge is thereby "transcorporeal," situated in what he calls "economies or movements of response, exchange and declaration."[13] This chapter submits then that, in speaking of Mary's knowing, one is dealing less with cognitive assent, and more with a personalist practice of mind and body in relation with others, as knowledge is transmitted in the warp and woof of the practices undertaken by those bodies and the response by hers.

One of the key features of Ward's phrasing of knowing in an economy of "response, exchange and declaration" that is relevant to Marian epistemology is that because of the primordial relationality between bodies,

10. Ibid., lxxii
11. Ibid., 373.
12. Simpson, *Merleau-Ponty and Theology*, 36.
13. Ward, *Christ and Culture*, 95.

world, and its inhabitants—Merleau-Ponty once wrote that "Man is a knot of relations"—the performances of Mary are never in isolation, but are instead inseparable from socialization.[14] In other words, Marian epistemology pays attention to her knowing, not just in terms of what she does, but also in terms of the social relations that frame what she does. Thus, Marian epistemology is not merely focusing on her lack of full comprehension, for there is also a question of *who* becomes the focus of her response to not fully comprehending. One of the ways this manifests itself in Marian epistemology is the recognition that she herself is not the locus of knowledge but, to paraphrase Merleau-Ponty, borrows herself from others.[15] More specifically, she recognizes that her knowledge is borrowed from the one who "gives wisdom to the wise and knowledge to them that know understanding" (Dan 2:21), namely God. In light of this recognition of a divine source of knowledge, Mary commits herself to that source as an important phase of her knowing.[16] This is why, by way of example, in the face of her still incomplete knowledge about how her conception of the child announced by Gabriel is possible, she nonetheless makes a commitment to God via her declaration: "I am the handmaid of the Lord, let what you have said be done to me" (Luke 1:38).

Remember however that, if one continues with this epistemological vector of knowing occurring in an economy of relations, then commitment cannot merely be to a transcendent other. The fact that knowing is a borrowing from another fundamentally comports the knower to another as another self. This other self thereby demands a response, a commitment that parallels the commitment to God, or more accurately is a participation in that commitment to God. As the Gospel of Luke illustrates, Mary's commitment to God in Luke 1:38 immediately spills over into practices of commitment to others in the immediate verse following. This commitment is expressed by Mary's setting out to her cousin Elizabeth's house in Judea in Luke 1:39, and remaining in Judea in order to be of service to Elizabeth. The reader sees in this passage a commitment to others through acts of service.

This commitment to God, it must be said, goes beyond a single act, and thus Mary's commitment to God similarly extends beyond her act of

---

14. Merleau-Ponty, *Phenomenology of Perception*, 483.

15. Merleau-Ponty, *Signs*, 159.

16. This point concerning a commitment to another as a component is knowledge is implicit in Merleau-Ponty's concept of the "intervolved" body. The body's thrownness into the world comports the body at a pre-theoretical level to that other in order for the subject to operate as subject, and this comporting commits the body to its surroundings, submitting to the body's situatedness as the subject dilates itself into the world. See Merleau-Ponty, *Phenomenology of Perception*, 430.

service to Elizabeth. We see a very subtle instance of this in John's narrative of the Wedding at Cana (John 2:1–11). There, Mary demonstrates her own commitment to God through her commitment in the incarnate Word, which is demonstrated by her action following her telling her son that the groom had run out of wine. Following Jesus' remark that his time had not yet come, Mary's commitment to her son is made manifest by her practices of commitment to others. Only this time, her commitment to other comes in the form of her exhortation to the servants "Do whatever he tells you" (John 2:5). Mary's commitment to God spills over in her commitment to others by her exhortation to others to follow Christ. While exhortation as a form of commitment to others might strike more contemporary ears as strange or even repugnant, such a link has been suggested in paragraph 25a of Pope Emeritus Benedict XVI's first encyclical, *Deus Caritas Est*.[17] In describing the nature of the Church, Benedict made reference to a "threefold responsibility" comprising the elements of *Leitourgia* (or "celebrating the sacraments"), *Kerygma-Martyria* (or the "proclamation of the word of God") and *Diakonia* (or the "service of charity"). These actions together bind individuals into the Body of Christ which is the Church. Benedict went on to say in his encyclical that these three elements are "presuppose each other and are inseparable."[18] By implication Mary, as icon of the Church, similarly demonstrates her service—her *Diakonia*—via her proclamation to follow Christ—her *Kerygma-Martyria*. The link between Mary's exhortation to others and her commitment to others, and ultimately to God, is further reinforced by an observation in *Mary Grace and Hope in Christ*. The statement notes in paragraph 25 that, in so instructing the servants, Mary's "initial role as the mother of Jesus has radically changed. She herself is now . . . a believer in the Messianic community. From this moment on, she commits herself totally to the Messiah and His word."[19] Note the important link made here, in that her declaration both commits her to the Messiah and incorporates her into a Messianic community with others. By her incorporation into the community of believers, Mary thereby expresses her solidarity with those believers.

The final element of Mary's practice of knowing in the face of incomplete understanding is manifested in the praise of the God who is the source of that knowledge. Note how when Elizabeth asks for a knowledge claim at Mary's visitation—"Why should I be honored with a visit from the Mother

---

17. Benedict XVI, *Deus Caritas Est*, no. 25a.

18. Ibid.

19. Anglican-Roman Catholic International Commission, *Mary, Grace and Hope in Christ*, 25.

of my Lord?" (Luke 1:43)—Mary's response comes not in a direct reply to Elizabeth, but in an act of praise of God's goodness, which we recognize as her famous *Magnificat* (Luke 1:46–55), the first line begins with an unabashed line of praise: my soul proclaims the greatness of the Lord (Luke 1:46). The *Magnificat* as a litany of praise of the power and goodness of God, and his regard for the lowly and the overthrow of the great is not an avoidance of the knowledge demanded by Elizabeth's request for knowledge. Rather, this litany of praise completes the nexus of knowledge outlined by Ward, a nexus which includes acts of declaration. It is interesting to note that Elizabeth foreshadows Marian epistemological practice of praise by following her own request for knowledge with a line of praise of her own: "blessed is she who believed that the promise made her by the Lord would be fulfilled" (Luke 1:45).

The tight nexus between practices of declaration, commitment, service and praise are not merely the hallmarks of good discipleship, nor are they extrinsic to the act of knowing. Rather, discipleship proceeds from a particular, properly ecclesial, epistemological posture. That the practices outlined above are bound up in Mary's response to the lack of complete understanding *a la* Descartes, suggests that these practices are more intimately tied to knowing than we might realize. These epistemological practices do not indicate a static bewilderment arising from a lack of comprehension, but constitute what Ward might term an active knowing in waiting. To borrow from the words of St. Paul's first letter to the Corinthians, there is in Mary's practice a recognition of her knowing in part, and also a waiting for perfection to come to do away with imperfect things and trusting that the one who is perfect—God—will one day fully make whole what we know in part (1 Cor 13:10). In so waiting for that perfection of knowledge, Mary's biography is a life underpinned not by full solitary comprehension but a "growth in understanding" in solidarity with others.[20]

Marian Knowing and Standpoint Feminism

Space prevents a full exposition of the ways in which Marian epistemology could uncover the epistemic disjunctures of many contemporary practices by Christians, disjunctures which, if the observations above are correct, prevent a faithful living out of the gospel, or prevent any meaningful traction with the surrounding culture which is increasingly abandoning any pretense to full comprehension. This pretense runs the risk of turning that

---

20. Anglican-Roman Catholic International Commission, *Mary, Grace and Hope in Christ*, 19.

culture away from claims or performances that purport to emit from a transcendent source when they become coupled with an epistemology grounded in ironclad certainty. Before concluding, however, this chapter will take its lead from Graham Ward to give at least an indication of one possibility of a critical alliance that a Marian epistemology could open up with some manifestations of postmodern theory, more specifically, the epistemology of standpoint feminism, whose exponents include Sandra Harding, Lynn Hankinson Nelson, and Nancy Hartstock.

Standpoint feminism provides a good demonstration of this promise at a number of key theoretical junctures. First, in a manner similar to the Marian epistemology submitted above, standpoint feminists are resistant to the idea of knowing as complete individual comprehension, since such knowledge has to be qualified by the practices of one's material, social, and cultural location, framed by gender, ethnicity, class, religion, and other subject positions, namely the kinds of horizons that Gadamer warned we cannot see past.[21] Interestingly, it is those standpoint feminists engaged in evaluating the methodology of the natural sciences that are the strongest voices that make this claim that, because of our situatedness, what passes for knowledge are not certainties encompassing all spaces and times, and thus should not go unqualified by any particular space or time.[22]

Such resistance is not done for its own sake, and this brings us to the second juncture. Because standpoint feminists assert that subject positions qualify universal knowledge claims, what are considered universal knowledge claims are relativized to being merely *dominant* knowledge claims. This then paves the way to standpoint feminism's more constructive aspect, namely the defense of more marginal claims on the same subject matter that the dominant knowledge claims either ignore or mute, much in the same way that the *Magnificat* "raises the lowly" in the estimation of the world. Also, because of the attention to what qualifies the subject positions embedded within knowledge claims, standpoint feminism may find traction with Marian epistemology insofar as the acquisition of knowledge is intimately tied to the attention to biography, what might be called knowledge from the perspective of particular lives and experiences.[23] What this emphasis on biography entails, however, is a recognition that knowledge is not only borne of hermetically sealed theoretical categories, but that theory is always embedded in the practices that make up the biography of the person— knowledge is understood here to be a *bio-graph*, a biological writing—and

---

21. Ward, *Cultural Transformation and Religious Practice*, 73.
22. See for instance, Harding, *Whose Science?*. See especially 124.
23. Ibid.

the sheer multiplicity of bodies in the biosphere thus cannot but multiply the sources of bodily embedded knowledge.

As biographies multiply perspectives, standpoint feminists at the same time eschew a crass subjectivism that critics of standpoint feminism say they hold. What prevents this is the fact that the markers of the subject position that in turn frame the knowledge gained by the subject are fundamentally *social* locations. What is paramount for a standpoint to exist, Ward observes is that for anything to be considered knowledge, it has to be shared.[24] This necessity for a shared framing of knowledge also necessitates a rejection of what Lynn Nelson calls "epistemological individualism," since there are also no individual knowers.[25] Furthermore, this crass perspectivalism is prevented because, as Nancy Hartstock argues, the standpoint is not just meant to create *alternative* accounts of knowledge, but is a "device that can allow for the creation of better (more objective, more emancipatory) accounts of the world."[26] And as mentioned before, standpoint feminism, like the Marian epistemology proposed here, makes no distinction between cognitive activity and practice, arguing that standpoints as sites of knowing only emerge through practices of collective struggle against dominant modes of knowing. In the course of this striving, standpoint feminists assert the possibility of achieving firmer notions of knowledge through what is called the "achievement" of standpoints, the growth in knowledge mentioned earlier. As one grows in knowledge and "achieves" these standpoints, such achievements are deemed transformative, as these standpoints unmask and unseat dominant knowledge claims that are deemed to be beyond contestation, in order to allow for other—and dare one say better—accounts of the world. This challenge to the seemingly unchallengeable parallels Mary's *Magnificat*, which calls for the unfolding of a new world where the mighty are cast from their thrones and the lowly are raised. And such a transformation via the achievement of the standpoint takes place, not through bureaucratic leverage, but through "persuasions, conversions, changes of mind, acts of will, displacements of desire involved in these recognitions of commonality that constitute the public belief in what is true."[27]

---

24. Ward, *Cultural Transformation and Religious Practice*, 76.

25. Nelson, *Who Knows*, 291. See also Harding, *The Science Question in Feminism*, 138.

26. Hartstock, *The Feminist Standpoint Revisited*, 74.

27. Ward, *Cultural Transformation and Religious Practice*, 137.

Conclusion

The above paragraphs sought to outline how a biblically based, Marian epistemology challenges the post-Cartesian presumption of knowledge as full comprehension by a solitary individual. It did so by outlining an exemplar within Scripture of a biography crafted from a foundation of "knowing in part" and a growth in understanding in an economy consisting of embodied practices of solidarity with others and with God. As earlier mentioned, this is no ordinary biography, for what are recorded here are the life events of what the Church considers her icon, the archetype which the Church aspires to emulate. In the course of fulfilling her mission in this world however, the Church may have allowed the adoption practices and institutions—bureaucracies, contracts, and metrics—that seep in forms of knowing where certainty and hermetically sealed knowers are considered the indispensable criteria of valid knowledge claims.

It is submitted here that following Mary as an icon of knowledge—she does bear the title of "Seat of Wisdom"—could assist the Church on two levels. First, Marian epistemology could be an aid in interrogating many modern presumptions in contemporary Church practice which presume knowledge as full comprehension of universally accessible truths, something that struggles to find traction in a postmodern milieu. As the above paragraphs have shown, a Marian epistemology bears the potential in providing a grammar that finds traction with postmodern culture insofar as postmodern culture defines itself by eschewing knowledge as solitary, full comprehension. Secondly, establishing this traction is not merely a strategic move, but a move that also brings the Church's grammar of knowing closer to the types of knowing presumed in its sources of revelation, particularly that of scripture. Since Mary is the icon of the Church, Mary thus presents for Christians a grammar with which to reflect on the extent to which they have in the course of spreading the kingdom of God, relied on practices or presumptions that are less than godly or even idolatrous, insofar as the kind of knowledge needed to found modern practices rely on a kind of knowledge which only God can possess.

With recourse to showing the potentiality for forming an alliance with standpoint feminism, this chapter has also asserted that the value in Marian epistemology not only just finds traction by ceding to the logic of postmodernity, but also by providing a critical reinforcement to it. By way of example, it has shown how Marian epistemology can further standpoint feminism in one important respect. Whilst standpoint feminists rightly demonstrate how growth in knowledge is derived from an immanent process of struggle and of immanent solidarity with others, the Marian standpoint goes further, acknowledging that such processes of knowing can only be held in place with reference to a transcendent horizon of knowledge. As such, Marian practices of solidarity with others who live within postmodern culture can only be assured when the Church stays true to its own pilgrimage towards the last things, praising the God from whom all blessings, including knowledge, flow.

Bibliography

Anglican-Roman Catholic International Commission. In *Mary, Grace and Hope in Christ: The Seattle Statement of the Anglican-Roman Catholic International Commission*, edited by Donald Bolen and Gregory Cameron, 7–88. New York: Continuum, 2007.

Benedict XVI. *Deus Caritas Est*. 2005. Online: http://www.vatican.va/holy_father/benedict_xvi/encyclicals/documents/hf_ben-xvi_enc_20051225_deus-caritas-est_en.html.

Gadamer, Hans-Georg. *Truth and Method*. Edited by Joel Weinsheimer and Donald G. Marshall. 2nd rev. ed. New York: Crossroad, 1989.

Harding, Sandra. *The Science Question in Feminism*. Ithaca, NY: Cornell University Press, 1993.

———. *Whose Science? Whose Knowledge?* Ithaca, NY: Cornell University Press, 1991.

Hartstock, Nancy. *The Feminist Standpoint Revisited and Other Essays*. Boulder, CO: Westview, 1998.

Levinas, Emmanuel. *Totality and Infinity: An Essay on Exteriority*. Pittsburgh: Duquesne University Press, 1969.

Merleau-Ponty, Maurice. *Phenomenology of Perception*. London: Routledge, 2012.

———. *Signs*. Evanston, IL: Northwestern University Press, 1964.

Nelson, Lyn Hankinson. *Who Knows: From Quine to a Feminist Epistemology*. Philadelphia: Temple University Press, 1990.

Pieper, Josef. *Faith, Hope, Love*. San Francisco: Ignatius, 1997.

Simpson, Christopher Ben. *Merleau-Ponty and Theology*. Philosophy & Theology. NY: Bloomsbury, 2014.

Smith, James K. A. *Desiring the Kingdom: Worship, Worldview and Cultural Formation*. Grand Rapids: Baker Academic, 2009.

———. *Speech and Theology: Language and the Logic of Incarnation*. London: Routledge, 2002.

Tan, Matthew John Paul. *Justice, Unity and the Hidden Christ: The Theopolitical Complex of the Social Justice Approach to Ecumenism in Vatican II*. Eugene, OR: Pickwick, 2014.

Ward, Graham. *Christ and Culture*. Oxford: Blackwell, 2005.

———. *Cultural Transformation and Religious Practice*. Cambridge: Cambridge University Press, 2005.

11

Mary the Temple of Scripture
The Biblical Art of Sacred Circumlocution

—Robert Tilley

Although it is not at first obvious, there is a strong structural relationship between how a culture understands the cosmos, what it sets out to realize in its architecture, and how it thinks its sacred texts should be read. The way in which we read the world around us and the way in which we interpret the Scriptures are closely entwined, and, as the ancient world understood, this relationship is made concrete in our architecture. Today, this relationship is informed by the value of consumption and a corresponding accent on speed-of-access such that our world is oriented to the ideal of immediacy. Just as this has shaped the way we view the cosmos, and influenced the kind of architecture in which we live and work, so too has it had its effect on the way in which sacred mysteries are approached. How then is this expressed in the study of Scripture? The argument here is that under the sway of modernity there is an increasing inability to trace out those more subtle meanings in the Scriptures that require time and patience to discern. One of the principle expressions of this inability being the failure to see how the maternal mystery of Our Lady, in respect of the Church, is portrayed in the New Testament. By reference to the architecture of the temple we can begin to trace out the ways in which sacred mysteries are conveyed in the sacred text of Scripture, and the means by which they are conveyed can be summed up under the phrase "the art of sacred circumlocution." The argument of this piece being that it is the figure of Mary who best represents the locus proper of this art and, it is for this reason, she can be called the Temple of Scripture.

It is generally held that that which defines the higher reaches of study and thinking is the discipline of critical reflection. We even hold it necessary to critically reflect upon reflection, asking ourselves why it is we approach a subject in a certain way with certain assumptions, and are these assumptions valid or invalid. We ask ourselves why it is we read a text in the way we do; indeed why it is we read *the world* in the way we do—a discipline often referred to as "hermeneutics." A discipline in which we accept that there is between a text and the world in which that text arises a real relation of some sort, a relationship that hermeneutics sets itself to discern. But in order to do hermeneutics we need to discern where it is we stand when we reflect: What it is that makes up the world in which we live and that informs the way we think and act? This is a task that requires not merely studying the *content* of our world but the very *structures* that "house" that content. We ask after the conceptual structures that provide the context in which we think and by which we discern meaning and value. We might say that in order to critically reflect we need to set ourselves to discern *the architecture* that houses the way in which *we* read and write, listen and think. In short, hermeneutics looks to discern and assess that which *houses* thinking. More particularly that which houses *our* thinking.

A recurrent theme in the critique of contemporary social-political and economic thinking is that which highlights the accent on speed and the concomitant availability of access to what it is we desire. We live in a 24/7 world where the demands of greater speed-of-access not only inform the market in both consumables and finance but work as well to shape the way in which value and meaning are conceived of and experienced.[1] It can be argued that our material culture betrays how it is we conceive of meaning and value, and perhaps this is no more evident than in architecture. We need only compare the way in which the architecture of shops changes over time;

---

1. Jonathan Crary writes that what is important is "how the rhythms, speeds, and formats of accelerated and intensified consumption are reshaping experience and perception." Crary *24/7: Late Capitalism and the Ends of Sleep*, 39.

from stately edifices meant to convey stability and thus trust, through to mega-malls of gloss and shiny surfaces, to the current trend for ephemeral pop-up shops (and of course the virtual world of internet shopping). The contents of these shops likewise changes insofar as their design, function, and durability answers to ever-quicker changes of fashion and concomitant demand. We might say that it is not gravitas that is sought for but effervescence, and that in both architecture and what it houses.

In tracing out the logic of postmodernism and late-capitalism, Frederic Jameson begins by way of studying the architectural meaning of a hotel and mega-mall in Los Angeles, a building that came to fruition in the late 1980s.[2] Jameson's is a critique, however, that has the feel of something dated, perhaps because it is *not* a celebration of all things new and bright but *is* a work of critical reflection. It is a critique that demands time and effort to understand, hence its meaning is not easily accessible and for this reason the book can come across as something of a totem to academic and theoretical elitism. Whereas once it read as something insightful and even thrilling, now, in the age of universities as dispensers of products for an ever expanding consumer driven market, the book comes across as too demanding and thus *passé*. So it is that the increasing accent on speed-of-access affects even the reception of an *earlier* critical reflection on speed-of-access.

If, as Marshall McLuhan famously noted, the medium is the message then it is so, here at least, because the medium necessitates that any content that it "houses" has its meaning and message shaped by the demands of speed-of-access. A message must be able to be transmitted, received and assimilated in the fastest possible way if it is to find the largest possible audience. If it is to accord with the value of efficiency. The ideal, then, is a frictionless medium one that would enable *immediate* access. An ideal brought all the closer to realization with the advent of IT, the birth of the virtual marketplace and the rise of its twin the social-media "commons."

The valorizing of immediacy is especially problematic in that it obscures the role of structure in the creation and shaping of meaning and, in doing so, it compromises the ability to critically reflect upon a text as well as on our reading of that text. It might be said that immediacy of apprehension is conducive of conceit in that it inculcates a sense of exegetical ability that is not deserved. For it is when we encounter friction in our reading that we see the need for critical effort. It is only when we are brought to a stop that we can begin to see where it is we stand and what it is that "houses" our thinking.

---

2. The building in question was the Bonaventure Hotel in Los Angeles, one that exemplifies, as Jameson puts it, "postmodern hyperspace." Jameson, *Postmodernism*, 44.

There is a good deal written on this topic, and that often of a very high standard. Only, what is rarely if ever reflected upon is how the value of speed-of-access and the ideal of immediacy shapes not only the way we read but at the same time the way we assume a text is structured; the way in which we conceive of the *architecture of a text*. Is the meaning of a text akin to the contents of a mall, accessible to any paying punter, or as ephemeral and ever-changing as the contents in a virtual market? What kind of structure is it that shapes the way we think about the contents of the text we are reading? If we read informed by the ideal of immediacy and ease of access then we will read quickly (if at all) and simply assume that the contents are what they are; we will not pay attention to the way the overall structure of the text may belie the ostensible meaning of those contents.

To go deeper into the foregoing by way of the example most salient to the argument of this chapter, we ought to turn to the beginning of the modern period proper, in the mid to late Renaissance. In the Reformation we see an increasing impatience (one inherited from the earlier humanist scholars) with religious mediation especially in respect of the salvific meaning of the sacred text the Bible. As the doctrine of *sola scriptura* develops so too does the argument (which quickly becomes a truism) that the salvific meaning of the Bible is immediately accessible by any sincere reader.[3] For this is how God intended the Bible to be written. It is a doctrine that finds its clearest formulation in the Calvinist teaching of the perspicuity of Scripture.[4] Any other teaching is seen to be expressive of priestly obfuscation, the aim of which being the manipulation of the faithful. Although the chief target of this criticism was the Catholic Church, very early on (one thinks of the various Anabaptist movements) it became a charge levelled against Protestant churches as well.

The accent on the immediacy of reception of the salvific message of the Bible soon elided with what came to be known as the "inner-light" movement, the goal being that an individual could receive immediate instruction by the Holy Spirit within them, a process independent of any external mediation (including for some the need for the Bible). In the seventeenth

---

3. In his "Answer to the Superchristian, Superspiritual, and Superlearned Book of Goat Emser" Martin Luther wrote: "The Holy Spirit is the plainest writer and speaker in heaven and earth, and therefore His words cannot have more than one, and the very simplest sense, which we call the literal, ordinary, natural sense." In Wilson, *About Interpretation*, 118. See too in the same work the comments by Calvin in his Commentary on Galatians: "Let us know, then, that the true meaning of Scripture is the natural and simple one." And speaking of allegory Calvin writes that we must reject those corruptions that "lead us away from the literal sense." Ibid, 132.

4. On this theme and how it developed in the course of early modernity see Stanglin "The Rise and Fall of Biblical Perspicuity."

century the inner-light movement found an ally of sorts with the birth of *secular* modernity concomitant with the rise of empiricism and rationalism. Here the "inner-light" was not so much identified with the Holy Spirit but with reason as it operates unmediated in an individual.[5] This accent on immediacy, being informed in both cases by anti-clericalism, will come to full flower in the Enlightenment. Indeed, to stand alone, reliant only upon reason, defined what it was to be an enlightened and thus mature individual.[6]

It is this accent and its attendant logic that has come into its own today, in that the virtual medium and its speed-of-access not only shapes the meaning of the texts transmitted but also serves to define the nature of the relationship between these texts, which relationships ideally are friction free. We live and think in the hyper-modern world of hypertext where all texts are interwoven, and that by way of a medium that allows (almost) instantaneous access.

From the Reformation on we can see how this accent on immediacy plays out in the material culture of the time, again most clearly in its architecture. From the "stripping of the altars" and the removal of altar rails and images, to the white-washing of church walls and an accent on the word of God with little or no reference to the priestly celebration of the sacraments, there is an orientation to the immediacy of the "word." A "word" that, having been abstracted from the sacraments and the Church, corresponds to a concept of faith that is understood as being subjectively immediate to the individual concerned. Sacred architecture comes to concretize this logic by becoming increasingly *irrelevant*, the first signs of which being a growing opposition to material forms that instantiate a hierarchical and graded approach to the substance of the faith. Architecture comes merely to serve as a platform for the word of God as spoken, not as the word of God made sacramentally present in the liturgy of the Eucharist.

That which is expressed concretely so in architecture finds its correspondence in the way in which the sacred text is itself understood to be structured. Just as the idea of mediation through a graded and hierarchical structure is removed from architecture so too is it removed from the Bible. From the Reformation on there is an increasing rejection of the pre-modern concept of the Quadriga (wherein the Bible is held to be composed of various levels of meaning, hierarchically ordered, all of which culminate in the spiritual or allegorical meaning).[7] Such that by the seventeenth century the

---

5. See: Fix, *Prophecy and Reason*, 187–213; Reventlow, *The Authority of the Bible and the Rise of the Modern World*, 3–4, 21–26, 229.

6. Porter, *Enlightenment*, 99–111.

7. On the development of this rejection of allegory and the Quadriga in favor of "literal" clarity see: Shuger, *The Renaissance Bible*. Also, Reedy, *The Bible and Reason*.

Quadriga is seen to be a relic of the dark ages, an example of the priestly obfuscation of the clarity of gospel truth which is conveyed in the Bible by the most simple and thus immediate of means.

Even though the correlation between architecture and text may seem like a contemporary critical fancy it was, in fact, something well understood in the pre-modern world. And that especially so by reference to both the cosmos and its "micro-cosmic" correlate the temple.

In many quarters and at diverse times the assumption was that a philosophically and theologically informed text was to mirror the architecture of the cosmos and, thereby, the way that God (or the divine principle or reason) was present in that cosmos.[8] In both its structure and its contents—indeed in the very way those two aspects worked together—the sacred text was to instantiate both metaphysical and cosmological principles. The text thereby became something of a microcosm of the macrocosm, a principle that we tend only to associate with concrete temples.[9] The temple certainly did serve as the prime microcosm of the cosmos, but as the sacred text enjoyed an authority derivative of the temple then it is not surprising that the temple should become *the* structural correlate by which the text should order and shape its contents.[10]

There are a number of ways that the kinds of structures basic to a temple find their correlate in the sacred text, perhaps the most basic of all being the use of hierarchically organized grades which lead to the innermost sanctum, the Holy of Holies. The Jerusalem temple is said to house in its holiest place the Name of God as well as the words of God that comprised the Law of Moses.[11] The words of God were also said to proceed out of the temple on the lips of the prophet.[12] In a like manner the Scriptures themselves are likewise held to house the Name of God as well as the words of God. But it is one thing to talk of how *the contents* of a text correlate to the temple, another thing again to say how the structure that *houses* those contents expresses the temple. Here we might return to the Quadriga.

The Quadriga captured the structural logic of the temple well, for it is predicated on the assumption that the levels of meaning of the sacred text

---

8. See: Doob, *The Idea of the Labyrinth*; Colish, *The Mirror of Language*; Coulter, *The Literary Microcosm*; Otten, "Nature and Scripture."

9. Elior, *The Three Temples*; George, *House Most High*.

10. See: Douglas, *Leviticus as Literature*. On the Deuteronomist history, McCormick, *Palace and Temple*; Schwarzer, "The Architecture of Talmud"; Segol, *Word and Image in Medieval Kabbalah*.

11. Exod 25:16; 31:26; Deut 12:11; 1 Kgs 8:29.

12. See for example how Isaiah is commissioned in the cosmic Holy of Holies (Isa 6:1–10) and how the word of the Lord goes out from Zion (Isa 2:3–4).

are hierarchically ordered being oriented to the higher most point, namely that place where the full meaning of the text is present by reason that it is there that the reader truly meets with God. (As Christianity developed, temple imagery could elide with that of the cathedral.) To ascend through to this meaning required not only diligent attention to the subtleties of the biblical text but to one's own moral and spiritual disposition as well, just as the priest who served in the temple had to be pure of pollution and be ritually cleansed if he was to proceed into its depths. In both the concrete temple and sacred text the structure was hierarchically graded and informed by a logic *opposed* to immediacy and speed-of-access.

To read the Bible, then, in a manner that privileges immediacy means to read contrary to its structure and thus, in a profound way, to misread the contents therein. But what does this misreading look like? The example that readily comes to mind is that approach which reduces biblical meaning to lists of bullet-point propositional statements. Statements that are easily digested and comprehended, not least because today their reception is facilitated by power-point presentations designed to be entertaining. This is a salient example to be sure, but being so ready at hand it can serve to forestall a deeper critique of the way our reading is shaped by the dictates of immediacy. A better example can be given by way of Mary the Mother of our Lord.

It is significant that from the Reformation on, as the Bible becomes increasingly subject to the dictates of immediacy, the status of Mary diminishes. There is a growing tendency to reject both the mediatorial role of Mary and the consequent high devotion paid to her within the Catholic Church. This is not the place to rehearse the history of Mary in Protestant (and modern biblical critical) exegesis, just to observe that the principle reason for rejecting the role of Mary as it was presented in Catholic theology was by way of an appeal to the Scriptures themselves. The arguments might be diverse but informing these arguments was an appeal to the relative absence of Mary from the New Testament. We might characterize this approach as "counting up content rather than tracing out structure"; a quantitative rather than what might be called an aesthetic approach. Certainly, for most Protestants Mary was to be honored in respect of being the mother of Jesus. It was an honor, however, void of any special mediatorial role in the mission of her son and thus in respect of a believer's redemption through the immediate appropriation of the salvific meaning of the word. A fact, it was argued, borne out by the *comparative* absence of any mention of her in Scripture. It is this appeal to the "comparative absence" of Mary that provides the best example of the way in which an accent on immediacy can blind us to the temple-like structure of the sacred text.

The issue for us is, how does the hierarchically graded nature of the temple get translated into its textual correlate? How is a text composed such that it requires an approach that necessitates the traversing of grades in order to reach the meaning proper of the text—that is the meaning of which all other meanings are ultimately derivative—which meaning has to do with the presence of God? After all, it is not too difficult to see how the architecture of the temple, in order to convey the sense of the sacred, uses devices like structural oppositions to create harmonious tensions; partitions and windows (or the absence thereof) to serve the play of light and darkness; the use of frames to create things like aedicules and what we might call *mise en scènes* (and even *mise en abymes*); having boundaries and borders run up against each other to create liminal spaces, and other like devices. But how are *architectural* structures like these translated into *textual* structures?

The argument here is that the architectural structures associated with the temple find their textual correlate in those devices that create a dynamic of what can be called "sacred circumlocution," which dynamic is accompanied by the employment of "exegetical prompts."[13] What is meant by these terms can best be explained by way of example—to be precise, two examples—the first from St. John's Gospel and the second from St. Luke's.

The contents of St. John's Gospel serve to bring out the sacramental dimensions of the early faith and they do so around the theme of the temple.[14] The Gospel is structured along priestly and liturgical lines in order to bring out the significance of baptism and the Eucharist and does so in order to show how these things allow one to participate in God through being brought into the relations of the Son to the Father through the Holy Spirit. It is in this matrix that Mary is presented both at the beginning of Jesus' ministry proper and at its conclusion at the cross. In other words she serves as a frame for her son's mission. A mission that concerns among other things the revelation of the glory of God in Jesus, which glory is fully revealed at the cross.[15] And glory, of course, in the Old Testament refers to God's presence in the temple.[16]

---

13. There are many excellent books that attempt to map out the subtle structures of biblical narrative, one thinks especially of the works by Robert Alter (especially his *The Art of Biblical Narrative*), but here I would draw attention to Geller's *Sacred Enigmas*.

14. On the temple theme in St. John's Gospel: Coloe, *God Dwells with Us*; Zimmerman, "Symbolic Communication between John and his Reader." For a nuanced overview of the sacramental themes in John's Gospel see: chapter 5 in Bauckham, *Gospel of Glory*.

15. For example: John 2:11; 12:28, 41; 13:31–32; 16:14–15; 17:1–5, 22–24.

16. For example: Ezek 43:4; 1 Kgs 8:11; 2 Chr 5:14. There are of course other, we might say, veiled references to things priestly, such as the fact that the water turned into wine is meant for purification (John 2:6) and that this is the first of seven signs, seven

There is much written on this matter so we will focus only on a few points. Mary is present at the wedding at Cana where she famously tells her son about the absence of wine. He answers her in an apparently abrupt way, saying "Woman, what is there to me and to you [*that is, between you and me*], my hour is not yet come."[17] However we might translate the "to me and to you" the sense is of some relationship in which Jesus and his mother will be especially entwined. Whatever the nature of this relationship it has something to do with Jesus' hour which, we learn, has not as yet come. What tends to be missed here is that there *will* be some special relationship between Jesus and his mother when his hour *does* come. Of course it is clear from the way John has structured his Gospel that the "hour" refers to the cross.[18] A point brought out not least by the way that at the cross Jesus again addresses his mother as "Woman" doing so to make her the mother of the beloved disciple and the beloved disciple her son. We are then told that at that very "hour" he took her under his roof.[19] As the beloved disciple is the only apostle present (accepting that it is John) then the new relationship between Jesus and his mother is one that now takes in all the Church, a point that Revelation will later bring out.[20]

Perhaps the oddest thing about the passage is that though we expect otherwise Jesus *does* do the miracle. Indeed, Mary it seems expects him to do so for she tells the servants to do what it is her son tells them even when it seems she has been rebuked. We are then told that it is there that the disciples first see the glory of Jesus revealed, what's more it is here that his mission proper begins.[21] It is an odd passage and it prompts us to look deeper if we are to make sense of the apparent anomalies; the way in which the passage is structured and composed acts as an exegetical prompt. More importantly the structure serves to intimate something *unspoken* informing the composition and contents. Implicit in the passage is that there is something that Jesus and his mother both know and are having to reckon with; namely when it is appropriate to begin his mission proper, one that will culminate in his "hour" at the cross. Both implicitly know that something has to act as a prompt to set things in motion. It is as if Mary knows that in

---

being the priestly number par excellence in the Torah. But it is not the intention of this paper to be exhaustive in its engagement with the biblical passages cited.

17. John 2:4.
18. John 7:30; 8:20; 12:23, 27; 13:1; 17:1.
19. John 19:26–27.
20. In Rev 12:1–5 the woman gives birth to the messiah, that is to only one child. But later, in 12:17 we are told that she has many offspring, namely those who hold to the testimony of Jesus. In other words, the followers of her son become her children.
21. John 2:11.

simply telling Jesus about the lack of wine (for in fact she does *not* explicitly ask him to do anything) that this will serve as a trigger for a miracle that will inaugurate her son's mission. She also seems to understand what it is her son means by the obscure reference to his hour bringing about a new relationship between them. As for the sacramental import of the miracle that is well known (and by some, contested) and needs no repeating here, except to note that it points to Jesus' death, thereby further confirming the fact that this passage proleptically anticipates the events of the cross.

The passage is so constructed that it calls for an explanation of what seems, at first reading at least, as apparent anomalies. Then, when one does look closer one finds oneself pointed to the culmination of Jesus' mission, which mission is presented by reference to temple imagery. The passage can only begin to be understood if it is read as one half of a frame; if it is read in tension with what will come later.

As for the intimation of a new relationship between Jesus and his mother, one brought about by the cross, this too is significant in light of the fact that John presents the work of the cross as inaugurating a new relationship, one in which a rather paradoxical entwinement occurs. John's Gospel is characterized by a "reciprocal" language wherein, for example, Jesus is said to be in the Father, and yet the Father is in him.[22] A relationship that will be expanded out as it were to include his disciples. They too will be in Jesus and yet he in them.[23] This will be effected by his coming death and the subsequent sending of the Holy Spirit. This new relationship will include the apostles and those who "Believe upon me through their word," which is to say the Church.[24] Thus, just as the Father and the Son are one, so too will they be one for they now participate in the divine relations of the Son and the Father.[25]

We know that this paradoxical relationship with Jesus is made possible through the sacraments of baptism and the Eucharist: we are in Jesus through baptism, and he in us by eating and drinking of his flesh and blood. And yet, although such mysteries are made explicit by St. Paul,[26] and that

---

22. John 14:11.

23. John 14:20. On this intertwined relationship see: Gruenler, *The Trinity in the Gospel of John*.

24. John 17:20.

25. John 17:11, 21–22, 26.

26. For example in Gal 3:26–27 Paul talks of our being "in Christ" by reason of baptism, yet later he speaks of Christ being formed within us (4:19). Compare as well Eph 1:11–14 and Col 1:27. The answer to this mysterious inner-outer reciprocity appears to devolve upon the mystery of the Eucharist as intimated in 1 Cor 11:27–34 and 12:12–13. A mystery that has to do with the Church.

a long time before John wrote his Gospel, nevertheless John speaks of such things by way of circumlocution, hence the references to living and healing water,[27] and the extended disquisition on the eating and drinking of Jesus' flesh and blood.[28] But it is a circumlocution that operates within narrative structures and themes that echo the architecture of the temple. The Holy of Holies being, of course, the cross and it is here that the mystical participation in the divine relations finds its locus proper.[29] It is in the heart of the temple that the height of the intimate and reflexive relationship is reached.[30]

We need not argue that John writes to counter an incipient Gnosticism (though to my mind that is very likely) to see that he accents the flesh and blood body and sacrifice of Jesus and does so in order to accent the reality of the Incarnation. This, after all, is the intent of the Prologue. But as the later Church understood in respect of the title "Theotokos" for Mary, implicit in the doctrine of the Incarnation is a realization of the special status of the one from whom the Word Incarnate received his flesh.

It is the argument of this chapter that John structures his Gospel in order to intimate the sacredness of the mystery of Mary's role, doing so by way of the structure of the temple. Mary is the temple that housed the Word of God, the very glory of God. Hence she houses the meaning proper of the words of God that make up Scripture. It is from her that the flesh and blood that fulfills Scripture is derived. By way of the art of sacred circumlocution, John intimates the role she has both at the beginning and close of her son's earthly mission. And then, with the new relationship established, the role of mother in respect of the Church in its continuation of Jesus' mission. Now, not only are the Apostles brought into the relationship between the Son and the Father, but also into the Son's relationship with his mother. The first relationship is explicitly referred to; the second implicitly so. The explicit has to do with the Father, which is to say the masculine, while the implicit has to do with the mother, the feminine. It is a collaborative not oppositional parallelism, one in which the Creator and the creature work together. A structural parallel that witnesses to the mystery of the unity of the one who

27. John 4:14; 5:4; 7:37–39.
28. John 6:32–63.
29. I might note that this is something intimated by St. Paul in 2 Cor 3:1–18 where the argument culminates in the heart of the tabernacle, face to face with Jesus. A passage that also informed by a relationship founded upon an intimate mystical participation marked by mutual reflexivity founded upon membership in Jesus' body, one necessitating the Eucharist (1Cor 11:23—12: 27).
30. Again one might note how St. Paul in Ephesians intimates this intimate participation with God, through the Church, by way of nuptial language, calling it a mystery (Eph 5:21–32). And of course Revelation ends by reference to the Bride of Christ and the Spirit (Rev 22:17).

is both truly God *and* truly man; to the Word made flesh who in this flesh fulfills the words of God that make up Scripture.[31]

The point is that the structures delineated above are clearly intended, designed by the author to convey the sense of the sacredness of the mysteries therein as well as something of their character. Whatever else we might say about it, the narrative structure is *not* written with an accent on the immediacy of apprehension. The more sacred and profound the mystery being imparted is, the more that is required of the reader. The more the reader pays attention to the architecture of the text the more the meaning in the text grows, and the less the reader feels he or she has mastered the text. The sense is of a mystery that resists being reduced to mere propositions that can quickly be apprehended; quite to the contrary, the effect of these temple-like structures is to give rise to meanings. They are conducive to a fruitfulness of meaning.[32]

Something of how this works can be seen in the way John employs forms of parallelism that work to create a reflexive dynamic, one in which each side of the "frame" illuminates the other and, in doing so, each gives rise to new but continuous meanings. "Continuous" in that the meanings that arise are not arbitrary but grow out of those meanings that precede them. Just as in the Quadriga (and the rabbinic Pardesh) the various levels of meaning were not opposed to each other but were continuous one with the other in a hierarchically graded relationship where each level reflected on the others.[33] It is important, then, to note that a very similar kind of structure is found, albeit in something of a distilled form, in those aforementioned passages where the Son and the Father are in a mutually interpenetrating relationship and where the Church is brought to participate in this relationship.

The second example is from St. Luke's Gospel. St. Luke opens his Gospel by reference to Zechariah serving as a priest in an outer court of

---

31. Hence the accent around the account of the cross on the Scriptures being fulfilled: John 18:9; 19:24, 28, 36, 37; 20:9.

32. It is perhaps pertinent to note here that the Holy of Holies of the temple was identified both in Scripture and extra-biblical writings with Eden, both being the place of divine fruitfulness and fecundity. Furthermore, Scripture too came to be depicted in Edenic terms, being a garden of delights. See Beale, "Eden, the Temple, and the Church's Mission in the New Creation." It probably does not need pointing out, but the womb too becomes the place in Scripture where, through the miraculous work of God, the barren or virginal becomes the location of fruitful salvation.

33. "Pardesh" is an acronym that serves to spell out the four levels of meaning in Scripture. "Pardesh" also means "orchard" and points to Eden, for the significance of which see the previous footnote.

the temple in Jerusalem,[34] and he closes his Gospel by telling us that after Jesus' ascension the Apostles stayed in Jerusalem continually praying in the temple.[35] There is a frame, then, and this by reference to the temple. As scholars have noted, Luke structures both Gospel and Acts by reference to the temple; in the former by way of approach, while in the latter by way of departure. Again, it is not our intention to rehearse in anything like an exhaustive fashion the way in which the temple orders Luke's content.[36] But what we might note for our purposes is how Luke is the only Gospel writer to include the references to the Holy Family's visit to the temple shortly after Jesus' birth, and how, when he was twelve, he was left behind within the wider temple area.[37]

Whatever else this inclusion of temple events into the early part of the Gospel serves, it alerts the reader to the structure that Luke employs to make his point. Thus, we begin with Zechariah in the outer court of the temple, where he meets with the angel Gabriel who tells him that he, that is Gabriel, stands in the presence of God (that is, in the heavenly counterpart of the earthly temple).[38] In the next scene, Gabriel then visits Mary where he tells her that the Holy Spirit will come upon her and she will be overshadowed by the "power most high." These being terms redolent of the cosmic Holy of Holies, similar to those we find in the Dead Sea Scrolls.[39] Luke then has the now pregnant Mary visit Elizabeth presenting this meeting by way of an allusion to the account in 2 Samuel 6 of David's joy at the Ark of the Covenant coming to Jerusalem.[40]

The beginning of the Gospel establishes by way of both explicit content and implicit allusion the sense of sacred place identified with the innermost

34. Luke 1:5–10.

35. Luke 24:53.

36. On Luke and the temple see: Chance, *Jerusalem, the Temple, and the new Age in Luke-Acts*. And chapter 6 in Esler, *Community and Gospel in Luke-Acts*.

37. Luke 2:22–39; 41–49.

38. Luke 1:19.

39. The allusion seems to be to Exod 40:34–35 where the glory of God comes down and fills the recently erected tabernacle. In respect of the Dead Sea Scrolls and some of the Pseudepigrapha (especially Enoch and Jubilees) is that the spirit and glory of God, the Ark, God's presence and the divine throne room are presented in terms of Merkabah and early Hekalot imagery. The imagery is vivid, mystical, and, to us at least, strange and even unsettling as it conveys the sense of the awesomeness of divine presence. Whereas, here in Luke, the presence of God and the Ark etc., are presented in terms of a young virgin. One need only contrast, say, the books of Enoch or the Songs of the Sabbath Sacrifice in the Scrolls with Luke 1 to see this difference writ large.

40. Luke 1:39–56. On the allusions to the Ark coming to Jerusalem see: Bastero, *Mary, Mother of the Redeemer*, 112–14.

recesses of the temple. But the structure likewise serves this purpose, in that we proceed inwards from Zechariah in the outer court/s, via Gabriel, whom we are told has his office proper in the cosmic Holy of Holies, into the new innermost sanctuary that is the place of the presence of God. This sanctuary being Mary. Furthermore, Luke also tacitly brings out the role of Mary in the birth of the Church in that in Luke/Acts the role of the Holy Spirit is especially pronounced being the "dynamic" proper of both Jesus' and the Church's mission. It is thus significant that Mary is the first person depicted in the Gospel to be a recipient of this Spirit.[41] Later, in Acts, we will see Mary present at Pentecost at the birth of the Church when the Spirit comes upon those assembled in a manner similar to how he came upon her.[42] The implicit meaning being that she, through the Holy Spirit, is the mother of Jesus and, being so, she recapitulates this role in respect of the Church, such that she is also the mother of the Church.

In both the above examples the art of sacred circumlocution serves to present the mystery of Mary being the mother of the Church. It is a mystery presented within a complex of literary structures which serve to create a correlate of the temple within the strictures of a text, thereby conveying their meaning "at a slant" (to borrow from Emily Dickinson). Although space does not permit me take this any further, I would also argue that a similar way of presenting Mary's maternal role in respect of the Church can be found in Rev 11:19—12:16 and Gal 4:21–31. Why this phenomenon should be so developed in respect of Mary is a matter of speculation but there are a number of things we can say by way of conclusion.

We might begin by noting that in the Bible a concept finds its perfection in a person not in, say, an abstract universal truth. Hence, Jesus is the way the truth and the life.[43] And he is also the temple proper.[44] But we might also note that the Church is also referred to as the temple,[45] is also referred to as the "way,"[46] is where one is baptized into life,[47] and is also seen to be the location proper of the truth.[48] Of course many other like passages can be cited but the theme common to them all is that the Church,

---

41. On the Spirit in Luke/Acts see by way of example: Luke 1:15, 35, 41, 67; 2:25–27; 3:16, 22; 4:1, 14: Acts 1:2, 5, 8: 2:1–4, 17, 38; 4:8 etc.

42. Acts 1:14; 2:1–2.

43. John 14:6.

44. John 2:21.

45. 1 Cor 3:10–17; Eph 2:11–22.

46. Acts 9:2; 19:9.

47. Gal 2:20–21 and 3:26–27.

48. 1 Tim 3:15.

being the body of Christ, recapitulates and makes fully present all that has its perfection in Christ.

There is a hierarchical order of derivation to the mystery of salvation, one in which the perfections (as it were) of Jesus are recapitulated in the Church and thereby made present to all the cosmos. The thing is that whereas the Church has all its perfections derivative of the sinless, sacrificed and then glorified and ascended flesh and blood of Jesus, Jesus has *his* perfect and sinless flesh and blood derivative of Mary. Jesus' body is the temple, but it is so by reason that his mother's body was the temple proper. She becomes the place in which the Name and Word of God resides. She becomes the Ark of the Covenant and thus the true throne chariot of God. She becomes the house that is filled with the glory of God and his Spirit. All of which things she is by reason of the presence of God incarnate, and all of which things the Church will become through the ministry of the same God incarnate. A ministry that culminates in Jesus' sending of the Holy Spirit thereby recapitulating his conception in the womb of his mother by way of the Spirit bringing to birth the Church. It is this pattern that informs the Scriptures, a pattern that echoes the temple structure (and, though we have not been able to discuss this, also the liturgy therein).[49]

The architecture of salvation is mirrored in the architecture of the Scriptures; the temple houses the contents therein and gives to them their proper meaning. Only, this meaning is not immediate but is instead mediated through the art of sacred circumlocution. We might say that mediation is of the very essence of salvation and of all that is implied in salvation. We might ask *why* mediation is of the essence of salvation. And although brief, our answer can form the conclusion to this piece.

Whatever else is fundamental to mediation one things stands out, it is the necessity of communion: the communion of God the Trinity; the communion of God with humanity; and of humanity with humanity, and these relations find their locus proper in the communion of the Church, the body of Christ. In contrast, when the salvific meaning of the Bible becomes defined by its being able immediately to be appropriated, and that by an individual standing alone before God, then the Bible has effectively been abstracted from the Church and from the necessity of communion. The Bible has been abstracted from Mary and thereby from her maternal presence. But this cannot be so for, as we have argued, *Mary is the Temple of Scripture*. To divorce the word of God from Mary's maternal care for the

---

49. The mystery of Mary's role in the redemption won by her son seems to be first made explicit (at least in the texts we have) in the writings of St. Irenaeus and that in respect of the logic of recapitulation. See Steenberg, "The Role of Mary as Co-Recapitulator in St. Irenaeus of Lyons."

Church is to render the word unfruitful. It is to take sacred things out of that which properly houses them, turning them into so many pop-up products immediately accessible in the mall of the profane.

Bibliography

Alter, Robert. *The Art of Biblical Narrative*. New York: Basic, 1981.
Bastero, Juan. *Mary, Mother of the Redeemer*. Dublin: Four Courts, 2006.
Bauckham, Richard. *Gospel of Glory*. Grand Rapids: Baker Academic, 2015.
Beale, Gregory. "Eden, the Temple, and the Church's Mission in the New Creation." *Journal of the Evangelical Theological Society* 48 (2005) 5–31.
Chance, J. Bradley. *Jerusalem, the Temple, and the New Age in Luke-Acts*. Macon: Mercer University Press, 1988.
Colish, Mary. *The Mirror of Language*. New Haven, CT: Yale University Press, 1968.
Coloe, Mary. *God Dwells with Us: Temple Symbolism in the Fourth Gospel*. Collegeville, MN: Liturgical, 2001.
Coulter, James. *The Literary Microcosm*. Leiden: Brill, 1976.
Crary, Jonathan. *24/7: Late Capitalism and the Ends of Sleep*. London: Verso, 2013.
Doob, Penelope. *The Idea of the Labyrinth*. Oxford: Oxford University Press, 1992.
Douglas, Mary. *Leviticus as Literature*. Oxford: Oxford University Press, 1999.
Elior, Rachel. *The Three Temples: On the Emergence of Jewish Mysticism*. Oxford: The Littman Library of Jewish Civilization, 2004.
Esler, Philip. *Community and Gospel in Luke-Acts*. Cambridge: Cambridge University Press, 1987.
Fix, Andrew. *Prophecy and Reason: The Dutch Collegiants in the early Enlightenment*. Princeton: Princeton University Press, 1991.
Geller, Stephen. *Sacred Enigmas: Literary Religion in the Hebrew Bible*. London: Routledge, 1996.
George, A. *House Most High: The Temple in Ancient Mesopotamia*. Winona Lake, IN: Eisenbrauns, 1993.
Gruenler, Royce. *The Trinity in the Gospel of John*. Grand Rapids: Baker, 1986.
Jameson, Fredric. *Postmodernism: Or, the Cultural Logic of Late Capitalism*. Durham, NC: Duke University Press, 1991.
McCormick, Mark. *Palace and Temple*. Berlin: De Gruyter, 2002.
Otten, William. "Nature and Scripture: Demise of a Medieval Analogy." *Harvard Theological Review* 88 (1995) 257–84.
Porter, Ray. *Enlightenment: Britain and the Creation of the Modern World*. London: Allen Lane, 2000.
Reedy, Gerard. *The Bible and Reason*. Philadelphia: University of Pennsylvania Press, 1985.
Reventlow, H. Graf. *The Authority of the Bible and the Rise of the Modern World*. London: SCM, 1984.
Schwarzer, Mitchell. "The Architecture of Talmud." *Journal of the Society of Architectural Historians* 60 (2001) 474–87.
Segol, Maria. *Word and Image in Medieval Kabbalah*. New York: Palgrave Macmillan, 2012.
Shuger, Debora. *The Renaissance Bible*. Berkeley: University of California Press, 1994.

Stanglin, Keith. "The Rise and Fall of Biblical Perspicuity." *Church History* 83 (2014) 38–59.

Steenberg, M. C. "The Role of Mary as Co-Recapitulator in St. Irenaeus of Lyons." *Vigiliae Christianae* 58 (2004) 117–37.

Wilson, Barrie, ed. *About Interpretation.* New York: Lang, 1989.

Zimmerman, Ruben. "Symbolic Communication between John and his Reader: The Garden Symbolism in John 19–20." In *Anatomies of Narrative Criticism*, edited by T. Thatcher and S. Moore, 221–35. Atlanta: Society of Biblical Literature, 2008.

12

Towards a Patristic Theology of Barrenness

—Kevin Wagner

The industry of fertility care has made significant progress in the effort to overcome physical infertility. Unfortunately there has been insufficient advancement in the spiritual care of the physically barren. A cursory reading of the Scriptures often provides little consolation for those who suffer this condition. Here we will draw on a selection of homiletic, exegetic, and pastoral writings from the Church fathers in order to trace the outlines of a patristic theology of barrenness. We do this with a view to understanding how God can make infertility a fruitful experience. Our study will begin by looking at Origen's interpretation of the cure of the women in Abimelech's household as recorded in Genesis 20. This will be followed by an examination of John Chrysostom's thoughts on suffering, which will assist us in understanding the positive value of infertility. Finally, we will analyze de virginitate *literature of the fourth and fifth centuries, writings which extol the value of consecrated celibacy. A study of this state of life, epitomized in the person of Mary, is useful as there are commonalities in the experience of childlessness felt by the consecrated virgin and the barren married person.*

The phenomenon of physical barrenness is widespread in modern times. As such it demands the attention of theologians who can apply appropriate resources to the task of understanding how God can work in and through this unfortunate human condition. In the spirit of *ressourcement* we will endeavor here to outline some preliminary steps towards a patristic theology of barrenness. Our approach will be in three parts. Part One will examine Origen's homily on Genesis 20, which provides an innovative explanation for the barrenness of Abimelech's wife and handmaidens. His appeal to the spiritual sense of the passage offers a corrective to the view that the state of barrenness is innately one of hopelessness. This is helpful as a literal reading of scriptural passages dealing with barrenness is often of little consolation to those suffering from infertility; in the final analysis the barren person is usually blessed by God and conceives. Next, in Part Two, we will draw on Chrysostom's thoughts on suffering which point to a way of understanding how barrenness can be a blessing. Finally, in Part Three, we will investigate a selection of patristic *De virginitate* texts in order to garner some insights into physical and spiritual parenthood, the difficulties of physical parenthood, and the maternal nature of the Church.

In the Scriptures barrenness is a quality attributable to both an individual and a people. Standing in contrast to fecundity, barrenness is not simply a lack, but rather a state in which God can act.[1] In a real sense, barrenness is a position of potential for those who seek God's will. We see, for instance, that for the barren Hebrew patriarchs and matriarchs their state is reversed after God showers forth unfathomable blessings. Also, in the Old Testament figure of daughter Zion, who is a type of the Virgin Mother, children are promised to her in her barrenness.[2] Barrenness therefore stands as a precondition for God showing his merciful power. A theology of barrenness, it would seem, should among other things seek an answer as to why

1. We notice that the most common Greek words for barrenness, στεῖρος and its cognates, lack the alpha primitive which denotes lack or deprivation in a thing. Gregory of Nyssa believed it to be common knowledge that "words formed on the alpha primitive denoted 'the absence of noninherent qualities rather than the presence of inherent qualities.'" While not a proof for the notion that the Greeks did not deem barrenness to be primarily a lack, it is nevertheless interesting. Pelikan's unique referencing style means that it is not clear where Gregory stated this. Pelikan, *Christianity and Classical Culture*, 40.

2. "To say that Mary is the Daughter of Sion is to affirm that she embodies the mystery of the Church under the aspect of the Old Testament expectation of Christ, which mystery has been personified in the Daughter of Sion figure, and that Mary's calling possesses the ecclesial dimensions which are prefigured in the Daughter of Sion imagery." Deiss, *Mary, Daughter of Sion*, xi.

God permits barrenness and, if it is really a God-given state, how we may embrace barrenness in order to receive most fully the blessings which flow from it. It is such a theology we will look to trace the outlines of through a reading of patristic homiletic, exegetic, and *de virginitate* texts.

Part One—Barrenness:
A State of Waiting for Fulfilment in Christ

Genesis 20 chronicles Abraham and Sarah's encounter with the Philistine King Abimelech. This narrative is situated directly after the account of the destruction of Sodom and Gomorrah and immediately before the account of the conception and birth of Isaac. While a comparative analysis of this text with both Genesis 12:10–20 and Genesis 26:6–11 would be fascinating, of more interest to us is Genesis 20:17–18:

> Then Abraham prayed to God; and God healed Abimelech, and also healed his wife and female slaves so that they bore children. For the Lord had closed all the wombs of the house of Abimelech because of Sarah, Abraham's wife.[3]

The text of Genesis offers no rationale for God rendering barren the womenfolk of Abimelech's house. Similarly, Abraham's weak explanation for deceiving Abimelech (vv. 11–13) does little to assure the reader of the patriarch's virtue in this sordid episode. Origen recognizes these shortfalls in the text of Genesis 20 and sets out to offer a "fitting and honorable interpretation."[4] While the Jews, he claims, only interpret the text literally (*secundum litteram solum*), Origen gives a spiritual interpretation inspired by Galatians 4:22–24.[5] It is to this we now turn our attention.

For Origen, each of the characters in this narrative symbolizes something. Sarah, who is joined to her spouse Abraham, "represents *aretē*, which

---

3. Gen 20:17–18 (RSV).

4. decora et honesta interpretatione. Origen, *In Genesim Homilia* VI.3, in Origen, *Homilies on Genesis and Exodus*, 126 (= Origen, *Gen.* VI.3 (Heine, 126)), cf. Migne, *PG* 12.197.

5. Si quis hæc secundum litteram solum audire vult et intelligere, magis cum Judæis quam cum Christianis debet habere auditorium. Si autem vult Christianus esse et Pauli discipulus, audiat eum dicentem, *quia lex spiritalis est*. Et cum de Abraham atque uxore ejus ae filiis loqueretur, pronuntiat hæc esse allegorica. "If anyone wishes to hear and understand these words literally he ought to gather with the Jews rather than with the Christians. But if he wishes to be a Christian and a disciple of Paul, let him hear Paul saying that "the Law is spiritual" [and] declaring that these words are "allegorical" when the law speaks of Abraham and his wife and sons." Origen, *Gen.* VI.1, 3 (Heine, 121–22), cf. Migne, *PG* 12.195.

is the virtue of the soul" possessed by the wise.[6] Origen affirms that "it is proper that until we reach perfection, virtue of the soul be within us and personal."[7] However, he posits that those who have attained perfection should seek to share and teach virtue.[8] By this hermeneutical sleight of hand, Origen justifies Abraham's decision to declare Sarah (*aretē*) to be his sister (who he can share) rather than his wife (who he cannot). Abimelech, who, unlike Pharaoh, had sought virtue with a pure heart,[9] represents those wise men who practice philosophy and recognize the fatherhood and kingship of God.[10] Accordingly, the king's wife and his handmaids are identified with the tools of the philosopher, his wife with "natural philosophy" and his handmaids with the various forms of dialectic.[11]

Having established the symbolism of the characters of the narrative we are now prepared to interpret verses 17–18. Origen, as he always does,

---

6. At times, in this homily, Origen analyzes the etymology of names to provide or reveal the symbolism of characters. For instance, "I think, therefore, that Sara, which means prince or one who governs empires, represents *aretē*, which is the virtue of the soul. This virtue, then, is joined to and clings to a wise and faithful man." Puto ergo Saram, quæ interpretatur *princeps* vel *principatum agens*, formam tenere ἀρετῆς, quod est animi virtus. Hæc ergo virtus conjuncta est et cohæret sapient et fideli viro. Origen, *Gen.* VI.1 (Heine, 122), cf. Migne, *PG* 12.195. Heine notes that Origen draws on Philo for this etymology. Heine, 391.

7. Et est conveniens ut donec ad perfectum veniamus, intra nos sit animi virtus, et propria sit. Origen, *Gen.* VI.1 (Heine, 122–23), cf. Migne, *PG* 12.195.

8. Cum vero ad perfectum venerimus, ita ut idonei simus et alios docere, tunc jam virtutem, non ut uxorem intra gremium concludamus, sed ut sororem etiam aliis volentibus copulemus. Origen, *Gen.* VI.1 (Heine, 123), cf. Migne, *PG* 12.195–96.

9. Origen, *Gen.* VI.3 (Heine, 125), cf. Migne, *PG* 12.196. Porro Abimelech, id est qui munde et philosophice vivebat, poterat quidem accipere, quia in corde mundo quærebat, sed nondum tempus advenerat.

10. Origen took the name Abimelech to mean "my father is king," thereby justifying his view that Abimelech recognised the kingship of God. According to Origen, Abimelech "represents the studious and wise men of the world, who by giving attention to philosophy, although they do not reach the complete and perfect rule of piety, nevertheless perceive that God is the father and king of all things." Abimelech interpretatur *pater meus rex*. Et videtur ergo mihi quod hic Abimelech formam teneat studiosorum et sapientum sæculi, qui philosophiæ operam dantes, licet non integram et perfectam regulam pietatis attigerint, tamen senserunt Deum patrem et regem esse omnium, id est qui genuerit et regat universa. Origen, *Gen.* VI.2 (Heine, 123–24), cf. Migne, *PG* 12.196. Heine affirms Origen's etymology of the Hebrew name Abimelech. Heine, 392.

11. Quantum possumus in tam difficilibus locis sentire, putamus uxorem Abimelech naturalem posse philosophiam dici; ancillas vero ejus, diversa et vana pro qualitate sectarum commenta dialecticæ. "So far as we can perceive in such difficult passages, we think natural philosophy can be called Abimelech's wife, but his handmaids represent the contrivances of dialectic which are diverse and various by virtue of the nature of the schools." Origen, *Gen.* VI.3 (Heine, 124), cf. Migne, *PG* 12.197.

recognizes that the Incarnation is the key to interpreting the spiritual sense of the Hebrew Scriptures. Hence, the gentile Abimelech, who in his purity was qualified to receive virtue, was unable to receive Sarah because "the time [of the Christ] had not yet come."[12] It is only through the Christ-event, Origen contends, that "complete and perfect virtue might pass over to the Church of the Gentiles."[13] At the coming of Christ then, "both the house of Abimelech and his handmaids whom the Lord healed" through the prayer of Abraham would bear children for the Church.[14] The barrenness experienced by Abimelech's wife and handmaids is thus equivalent to the barrenness experienced by those subject to the "law of the letter" embodied in the Hebrew Scriptures.[15] This barrenness could only be overcome by Christ who freed souls to "marry the spirit and receive the marriage of the New Testament," and only in this marriage with Christ could spiritual children be born for the Church.[16]

A final point; Origen does not explain how Abraham's prayer was effective in giving life to the barren wombs of Abimelech's wife and handmaidens. Indeed, Origen is explicit in determining that grace "was designed to be delivered to the Gentiles not by Abraham who, although he was great was, nevertheless, a servant, but by Christ."[17] However, Origen affirms that all nations shall be blessed in Abraham, but "established in Isaac, that is, in Christ," Abraham's seed.[18] Now we note that the Scriptures record the conception of Isaac immediately after this narrative (Gen 21:1–2). It seems plausible then that Origen would attribute the effectiveness of Abraham's prayer to Isaac—this figure of Christ—who was conceived practically contemporaneously with the healing of Abimelech's household.[19]

12. Manet ergo apud Abraham virtus, manet in circumcisione, donec tempus veniat, ut in Christo Jesu Domino nostro . . . integra et perfecta virtus ad Ecclesiam gentium transeat. Origen, *Gen.* VI.3 (Heine, 125), cf. Migne, *PG* 12.197.

13. Ibid.

14. Tunc ergo et domus Abimelech, et ancillæ ejus, quas sanavit Dominus, parient Ecclesiæ filios. Origen, *Gen.* VI.3 (Heine, 125), cf. Migne, *PG* 12.197.

15. Legem litteræ. Origen, *Gen.* VI.3 (Heine, 124), cf. Migne, *PG* 12.197.

16. Ut ita demum libera jam anima spiritui nubat, et novi testamenti matrimonium sortiatur. Origen, *Gen.* VI.3 (Heine, 125), cf. Migne, *PG* 12.197.

17. Hæc enim gratia non per Abraham, qui quamvis esset magnus, famulus tamen erat, sed per Christum gentibus parabatur. Origen, *Gen.* VI.2 (Heine, 124), cf. Migne, *PG* 12.196.

18. Tamen in Isaac ei ponitur repromissio, id est in Christo. Origen, *Gen.* VI.2 (Heine, 124), cf. Migne, *PG* 12.196.

19. We recognize, of course, that this is speculation. Faced with the need to speculate in order to make sense of Origen's exegesis, we can draw some consolation from Origen himself who wrestled with the limits of what he could draw from the challenging text of

Part Two—John Chrysostom on Suffering

John Chrysostom offers an important key to unlocking the mystery of suffering; one that might be applied fruitfully to the problem of barrenness. In his homily on Isaiah 45:6–7, Chrysostom makes the claim that "[s]ome things are good, others bad, others in-between; while some of them are thought bad by many people, in fact they are not, only being described and presumed to be."[20] Examples of good things which "could never be bad" include self-control and almsgiving, while "licentiousness, inhumanity [and] cruelty" are bad and never able to be good.[21] Chrysostom's third category—those things which are in-between (τὰ μέσα)—comprises those things which become either bad or good "depending on the attitudes of the one who uses them."[22] In this category, Chrysostom includes "poverty and wealth, health and sickness, life and death, glory and honor, slavery and freedom, and suchlike."[23]

Chrysostom clarifies his position on what constitutes an "in-between thing" in the context of a discussion on the moral value of wealth and poverty.

> While by many people poverty is thought evil, in fact it is not; rather, if you look at it dispassionately and with sound values [νήφει καὶ φιλοσοφεῖ],[24] it has the effect of removing evils. . . . [I]f poverty were an evil, it would follow that all those living in poverty were evil, whereas if many of those living in poverty attained heaven, surely poverty is no evil.[25]

Genesis 20: "So far as we can perceive in such difficult passages..." Quantum possumus in tam difficilibus locis sentire. Origen, *Gen.* VI.3 (Heine, 124), cf. Migne, *PG* 12.197.

20. Τῶν πραγμάτων τὰ μέν ἐστι καλά, τὰ δὲ κακά, τὰ δὲ μέσα· ὧν ἔνια πολλοῖς μὲν εἶναι δοκεῖ κακά, οὐκ ἔστι δέ, ἀλλὰ λέγεται μόνον καὶ ὑποπτεύεται. John Chrysostom, *In illud Isaiae: Ego dominus deus feci lumen* 3, in Chrysostom, *St. John Chrysostom Old Testament Homilies Vol. 2*, 31 (= Chrysostom, *In illud Isaiae* 3 (Hill, 31)), cf. Migne, *PG* 56:146.

21. Οὐκοῦν τρεῖς αὗται μοῖραι· τὰ μὲν γὰρ καλὰ οὐκ ἂν γένοιτο κακά, οἷον σωφροσύνη, ἐλεημοσύνη, καὶ ὅσα τοιαῦτα· τὰ δὲ κακὰ οὐκ ἄν ποτε γένοιτο καλά, οἷον ἀσέλγεια, ἀπανθρωπία, ὠμότης· Chrysostom, *In illud Isaiae* 5 (Hill, 35), cf. Migne, *PG* 56:149.

22. τὰ δὲ ποτὲ μὲν τοῦτο, ποτὲ δὲ ἐκεῖνο γινόμενα, παρὰ τὴν γνώμην τῶν χρωμένων. Chrysostom, *In illud Isaiae* 5 (Hill, 35), cf. Migne, *PG* 56:149.

23. Ἆρα τῶν μέσων ταῦτά ἐστι, πενία καὶ πλοῦτος, ὑγίεια καὶ νόσος, καὶ ζωὴ καὶ θάνατος, δόξα καὶ τιμή, δουλεία καὶ ἐλευθερία, καὶ ὅσα τοιαῦτα. Chrysostom, *In illud Isaiae* 4 (Hill, 32), cf. Migne, *PG* 56:147.

24. Νήφει καὶ φιλοσοφεῖ is perhaps better translated "in a balanced and philosophical manner."

25. Ἡ πενία δοκεῖ μὲν πολλοῖς εἶναι κακόν, οὐκ ἔστι δέ· ἀλλ' εἴ τις νήφει καὶ

Applying Chrysostom's logic to barrenness *per se*, it would seem that he would agree that barrenness is able to remove evils.[26] Certainly, if one adapts the final sentence of the quote above, Chrysostom would accept that "if barrenness were an evil, it would follow that all those who are barren were evil, whereas if many of those who are barren attained heaven, surely barrenness is no evil." As we shall see in our study of patristic *de virginitate* texts, barrenness was deemed to be an effective means of purification from evil. Furthermore, the witness of virgins from the beginning of the Church (as testified to in the Pauline epistles) affirms the place of virgins among the saints.

Part Three—Patristic de virginitate literature

Patristic *de virginitate* literature is, in some sense, a logical place to begin seeking a theology of barrenness simply for the fact that both the virgin and the barren man or woman experience the pain of physical childlessness, albeit in different ways and to different degrees.[27] But what can this literature offer? In the interest of brevity, we will identify just three prominent features of these texts. In the first instance, these texts give a developed account of spiritual motherhood and stress the superiority of this motherhood over the merely physical. Next, they highlight the difficulties of physical motherhood, not simply as sources of sadness, but as distractions which serve to divert the individual from the proper *telos* of human existence, the vision of God himself. Third, the Church's virginal maternity is emphasized. These three areas will thus form part of the framework about which we will begin to construct a patristic theology of barrenness. Before we begin, a few brief comments on virginity are in order.

φιλοσοφεῖ, καὶ κακῶν ἀναιρετικόν . . . Πάλιν ἡ πενία εἰ κακὸν ἦν, ἔδει τοὺς ἐν πενίᾳ ἅπαντας εἶναι κακούς· εἰ δὲ πολλοὶ τῶν ἐν πενίᾳ ὄντων τῶν οὐρανῶν ἐπελάβοντο οὐκ ἄρα ἡ πενία κακόν. Chrysostom, *In illud Isaiae* 3 (Hill, 31–32), cf. Migne, *PG* 56:146–47.

26. We may note too that Chrysostom does not limit the medicinal effects of suffering to poverty. For instance, "hunger is not only no evil but even acts to abolish evils, correcting ailments in the manner of a medicine."

Ὁρᾷς ὡς οὐ μόνον [οὐ] κακὸν ὁ λιμὸς, ἀλλὰ καὶ κακῶν ἀναιρετικὸς, ἐν τάξει φαρμάκου τὰ νοσήματα Διορθωσάμενος. Chrysostom, *In illud Isaiae* 6 (Hill, 36), cf. Migne, *PG* 56:150.

27. For our study we will look particularly at the following works, recognizing that some authors wrote separate works extolling the excellence of marriage which provide a useful counterpoint to their texts on virginity: Ambrose of Milan, *De virginitate* and *De virginibus*; Athanasius, *First and Second Letters to Virgins* and *On Virginity*; Augustine, *De bono coniugali* and *De sancta virginitate*; Cyprian, *De habitu virginum*; Gregory of Nyssa, *De virginitate*; St. Methodius, *The Symposium—A Treatise on Chastity*.

From the earliest years virginity was held in high esteem in the Christian community. In the words of Louis Bouyer, virginity was justified

> as an effort to realize immediately and totally the reality of which marriage offers an image and a partial realization; the union of Christ and the Church, of the Word of God and humanity redeemed from sin by the cross of Jesus.[28]

Virginity was, therefore, a sign that pointed both to the spiritual marriage made between the Church and her Spouse, and to the salvific power of Christ's redeeming sacrifice. Drawing particularly on chapter 7 of Paul's first letter to the Corinthians, the fathers sought in the *De virginitate* literature to establish the value of consecrated virginity while balancing this with a positive account of marriage.[29] As a close reading of these texts reveals, some achieved this balance more successfully than others.[30]

Physical and Spiritual Parenthood

Western civilization, at least, has always believed physical parenthood to be both a natural human desire and a blessing. According to Plato, the desire for physical progeny is linked to the desire for immortality.[31] Augustine builds on this, recognizing that mortal beings possess a natural inclination to provide a successor which, when "accompanied by worship of God . . . is destined to be fruitful thirty times over."[32] In the Hebrew Scriptures we find numerous stories which celebrate the blessing which is experienced in the birth of children. For example, the promise of descendants to Abraham and the subsequent birth of Isaac stands out as a clear reminder that progeny are both a natural desire and a gift and blessing from God. In sum, on the

---

28. Bouyer, *The Spirituality of the New Testament and the Fathers*, 304.

29. There are, of course, in this literature on virginity extremes to be found regarding the esteem with which marriage should be held. Much of this, we would suggest, can be put down to the genre; one would expect literature written specifically to praise the virginal state to elevate this state above marriage. We note, however, the warning of Bouyer who strongly refutes the notion that consecrated virginity is "connected with the dualistic theses of heretical gnosticism." Ibid.

30. Methodius, in his *Symposium*, is probably less successful in this regard than someone like Augustine who wrote treatises both on the good of marriage and the good of virginity.

31. "[M]ortal nature seeks as far as possible to live forever and be immortal. And this is possible in one way only: by reproduction, because it always leaves behind a new young one in place of the old." Plato, *Symposium* 207d, in *Plato: Complete Works*, 490.

32. Augustine, *The Excellence of Marriage* 22.19, in Augustine, *Marriage and Virginity*, 50.

Judeo-Christian worldview, physical parenthood is both the fulfillment of a rightful and basic human desire, and a confirmation of God's blessing.[33]

There is, however, another type of parenthood which is not so explicitly found in the Judeo-Christian Scriptures; the spiritual. Spiritual parenthood, as exemplified in the consecrated virgin, is more fruitful than that achieved in the physical begetting of children. Gregory of Nyssa discusses spiritual parenthood from a maternal perspective. Spiritual motherhood, Gregory posits, brings to birth not mortal bodies, but "life and incorruptibility."[34] It is a vocation which is not restricted to the consecrated virgin, nor is it limited to women. Rather, according to the Nyssan, spiritual bringing-to-birth "occurs when someone through the life-giving quality of the heart takes on the incorruptibility of the Spirit and begets wisdom and justice and holiness and redemption."[35] Anyone, Gregory continues, can potentially "become a mother in reality" since—and here he references the Synoptic Gospels—anyone who does the will of God becomes Christ's brother, sister, and mother.[36] Indeed, in the words of Augustine, "every devout soul that does the will of his Father by the fertile power of charity is Christ's mother in those to whom it gives birth, until Christ himself is formed in them."[37] Spiritual motherhood, therefore, is accessible to all Christians who are open to following the will of God and to carrying the Word, the Spouse *par excellence*, in their heart.[38]

So are the fruits of spiritual motherhood superior to those of physical motherhood? Gregory is helpful in this regard. First, he references 1 Timothy 2:15, where Paul affirms that the child-bearing woman who persists in faith, love, and holiness, with self-control (*sōphrosúnē*) will be saved.[39] For Paul, it is not the bearing of children that saves the woman, but rather it is her faith, love, holiness, and self-control that leads to her salvation. Gregory, however, applies this pericope to the virginal mother who, he posits, will be saved by bearing "life and incorruptibility" through her "participation

---

33. The Scriptural understanding of progeny is that children are always a gift that God can freely give or take away. God does not "owe" parents children; that is, children are neither a reward nor a human right.

34. Gregory of Nyssa, *De virginitate* 13, in Gregory of Nyssa, *Fathers of the Church*, 48 (= Nyssa, *De virginitate* 13 (Callahan, 48)).

35. Nyssa, *De virginitate* 14 (Callahan, 50).

36. Nyssa, *De virginitate* 14 (Callahan, 50); cf. Matt 12:48–50; Mark 3:33–35; Luke 8:21.

37. Augustine, *De sancta virginitate* 5,5, in Augustine, *Marriage and Virginity*, 70 (= Augustine, *De sancta virginitate* 5,5 (Kearney, 70)).

38. Augustine, *De sancta virginitate* 3,3 (Kearney, 69).

39. ἐν πίστει καὶ ἀγάπῃ καὶ ἁγιασμῷ μετὰ σωφροσύνης. 1 Tim 2:15.

in the Spirit."[40] We would suggest that this "participation in the Spirit" is equivalent to the life of faith, love, holiness, and self-control described by Paul. A key difference then between physical and spiritual motherhood lies not in the spiritual life of the mother—both are called to bear the spiritual gifts, especially *sōphrosúnē*—but rather in the type of fruit each bears.[41]

Athanasius confirms this, declaring that: "We will all bear fruit to the Lord who sowed" the seed of the Word.[42] He continues, offering an alternative interpretation of the parable of the noblemen and the ten servants in Luke 19:12–27: "Moreover, it is the same Lord who says to the virgin, 'Be set over ten cities,' and to the married woman, 'Be set over five cities.'"[43] Augustine also affirms that the reward given to the virgin and married will be of differing magnitude. He does this in *De sancta virginitate* in the context of seeking to understand God's promise to faithful eunuchs in Isaiah 56:4–5. On Augustine's view, God's promise of a better place for eunuchs in the Kingdom implies "that married persons will be given a place [in the Kingdom] too, though a much inferior one [to that of the eunuch]."[44]

So what is this superior position that the eunuch will receive? Augustine would argue, on the basis of further reflection on Isaiah 56:4–5, that it is an everlasting name, a *nomen aeternum*. This name is "certainly some special higher honor" not shared "in common with the multitude, even though they dwell in the same kingdom and the same home."[45] The promise of a name to eunuchs expressed in Isaiah 56 has obvious parallels with God's promise of a name to Abraham given in the context of the Abrahamic covenant.

In sum, the fathers affirm the value of physical parenthood, especially when those who have married have been faithful and, in Augustine's words,

---

40. Nyssa, *De virginitate* 13 (Callahan, 48).

41. Immediately after his reference to 1 Timothy, Gregory cites Ps 112:9, "He establishes in her home the barren wife as the joyful mother of children." Gregory, *DV* 13 (Callahan, 48). ὁ κατοικίζων στεῖραν ἐν οἴκῳ, μητέρα τέκνων εὐφραινομένην. Ps 112:9 (LXX). Interpreting this verse, Gregory declares "[t]he virgin mother who begets immortal children through the Spirit truly rejoices [εὐφραίνεται] and she is called barren by the prophet because of her moderation [sōphrosúnēn]." Nyssa, *De virginitate* 13 (Callahan, 48), cf. Migne, *PG* 46.377. The virgin mother is thus equated to the "barren wife" of Ps 112:9 because she possesses *sōphrosúnē*; it is because of this virtue that she is able to bear spiritual and immortal children.

42. Athanasius, *First Letter to Virgins* 20, in Brakke, *Athanasius and the Politics of Asceticism*, 280 (= Athanasius, *First Letter* 20 (Brakke, 280)).

43. Ibid.

44. Augustine, *De sancta virginitate* 24,24 (Kearney, 82).

45. Augustine, *De sancta virginitate* 25,25 (Kearney, 83); cf. Augustine, *De sancta virginitate* 26,26 (Kearney, 83–84).

have "had children chastely and legitimately and brought them up in the fear of God, teaching their children to put their trust in God."[46] While these physical parents have a share in the kingdom, this share is of a different order to that given to spiritual parents; the righteous eunuch and, by extension, all spiritual parents, are given a *name*. Let us now consider how physical parenthood can be an obstacle to achieving this name.

The Difficulties of Physical Motherhood and the *Telos* of Human Existence

In his *De virginitate* Gregory of Nyssa provides one of the more striking patristic accounts of the difficulties of the married state.[47] Combining the classical *epithalamium* genre with that of the funeral speech, Gregory vividly articulates the sadness which can speedily come after the joy of the wedding banquet.[48] For instance, he notes:

> When the bridegroom looks upon the face of his beloved, the fear of separation immediately comes over him; while he listens to her sweet voice, he is aware that sometime he will not hear it; when he is delighted by the sight of her beauty, then, especially, does he shudder at the expectation of misfortune.[49]

Further reading of the text reveals that Gregory is by no means morbid. Rather, the Cappadocian is realistic, pointing out what is often too quickly dismissed; physical life is subject to temporal and material concerns, the greatest of which is death. Ambrose too, in order to provide a contrast between the temporal advantages of the married woman and those of the virgin, describes the difficulties of married life. In *De virginibus* he declares:

> Although a noble woman may boast of her fruitful womb, the more she has borne the more she labors. Let her calculate the

---

46. Augustine, *De sancta virginitate* 24.24 (Kearney, 82).

47. Nyssa, *De virginitate* 3 (Callahan, 14–15).

48. "Technically speaking, an epithalamium was a song, poem or speech made at the entrance of the bridal chamber—the *thalamos*—at the point just before the bride and groom were due to enter and the marriage would be consummated. The term is also used more generally, however, to describe a range of poetry and prose forms which refer to a wedding. The basic function of these genres is praise: not just praise of the bride and groom themselves, but also praise of the couple's families, of the institution of marriage, and of a god or gods associated with marriage." Ludlow, "Useful and Beautiful," 221.

49. Nyssa, *De virginitate* 3 (Callahan, 14–15).

consolations that her children give her, but let her also calculate her trials.⁵⁰

Elsewhere, after affirming that marriage is not sinful, Ambrose explains that the labors of the married woman include "the grievous labours of childbirth" and "the heavy task of forming and educating children."⁵¹

The key point to be garnered from such accounts of the difficulties of marriage and childbirth is that these encumbrances can distract one from the *telos* of life, the undisturbed vision of God.⁵² Of course, while both the consecrated virgin and the married infertile person are freed from the burdens of childrearing, the married infertile person still faces the aforementioned difficulties of marriage.

On the view of the Nyssan, consecrated virginity, which is devoid of all these distractions, provides a means for the soul to transcend and overcome "the lowly guilt of the flesh" in order to ascend to the divine.⁵³ Indeed the Nyssan's anthropology hangs on this conviction that the soul cannot gaze on the divine if it is "nailed down by the pleasure of the flesh and indulging in a desire for human passions."⁵⁴ The flesh, therefore, must be overcome if one is to gaze on God, "the chief and first and only beautiful and good and pure."⁵⁵

Augustine too held that consecrated virginity was a path to material transcendence. John McQuade, a translator of Augustine's *De sancta virginitate*, notes that "the essence of virginal consecration" entailed "the throwing of one's whole being into intimate, loving union with God, so that He becomes the center of thought and action."⁵⁶ McQuade continues,

> [i]n this union the soul finds its deepest satisfaction and noblest self-expression. It achieves a fruitfulness immeasurably superior to that of carnal generation. Like Mary, like the Church, it

---

50. Ambrose, *De virginibus* 6.25, in Ramsey, *Ambrose*, 80 (= Ambrose, *De virginibus* 6.25 (Ramsey, 80)).

51. Ambrose, *De virginitate* VI, 32, in Ambrose, *On Virginity*, 20 (= Ambrose, *De virginitate* VI, 32 (Callam, 20), cf. Sirach 30.

52. This is equivalent, we could argue, with deification, becoming like God. For the *telos* of persons in the anthropology of Gregory of Nyssa see Blank, "The Etymology of Salvation," 78.

53. Nyssa, *De virginitate* 5 (Callahan, 28).

54. Nyssa, *De virginitate* 5 (Callahan, 28).

55. Nyssa, *De virginitate* 11 (Callahan, 42).

56. McQuade, "Introduction—Holy Virginity," 141.

becomes in a special way, in a spiritual way, the mother of Christ in His members.[57]

The goal then of consecrated virginity and, by extension, all spiritual parenthood, is a vision of God which involves the entirety of one's being such that the person bears spiritual fruit incomparably superior to physical progeny. As McQuade recognizes, this fruit is not borne merely for the pleasure of the individual; or even for the betterment of humanity generally; but rather it is borne for the kingdom of God. We may now consider how the Church brings to birth children for the kingdom in her role as virginal mother.

The Church as the Virginal Mother

Cyril of Alexandria deemed the Church to be the mother once barren which is now the mother of many children.[58] Developing this notion, John Chrysostom, drawing on the example of Sarah, declared "[f]or just as she [Sarah] gave birth in her old age when she was barren, so too the church, though barren, has given birth for these, the final times."[59] Ambrose interpreted this paradox of the Church as a barren mother to mean that the Church is

> unsullied by intercourse, fruitful in bearing, a virgin in chastity and a mother in offspring. And so she bears us as a virgin who has been impregnated not by a man but by the Spirit ... she is wedded to the Word of God as to an eternal bridegroom without endangering her chastity, and she is barren of injury and pregnant with reason.[60]

Augustine believed similarly, asserting that for both Mary and the Church "virginity is no obstacle to fecundity" and "fecundity does not dispense with

---

57. Ibid.

58. ἡ πρότερον μὲν στεῖρα, νῦν δὲ πολύτεκος. Cyril of Alexandria, *Catechetical Lecture* XVIII.26, in Migne, PG 33.1048.

59. Ὥσπερ γὰρ ἐκείνη στεῖρα οὖσα ἔτεκεν ἐν γήρᾳ, οὕτω καὶ αὕτη στεῖρα οὖσα ἔτεκεν ἐπ' ἐσχάτων τῶν καιρῶν.

John Chrysostom, *Non esse desperandum* 4, in *Genesis 12–50—Ancient Christian Commentary on Scripture*, 90, cf. Migne, PG 51:368 and Petit, *La chaîne sur la Genèse*, 187. Chrysostom's reference here to the final times (ἐπ' ἐσχάτων τῶν καιρῶν) may be taken to mean both the Church of the fourth/fifth century, and the kingdom of heaven. Certainly the plunging of the catechumen into the baptismal font at Easter gave, and continues to give, birth to a new member of the earthly congregation who is set apart for membership of the heavenly court.

60. Ambrose, *De virginibus* 6.31 (Ramsey, 81–82).

virginity."⁶¹ The Church is thus virginally barren through her chastity, and mother through the offspring of her union with the Word.

The fecundity through barrenness of the Church is prefigured not only by Sarah, but also Rachel and Hannah. In the three pairs of women, Sarah and Hagar, Rachel and Leah, and Hannah and Penina, one was barren and the other fertile.⁶² In each instance, the one who was barren ultimately comes to enjoy God's favor, while—Ratzinger states—the fruitful wife "recedes into the ordinary or even has to struggle against the curse of repudiation, of being unloved."⁶³ While this turn of events may appear initially to be of little consolation to the infertile couple, Ratzinger's explanation of this trio of pairs is helpful and bears quoting in full:

> The theological implication of this overthrow of values [where the infertile is blessed and fertile repudiated] becomes clear only gradually; from it Paul developed his theology of spiritual birth: the true son of Abraham is not the one who traces his physical origin to him, but the one who, in a new way beyond mere physical birth, has been conceived through the creative power of God's word of promise. Physical life as such is not really wealth; this promise, which endures beyond life, is what first makes life fully itself (cf. Rom 4; Gal 3:1–14; 4:21–31).⁶⁴

So theological speculation on the infertile members of these pairs leads us to consider spiritual birth as the true fruit of God's promise; a promise which integrates and fulfills the individual both in this life and the next.⁶⁵

Ambrose reflects further on the relationship between Rachel and the Church. For Ambrose, in the time before her pregnancy "Rachel is seen to be a type of the Church, to whom it is said, 'Sing, O barren one, who did not bear; break forth into singing and cry aloud, you who have not been in travail!'"⁶⁶ Although jealous of her sister Leah, who had borne many children, Ambrose asserts that Rachel experienced in her barrenness the wound of love.⁶⁷ The Milanese bishop posits that this wound of love was

---

61. Augustine, *De sancta virginitate* III.2, in Augustine, *De bono coniugali and De sancta virginitate*, 67–69.

62. Ratzinger, *Daughter Zion*, 18.

63. Ibid., 18.

64. Ibid., 18–19.

65. Gal 4:22–27 confirms this as it draws a link between Hagar and Rachel, and the city of Jerusalem and the heavenly Jerusalem. The author of this rich and profound passage quotes Isa 54:1 *verbatim*.

66. Ambrose, *De virginitate* XIV.91 (Callam, 46).

67. Ambrose, *De virginitate* XIV.91 (Callam, 45–46).

struck by God's Word which scrutinized her heart and preserved her.[68] Rachel was thus purified and preserved by the Word of God just as Jerusalem was through her time in exile.[69] All those who are saved, Ambrose contends, arrive in heaven wounded by the sword of the Word. The Word removes the garment of the body and cuts away the dross of secular wisdom and fleshly desire from the heart and mind so that one might gaze on Christ in "utter simplicity."[70] Similarly, the Church is wounded by the Word of God which purifies her, removing from her "the garment of philosophy," "the dress of secular wisdom."[71]

Concluding Remarks

Aidan Nichols declares the task of theology to be "the disciplined exploration of what is contained in revelation."[72] The fathers wrote, preached, worshiped, and ministered in that privileged period in which the canon of Scripture was being, or had been recently, finalized. Their insights into difficult pastoral realities like barrenness are therefore to be esteemed. While their theology was often not as disciplined as we may wish it to be, there is little doubt that they understood themselves to be exploring the limits of revelation.

In our analysis of Origen's homiletic work on Genesis 20, we have established that barrenness is only made fruitful through the encounter with Christ. This fecundity requires, Origen posits, the presence of virtue before the grace of the Incarnation can work effectively. Chrysostom's teaching, on those things which are good or bad depending on the attitude of the one receiving them, demonstrates how barrenness can remove evils. We may understand this to mean that well-received barrenness can actually work to make the barren one virtuous. Barrenness, therefore, need not be a barrier to fruitfulness; it was not for Mary, nor the Church, and it need not be for any faithful Christian. All persons, in fact, are called to spiritual parenthood and each is able to actualize this as grace builds on virtuous nature.

So where does that leave us in our efforts to trace the outlines of a patristic theology of barrenness? I would suggest that such a theology must be founded on a sound understanding of spiritual parenthood, not as an

---

68. Ambrose, *De virginitate* I.3 (Callam, 8), cf. Ambrose, *De virginitate* XIV.91 (Callam, 45).
69. Blenkinsopp, *Isaiah 40–55*, 360.
70. Ambrose, *De virginitate* XIV.88, 92 (Callam, 44, 46).
71. Ambrose, *De virginitate* XIV.92 (Callam, 46).
72. Nichols, "What Theology Is," 387.

alternative to physical parenting, but rather, as a call for all who wish to follow Christ. In their *de virginitate* literature the fathers propose a way or path to achieving spiritual parenthood, albeit in the particular context of extoling the value of consecrated celibacy for the kingdom. This path requires faith, love, holiness, and self-control, along with the theological virtue of hope. In particular, the fathers have indicated that the spiritual parent can hope as Abraham did for an eternal name. He or she can also hope for a reversal in values, that the barren may become fruitful, as occurred for Sarah, Rachel, Hannah, and Mary. The path to spiritual parenthood also demands abandonment to the Spirit in order to follow the will of the Word completely. Such an abandonment, is equivalent to allowing the Word to cut away the dross of physical attachments—applying a lover's wound—opening the door to the bridal chamber, permitting the Christian to unite with Christ the Spouse. In sum, the fathers propose the virtuous life as a means for begetting children for the kingdom and assuring one's *nomen aeternum*. And what better model for this type of life than Mary?

Bibliography

Ambrose of Milan. *De virginitate*. In Ambrose, *On Virginity*, translated by Daniel Callam. Ontario: Peregrina, 1991.

———. *De virginibus*. In Boniface Ramsey, *Ambrose*, 71–116. New York: Routledge, 1997.

Aquinas, Thomas. *Summa theologiae: Latin text and English translation*. 60 vols. Translated by English Province Dominicans. Oxford: Blackfriars, 1964–.

Athanasius. *First Letter to Virgins; Second Letter to Virgins; On Virginity*. In David Brakke, *Athanasius and the Politics of Asceticism*, 273–309. Oxford: Clarendon, 1995.

Augustine. *De bono coniugali*. In Augustine, *De bono coniugali and De sancta virginitate*, translated and edited by P. G. Walsh. Oxford: Oxford University Press, 2004.

———. *Marriage and Virginity*. Translated by Ray Kearney, edited by D. G. Hunter and J. E. Rotelle, introduction by D. G. Hunter. New York: New City, 1999.

———. *De sancta virginitate*. In Augustine, *De bono coniugali and De sancta virginitate*, translated and edited by P. G. Walsh. Oxford: Oxford University Press, 2004.

Blank, David L. "The Etymology of Salvation in Gregory of Nyssa's *De Virginitate*." *Journal of Theological Studies* 37 (1986) 77–90.

Blenkinsopp, Joseph. *Isaiah 40–55*. The Anchor Bible. New York: Doubleday, 2000.

Boadt, Lawrence. *Reading the Old Testament: An Introduction*. New York: Paulist, 1984.

Bouyer, Louis. *The Spirituality of the New Testament and the Fathers*. Translated by Mary P. Ryan. New York: Seabury, 1982.

Cyprian. *De habitu virginum*. In Saint Cyprian of Carthage, *Fathers of the Church, Volume 36: Treatises*, edited by Roy J. Deferrari, translated by Sister Angela Elizabeth Keenan, 24–52. Baltimore, MD: Catholic University of America Press, 1958.

Deiss, Lucien. *Mary, Daughter of Sion.* Collegeville, MN: Liturgical, 1972.

Gregory of Nyssa. *De virginitate.* In Gregory of Nyssa, *Fathers of the Church, Volume 58: Ascetical Works,* translated by Virginia Woods Callahan, 1–75. Baltimore, MD: Catholic University of America Press, 1967.

John Chrysostom. *St. John Chrysostom Old Testament Homilies, Vol. 2, Homilies on Isaiah and Jeremiah.* Translation and introduction by Robert Charles Hill. Brookline, MA: Holy Cross Orthodox Press, 2003.

Ludlow, Morwenna. "Useful and Beautiful: A Reading of Gregory of Nyssa's On Virginity and a Proposal for Understanding Early Christian Literature." *Irish Theological Quarterly* 79 (2014) 219–40.

McQuade, John. "Introduction—Holy Virginity." In Augustine, *Fathers of the Church, Vol. 27,* edited by Roy J. Deferrari, 135–41. Washington, DC: Catholic University of America Press, 1955.

Methodius. *The Symposium—A Treatise on Chastity.* Ancient Christian Writers, Vol. 27. Translated and annotated by Herbert Musurillo. London: Longmans, Green and Co., 1958.

Migne, J. -P., ed. *Patrologiae cursus completus. Series Graeca* [PG] 161 vols. Paris: Migne, 1857–66.

Origen. *In Genesim Homilia VI.* In Origen, *Homilies on Genesis and Exodus,* translated by Ronald E. Heine. Washington, DC: Catholic University of America Press, 1982.

Nichols, Aidan. "What Theology Is." *New Blackfriars* 69 (1988) 383–92.

Pelikan, Jaroslav. *Christianity and Classical Culture: The Metamorphosis of Natural Theology in the Christian Encounter with Hellenism.* Gifford Lecture Series. New Haven, CT: Yale University Press, 1993.

Petit, Françoise. *La chaîne sur la Genèse / Éd. intégrale IV, Chapitres 29 à 50.* Louvain: Peeters, 1996.

Plato. *Symposium.* In *Plato: Complete Works,* edited by John M. Cooper, 457–505. Indianapolis: Hackett, 1997.

Rahlfs, Alfred, and Robert Hanhart. *Septuaginta: id est Vetus Testamentum Graece iuxta LXX interpretes* [LXX], editio altera quam recognovit et emendavit Robert Hanhart. Stuttgart: Deutsche Bibelgesellschaft, 2006.

Ratzinger, Joseph, Cardinal. *Daughter Zion: Meditations on the Church's Marian Belief.* Translated by John M. McDermott. San Francisco: Ignatius, 1983.

Sheridan, Mark, and Thomas C. Oden, eds. *Genesis 12–50.* Ancient Christian Commentary on Scripture. Downers Grove, IL: IVP, 2002.

13

Lex orandi, lex credenda. Dulia, Hyperdulia, et Latria

—Christopher John Wolter

This chapter intends to show the doctrinal place of the Blessed Virgin by looking at the honor given her in the Eucharistic rite of the Western Church. It is argued that Our Lady is not worshiped, but that the exalted celebration of her accords with the traditional doctrine and that this is just. We will conclude that she has an indispensable place at the heart of our sacrificial worship, displaying the work of God.

Introduction

*L*ex orandi, lex credenda—the law of prayer is the law of belief. This is the ancient Christian axiom that speaks of the intrinsic relationship between our prayer and our belief. The Church believes as she prays; how the individual prays shows what they truly believe, just as what we are taught to pray informs our faith.[1] What do we pray and believe in relation

---

1. That what we pray corresponds with what-we-truly-believe is obvious. It would be a complete fallacy for one to suggest that God is an Earth Mother, for example, if then in the depth of the night, in one's hour of need, kneel down, and say "our Father . . . ."

The phrase, *lex orandi, lex credendi*, was first used by St. Prospero of Aquitaine, the fifth century (c. 390—c. 455) disciple of, and apologist for, St. Augustine. For Prospero, that there is unformality throughout world in what he called "*obsecrationum quoque sacerdotalium sacramenta*" the sacraments of priestly prayers or petitions—that is the formal liturgy—is the means by which right belief is established. ". . . *obsecrationum quoque sacerdotalium sacramenta respiciamus, quae ab apostolis tradita, in toto mundo*

to the Blesses Virgin Mary? This chapter will consider this question from the perspective of the Western Eucharistic liturgy, thereby situating our worship of Mary as with her at the foot of the cross of her divine son.

Dulia, Hyperdulia, et Latria—honor, super-honor, and worship—Catholics say they worship God alone, show honor to the saints, and accord a heightened honor to the Blessed Virgin Mary. But, what exactly do we mean by *dulia, hyperdulia,* and *latria*? To answer that we can do no better than to look at the place of the saints, the Blessed Virgin Mary, and of Almighty God as they are presented to us in the liturgy. Looking at the liturgy—the ceremonies of the Church—is an excellent way of demonstrating what we truly believe.

Latria, is usually translated into English as "worship." Though the etymology of "worship," literally "worth-ship," to give something its worth, is not exclusively about God, this is how we use the word today (as a translation of *latria*).[2] The very idea of giving something its worth relies on a notion of justice. It would be an injustice to give God's worth to a creature. *Dulia*, on the other hand, from its Greek root, means to venerate or to give homage and is most often translated as veneration. It can also easily be translated as "showing honor." How do *latria* and *dulia* differ?

Catholics are often accused of worshiping the Blessed Virgin. Indeed, sometimes our veneration can seem to tread a fine line between worship and giving honor. If all one experiences of worship is offering a few prayers and singing some hymns, then undoubtedly we traditional Christians give that worth to Our Lady. So we will look to the liturgy, as much as to define the difference as to show that what we give Our Lady is not the same as what is given to almighty God. More particularly though, we will look at this in the context of what is just.

---

atque in omni catholica Ecclesia uniformiter celebrantur, ut legem credendi lex statuat supplicandi." Migne, *Patrologia Latina* 51, 209–10. For this ancient Christian writer, it is essentially the liturgy that communicates, hands on, and crystallizes the faith. Thus, to quote the Catechism of the Catholic Church, 1124, the Liturgy is seen as "a constitutive element of the holy and living Tradition." One could argue that in no other field of theology is there so close a link to faith as there is in a theology of the faith celebrated in practice, that is, in a theology drawn from the liturgy.

2. The archaic use of the term can still be seen in the traditional marriage vowels where the couple respectively promise worship the other with their bodies. Literally: "with my body I thee worship" (sounds like something out of a contemporary pop song; Hozier, "Take Me to Church" for instance). Worship in that sense—giving what's due—is easily interchangeable with *dulia*. Yet, to God only is due what is due to him only, as befits his worth a worth-ship of latria. This issue is further confused if considered practically, what does, what exactly does giving God his worth entail? That is where our theology of *latria* will come into play.

A Thing of Justice

It is well known that St. Thomas Aquinas followed the ancients in saying that the virtue of religion or piety is a sub-virtue of justice.[3] In fact, it can be argued that the virtue of religion is the most excellent instance of justice (even though it is an odd form of justice as God cannot be repaid in measure equal to his due).[4]

As Josef Pieper has pointed out, justice, for its part, can be described as being good in light of others, or the ability to live truly with others;[5] that is, acting in accord with one's true being as well as that of the other. Reflecting then on the communal nature of humanity, justice is being good in community.[6] The community of being—that is all that God has made, inclusive not only of people but of everything—entails that true justice be given in a fashion that accounts for our creatureliness. To display a level of justice there must be a constellation of created things with greater or lesser renderings. God, as Creator, is then the reference point for any true justice. As God is behind a deliberately ordered creation, any true justice given to God must include a respect for his work. Seeing and recognizing everything's just value, rightly ordering the good, we can then become people of love, where love is understood as relishing in goodness.

According to Thomas's thought, true love, or charity, consists in loving God's goodness, even if that goodness is found in things external to God, such as one's neighbor.[7] God communicates his goodness to all that is good. However, he does not communicate his uniqueness, nor the infinity of his goodness.[8] Thus, only he can be honored as he ought to be honored, in a way unique to God.[9] That is the role of worship. It is a recognition of our debt to God. Rendering justice at the very core of goodness and being itself, it is a call to order the entire cosmos rightly.

Recognizing our utter indebtedness to God, one is called to act upon it, but dependent on God, we cannot give him anything he has not already given us. Yet still, the one who acknowledges he is entirely God's wants to be entirely God's. True devotion encompasses one's entire existence. The devotion to serve is at one with the recognition of our deficiency, even our

---

3. Aquinas, *Summa Theologicae*. II–II, q80.
4. Ibid.
5. Pieper, *The Christian Idea of Man*, 18.
6. Ibid., 19.
7. Gilson, T*he Christian Philosophy of St. Thomas Aquinas,* note 5, 488.
8. Aquinas, *S.T.* II–II, q81, a4, ad3.
9. Gilson, T*he Christian Philosophy of St. Thomas Aquinas,* 488.

inability to worship God.[10] So, not capable of giving him anything,[11] how can we worship? Here enter the Christian mysteries.

We believe that fellowship with God, and with one another in God, is possible by the self-giving sacrifice of Christ who is truly God and truly human. His cross brings us salvation from sin, the possibility of entry into heaven and relationship with the divine. By this hoped for salvation from sin and entry into heaven, as well as the already partial relationship with God, the divine activity does more than restore our dignity. By our Lord's sacrifice God honors us beyond our previous worth.

For St. Thomas Aquinas, while a sacrifice properly speaking is something done to pay the honor which is properly due to God,[12] in a certain sense every work performed for the purpose of being united to God can be justly referred to as a sacrifice, as unity with God is the end or goal of sacrifice.[13] (In our liturgies we have the twin notion of sacrifice and communion.) In this sense Christ's life and subsequent death is the truest of sacrifices.

Now, the Church firmly believes that "the Eucharist is a sacrifice because it re-presents (makes present) the sacrifice of the cross, because it is its memorial and because it applies its fruits."[14] Yet today it is not popular to talk about "sacrifice." Here one finds the source of much of the confusion, especially the accusations that we worship Our Lady or, within some trends of contemporary Catholicism, that we should reject Marian devotion

---

10. Gilson, *The Christian Philosophy of St. Thomas Aquinas*, 336.

11. Justice can be seen to include the interior disposition of the person. Arguing from Aquinas that faith is the origin of justice, Brook that for the Saint there is such a thing as an infused justice or metaphoric justice that does not have to have an expression in just acts done to others, that is to say it can be had by one alone in the wilderness or in a hermit's cell, but is a "rectitude of order in the interior disposition." It is whereby we put God before all things and that which is highest in us before all that is lowest.

12. Aquinas, *S.T.* III, q48, a3. In any religious sacrifice there is an attempt at union with God or a god, which in itself is an attempt at a right relationship, as ordered to justice. The sheer fact that they are accompanied by a ritual denotes that there is at least a sacrifice of time and effort ("correct" rituals usually imply a certain amount of concentration, precision, and dedication to detail) for the spiritual purpose alone. It takes a festival with all its disinterested qualities, consuming our abilities, and taking us away from the materially useful.

The Christian *cultus*, unlike any other, is at once a sacrifice and a sacrament in so far as the Christian *cultus* is a sacrifice held in the midst of the creation which is affirmed by this sacrifice of the God-man—every day is a feast day; and in fact the liturgy knows only feast days, as already pointed out, even working days being *feria*. In so far as the *cultus* is a sacrament it is celebrated in visible signs. Pieper here sites Aquinas, *S.T.* III, q79, a5.

13. Aquinas, *S.T.* III, q48, a3; Augustine, *De Civ*, X.

14. *Catechism of the Catholic Church*, # 1366.

altogether. If we are not talking about sacrifice and offering, then what practical difference is there between our worship and our more general giving of honor? We certainly do not offer Our Lady on an altar, or take and eat her flesh. Nor do we really manifest our devotion to her with an awestruck disposition of silence, or spend long hours on our knees in adoration *per se*. Those are the things of our worship.

Wonder and Awe

The awe struck disposition that we should encounter in worship is itself just. The human heart cannot desire to be separated from the ultimate ground of all being, who is God. As we know, the natural desire for those things that sustain us and, by extension, for those things we take pleasure in, can be destructive. But in supernatural faith destructible desires are tempered by that biblical virtue (or supernatural gift) of "fear of the Lord," the first stage of wisdom (Prov 1:7; 9:10; Ps 111:10; cf. Job 28:28), and thus leads to a supernatural absorption in the love of God.[15] The awestruck wonder before our Father who art in heaven, reverencing his name and thus what the name signifies above all else, is a deliverance from every evil.[16] There is genuine fear involved, a fear of the loss of friendship with God. But that implies that friendship with God is possible; hence we use the term "filial fear."[17] It is the flip side, as it were, to that hope of salvation from sin, entry into heaven, and relationship with the divine; and hence the foundation of all Christian courage. As finite creatures that once were not, in justice we cannot hold to a relationship of presumption upon ultimate Being. Fear of the Lord is ultimately fulfilling of our creatureliness.[18]

It is not incidental, then, that it is in the awestruck silence that we are at our most introspective. Pieper speaks about contemplation and silent wonder as an attitude of the mind that is both the occasion and the capacity

---

15. Aquinas, *S.T.* II–II, q19, aa6–10.

16. For Aquinas following St. Augustine, the Seven Gifts of the Holy Spirit (the perfection of the virtues where God is active in us), the seven petitions of the Pater Noster, and the seven precepts of the Beatitudes all correspond numerically one to the other. In that, fear of the Lord, as the fist stage, is the spiritual poverty spoken of in the first Beatitude and whereby God's name is hallowed above all else. This unfolding of prayer, blessedness, and gift, all ends in that supernatural absorbesion in the love of God whereby the peacemaker child of God enjoys the supernatural wisdom of seeing things as God sees them. Ibid., q 83, a9; 9, ad3.

17. Ibid., q 19, aa 7–8, 10.

18. Pieper, *The Christian Idea of Man*, 27–28.

for steeping oneself in the whole of creation.[19] He argues that it is an appreciation of reality that is not about grabbing and taking, but is instead open to everything. It implies serenity that stems from our inability to understand, and recognition of the mysterious nature of the universe and our contentment before such wonder.[20] This all comes to us as wisdom in the context of the divine giver, before whom we stand as gift to the world and receiver of gifts, receiving of the world, and even receiving, in some sense, God.

It is in encountering the sacrifice of Christ—revelation of the mutually self giving inter-Trinitarian relationship—that we get to the heart of our inner connectedness to being and the gratuitousness of God. While in the Mass we are confronted with the ultimate call for silence, we can be lead to that awe by such things as Marian devotion. Especially in the Rosary, I would argue, we are drawn ultimately to consider God's condescension to us. However, the Rosary itself is not an act of worship. In it we merely contemplate the outpouring and self-giving of God, through Christ Jesus and especially in she who is most gifted, highly favored, or full of God's gratuitousness, the Blessed Virgin Mary.

So, Marian devotion can be performed in careful silence too. We see that the Rosary can be said quietly and carefully (though not by everyone) with an aroused sense of wonder. Moreover of course, the liturgy itself is clothed in other things than just silence. What then is exactly the difference?

Joseph Ratzinger is arguably the most influential contemporary commentator on the liturgy.[21] In response to some of the liturgical crises of our day he has spoken much of the notion of silence and right worship. That discussion has practical implications.[22] He speaks about "content-filled silence" and the effectiveness of silence accompanied by action; and he speaks too about a Christ-like attitude, exposed though hidden, before the sight of God and men.[23] For him silence makes sense as the Mass should for the individual be seen as part of an interior process, where we see ourselves as the real gifts in the "Word-centered sacrifice" in sharing in Jesus Christ's act of self-offering. The emphasis here is on God transforming us at the very

---

19. Pieper, *Leisure the Basis of Culture*, 46–47.

20. Ibid., 47.

21. As well as later going on to become Pope and amongst numerous publications on the subject, Ratzinger's 1999 work *Einführung in den Geist der Liturgie* (Introduction a Spirit of the Liturgy), in its English language publication *The Spirit of the Liturgy* (Ignatius) was so successful that it went through four editions in its first year.

22. Particularly in *The Spirit of the Liturgy* he talks about it in relation to communion and the preparation of the gifts and offertory. Ratzinger, *Spirit of the Liturgy*, 210–11.

23. Ibid., 213.

heart of our being. Ratzinger uses such phrase as "inner process"[24] and "interior conversion."[25] Yet, that transformation cannot take place without our responsive act of self-giving. The difference is really about interior disposition, though it will practically pertain to the Mass text, as we shall see. The Rosary and other Marian devotions help to bring about that disposition, but the offering of Christ, on the cross and on our altars, actualizes that disposition. This means that the lack of meaningful silence in our liturgies can be see as indicative of the loss of a sense of sacrifice as much as a loss of the sense of the sacred and of the awesomeness of God.

This divergence into talking about silence and awe brings us to an important point concerning justice. When we are incapable of worshiping with silent awe, we treat God not as a creature who is subject to and who participates in his goodness should; we need to be able to stand back in wonder; this satisfies some of our duty to worship. Without silent awe before God, any act of honor, whether toward the Blessed Virgin or anybody else, may seem blasphemous; but the problem is not identified in showing the Blessed Virgin too much honor. An issue arises only when we do not show God something entirely else. The lack of meaningful silence can be seen as indicative of the loss of a sense of sacrifice and thus a loss of true justice.

Religious Sacrifice

We might think of the liturgical sacrifice as a turning point in the created order where we free rational creatures, in justice, render back to the Eternal Being, that is God, the entirety of created beings. It is where we make Christ's cosmic action our own. This is done in celebration of the Essential Being, the Eternal Goodness that is God, and in so doing we honor the entire created order as it issues from him and is willed by him. As this created order, with all that has being and goodness, issues forth from God, so too the worship, whereby all returns to him in celebration, must itself be instituted by God. And so he sent his only begotten Son that all might be saved (cf. John 3:16.). That very Word incarnate is the greatest granting of honor to our human existence by the divine, as well as humanity's definitive act of turning to God.

The right ordering achieved through religious sacrifice, when embodied as a virtue, becomes a right ordering of the self in relation not only to God, but to the immensity of created being. Included in this discussion, however, has been the supernatural, God's activity within us. This is only

24. Ibid., 211.
25. Ibid., 210.

really possible if there is some likeness between us and God. This changes our entire life as well relationship with God. It changes our disposition towards all that he has granted unity of being, particular existences, and particular goods. It forms within us an ever greater movement towards God, a temperate rejection of false fears (fearing nothing but the loss of God), a courage that allows one in hope to be just against all odds, and a prudence born out of the love of truth of things, in accord with a flourishing image of God. True justice includes the interior disposition of the person.

The Blessed Virgin, and Our Sacrifice

So, we are called to make Christ's sacrifice our sacrifice. In a most profound sense it is already the Virgin Mary's sacrifice too. She, the Woman, alone amongst those at the foot of the cross, could say "this at last is bone of my bones, flesh of my flesh" (cf. Gen 2:23.), or "this is my body, given up for you, this is my blood, poured out for you" (cf. 1 Cor 11:24–26; Matt 26:26–28; Mark 14:22–24; Luke 22:19–20). Simeon had prophesied that, as her Son would be a sign of contradiction, so too a sword would pierce through her own soul (Luke 2:35). On a human level we might wonder what would have been the greatest of our Lord's sufferings? Neither the nails through his hands, nor the lashes on his back could have compared to the shame of seeing one's own mother watching and knowing she knows his pain and her pain is his. Yet, in that is also brought a consolation. Just as an angel was sent to console our Lord in the garden (in his hour of great struggle to be at peace with the Father) so too his mother (she who had always done God's will) was an accompanying presence when his hour had truly come. If we believe that the Eucharist truly represents Christ's passion, then she must be linked to the *anamnesis* or re-presentation of that passion. Yet, the sacrifice is her son, the point of unity with God is her son.

The Honor Given to Her

Honor is due to the Virgin Mary because it is first and foremost given to her by God. Biblically, she is the most highly favored "full of Grace" (Luke 1:28), most blessed amongst women (v. 42), whom all generations will call blessed (v. 48). Moreover, she is the perfect display of faith; thus she is meritorious, and the favor itself is a just act on God's part. This is seen in her consent to the angel's message, "behold, I am the handmaid of the Lord" (v. 38) in her ponderings on the mysteries of our Lord's youth, in her heart (cf. Luke 2:19, 51) and in her faithfulness to the end, at the foot of the cross (John

19:25). Elizabeth, moved by the Spirit, said "And blessed is she who believed that there would be a fulfillment of what was spoken to her from the Lord." (Luke 1:45). Thus, by God's own word, an altogether greater honor is her due, and that reflects back on God. This is the goodness of her being.

One clear example of the extraordinary honor given to the Blessed Virgin by us is the number of feast days dedicated to her. There are at present approximately (dependent on several factors) seven memorials (some optional), three Feast days, and three solemnities (extra high Feast days). This does not include Christmas, the Epiphany, the Presentation of our Lord at the Temple, or the Feast of the Holy Family, all of which she features in. This is not to mention also that every Saturday that does not have a particular allocation can be offered as a "Saturday Mass of Our Lady." In comparison, St. Peter and St. Paul each have one feast day and share a solemnity, St. John the Baptist has a Solemnity for his birth and a feast for his beheading, and St. Joseph a Solemnity celebrating him under the title of "Husband of Mary" and a memorial dedicated to him as patron of workers. All other Saints celebrated in the general Roman calendar have but one day each. She very much dominates the sanctoral calendar.[26] To the saints are given *dulia*, to Our Lady is given a *hyperdulia*. Her singular privileges, her extraordinary salvation from sin (the Immaculate Conception), her assumption into heaven, her being made Mother of God—these are the three great Marian Solemnities, are all gracious honors given to her by God. Hers are salvation from sin, entry into heaven, relationship with the divine.

The honor given in the extrinsic dedication of these feasts is reflected back on God. This is no more evident than in the great many collects (or opening prayers as they are sometimes called) proper to each feast. The collects follow a sequence beginning with an invocation addressing the Father, followed by what is called the *postulatio*, a thanksgiving for such and such a blessing, before the petition and Trinitarian doxology. For many of the feasts of the Saints the *postulatio* will be something like: "You [God] who have worked *such and such* a miracle in the life of . . ." or "you who have given us an example of . . . in . . . ." The prayer may well go on to ask the Triune God to pay head to the Saint's intercession, but ultimately it is a petitioning of God. While applicable to the collects of all the saints, a fine example of this is evident in our possibly most ancient Marian collect. Whether you call this day the Solemnity of the Mother of God, Feast of the Circumcision or

---

26. All the numbers and titles in this paragraph are taken from the calendar of the Ordinary Form of the Roman Rite. I might also add that in Australia the feast of Our Lady Help of Christians, as national patron, is raised to the rank of a solemnity.

New Year's Day—the collect of this octave day of Christmas has remained the same for centuries.[27]

> O God, who by the fruitful Virginity of the Blessed Mary hast given to mankind the rewards of eternal salvation; grant, we beseech thee, that we may experience her intercession, by whom we received the Author of Life, our Lord Jesus Christ, thy Son. Who lives, etc.[28]

While the *postulatio* point of reference, the fruitful virginity, is undoubtedly the work of God, as illustrated in Luke's Gospel, it does include the human agency of the Blessed Virgin Mary. Thus she merits, and thus we go on to petition our Lord that we may experience her intercession.

The liturgy rarely addresses Our Lady directly. The closest thing we have to a formal prayer directed to her are the antiphons occasionally employed by the Church on Marian Feasts. Of course, there are many hymns and prayers that we add on to the liturgy that address her. The liturgy is often clothed in the glory given her. We are primarily talking about the Mass, but the same holds for the divine office too. In the formal part of that prayer there are no actual prayers addressed to the blessing virgin, though it is often clothed in song and word that sing her praise. Our Lady's *Magnificat* is a good example of this (Luke 1:46–56). It is her biblical canticle of praise that nonetheless speaks about her soul glorifying, magnifying or highlighting the Lord, who has done such great things for her. It is a relishing in the goodness given to her.

The Canon of the Mass

At its barest bones it is possible to have a Mass in which Mary receives but one mention only. Yet, this one mention—close to the heart of the Mass—is during the Eucharistic Prayer. Today we have several options for this prayer, but all follow a like pattern, based on that of the traditional Western

---

27. The Ordinary Form of the Roman Rite celebrates this day as a Marian Feast, the Solemnity of Mary the Mother of God. The antique Extraordinary Form continues to celebrate it as the Octave Day of Christmas, under the title of the Circumcision. However, even in that use the prayers of proper of the Mass are ostensibly Marian in nature. Only the Gospel, "On the Eighth Day . . ." mentions the Circumcision.

28. *Deus, qui salutis aeternae, beatae Mariae virginitate fecunda, humano generi praemia prastitisti: tribue, quaesumus, ut ipsam pro nobis intercedere sentiamus, per quam meruimus auctorem vitae suscipere, Dominum nostrum Jesum Christum, Filium tuum. Qui tecum. Missale Romanum*, all typical editions.

anaphora, known as the Roman Canon.²⁹ As a concluding point we will focus on this singular mention.

Following the singing of the *Sanctus*—with the angels and the entire company of heaven—and then the priest's prayer *Memento Domine*, asking the Lord to be mindful of all those present, comes the *Communicantes*, an invocation of the Church triumphant, literally "in communion with." The initial emphasis of the prayer is on communion with the saints, but at the same time we are made aware of the hierarchical divide between us and them "whose memory we venerate." Before asking their constant help and intercession, a list of names is given. "In the first place the glorious ever virgin Mary, mother of our Lord and God, Jesus Christ." "In the First Place," the text does not just name Our Lady first, but makes a point of it. What follows from there is a well ordered and structured list of two sets of twelve names.³⁰ First, twelve apostles, in the usual Gospel order, but with Paul placed in the second place, filling the gap in the number left by the absence of Judas Iscariot. Then, in the next set of twelve, comes six bishops, five of them popes and then a non-Roman, Cyprian, contemporary of Cornelius (who is therefore the only one taken out of chronology and rank order so as to be set next to his friend). Amongst the other six martyrs, there are two clerics, Laurence and Chrysogonus; then follow John, Paul, Cosmos and Damian.³¹ Later on, after the consecration in the prayer *nobis quoque peccatoribus*, we find again an invocation of two groupings of saints, this time with that other symbolic number of seven a piece. There is a deliberate ordering and structure in a well planned arrangement. As the greatly influential liturgical historian Joseph Jungman pointed out, the listings show the work of a systematic hand.³² The main point for us is that the Blessed Virgin is in communion with and "in the first place," but also is set apart, not numbered amongst either set of twelve, or of the later twin sets of seven, the last of which consists of entirely women's names. This is just, as she, in the first place is the most blessed amongst them, uniquely honored by the Almighty

---

29. In that there are several key elements: Thanksgiving, acclamation, epiclesis, institution narrative or consecration, anamnesis, the oblation, intercessions and doxology. The shortest of the Eucharistic prayers, the second, the one (very loosely based on the canon of Hippolytus) mention's Our Lady once in the anamnesis after the consecration. The longest of them, the fourth, extols her in the thanksgiving before.

30. Symbolic of the twelve tribes of Israel, (prefiguring the Church) and the structure of the heavenly Church, the new Jerusalem, coming down out of heaven with twelve gates and twelve towers as well as the twelve apostles (explicitly named). This is the Church in its fullness.

31. Jungman, *The Mass of the Roman Rite*. Vol. I, 172–73.

32. Ibid. 174–77.

and uniquely related to the sacrifice of Christ, and it is by sacrifice, Christ's sacrifice, that we worship God.

Conclusion

Mary has a fundamental place next to the Sacrifice, that place where we truly worship God in the awestruck silence of our hearts. So we clothe the liturgy in the honor that God has given her, relishing in the goodness of her being and making it our own. Saved from sin in the Immaculate Conception as the first fruits of the cross she is uniquely honored by God and so stands at the foot of that cross, a part of her son's pain, but also a consoling presence. Thus, she is received into heaven bodily, in the first place ahead of all the other Saints, and stands by the altar of God in heaven and interceding for us. Our recourse to her is in keeping with her life, which is in keeping with her God given gifts, which is justly in keeping with the honor that is her due.

Bibliography

Aquinas, Saint Thomas. *Summa Theologicae*: First complete American ed. Vol. I, II, & III. New York: Benziger Brothers, 1947.
Catechism of the Catholic Church. 2nd ed. Strathfield, NSW: St. Paul's, 2000.
Gilson, Etienne. *The Christian Philosophy of St. Thomas Aquinas*. Translated by L. K. Shook, C.S.B. Notre Dame, IN: Notre Dame University Press, 2002.
Jungmann SJ, Joseph. *The Mass of the Roman Rite: Its Origins and Development*. Vol. I & II. New York: Benziger Brothers, 1955.
Pieper, Josef. *The Christian Idea of Man*. Translated by Dan Farrelly. South Bend, IN: St. Augustine's, 2011.
———. *Leisure: The Basis of Culture: The Philosophical Act*. Translated by Alexander Dru. San Francisco: Ignatius, 2009.
Ratzinger, Joseph. *The Spirit of the Liturgy*. Translated by John Saward. San Francisco: Ignatius, 2000.

www.ingramcontent.com/pod-product-compliance
Lightning Source LLC
Chambersburg PA
CBHW050346230426
43663CB00010B/2009